Ignatian Exercises:

CONTEMPORARY ANNOTATIONS

Edited by David L. Fleming SJ

The Best of the Review - 4

Review for Religious
3601 Lindell Boulevard
St. Louis, Missouri 63108

ISBN 0-924768-06-1

Foreword

*I*n 1981 the first book in the series of The Best of the Review was published with the title *Notes on the Spiritual Exercises of St. Ignatius of Loyola*. I was the compiler and editor of articles on the Ignatian Exercises which had been published in Review For Religious from the late 1960s up to the early 1980s. Father Daniel Meenan SJ, then editor of the journal, gave me strong encouragement in this endeavor. Both of us were surprised at the enthusiastic response to this kind of resource book. The demand has remained through a fourth printing.

Although volumes on religious life and spiritual direction have been published in the intervening years, I desired to return to the topic of the Spiritual Exercises and collect valuable articles which have been published in Review for Religious from the mid-1980s up to the mid-1990s. The result is the current volume.

I have used the expression "contemporary annotations" as part of the title. *Annotations* is an Ignatian expression for the helps which he intends for the one who gives the Exercises, that is, the person frequently referred to today as the retreat director. I envision this collection of articles to continue for our times the kind of help which Ignatius so pithily provided in his own text. I believe that the articles in the *Notes on the Spiritual Exercises* gave a basic understanding and insight into the Ignatian text. The articles collected in this volume tend to demand a familiarity with the text and with the movement of an Ignatian retreat. Perhaps they exhibit a sophistication that reflects the current development in the study and practice of the Exercises.

As an introduction to this collection, I have written an original article which describes the foundational movement in our Christian lives and in the Ignatian Exercises—our response to the call of Jesus to be with him. Sometimes the Exercises are presented with such an emphasis on decisions about particular vocations or choices about a way of life that we obscure the basic context of our desire to grow as disciples of Jesus, grounding any decision or choice. Probably most of the shorter Ignatian retreats enter us into some point along the movement of our growth as disciples. I hope to have highlighted some of those points of growth, whether within or outside the Ignatian retreat.

Just as the original annotations of Ignatius take in a wide variety of topics, so the articles in this collection range in a similar way over vision, attitudes, examinations, movements, prayer, discernment, and adaptation. Just as Ignatius noted some helps that would extend beyond the immediate experience of the retreat, so too some articles here included certainly expand the topic beyond the retreat situation.

I hope that this collection of articles—contemporary annotations for the Ignatian Exercises—will provide a resource valued by both those who are involved in Ignatian retreats and those who desire to study about the Ignatian text.

I remain grateful to all the staff of Review for Religious who take on added responsibilities to their ordinary duties whenever we publish a book.

David L. Fleming SJ

contents

movement

prayer

jesus

discernment

adaptation

A Prayer to Jesus on the Cross

(inspired by the *Anima Christi*)

Note: St. Ignatius Loyola had a special love for the traditional prayer *Anima Christi* or *Soul of Christ*. The prayer expresses the desire for a growing intimacy between ourselves and Jesus. The prayer is a kind of mirror of the movement of the Spiritual Exercises.

Soul of Christ, give life to me.
Body of Christ, be food for me.
Blood of Christ, make warm my heart.
Water from the side of Christ, wash me clean.
Passion of Christ, make me strong
O good Jesus, hear my prayer.
Within your wounds, hide my hurts.
Turn your gaze upon my face.
Save me from what may betray you.
At death's door, be there to call me.
Open arms to draw me close.
Present me to your friends and family
That I may sing your love forever.
                              Amen.

—paraphrased by David L. Fleming SJ

Introduction

Following Christ More Nearly:
Discipleship in Ignatian Spirituality

*A*ll too often we take for granted that we are Christians. When we see age-old Christians killing each other in Northern Ireland and in Bosnia, and perhaps more recent Christians as in Rwanda, we say that "blood" (that is, our tribe, our race, our culture) runs thicker than "water" (that is, baptism in Jesus Christ). Why do we find it so hard to have "Christian" be the bonding between African-American and White-American, between White-American and Hispanic-American, between African-American and Asian-American—when all are believers in Christ and all go to Christian, perhaps all even to Catholic, churches? Why is our Christian identity so fragile?

Sometimes we define ourselves even in the church too much by our relation to a secular world. For example, we still talk about *lay* people in the church, with the definition of "lay" coming from involvement with the world. We pass over too lightly the difference between personal choice and a call from the Lord. We like to stress that we are formed, that is, "made real," by our choices more than by our calls. But from our Christian faith, we believe that we are defined more by our call, our relationship to God, than even by our choices. Lay person, priest, religious—each is defined primarily in terms of call, relationship to God. Our choices, then, become important in trying to respond to and live out our calls.

In the gospels, we see clearly that Jesus calls people to be disciples. But what is it to be "called" a disciple? Ignatius Loyola in his retreat manual the *Spiritual Exercises* offers us a way of entering more fully into the process of being called a disciple of Jesus. I want to share in some broad strokes my understanding about this Ignatian way of growing in our calling to be Jesus' disciples.

What does the word *disciple* mean? At its root, it means more than just being a follower; it comes from a Latin and before that a Greek root, with a meaning of *one who learns*. And so anyone who claims to be a disciple is one who rejoices in always being a learner.

Jesus calls people to follow him, and he carefully forms and teaches them—they are identified as his disciples. Fifteen-hundred years later, for our entering into the process of growing as a disciple of Jesus, Ignatius Loyola worked out a fourfold movement: 1) learning to be fired by great visions and ideals; 2) learning to be a companion and to work with; 3) learning to be a companion and to suffer with; and 4) learning to be a companion and to rejoice with.

Those familiar with the Ignatian Exercises may hear echoes in the four movements of the dynamic of the retreat in terms of its Four Weeks. Since through the Second to the Fourth Weeks Ignatius enters us into the life of Jesus first in his active ministry, then in his passion, and finally in his resurrection, it is important for us to see this journey with Jesus in terms of a growth in discipleship. The Weeks do not simply represent chronological movements in Jesus' own life; they are not stages in Christ's life meant only to confirm our retreat resolutions. In our entering into the Weeks dealing with the life of Jesus, Ignatius was teaching us how to continue to develop as disciples of Jesus through all the experiences of our lives.

Let me make two preliminary observations before we take up each of the four movements in our growing as disciples. To describe a growth process is rather difficult. A stairway model seems quite inadequate because we have a better sense today that growth is not a lock-step forward movement; there are lots of fits-and-starts in human growth and in Christian growth. The old notion of spiritual life identified with the purgative, illuminative, and unitive stages seems too static and platonic to describe real-life experience. We know the experience of taking a lot of our past with us, so that new as the situation is we feel at times that we "have been here before." An image for growth and development that I find more helpful is a cone-model adapted from the writings of Teilhard de Chardin. We are moving forward (the vertical direction of the cone), and we take with us our past experience (the circularity of the cone). By putting the two movements together (forward and upward) we are always learning at a new level, with a richer or deeper sensitivity to the experience similar as it may be. Of course, there is the sad possibility that we can also "grow" in a downward movement along our cone analogy. The point is that we are just not repeating the exact same experience when we are "learners."

How does Jesus call? Just as some scripture scholars identify Jesus' calls pictured in the gospels in two ways, so there remain evidences today for two kinds of calls still found in the church: 1) there are the calls "made by the lake"; 2) there are the calls "on the mount." In all the early calls particularly in the gospels of Mark, Matthew, and Luke, we seem to find Jesus along the lakefront calling to people to follow. These people are all living in ordinary circumstances, plying their trades, doing their daily duties, and Jesus calls them to be his disciples—a discipleship to be lived right in the midst of the ordinariness of life. Then there appear the calls on the mount. This call seems to come in the context of a crowd of people; it is a calling to come forward out of the group, and it is to be in some responsible mission with Jesus in terms even of other disciples (in the gospels, the group experiencing this call were identified as the Twelve). Regardless of the type of call to discipleship in the gospels or today, the growth or development process keeps the same dynamic.

Jesus is the one who calls us to be his disciples, and the first movement as Ignatius delineates it is learning to be fired by great visions and ideals.

Now let us enter into a reflection on each of the four movements of growing as a disciple in Ignatian spirituality.

1. Learning to Be Fired by Great Visions and Ideals

Jesus is the one who calls us to be his disciples, and the first movement as Ignatius delineates it is learning to be fired by great visions and ideals.

The opening vision piece of the Ignatian Exercises, preliminary to entering into any of the Weeks, is called the Principle and Foundation. It is a vision piece about God and us and the whole world; it is a vision piece of how we all are interrelated; it is a vision piece that contains the seeds of how Jesus Christ is central to all the relationships—the Word in whom all things are created, the Word made flesh. It is a vision piece where God remains an active participant in creation—to use Ignatius's favorite imagery, a God who labors for us and with us and with all the rest of creation in bringing about God's reign—the *kingdom of heaven* term used by Jesus. The vision piece presents a God who is totally identified as "giver" and a creation identified as gifts. The thanks, the reverence, the respect for a gift—something freely and lovingly given, always representing in some small, often obscure way, something of the giver—are stimulated by our recognizing and acknowledging this gift-reality in ourselves, in other people, and in all the created elements of our world.

Some gifts we respect, reverence, and love—like the gift of people in our lives. Some gifts we respect and use—all the various material goods that support and sustain our human lives, give us joy, and help us in our life's journey. Although people are God's gifts, not all human relations work out. Some people relate to us in not good ways, sometimes through no one's fault. We do not have to make a judgment that these are bad people; they just are not good for us as part of our journey with God. So too with all of God's gifts in creation—all gifts are potentially good, but perhaps this or that gift is not good for us in terms of our growth and development. And so our vision piece includes all the goodness of God, ourselves, and the rest of creation. It includes how we are interelated and how we are bound together in a movement with God. The vision includes the reality that human choices for growth are a necessary part of our working with God in this movement described by St. Paul as culminating when "all things are yours, and you are Christ's, and Christ is God's" (1 Co 3:23).

This is the vision piece which we find at the beginning of the Spiritual Exercises, and it is the first of Ignatius's ways of drawing us to be fired by great visions and ideals. This is Christ's world—this is the world we want to be in with him.

How does Ignatius want us to make this vision ours? We need to take it in slowly, meditating on it, better—ruminating on it, letting it permeate us in our time of prayerful reflection. Consonant with our cone image of a growth model, Ignatius will continue to present "visions and ideals" in the succeeding Weeks as a source of firing us up in our following of Jesus.

2. Learning to Be a Companion and to Work With

Ignatius leads us into a call of Jesus himself to followers. At the beginning of the Second Week, Ignatius draws another vision piece to fire our imagination and our hearts. He distills all the call scenes in the gospels and presents a structural meditation identified in his book the *Spiritual Exercises* as "The Call of the King." It is commonly referred to as "the Kingdom meditation."

Ignatius has us consider Jesus, gracious and winning, making his appeal to all peoples—no matter their age, their country, their occupation—to come and to be with him. "Being with me," Jesus says, "means that you live the way I live, share experiences with me of success and failure and of joy and sorrow; you will be with me in good times and in bad, but the victory is assured. I want to tell you," Jesus says, "I did it, I won, and I want you to be with me—forever."

Ignatius proposes two responses which people might give to this call of Jesus: 1) the reasonable response: who in his or her right mind could refuse such a call? 2) the generous response: the desire to be intimate, the desire to do more. Ignatius again just has us ruminate, reflect on, and make our own the way Jesus calls—always "to be with"—and we know the kinds of response possible. A disciple, one who wants to follow Jesus, is fired up by this vision. And we?

It is interesting to note that within this Second Week Ignatius in having us consider Jesus' call to be disciples does not suggest first a repentance, conversion, or penance. We know that the gospels begin the public life of Jesus by introducing John the Baptizer with his call to repentance and Jesus' own baptism by John and then Jesus' forty-day experience in the desert; we also recall that Jesus is described as proclaiming a first message of "repent, be converted, and believe the good news." But in the moment of calling disciples, Jesus first draws them by vision and ideals. For example, in his first being called, Peter declares that he is a sinful man; nonetheless Jesus does not focus on his confession at all, but rather holds out an ideal of an intriguing and mysterious "fishing for people." Matthew similarly seems to go through no penance period first. Rather at his own banquet to celebrate his following of Jesus he is fired by Jesus' holding up the ideal of sick people needing help. So our gospels seem to show Jesus drawing people to be his disciples by calling them and presenting them first with visions and ideals. The greater conversion and a new sense of penitence is still ahead in learning to grow as a disciple. This same style of movement pictured in Jesus' call to his disciples is the process captured by Ignatius in our own first steps in growing as disciples.

Ignatius suggests that we speak out our desires for our following of Jesus. What is it that we want of Jesus? "To know thee more clearly, to love thee more dearly, and to follow these more nearly—day by day." That is the grace we seek for our being a disciple—to know more, to love more, and so to be able better to follow—and all this, in a daily way. We pray that we might live more and more as companions of Jesus.

How does Ignatius image that we do this "learning to be with"? His method is through a way of praying the gospels, a way of praying now identified as Ignatian contemplation. Briefly Ignatius has us place ourselves into the gospel scene, being totally present to the scene as it is. We see the people, we hear the words spoken, we watch the facial expressions, we look at their gestures, we pick up on their feelings. Contemplation is Ignatius's favorite way of learning how to be a disciple because it is quiet, observant, reverent, passive, drinking in, absorbing, immersing oneself in, a living in the situation, a being a part of. It reminds me of how one might teach someone how to be polite. You could buy *Emily Post's Etiquette* and demand a memorization; or you could have the person live with a family whose members are always polite with one another. Such a person would not know rules, but would instinctively be able to do the "polite thing," no matter the situation. This second way captures how totally Ignatius wants us to learn to be Christlike. We are growing as companions.

Ignatius has a certain refinement about the gospel mysteries of Jesus' life he would have us focus on. He chooses gospel texts with emphasis on Jesus' actions with others. He tends to avoid passages that are just "talking" passages, whether it be Jesus telling parable stories or Jesus preaching. Why does Ignatius pick and choose these active passages? Because, I believe, he wants us "to do like," "to work with" Jesus in the way that Jesus is active, in the way Jesus does it, in the way Jesus works. Being with Jesus, a disciple grows in behaving like him in every situation. Jesus' disciples are not solipsists; they are always ones who work with. Being with Jesus not only makes us his companions, but it places us as companions with all those whom Jesus calls.

In the course of the Exercises, Ignatius now introduces us to another of his structural meditations, one traditionally called The Two Standards. Once again Ignatius tries to summarize in capsule form the values dearest to Jesus for one who is with him as his disciple. Ignatius tries to make sense out of the values which Jesus identifies for his own life. Jesus talks about poverty and lives it, about service as a way of life, about laying down one's life, about taking up a cross daily. In the manner of Peter, we are all tempted to say "Jesus, forget it. These are not values; you won't get any disciples that way."

So Ignatius reflects on the values with which we live; he presents them through the call of Lucifer, the false angel of light. Lucifer calls devils, his followers, to entice and enslave people by having them focus on whatever it is that they imagine gives them value, what they have or possess, their "riches." Then the next step is that they get respect and honor from others because they have this "valuable thing" (like fame, beauty, titles, accomplishments), and they expect to be fawned over, they demand it, or they pay for it. Finally they get so swelled up with their own importance that pride or self-sufficiency wipes out any reference to God or others. And so Lucifer can draw such people to choosing and living out any number of other evils.

Knowing the subtlety of this angel-of-light approach, so enticing and enslaving of human beings, Jesus chooses opposite values to focus on our true human identity. The Son who emptied himself to become human, becoming like us in all things but sin, being condemned to death, even death on a cross, that God might raise him up and give him the name above all other names—this is the movement of Jesus. Choose poverty (everything is gift of God), then humiliation results (it is true, we have nothing of ourselves so we take in no false esteem from people), and humility becomes our gift—the grounding truth that we are children of God in Christ. That identity no one can take from us; that identity gives us all our value. Such disciples, following Jesus' value system and grounding in his identity-source, are truly free and on fire with these ideals. The more Jesus' experiences are reflected in our own lives the greater grace we see is ours; we find joy in our being with and working with Jesus. We are his companions; we are growing as disciples who work with. . . .

3. Learning to Be a Companion and to Suffer With

In the context of the Third Week of the Exercises, Ignatius would have us look to the next movement of growing as a disciple: learning to be a companion and to suffer with.

As we know, few disciples stayed with Jesus as he enters into his passion: Mary his mother—the first disciple, Mary Magdalen,

Mary the wife of Clopas, and John remain at the foot of the cross. As we enter into our contemplations on the passion narratives of Jesus, we are invited by Ignatius to pray hard for the grace to enter inside the passion events—to be with Jesus in his interior anguish, his feeling of abandonment, his feeling of people's anger or hatred, his feeling of being alone. Jesus wants to let us in, so that we can learn how to be ever more his disciple. We need to labor to stay with Jesus at this time.

Quite often the reason we find it hard to stay with Jesus is that we can do nothing. We can only be there, with compassion. It is a very rich and privileged moment in being a disciple, staying with Jesus, even to death. It is a further movement from the earlier understanding and doing (with Jesus) "for the kingdom," for the reign of God, to now giving and paying the cost (with Jesus), and so truly "entering" into the reign.

Jesus' passion is the greatest labor of his life: "This is the work I have come to do." It is a divine paradox that Jesus' greatest work or labor is passion and death. This throws a wholly unexpected light upon our being disciples. When do we do our greatest labor in following Jesus, in being his disciples? Although we pride ourselves in our works, the question of human living is our integrating the larger half of our lives, what happens to us. Learning to be a disciple is learning how to suffer with: suffer with Jesus, suffer with ourselves and all that we would want different about ourselves, suffer with others, suffer with our world. This movement of learning to be a disciple involves the hard process of being able to stay with; it is a movement of compassion. We are growing as disciples when we learn to suffer with . . . .

4. Learning to Be a Companion and to Rejoice With

In the context of the Exercises of the Fourth Week, Ignatius would have us consider the next movement in our growing as disciples: "learning to be a companion and to rejoice with." While we feel uncomfortable and want to escape from the suffering of others that we can do nothing about, often even with greater difficulty do we find ourselves able to enter into someone else's happiness or good fortune. Aware of this human response, Ignatius would have us enter into the gospel resurrection accounts—noting how Jesus wants to console his followers, his disciples. He would like them to enter into his joy of victory.

If we have experienced the previous gift of compassion in our growth as disciples, then we will know this next movement of discipleship—not only in the being able to rejoice with Jesus, with others, with our world, but we also experience consolation, the consoling presence of Jesus even in the midst of our everyday struggle. Jesus is consolation to us in a way that we have been compassion to him. He does not change our personal history and experience. The miracle is not saving us from all the implications of human events and history, both the consequences of our own actions and the chance misfortunes of life; the miracle for the disciple is that this compassionate, consoling Jesus stays with us in the midst of it all. Jesus—Emmanuel—is truly God-with-us.

The Exercises, like the following of Christ, do not have a completion moment. To underscore the continuing process of growth, Ignatius has drawn one more vision piece as the final exercise of the retreat. When we consider the movements in growing as a disciple, this vision piece serves to reinforce the fact that we are always learners and we need to keep getting fired up by our visions and ideals. This vision piece, called The Contemplation on the Love of God, is rather like a summary of all that we have considered: God's giving of creation's gifts to us, God's self-giving to us, God's laboring for us, and God's unceasing giving and gifting. This is the world of the risen Christ; this is the world of the new creation. This is our Good News to proclaim as Christ's disciples. We are companions who have learned to rejoice with. . . .

In Ignatian spirituality, then, how do we grow in being disciples of Jesus? In summary we find that the elements are:

1. Ignatian insight: rejoice in always being a learner;
2. Ignatian method: use the context of prayer,
    a) ruminating about Christian visions and ideals;
    b) contemplating the mysteries of the life of Jesus
       in gospels;
3. Ignatian movements: go forward and upward,
    a) learning to be fired by great visions and ideals;
    b) learning to be a companion and to work with;
    c) learning to be a companion and to suffer with;
    d) learning to be a companion and to rejoice with.

This is how Jesus born human like us interacts with us. This is first Jesus' movement in dealing with us. Learning from him, this is how we take on the movement for ourselves and grow in being his disciples. We disciples never cease praying for the grace "to follow him more nearly—day by day."

vision

The Ignatian *Exercises* and Jesuit Spirituality

There is a tendency, noted more in passing remarks than in thematic studies, to equate Jesuit spirituality with the *Spiritual Exercises* of St. Ignatius of Loyola. I do not know whether anyone has ever made the equation in so many words, but one hears it said that the *Exercises* are the wellspring of Jesuit life, that Jesuit spirituality is to be found above all in the *Exercises*, that the *Exercises* are the basis of Jesuit spirituality, that Jesuits have a vision given them by the *Exercises*, and so on.

There is a profound truth in all these statements, but just because the truth in them is so very profound and so very true, it seems to me all the more necessary to state explicitly that it is not the whole truth and to think out clearly the relationship of the *Exercises* to Jesuit, and any other, spirituality. Otherwise part of the truth is easily taken to be the whole truth, and so we come imperceptibly to identify two distinct elements in Jesuit spirituality: the *Exercises*, and the complex history that culminated in Ignatius's *Constitutions* for the Society of Jesus. Then, since innocently deficient ideas still have consequences, we arrive at two practical errors: pointing the *Exercises* toward a spirituality they do not intend and depriving Jesuit spirituality of its specific character, as found most notably in the *Constitutions*.

Two simple lines of reasoning should, it seems to me, establish the point I am making. The first is a thought experiment that makes the case in a more graphic way than my abstract assertion. Let us imagine two men with the proper dispositions who both make the Spiritual Exercises. One of them emerges from the thirty days with a decision to seek admission to the Jesuits. The other emerges with a decision to join the Carthusians. Is this an impossible scenario? Will anyone tell the Holy Spirit, "You cannot do that; the *Exercises* are identified with Jesuit spirituality; you really cannot use them to direct someone to the Carthusians"? Or would anyone say that the Carthusian vocation here is due to a failure of the exercitant to be guided by the Spirit, that the Spirit was directing him elsewhere, that he is in fact a Jesuit manqué?

Will anyone tell the Holy Spirit, "You really cannot use the Ignatian Exercises to direct someone to the Carthusians"?

I mean this, of course, as a *reductio ad absurdum*, for no one would dream of taking such a position on what the Holy Spirit should or should not do, or of attributing a failure to respond properly if the exercitant does not decide to be a Jesuit. And a parallel statement could be made about two women emerging from their Ignatian retreat, one to become a Poor Clare, the other to become a social worker; or about a man and woman emerging with plans for matrimony.

My other line of reasoning takes us to actual history. We might ask: What were the first companions of Ignatius doing in the years that followed their experience of making the Exercises, say between 1534 and 1540, a period in which they were steadily seeking the divine will? Why, if the Exercises had already determined what the Jesuit spirituality and way of proceeding was to be, did they run through so many different options before they settled on that way? What, indeed, was Ignatius himself doing for nearly two decades after Manresa, wandering around Europe and the Holy Land before he found his destined way of life? And a still more pointed question: What was he doing in the dozen years of "blood, toil, tears, and sweat," during which he laboriously worked out the Jesuit *Constitutions*? The answer seems obvious in all these questions: Ignatius and his first companions were seeking something the Exercises had not given them.

I believe that we need to face these questions and work out with all possible accuracy what role the *Exercises* may play in Jesuit or any other spirituality[1] and how that role may be complemented by the distinct and specifying roles that different spiritual traditions may contribute—for Jesuits, in the way their *Constitutions*, above all, determine for them; for Carthusians, Poor Clares, and other religious institutes, in ways that they also have worked out for themselves and that I need not try to determine for them here.

Is there then a spirituality in the *Exercises*? Yes, indeed, the very highest. If we leave aside the case of those who are not disposed to go beyond the First Week (§18),[2] the aim of the *Exercises* is to bring exercitants, whatever their state in life is to be and wherever God will direct them, to choose to live under the standard of Christ: "We shall also think about how we ought to dispose ourselves in order to come to perfection in whatsoever state or way of life God our Lord may grant us to elect" (§135)[3]— which means embracing the way of Christ, in the highest poverty, spiritual poverty certainly and if God wills it in actual poverty as well; in willingness also to bear opprobrium and injuries in order to imitate him the better (§147); and again, when God is served equally by either of the two alternatives, to choose poverty with Christ poor rather than riches, opprobrium with Christ covered with opprobrium rather than honors, to be counted vain and stupid with Christ so counted rather than wise and prudent in this world (§167); and so forth.

The real question is: How does this spirituality relate to the various specific spiritualities to which various individual exercitants may be called? I will suggest a few ways of conceiving the relation, ways that follow more traditional lines of thought and shed some light on the matter, none of them quite satisfactory, but each adding an element of understanding. And then I will propose another approach to the whole question.

The obvious pair of terms to define the relationship in question is *generic* and *specific*: the *Exercises* have a generic spirituality, the following of Christ; then, giving more determinate content to this, we have the specific spiritualities of Jesuit, Carthusian, and so on. I have drawn on these concepts already to start discussion; they contribute some clarity, but they use the language of logic, which seems simply inadequate for so spiritual a question.

Another useful set of terms would be *infrastructure* and *superstructure*. To follow Christ is infrastructure for whatever way of life we choose to follow; on this basis one builds a superstructure of, say, the Jesuit way of proceeding. These terms from the world of civil engineering clarify our question rather nicely. Still, they make the following of Christ the invisible element, or at any rate not the focus of attention—a situation that does not correspond to any vocation emerging from the Exercises.

A third set might be the concepts of the *compact* and the *differentiated* that have now come into general use, mainly, I believe, through the influence of Eric Voegelin. Bernard Lonergan also has some helpful pages on the process from the compactness of the symbol, where very profound truths may be contained and grasped, to the enucleated and analyzed differentiations of scientists, philosophers, and theologians. He illustrates the process by Christology and the "transition from a more compact symbolic consciousness expressed in the New Testament to a more enucleated theological consciousness expressed in the great Greek councils."[4] Once again we have a pair of terms that provide some understanding—certainly the various spiritualities are differentiated from one another (one has only to adduce again the example of Carthusian and Jesuit)—but do they also contain the unwelcome hint that the various differentiations divide up something that the compact contained in its wholeness?

We need to work out with all possible accuracy what role the Exercises *may play in Jesuit or any other spirituality.*

A fourth pair, made familiar in social studies, is the *communal or collective* and the *particular or individual.* Our communal spirituality is the way of Christ; our individual spirituality is the particular way of life in which we follow Christ. This seems a promising line of thought, but working out the relation between the communal and the individual, we would need to see how the communal is explicit in the particular and how the particular contains without loss the whole of the communal.

No doubt we could add to this list and pursue similar paired meanings with considerable profit, but I wonder if in the end it would bring us to the heart of the matter. I wonder in fact if our aim here is not a bit off center, if we should not approach the problem from another perspective altogether. For in the various pairs we have considered, the first member seems to remain incomplete until the second is added, and the second has always to be concerned that it incorporates the whole of the first. Further, the second term in each pair is thought of as an end product with its meaning determined: what a Jesuit is, what a Carthusian is—these are already more or less clearly defined, belong to an established order, are in some measure static. Does such thinking deal adequately with the dynamism of the Exercises?

I would like to explore a somewhat different approach. In this line of thought it is the heuristic character and therefore the dynamism of the Exercises that will be the focus. But all dynamic movement, all searching, all heuristic activity suppose and take place within a horizon that determines the activity and defines the source of energy for the search; I therefore need to study first the idea of horizon. For both terms, *horizon* and *heuristic*, I draw directly on the work of Bernard Lonergan.

For the meaning of horizon, it will be best simply to quote Lonergan's account of the matter:

> In its literal sense the word, horizon, denotes the bounding circle, the line at which earth and sky appear to meet. This line is the limit of one's field of vision. As one moves about, it recedes in front and closes in behind so that, for different standpoints, there are different horizons. Moreover, for each different standpoint and horizon, there are different divisions of the totality of visible objects. Beyond the horizon lie the objects that, at least for the moment, cannot be seen. Within the horizon lie the objects that can now be seen.
>
> As our field of vision, so too the scope of our knowledge, and the range of our interests are bounded. As fields of vision vary with one's standpoint, so too the scope of one's knowledge and the range of one's interests vary with the period in which one lives, one's social background and milieu, one's education and personal development. So there has arisen a metaphorical or perhaps analogous meaning of the word, horizon. In this sense what lies beyond one's horizon is simply outside the range of one's knowledge and interests: one neither knows nor cares. But what lies within one's horizon is in some measure, great or small, an object of interest and of knowledge.[5]

It is easy to apply this idea to the world of the Spiritual Exercises. One enters upon them with a given horizon, vaguely or clearly conceived: "the range of one's knowledge and interests"; for example, maybe one is led by a spirit of repentance or by anxiety about one's salvation. One makes the First Week, remaining for the most part within such a horizon—with glimpses of something beyond, to be sure, in such passages as the colloquy at the end of the first exercise (§53). But if one responds to the call of Christ in the Kingdom exercise (§91), one pushes back the previous horizon to work within a new one, far wider, with far greater potential, a horizon that is all-encompassing, a boundary that is in fact no boundary for it encloses a territory that is boundless.

Now it is this ultimate horizon, and not any relative and confining horizon, that I would equate with the spirituality of the *Exercises*. The horizon of those who should not be led beyond the First Week is narrow and confining. What happens when one enters the Second Week with the mind and heart of those who would "show greater devotion and . . . distinguish themselves in total service to their eternal King and universal Lord" (§95)? What happens is the discovery of a new horizon, the horizon defined by Christ the Lord. The horizon is established in the exercises on Two Standards (§§136-148) and Three Ways of Being Humble (§§165-168); details are added in the Mysteries of the Life of Christ Our Lord (§261); and in the Third and Fourth Weeks communion with Christ (what the Germans call *Mitsein*) fortifies the attraction of the good with the power of love and the interpersonal.

Communion with Christ fortifies the attraction of the good with the power of love.

This does not happen without the grace of God and a conversion. For besides the ultimate horizon there are relative horizons. There are shifts in our relative horizon as we move, say, from school days to the work force, and this shift may occur as a normal development of potentialities. "But it is also possible that the movement into a new horizon involves an about-face; it comes out of the old by repudiating characteristic features; it begins a new sequence that can keep revealing ever greater depth and breadth and wealth. Such an about-face and new beginning is what is meant by a conversion."[6]

Against that background we turn to the idea of the heuristic, taking as our context the fact that the Exercises are a search. Thus, the first annotation tells us: Our purpose, after removing obstacles, is to seek and to find the divine will (§1), and the fifteenth annotation has advice for those who during the Exercises are seeking God's will (§15). Or, as is repeated over and over, recurring like a refrain, we are to seek what gives glory to God (§16). In the key stage of the Election, "While continuing our contemplations of [Christ's] life, we now begin simultaneously to explore and inquire: In which state or way of life does the Divine Majesty wish us to serve him?" (§135). And still, at the heart of the Exercises, in the meditation on the Three Classes of Men, we are seeking to "desire and know what will be more pleasing to the Divine Goodness" (§151).

We are, then, in an area in which the idea of the heuristic plays a central role. My Webster's dictionary defines heuristic as "serving to guide, discover, or reveal." A helpful point: the famous "Eureka" of Archimedes is from the same Greek root; it means "I have found [it]; I have discovered the secret." Now this line of thought is thoroughly developed in Bernard Lonergan, and I find his treatment of the idea helpful for understanding the process and dynamic of spiritual search that the Exercises are. In his usage a heuristic notion tries to give some advance notice of what we hope to find; it is an anticipation of the answer we seek to a question; it is not a determinate concept, like various concepts in physics or chemistry or biology; it is an indeterminate anticipation.

The nearly perfect word for this way of conceiving in anticipation what we have not yet determined in particular is *whatever*, and the nearly perfect use of *whatever* we can find right in Scripture. Paul, writing to the Philippians (4:8), exhorts them to focus on "whatever is true, whatever is honorable, whatever is just, whatever is pure, whatever is pleasing, whatever is commendable" (*NRSV*; in the Douai translation, "whatsoever"). Well, what *is* true? what is honorable, just, and so on? That will emerge with each new day, and meanwhile we are guided by its anticipation in that "whatever."

To come, then, to the present point, Ignatius and Paul are at one in conceiving by anticipation what they do not yet determine in particular. Apropos of the Election, Ignatius writes that we are to "think about how we ought to dispose ourselves in order to come to perfection in whatsoever state or way of life God our Lord may grant us to elect" (§135).

It is possible now to bring these two ideas together in a new understanding of the relationship of the *Exercises* and Jesuit or other spirituality. My brief statement of the case would be that the horizon of the *Exercises* and the spirituality they directly intend is established in the exercise on the Two Standards (§§136-148) and the exercises that directly relate to it; further, that the heuristic of the *Exercises* is epitomized in the Election (§§169-188), where we search for and discover and embrace the state of life God intends for us. And the relationship between the two is indicated in the Introduction to the Consideration of the States of Life: "We shall also think about how we ought to dispose ourselves in order to come to perfection in whatsoever state or way of life God our Lord may grant us to elect" (§135). Perfection as defined in the Two Standards and their retinue of exercises is the horizon; but "whatsoever state" God may direct us to is another matter: it represents the heuristic element.

The *Exercises* do not, therefore, *intend* any one spirituality; their objective ordination, what the scholastics would call their *finis operis*, is neither Jesuit nor Carthusian spirituality, nor any other; they intend what God will choose, and their finis operis is a "whatever." What we therefore first conceived as generic, as infrastructure, as compact, as communal, we now conceive as a horizon; and what we first conceived as specific, as superstructure, as differentiated, as individual, we now conceive as the area within that horizon that we discover to be God's will for us.

But in moving from one to the other we do not add something specific that was not contained in the genus, for everything is contained in the horizon; and, for those who respond fully, the whole spirituality of the horizon enters every vocation and every state of life. The situation is more like that of the incarnation: as the fullness of the Godhead dwells in Christ (Col 1:19), so the fullness of the horizon of Christ is the world in which we dwell, Jesuit and Carthusian and all others that respond fully to the call of the Kingdom exercise.

And similarly, the "superstructure" we conceived as our way turns out to be what we may call an "addition," but an addition to what is already complete (like the humanity of Christ added to the eternal and infinite Word). The "differentiation" we spoke of is not a dividing off of a part, but the incorporation of the whole, and the "individual" contains the fullness of the communal.

Thus, one is everywhere safe within the all-encompassing arms of the Christian horizon; one is never in exile, never outside the shores of home, never a wanderer like the prodigal son in distant lands. One does not, therefore, go beyond this horizon to be a Jesuit or to be a Carthusian or to find some other particular vocation. There is nothing there beyond it. It is the all-encompassing. Just as within any relative horizon of geography one can go north or south, east or west, without going beyond the horizon, so within the ultimate horizon established by Christ one can become a Jesuit or a Carthusian, but one cannot go beyond the horizon set by Christ; one can only contract that horizon by living an inauthentic Jesuit life or living an inauthentic Carthusian life.

Further use of the ideas of heuristic and horizon is readily made. In Lonergan's thought one can speak of heuristic *notions* and heuristic *devices*. There is the notion of being, the notion of the good, and so on; but there are also the heuristic structures that promote the discoveries we seek (his rather famous scissors action of heuristic method). One could say that God's will is the supreme heuristic notion guiding the exercitant and that the *Exercises* are a heuristic device, an instrument par excellence for finding God's will, maybe with a kind of scissors action too. (I do not, however, call the *Exercises* the supreme heuristic device, for we do not limit God's creativity to what was divinely done in Ignatius, and we do not know what successor God may be preparing for Ignatius.) Again, still in Lonergan's thought, one can speak of interrelationships in the set of horizons, of their complementary, genetic, and dialectical differences. But that would add length to an article that is already long enough, and introduce further specialized categories where they are already rather extensive.

> *God's will is the supreme heuristic notion guiding the exercitant, and the Exercises are a heuristic device.*

Notes

[1] Eventually such a study should come to the details of particular spiritualities, but that is a further step. Here I intend the word in a broad sense: "spirituality" includes, therefore, elements of doctrine and practice, of vocation and way of proceeding, of tradition and orientation, of rules and constitutions, and so on, without specifying what these may be for Jesuit, Carthusian, and other vocations.

[2] *The Spiritual Exercises of Saint Ignatius: A Translation and Commentary*, by George E. Ganss SJ (St. Louis: Institute of Jesuit Sources, 1992), no. 18 in the numbering that is standard for all editions. All English quotations will be from this edition; numbers will be given in parentheses in the text.

[3] In the Latin, "ut veniamus ad perfectionem in quocumque statu seu vita, quam Deus Dominus noster eligendam nobis dederit" (§135). The "quocumque" is the "whatever" I will presently discuss.

[4] Bernard Lonergan, *Topics in Education* (The Cincinnati Lectures of 1959 on the Philosophy of Education), ed. Robert M. Doran and Frederick E. Crowe (University of Toronto Press, 1992), pp. 55-58. On Eric Voegelin see Kenneth Keulman, *The Balance of Consciousness: Eric Voegelin's Political Theory* (Pennsylvania State University Press, 1990), pp. 92-93: "What the pattern of symbolizations indicates is the development from compact to differentiated forms. . . . The terms "compact" and "differentiated" refer not only to the symbolizations, but also to the characteristic forms of consciousness that generate them."

[5] Bernard Lonergan, *Method in Theology* (2nd ed. reprint, University of Toronto Press, 1990), pp. 235-236.

[6] Ibid, pp. 237-238. I add a few helpful quotations: "Horizontal liberty is the exercise of liberty within a determinate horizon and from the basis of a corresponding existential stance. Vertical liberty is the exercise of liberty that selects that stance and the corresponding horizon" (ibid, p. 40, with a reference to Joseph de Finance). "For falling in love is a new beginning, an exercise of vertical liberty in which one's world undergoes a new organization" (ibid, p. 122). "A horizontal exercise [of freedom] is a decision or choice that occurs within an established horizon. A vertical exercise is the set of judgments and decisions by which we move from one horizon to another" (ibid, p. 237). "Further, deliberate decision about one's horizon is high achievement. For the most part people merely drift into some contemporary horizon. They do not advert to the multiplicity of horizons. They do not exercise their vertical liberty by migrating from the one they have inherited to another they have discovered to be better" (ibid, p. 269).

Extremism in Ignatius of Loyola

*R*etreats can be deceptive. We withdraw from our daily meanderings and ascend to some lofty point from which we can see, from a spiritual perspective, where our journey has taken us and where it is going. We may feel a need for an outlook quite opposite to our culture's, even extremely so in some sense, if we are to live a vibrant spirituality in the midst of the world. From that vantage point, we search the gospels for some absolute ideal against which to test our everyday activities. And usually we come away with a vision simple and uncompromising.

Then we come down from the heights, and before long we start working on a balance between these opposites: not too talkative, but not too silent; not a workaholic, but not lazy; don't jump to conclusions, but don't accept everything mindlessly either. We look back on our retreat from quite a different perspective than we had while we were in it. Then we saw ourselves as refusing to compromise with the world; but now we feel maybe just a little more faithful or a little more loving, and we count that small gain as our humble best.

Is this retreat desire for some spiritual extreme an illusion we amuse ourselves with while perched far above the harsh realities of the city? Or is the opposite true: that our adaptations to everyday realities compromise something in us that is precious in the sight of God?

Ignatius of Loyola was one person, among many others in our history, who pushed for the no-compromise attitude:

> Just as people of the world who follow the world love and
> seek with such great diligence honors, fame, and esteem for
> a great name on earth, as the world teaches them, so those
> who are professing in the spiritual life and truly following
> Christ our Lord love and intensely desire *everything opposite*
> (GE 101).[1]

This sounds impressive, but many doubt that we can make such a black/white distinction today. Unlike Ignatius in his day, we perceive a certain continuity between religious values and secular values. Our society's hospitals, its welfare systems, our efforts to eliminate poverty and to establish political grounds for world peace all point to a growing convergence of what "the world" and what Christians intensely desire. Indeed, a case could be made that it is chiefly because of Christian values that the Secular City is gradually taking on humane, even spiritual goals for the human race.

So should we regard Ignatius' contentious approach to life as just a temporary stance made necessary by the chaos of the Church and of society in his time? I would like to argue a strong "No!" *Strong,* because unless we see some practical usefulness to an "everything opposite" attitude, we would lose our sense of what is radical about being Christian. We would gradually grow accustomed to "the world" as it is, and lose our critical sense. We would have no razor-edged criterion for weighing practical alternatives in our apostolates.

But what exactly does Ignatius mean by "everything opposite?" Paradoxically, he also counseled balance in many areas of life. So we can legitimately ask in what sense ought we be spiritual extremists, and in what sense men and women of prudent balance? Although I focus mainly on Ignatius, I have no doubt that most of the spiritual giants in human history would know what Ignatius was talking about.

A Dialectic of Desires

First of all, this "everything opposite" attitude does not refer to external social or cultural realities. It does not mean that we should be opposed to all modern institutions just because they are "of the world." In any case, these are always a mixed product of intelligence and malice, of good will and stupidity, and so in their regard we try not to throw out the baby with the bath. What Ignatius is talking about is rather the *inner realities* of consciousness. The "everything" which ought to be opposite to the "world" means inner *desires*. The disciple's desires ought to be completely opposite to the worldly penchant in us to "love and seek with such great diligence honors, fame, and esteem for a great name on earth, as the world teaches." Let me explain this more fully.

On the one hand, we revel in praise, we take pains to protect our reputations, and we easily pour our energies into making a name for ourselves. On the other hand, rebukes chasten us, insults sting us, and injuries humble us. However, even when these humiliations are unjustified, we do have to admit that the shock to our pride does have a therapeutic element in it. In some small way, we need a come-uppance now and then. To be "put in one's place" can shatter self-defeating illusions we cherish about ourselves. What is very important to notice here is that what honors do to our sense of ourselves, and what put-downs do, are completely opposite. It is these opposing senses of ourselves, I believe, that Ignatius means by "everything opposite."

What Ignatius gives in the General Examen, he expands upon in the meditation on the Two Standards (SE 136-148).[2] There he shows how different acquired tastes about lifestyle usually lead to quite deep and quite opposite longings about one's self-awareness. On the one hand. the taste for money leads to a desire for a great name. On the other, the taste for poverty usually leads to a longing for a certain anonymity—the kind that frees a person to live without crippling self-concern. And beyond the great name and the little name lie the *real* objects of one's deepest love—what Ignatius calls either a life of pride or a life of humility.

Learning the Dialectic of Desires

Now few people recognize that, in fact, they long either for pride or for humility. In one's everyday choices, most things seem morally gray, without serious consequences. And yet they do add up to a direction in one's life, a direction that sooner or later reveals whether a person is self-centered or not. So it takes some reflection to realize for oneself that underneath a great number of apparently harmless concerns there lurks one's fundamental inclination to pride. Likewise it takes some measure of self-reflection to notice the interior movements that in fact are a person's desire for humility. Once both these movements are recognized, we can see that they are entirely opposite pulls in consciousness. Moreover, we can then begin to recognize that this dialectic of desires underlies our every activity, and see how it profoundly determines the person we become and the stamp we leave on our world. Given the importance of this self-education in inner movements, it is no wonder that Ignatius prescribes more meditations on the Two Standards than on any other in the Exercises.

Still, we must admit, despite repeated meditations on the Two Standards and numerous exhortations on the value of resisting the pull to ownership and to be held in high esteem, even the spiritually mature do not easily maintain such a dialectical attitude toward their inner movements. And so we must ask why an "everything opposite" attitude is so difficult to live out.

It is one thing to acknowledge that life is a struggle, but quite another to name exactly what we are struggling with each day.

One reason is that we have failed to see the point of the Two Standards meditation. We may have "done it" during a retreat and felt we got the point. Perhaps we understood Ignatius' view of the spiritual struggle very well and saw its connection to making choices in life. So we act as though it is enough to grasp the *concept* of spiritual struggle; we sincerely hope to bring the concept to bear in our everyday situations.

What we forget is that life is concrete, not abstract. The people and the situations around us are a profoundly mysterious jumble of grace and malice, requiring in-depth reflection every day. Meditation is not analysis. Nor is it simply an appreciation of an abstract vision. Rather, meditation should be an ongoing and strenuous exercise in understanding the interaction between our concrete surroundings and our inner struggles.

Ignatius, in fact, appeals very little to the *concept* of struggle. By that I mean that he does not analyze the meaning of "acting against" considered as a principle from which actions can be determined. It is one thing to acknowledge that life is a struggle, but quite another to *name* exactly what we are struggling with each day. In his practice and teaching of discernment Ignatius seldom appeals to an abstract rule of life. Instead, he appeals to *imagination* and to *history* to show that life is essentially a dialectic of desires, because he wants us to realize it in our own lives.

For example, in the General Examen, he asks that the candidate for the Society of Jesus "ponder" how helpful it is to imitate the humiliated Christ. Does "ponder" mean conceptualize and analyze here? Not at all. The candidate is asked to *imagine* spiritually advanced men and women and to notice how in fact they "intensely desire" to be clothed exactly as Christ, because of the love they bear him. Ignatius does not tell the candidate to imitate Christ humiliated and poor. He directs him only to imagine what the loyal disciple desires.

Likewise in the Two Standards, the retreatant imagines the "servants and friends" of Christ, how they are naturally attracted in the direction opposite to pride, and how they attract others in the direction of humility. I believe that Ignatius is trying to help the retreatant distinguish between several otherwise nameless, interior experiences. By focusing on the disciple instead of the Master, Ignatius clearly means to have us consider which of our inner experiences, among the many that occur, corresponds to that particular attraction to Christ which the true disciple experiences. In other words, he wants us to *discriminate among inner desires*, not apply some facile, clean-cut rules about behavior.

I said that Ignatius appeals also to history to teach us about these two pulls in consciousness. He does this in two ways. First, he directs attention to the purposes which motivated Jesus in his work on earth so that we might better imitate him. True disciples "desire to resemble and imitate our Creator and Lord Jesus Christ . . . since it was for our spiritual profit that he clothed himself as he did"(GE 101). Notice that Ignatius calls Jesus "our Creator." This makes the choices of Jesus for poverty and humiliations a deliberate revelation of how *we* can best fulfill the purpose of our creation. Our Creator, Jesus Christ, came with this express purpose—to "give us an example that in all things possible we might seek . . . to imitate and follow him, since he is the way that leads us to life" (GE 101). For Ignatius, God desired to enter human history in person, taking on the only condition that truly gives life, a condition of poverty and humility. If there was any doubt which inner desire one can depend on, now we see clearly that Jesus Christ freely and wisely *chose* poverty and humiliations. History now has a model-member to guide it: Jesus Christ, not just Lord but Creator as well, in imitation of whose interior desires we find real life.

Ignatius appeals to history in another manner which, although it is less obvious in the texts, underlies everything in the General Examen and the Exercises. Like St. Paul, he boldly sets his own historical experience and that of his first companions as the measure of what abnegation means in the concrete. In Chapter Four of the General Examen, which Ignatius wrote with the overall intention that novices accept the idea of abnegation,[3] we find this reason given: "For where the Society's first members have passed through these necessities and greater bodily wants, the others who come to it should endeavor, as far as they can, to reach the same point as the earlier ones, or to go farther in our Lord" (GE 81). In other words, the candidate is told that he is entering a community which is not leading itself; it is being led by God. Like Israel, the Society's founding historical experience is normative for the Society's continuing style. Therefore for the simple reason that God moved the early companions to love poverty and humiliations in order to achieve the humility of Jesus, so too should the later companions, because this is not just human work but the very labor of God not only in our psyches but in our history too.

I see two kinds of meditations which these reflections should prompt. First, we should learn for ourselves how to recognize when we are pulled toward humility and when towards pride. To do this, it may help to compare our own inner experience to that of deeply spiritual persons. Their outwardly simple and self-effacing lifestyle is a manifestation of a militant obedience to a deep and steady love within. Authentic people avoid applause, not because they are shy but because they are courageously maintaining a spirit which is very precious to them.

Second, we should meditate on the various stories in which God acted for the Church through Ignatius, or through any of the men and women who understood the struggle within. Their story is part of our history, and our story draws its meaning from that shared history. God indeed has entered history permanently, not only in the person of Christ Jesus but also in the hearts of our spiritual ancestors. Ignatius and his companions, in particular, recognized that their experience of begging and mockery gave them great joy. And why? Because they felt a concrete share in the experience of their Creator and Lord. Once they decided to form a community, they wrote constitutions with the purpose of structuring, as far as possible, a continual reenactment by its members of their often difficult yet greatly joyful desires.

We can read Scripture in the same way. By attending to the inner experiences which lay behind the texts of Scripture, we can recognize the two pulls of consciousness and the meaning of each. For example, when Jesus heard the woman cry out, "Happy is the womb that bore you and the breasts that nursed you!" he replied, "Not as happy as those who hear the Word of God and keep it!"(LCD 11:27-28). As I read it, this text says that the chief concern of a happy consciousness is inner obedience, not family loyalty nor pride in the fruits of one's labor.

For another example, we hear the reading from Wisdom, "I esteemed her [wisdom] more than scepters and thrones: . . . I loved her more than health or beauty" (7:8-10). What else is this wisdom but the constant desire to live with the regular humiliations that come with living in the truth? Once we understand that what we call "salvation" is in fact the outcome of a tension in consciousness, we can read any scriptural stories and recognize familiar inner movements in ourselves. In this fashion, by seeing our present experience in the light of the gospels, we can grow to love the humble, self-transcending path.

An Empirical View of the Dialectic

Having said all that, there still remains a nagging question. Many deeply spiritual men and women in fact have meditated in this way, have lived in actual poverty, have been stung by the insults, and know the joy that can accompany these experiences, but they regard this as a *personal* asceticism only. They possess only vague notions of what the humble way has to do with peace in the world and the ongoing struggle of cultural and political leaders to achieve it. Perhaps they believe in the principle that pride pulls down nations, but they have no mental framework for understanding how it does so. Nor do they perceive how anyone's humility might ever build up a nation. As a result, while they may live out a dialectical attitude in their personal lives, they can make no connections between it and contemporary political science, psychology, sociology and economics. And so they seem to ache for the world but know nothing about how to improve it.

Our world, after all, is thoroughly empirical, unlike Ignatius' world, which it seems, doted more on eternal verities. Were Ignatius alive today, I believe that besides appealing to imagination and to history, he would add a functional explanation of how the dialectic of desires underlies social progress and decline. That is, he would seek to explain how an inner penchant for doing without funds or fame works to bring about a redemption in

Christ Jesus that would mean something to this world. Or, to use his terms, he would explain what role "discernment of spirits" plays in "redeeming" the world.

To work out that functional explanation of how discernment of spirits facilitates redemption, we have to express the movements of the good and bad angels in terms that the average person can find in experience. There are two experiences in particular which we must point out, each representing a pull or drawing in consciousness on the side of Christ's standard.

First is the experience of *intending the truth*. This experience relates to an extremely broad range of objects, and yet, as experience, it is quite distinct from many other kinds of inner experience. To "intend the truth" means to want to know reality, to search for answers to questions, and to respect the truth when we find it. This intending, this search, this respect, pulls against a counter-drift in us which settles for simple answers, for impressive words, for tricky solutions, and for comforting illusions.

Were Ignatius alive today, I believe that besides appealing to imagination and to history, he would add a functional explanation of how the dialectic of desires underlies social progress and decline.

Second is the experience of *intending the good*. This too relates to a broad range of objects and yet is quite a distinct feeling in consciousness. We "intend the good" when we weigh options for the sake of discovering what is objectively the best choice. In doing so, we pull against a counter-tendency which seeks the merely satisfying, the subjectively comfortable. To want the truly good often means to choose a more painful path, but a better one. And the criterion we use to tell which is better is not only an examination of pros and cons but also—and chiefly, I believe—an experience of fulfilled or frustrated desire in our hearts.

With these two experiences in mind—the intention of truth and the intention of good—we can analyze how an "everything opposite" attitude works redemption in concrete situations, and how a failure to be strongly contentious prevents redemption from taking over. Let me illustrate this in several different areas of life.

Some Illustrations

To a great extent we all have difficulty with our feelings. Speaking for myself, whenever I meet a stranger at a party, I seem to listen to our conversation with one ear and to my inner apprehensions with the other. It doesn't work very well because I often say things I immediately feel foolish about. Just when I hope to make a good impression, I feel I make a bad one. This happens because my mind was not fully on what we were talking about. I was also thinking about how to feel accepted, and so I blurted out things unrelated to the topic of our conversation.

Things are not much better with friends either, particularly when it comes to dealing with anger. When a friend gets angry with me, I want to strike back or at least defend myself. But neither reaction helps me *understand* what has gone wrong, and this failure to understand only makes it that much harder to work out an amicable solution.

The ideal, of course, is to be able to acknowledge the truth of my own feelings and the feelings of others. This means working both to name the feelings and to pinpoint what the feelings are focused on—not an easy task for anybody. Negative feelings in particular are often repressed, and yet they are our best indicators that something of value is going wrong. Because they are meant to alert us to harm, we should take them seriously, making every attempt first to acknowledge them and then to understand what they are all about. But this requires a no-compromise attitude towards those pulls inside us which spring to defend our poor egos. Those pulls create illusions which seduce us and cushion us against taking the sometimes painful responsibility of facing the truth and doing our real best.

For another illustration of how dedication to reality and to objective worth helps bring order and sense into an otherwise chaotic situation, consider how communities tend by nature to be self-centered. As a community we may be very realistic and quite responsible where each other are concerned, but this does nothing to prevent us from being aloof and oblivious to outsiders. Every community tends to reinforce its own biases, to congratulate itself on its victories, and to speak a language full of value judgments that no one questions. Members seldom wonder whence its resources come and where its garbage goes. They seldom question whether or not its enjoyments are paid for by the sweat and malnutrition of foreigners.

Unfortunately, for all the values inherent in community, there is very little in community itself that directs it beyond itself. These powerful gravitational forces toward self-centeredness can be found in communities of all sizes: couples in love, large families, ethnic groups, labor unions, nations—and even religions. But all such communities live among other communities. They contain subgroups, and they belong to larger groups. Without some cultural commitment to the larger, more common good, subgroups cut back their good will and limit their creativity to what benefits themselves alone. So the normal demand for large-scale cooperation is regularly sacrificed for some small-scale gain: first for this and then for that faction. Sadly and ironically, once this game of competition between groups begins, none of the groups benefits as much as each of them might have, had they all shared their wits and their good will with one another.

Historically, self-centered communities have enlarged their vision and commitments only when they have been provoked from within by a prophet. Usually the prophet gathers a select community of like-minded people together to become the leaven in the dough. But before the prophet speaks a single word or calls a single disciple, he or she obeys an inner pull toward truths and values that run counter to the prevailing attitudes. Prophets have reputations for being contentious. They get that way because they already fight an interior battle between illusions that are familiar and truths that are strange, between old, accepted ways of treating people and new, more dignified ways. So they cry out to the people they love, calling them to realize that they are playing a no-win game with other groups.

When prophets are successful, a reform movement will get underway only insofar as it deals with the community's concrete relations to other groups. The measure of its success will be the degree to which it demolishes any self-centered myths which its own authorities may propagate in the name of community strength or unity. But its members have to wake up intellectually. Only when they recognize these myths in themselves and wage an interior war against them will this peaceful revolution begin.

For my final illustration, I want to highlight the inner struggle that takes place in what we call the deep thinkers—scientists, historians, philosophers, and theologians, both the professional and the amateur. Contrary to popular opinion, deep thinkers often do not have an astronomically high I.Q. They work slowly but steadily. Nor are they born "bright"; they *become* aware of long-range implications and complex problems only by a steady fight against their minds' drift toward the easy answers.

Again, you can see my point. On the one hand, we all experience a pull toward a bogus form of knowing, the kind that relies on memory, rhetoric and bluffing. On the other, we also experience an "entirely opposite" pull towards asking honest questions, and searching for the best explanations, fighting against any worry that someone else might beat us to a solution. We all have felt the desire to belittle intellectual inquiry and to disregard journals of opinion, even as we secretly wish we had the staying power to work for a more than surface understanding of the world around us.

"Everything opposite" means a conversion— one that requires sometimes anger but often gentleness to maintain.

We cannot excuse our anti-intellectualism on the grounds of mental dullness. The so-called "dull" can be extremely bright when it comes to practical and immediate concerns. Here lies the road to pride again. On its own power alone, our intelligence would never stop asking questions about anything, no matter how remote. But when the fruits of our reflections are not immediate and palpable, then a prideful concern for our own welfare forces its way in and compels our intelligence to surrender. We yield to the forces in our consciousness that move us toward easy answers, silly responses, and make-believe solutions.

While we all recognize these pulls in ourselves, we should notice what happens when psychologists, historians, political scientists, economists and the like give in to them. Their short-sighted solutions to human crises make life more miserable not just for themselves but for countless other human beings. Yet no jury indicts them for malpractice. No preacher denounces them from the pulpit. Instead, we give them the benefit of the doubt that "they did their best." But upon their interior obedience to the canons of truth—an obedience monitored by themselves alone—hangs the future of anyone whom their theories and policies touch.

From this large-scale perspective, we can see better that every time someone settles for merely partial answers to problems, he or she usually introduces a solution which itself needs fixing by someone else. Of course, this is only a general explanation of how bad situations get worse, but it does explain how a contentious spirituality can work to better the world we live in. Only an "everything opposite" attitude towards this downhill intellectual slide will regularly bring about intelligent and long-range solutions to the problems that beset God's people.

Conversion to the Dialectical Attitude

"Everything opposite" means a conversion—one that requires sometimes anger but often gentleness to maintain. It means recognizing that one's interior is a battleground of two opposing kinds of movements, whose outcome has direct manifestations in one's psychic health, one's prophetic spirit, and one's intellectual freedom. These, in turn, have a direct effect on family harmony, social justice, and on the broad philosophies and theories that shape our human institutions. The conversion ought to be total, because there is no event in our everyday lives which does not derive its meaning from how we responded to it.

As Christians, we stand in a peculiar relationship to this conversion to a dialectical attitude. The functional explanation given above, of how discernment of spirits works to create a better world, could stand on its own without any reference to Christ Jesus. This is an asset insofar as Christians can share a vision, a language, and a praxis with non-Christians—which we must certainly do if we are to tackle issues of social justice with any seriousness. Such cooperation can even be the beginning of a dialogue about ultimates in truth and goodness leading to the Good News of Christ Jesus. But a functional explanation by itself is also a liability insofar as Christians might forget to name just who it is who moves the soul to face the truth and do one's true best. So it seems incumbent upon theologians and catechists to express the age-old doctrine of redemption in Christ Jesus and the Spirit in functional categories drawn from the dynamics of consciousness and the workings of history. This is a large order, but fortunately one already being taken up by many today.

A final word of caution: Such an "everything opposite" attitude is not learned overnight. It takes time to name which inner experiences correspond to "intending the truth" and which to wishful thinking; which to "intending the good" and which to securing the merely comfortable for ourselves. And we learn by our mistakes. But without the slightest exaggeration we can say that in this matter there should be no compromise. Only an extremism about our inner movements can give us the day-to-day balanced judgment and love that redeem the world.

Notes

[1] *General Examen.* This document was written by Ignatius for the purpose of teaching candidates for the Society of Jesus what Jesuit life would require. It was meant to be given in a retreat setting, requiring some serious meditation. See George E. Ganss SJ, ed., *The Constitutions of the Society of Jesus* (St. Louis: Institute of Jesuit Sources, 1970) pp. 75-118. My references above refer to paragraph numbers.

[2] Spiritual Exercises. See Louis J. Puhl, ed., *The Spiritual Exercises of St. Ignatius* (Westminister, Maryland: The Newman Press, 1959). References are to paragraph numbers.

[3] Joseph de Guibert, *The Jesuits: Their Spiritual Doctrine and Practice* (Chicago: Loyola University Press; St. Louis: Institute of Jesuit Sources, 1964) p. 141.

Realism in Ignatius of Loyola

The story of Ignatius' conversion is deceptively familiar. In 1521, while he was defending the castle of Pamplona against the French troops of King Francis I, his leg was broken by a cannonball. During his convalescence, he read a Life of Christ and a Lives of the Saints. He then resolved to go to the Holy Land to imitate the great deeds of saints for God. After an all-night vigil before our Lady at the monastery of Montserrat, he stopped at the little town of Manresa. There he worked in a hospice and spent hours in penance and prayer in a cave. For eleven months he struggled with intense scruples and spiritual consolations, all the while composing his famous *Spiritual Exercises*.

Ignatius himself gives a more detailed account of these events in a brief story of his life. What I find to be a goldmine of wisdom about the spiritual life is the first thirty-seven paragraphs,[1] which cover the time he spent at Manresa. His scribe, Luis Gonzales, notes in the Introduction that Ignatius resisted requests to dictate his story but gave in only after an occasion on which he told Gonzales about how he learned to struggle against the evil spirits regarding vainglory. It was as though he was finally moved with both a strong desire and a clear purpose for talking about himself. That purpose, I believe, is not to encourage but to enlighten, not to give guidelines for behavior but to explain how behavior is governed by the workings of the soul, so that anyone reading his story might learn to listen intelligently to the voice of God within. In fact, it is misleading to call this account an "autobiography." Nadal had asked Ignatius to "make known all that had taken place in his soul up to that moment."[2] Something like Augustine's *Confessions*, his story is an exploration of the general workings of the soul through an investigation of his own inner experience.

We can find out *what* he discovered about the soul in his "Rules for Discerning Spirits,"[3] appended to his *Spiritual Exercises.* But to find out how he made these discoveries, to understand the learning process, then this autobiography is the work to read. His purpose there is to teach, by the example of his own history, how to discover for ourselves the wisdom he encapsulates in the Rules for Discernment. What Ignatius discovered about the soul was made possible by an intellectual curiosity and an unflinching dedication to truth which gave his spiritual development a solid intellectual foundation. If I had to put in a single word what he is trying to say there, I would call it "realism." What follows is a plausible account of the steps in his development as he describes them. Here and there I will also refer to the parts of the *Exercises* which clarify what happened to him at Manresa. As we go, the meaning of "realism" and its significance for our own spiritual development will become clear.

Noticing

As Ignatius lay recuperating from his battle wounds, he not only read about the life of Christ and the lives of the saints. He also fantasized for long hours about doing gallant deeds for an unnamed noblewoman, and of other deeds which he discreetly puts under the category of "knight errantry" (A:5). He noticed that the thoughts of chivalry excited him at the time but left him sad and dry later, while the thoughts of great escapades for God left him with an abiding peace. He says he paid no attention to this difference at first, but then (referring to himself in the third person as he does throughout the autobiography) he says, "one day his eyes were opened a little and he began to wonder at the difference and to reflect on it, learning from experience that one kind of thoughts left him sad and the other cheerful." He remarks that this was the beginning of a "step-by-step" (A:8,55) process by which he eventually learned the art of discerning spirits.

I want to underscore the fact that this first step in his spiritual education was simply a matter of noticing two quite different feelings which lingered long after his fantasies. He makes no mention here of examining his conscience or of feeling any interior sorrow for his past sins. Nor has he received any extraordinary visions at this time. What he remembers as the beginning of a profound spiritual education is a growing intellectual curiosity about the spiritual feelings left over from two kinds of daydreaming.

But this was only a beginning. He notes that the growing desire to serve God which he experienced at this time was completely focused on external deeds—deeds as extreme as the deeds of chivalry that delighted him earlier—and that this new intellectual curiosity did nothing at first to change this simplistic zeal. "All his thought was to tell himself, 'St. Dominic did this, therefore, I must do it. St. Francis did this; therefore, I must do it'"(A:7,17). He describes himself as doing penances "not so much with an idea of satisfying for his sins, as to placate and please God" (A:14). To his mind, the outer world was where real action happens, while the inner self comprised just the feelings and thoughts which react to that world. Like a child, he regarded his feelings and thoughts as simply *himself*. He had no idea that the self, too, might be part of an objectifiable world subject to inquiry, understanding and growing realizations. "Up to this time he had continued in the same interior state of great and undisturbed joy, without any knowledge of the inner things of the soul" (A:20).

He describes here a little story of decision making so ignorant of the soul that we can't help think of him laughing at himself as he tells it (A:15-16). Once recovered from his leg surgery, he mounted a mule and headed for the monastery of Montserrat, where he intended to dedicate his life to God during an overnight vigil there. He fell in with a Moor and they began arguing whether the Virgin Mary lost her virginity in giving birth to Jesus. The Moor seems to have won the argument and spurred his mule on ahead. Steaming with indignation, Ignatius could not decide whether to give the Moor "a taste of his dagger" for what he had said about Our Lady or to let the matter pass. "Tired out from this examination," he did what many of us do on occasion. He rode to the fork in the road and let his mule furnish the best decision for him.

Well, the mule chose the better part of valor and brought him on to the monastery where Ignatius laid aside his dagger and fine clothes and spent the night in a vigil of dedication before the altar of Our Lady of Montserrat. From there he headed for Barcelona, taking a side road so as not to be recognized—a road leading to the fateful town of Manresa. As you know, he ended up spending eleven months there, learning the fundamentals of the spiritual life and writing exercises for others to learn the same for themselves.

Objectivity

For the first time in his life, Ignatius began to experience visions, though these first visions turned out to be less than trustworthy (A:19-20). Very frequently during broad daylight, he says, he saw a serpentine figure, covered with bright objects something like eyes, and was greatly consoled by the vision. But not to be carried away with the consolation, he noticed two unsettling features of these experiences. First, when they receded, he was left displeased. Second, during these same days he was also bothered by an inner voice saying, "How can you stand a life like this for the seventy years you have left to live." He reacts with the pugnacious instincts of a noble knight under attack. He retorts to this enemy, "You poor creature! Can you promise me even one hour of life?" He noted that this reaction brought him peace and that these days he made great efforts to preserve the serenity of his soul.[4]

However, this small victory marked just the beginning of an all-out war against him by the Tempter (A:21). Immediately after, he says, "He began to experience great changes in his soul." For a time, he felt intense distaste for spiritual things, and then as suddenly "as one removes a cloak from somebody else's shoulders" he experienced intense spiritual consolation. Ignatius remarks, "Here he began to marvel at these changes which he had never experienced before, saying to himself, 'What new kind of life is this that we are now beginning?'" He points out that while he had "a great desire to go forward in the service of God" he still "had no knowledge of spiritual things." Knowledge, no, but curiosity, yes: a curiosity not about what anyone said or wrote about the spiritual life, nor about any virtues or principles, but about the actual inner events which he experienced. And besides a curiosity, he acknowledges that he was very scrupulous about not departing from the truth (A:12,99). His sense of reality underwent a fundamental transformation inasmuch as he began to regard inner experience with no less objectivity and wonder than he formerly regarded the external deeds of chivalry.

In the crucible of these struggles with consolation and desolation, he worked out not only his own personal resolution to problems, but an objective understanding of what goes on in anyone who seeks God, and how they might question their own experiences. Scruples began to toss him between certitude and doubt about whether he had really confessed all the minutest sins of his life. So he prayed seven hours a day on his knees and abstained from eating and drinking for a week, but this bias for external actions got him nowhere (A:22). As this struggle led him to the brink of suicide, he made a desperate but morally courageous leap. Of the two kinds of inner sensations he experienced during his convalescence, he realized that the scruples clearly stripped him of all the good cheer which resulted from reading the lives of the saints. Encouraged, probably, by his success in rejecting the earlier temptation to give up a lifetime of trial, he began to look behind the *content* of these torturing thoughts, which were likely true enough, and to wonder about their *source* (A:24,25). He notes that "he began to look about for the way in which that [evil] spirit had been able to take possession of him" (A:25)—a habit of scrutiny he will later recommend to anyone interested in serving God (E:333-334). He then made up his own mind, which had become very clear, he says, never to confess his past sins again, "and from that day on he remained free of those scruples, holding it a certainty that our Lord in his mercy had liberated him" (A:25).

In the crucible of these struggles with consolation and desolation, he worked out not only his own personal resolution to problems, but an objective understanding of what goes on in anyone who seeks God, and how they might question their own experiences.

We can see here how intently Ignatius wanted to show how his understanding, and not just some vague good will, was the key to his freedom. By taking responsibility for understanding his own inner experiences, he completes the crucial differentiation which had begun earlier between his "self" and the feelings and thoughts that occurred to that self. He saw the self as capable of freely choosing to accept or reject feelings and thoughts. Implicit in this drama lies the unconceptualized idea that reality is simply whatever occurs and whatever really is, no matter whether "in here" or "out there" or "up there." From this time forward he watches the arrival of thoughts and desires into his consciousness like a high-stakes poker player watching the fall of the cards.

A Theology of History

At this point, we post-Freudians may wonder about the reality of these good and evil spirits. But Ignatius never doubts their reality and would not have been interested in debating doctrines anyway.[5] His belief in spirits is instrumental to his far larger concern to get intelligently involved in salvation history. Ignatius does not describe this larger concern in the autobiography, but it is quite evident in the *Exercises*, which he was composing at the time.[6] He envisioned salvation history from two angles: first, through a parable of the inner struggle of every man and woman; and second, through an extraordinarily matter-of-fact approach to the events narrated in the Gospels. First, let us look at his parable on the universal inner struggle, the meditation on the Two Standards.

At Manresa, while struggling with the spirits in his own life, Ignatius also discussed spiritual matters with many people with significantly positive results (A:26,29). No doubt he explained what he learned about the spirits. But he also seems to have learned firsthand from this ministry how both the good spirits and the evil spirits themselves have a worldwide ministry in mind. We can see this in the universal and aggressive scene which the Two Standards presents. It is far more than a lesson designed for retreatants to resist temptation and cooperate with grace. It is a theology of history, a worldview, a philosophy of life in metaphor projecting a vision of how all the thoughts and feelings which the various spirits initiate influence all the actions of people. It envisions every person, in every possible life, as engaged in this fundamental battle. On the side of evil, Ignatius sees innumerable demons sent out across the face of the earth, so that "no province, no place, no state of life, no individual is overlooked" (E:141). On the side of good he presents Jesus, described as "the Lord of all the world," who "chooses so many persons, Apostles, Disciples, and so forth," and who "sends them throughout the whole world, spreading his sacred doctrine through all sorts and conditions of persons" (E:145).

In this battle, both sides employ strategies. Lucifer sends demons out to snare people by drawing them first to desire riches, and then to want honors that they may finally arrive at pride. Christ's strategy is just the opposite, ploy for ploy. Christ sends disciples out to attract people to spiritual and even actual poverty, then to desire humiliations so that they may achieve humility (E:136-148).

For Ignatius, the parable of the Two Standards represents not just one way of looking at good and evil in the world. It is more than a device to provoke religious feelings. As a parable of the first order, it combines such insights and feelings into a powerfully integrating symbol meant to provoke action. In the colloquy which concludes the exercise, Ignatius has the retreatant beg for the poverty and the insults which are the earmarks of "true life" as exemplified in Christ (E:139). To drive this point home, he prescribes this colloquy at the end of at least forty one-hour exercises during the retreat (E:147,148,156,159)! Like Karl Marx, Ignatius' realism aimed not just at understanding history but at changing it.

He envisioned salvation history from two angles: first, through a parable of the inner struggle of every man and woman; and second, through an extraordinarily matter-of-fact approach to the events narrated in the Gospels.

The second way in which Ignatius looked at salvation history is by regarding the Gospel events as real human history. We can see this in his introductions to the contemplations of scriptural passages in his *Exercises*. Ignatius always directs the retreatant to start with the "history" of the matter to be contemplated.[7] Now, by "history," he did not mean "here is a story with a good moral." First and foremost, he meant "what really happened; what you, God, actually did."[8] This is evident in his choice of passages for contemplation. Of the fifty-one scriptural passages he lists in the appendix, and the five passages in the body of the text, he skips all the parables of Jesus and every teaching but one (Sermon on the Mount, §278). He expects a retreatant to find fruit in such laconic references as "Christ our Lord and the disciples were invited to the marriage feast," or "He was obedient to his parents," or even "Guards were stationed." Furthermore, he warns the director of the *Exercises* to refrain from "dilating upon the meaning of the history" and instead direct the exercitant to begin with the "true foundation of the history," and only then to go on to reflect on the meaning of the event contemplated. "It is not abundance of knowledge," he adds, "that satisfies the soul, but the inward sense and taste of things" (E:2).

Ignatius well knew the difference between reasoning on abstractions drawn from a story and acknowledging that an event actually occurred. It is one thing, for example, to reflect on how Mary's humility made her an apt choice for God to work the Incarnation. It is quite another to contemplate the raw fact that God actually became incarnate in this specific "house and room of our Lady in the city of Nazareth in the province of Galilee" (E:103). Ignatius himself showed an intense love for the actual places Jesus walked. Twice he bribed guards to let him see the footprint supposedly left by Jesus on Mount Olivet (A:47). Ignatius's spirituality has been called "Baroque" because it focuses so heavily on the visible and the sensible. But the deeper meaning of "Baroque" is that it begins from a conviction that God actually walked our land. This inner intellectual judgment is the real ground for the so-called "affective" and "sensual" approach Ignatius is famous for. Ignatius was indeed interested in feelings, but he did not *feel* about feelings, he *thought* about them.

By focusing on the parable of the Two Standards and on "historia" in the *Exercises*, I did not intend to sweep our question of angels and devils under the carpet. To fully understand Ignatius' realism, we should understand what the reality of spirits meant to him. Ignatius was mainly committed to the realism of a world in which our desires and thoughts are not our original creations; we remain essentially free to allow or reject them. In other words, his realism is not about spirits as much as about human freedom. Let me explain this from the point of view of contemporary psychology.

First of all, whether or not we believe in angels and devils, at least psychological health requires that we achieve some intellectual distance on our thoughts and feelings if we are to negotiate them responsibly. To grow out of our childish reactions to stimuli and into mature monitoring of our own reactions, we should be able to stand back from our inner reactions and notice what is going on in us. We need to insert this reflective moment between the events we experience (either within or without) and our response to those events.

Secondly, besides this psychological task, we also face a moral task. Once we recognize our spontaneous feelings and thoughts, we still must decide which ones we are going to let guide our living and which we will reject. For a responsible person, this means suppressing the feelings and thoughts about mere biological comfort or mere egoism and cooperating with those that respond to the objectively worthwhile. For example, if I am irritated by the noise in the apartment next door, I not only have to admit my feelings to myself; I must also decide whether or not to express my irritation and ask for some consideration.

But for Ignatius these psychological and moral challenges were embedded within a wider interpersonal challenge. The world of medieval Christianity was populated, not with abstract, undiscoverable "forces," but with concrete angels and devils who had will and intention of their own. So, not only do our feelings and thoughts originate outside of us in such a way that we are free to cooperate with them or not as we please; they originate from living beings who are intent on achieving their own purposes—some towards loving and serving God and some towards spiritual discouragement and the pursuits of pride. Whether or not these spirits have ontological existence as persons, at least it is easier to deal with the mysteries of grace and malice—which always remain mystery—through the metaphors of purposeful spirits than with the hypothesis of a stubbornly opaque "unconscious" that has come down to us from Freud.

No doubt, before this Ignatius had a notional assent to the existence of angels and devils, but now he has set his understanding of these creatures within his own experience of how the soul negotiates its own freedom. It is very important to notice here that this is an insight not into his personal psychology but into the psychology of human nature in general. Having made the personal breakthrough to a realism about the occurrence of his own feelings and thoughts, he achieves a comprehensive viewpoint on the general nature of all spiritual reality as a struggle between contrary spirits, each with conscious designs on the essentially free person. With this comprehensive understanding he is now ready to close in, as it were, on the forces of evil.

Categories of Experience

To work out a practical strategy for dealing with personal spirits, Ignatius realized that he needed to use names, or categories, which were either drawn from experience or were defined in terms of experience. In particular, he shows extreme care to distinguish the exact functions played by human desires and human thoughts. In doing so, he created a consistent and useful metaphysics of the spiritual life. What he found there runs counter to most contemporary psychology.

To the contemporary mind, for example, human desires belong to humans. The more we experience good desires and act on them, the more we consider ourselves moral persons. On the darker side, the more we experience degrading desires, the more degraded we think we really are. Ignatius, however, considered every desire for moral behavior to be a gift from God, not really our own possession, just as every degraded desire comes not from ourselves but from the evil spirits. We can make these desires our own, of course, but prior to that choice we are free—neither good nor evil for having experienced them.

The contemporary mind also names self-centeredness as the basic moral failing, as if other-centeredness is the basic moral success. Ignatius himself says that in principle, spiritual progress "will be in proportion to one's surrender of self-love and one's own will and interests" (E:189), but he does not raise other-centeredness as a norm for moral achievement. Instead, he scrutinizes where our desires originate. Even good desires for others come under his skeptical eye, on the chance that they might originate from the evil spirit and would bring in chaos disguised as peace. The point is not how much the desires of others supersede our personal desires, but how much divine desire we allow into consciousness.

The book of the *Spiritual Exercises* reveals the absolutely central role of desire which Ignatius sees not only regarding a person's praxis[9] of discerning spirits but also regarding his or her practical worldview. He gives a number of principles and parables that focus on a Christian's desire.[10] The director of the *Exercises* is expected to monitor closely the desires of the retreatant, waiting until certain specific desires are present before moving the person further.[11] He insists that good desires are gifts donated by God.[12] He also portrays both God and the evil spirits as having specific and urgent desires[13] about a person, and in doing so, he sets each person within a universal and enduring spiritual battleground. In other words, in the worldwide spiritual struggle, both God and "our ancient enemy" strongly desire to capture us, and once they do, they lead us further by implanting their own desires to become our own.

Besides discovering the central role of desires in the spiritual life, Ignatius also learned many lessons about how to deal with thoughts. Fortunately, we have not only his description in his autobiography (A:20-26) of how he learned about thoughts but also his extremely precise theory[14] and his practical advice[15] about it in the *Exercises*. "I presuppose that there are three kinds of thoughts in my mind, namely: one which is strictly my own, and arises wholly from my own free will; two others which come from without, the one from the good spirit, and the other from the evil one" (E:32). Elsewhere in the *Exercises* he points out that our thoughts are very largely governed by the consolation or desolation which we cannot cause in ourselves (E:317,333,334).

At some point during Manresa, Ignatius noticed that the good and evil spirits both prefer to move our affects, leaving our affective orientation to direct our thoughts. However, there are two significant exceptions to this rule. First, there are times when the spirits can introduce thoughts in our minds somewhat independent of whether we are in consolation or desolation (E:347). Second, and more importantly, Ignatius shrewdly noticed that the spirits resort to introducing thoughts chiefly when a person's moral horizon was opposite their own. So, for example, the good spirit often fills the morally good person with consolations, while the evil spirit will pry open that good conscience with disturbing thoughts in order to flood it with anxieties and sadness. For a generally immoral person the strategies are reversed, with the evil spirit flooding him or her with hedonistic consolations and the good spirit prying that conscience open with stinging thoughts in order to bring the consolations of an upright life.[16]

Am I belaboring the obvious by saying that Ignatius understood the difference between thoughts and desires? I think not. Granted, we all experience the difference, but few people ask themselves about the relationships between the different roles played by thoughts and desires when they reflect on their spiritual struggles. Fewer still generalize from their own experience to understand thoughts and desires within a comprehensive view-

Ignatius considered every desire for moral behavior to be a gift from God, not really our own possession, just as every degraded desire comes not from ourselves but from the evil spirits.

point. It was Ignatius's achievement to elevate the terms "desire" and "thoughts" from their everyday meanings to the status of reliable categories in an anthropology of the spiritual life. What makes these categories so reliable is that they are (1) verifiable in anyone's conscious experience, (2) related to each other in a consistent and discoverable pattern, and (3) extremely useful in the praxis of making decisions that affect one's world.

Not only did Ignatius elevate the experiential terms, "thoughts" and "desires," to the level of explanatory categories, he also took a current theological category and grounded it in verifiable experience. I am speaking of the term "grace," one of the most disputed terms of his day. As Ignatius uses the term in the *Exercises*, he nearly always[17] refers to what we would call "actual" grace, that is, to some help from God at a particular time and place. More importantly, he specifies exactly which acts of consciousness a retreatant ought to notice. The list of these acts of consciousness is quite revealing:

> the grace to *remember* how often I have fallen into sin (#25);
>
> the grace to *know* my sins and to *cast* them out (#43);
>
> the grace that all my *intentions*, *actions*, and *operations* may be directed purely and solely to the Divine Majesty (#46);
>
> the graces of (1) *inward knowledge* of sins; of (2) *feeling* the disorder of my actions; and (3) a *knowledge* of the world; and, with each of these, a *feeling* of abhorrence *and* the ability to amend my life (#63);
>
> the graces of *inward contrition*, of *weeping* for my sins or over Christ's sufferings, or to *resolve a doubt* (#87);
>
> the grace to imitate Christ and, implied, the *knowledge* of Satan's machinations and the *knowledge* of the true life which Christ shows (#139);
>
> the grace to *choose* what is more for God's glory (#152);
>
> the grace to be *glad* and to *rejoice* intensely (#221);
>
> the grace to *know* where I have failed (#240);
>
> the grace of great *devotion, intense love,* **tears** and *spiritual consolation*, which require, he says, an "intimate perception" of the fact that these are indeed grace from God our Lord (#322).[18]

Notice that all these passages describe an inner experience whose occurrence is rather easy to discern.[19] Just as the ordinary experiences of thoughts and desires often have divine origins, so divine grace has its effect in ordinary experience. The point here is that Ignatius discovered that the only categories that could do justice to both grace and nature were terms that pointed to events locatable in inner experience.

Rules for Understanding Movements

We have been looking at the roles which the categories "desire," "thought," and "grace" play in the Ignatius' praxis of discerning spirits. We must now see how he put this functional analysis into practice. While he was at Manresa, Ignatius began spelling out guidelines for seeking God and/or God's will in three different kinds of experiences: (1) in an undoubtable consolation, (2) in a struggle between consolation and desolation, and (3) in a time of tranquillity (E:175-178). I want to focus on the first kind as normative[20] because it will best give the realistic horizon against which all the other two kinds of experiences should be interpreted.

Among the many spiritual consolations Ignatius experienced at Manresa, he noticed that in some, he was left with no doubt that its source was God and not an evil spirit, while in others, consoling as they were, he still could discern an absence of conviction or certitude. Ignatius described the experiences which erased all doubt as lessons from God treating him just as a schoolmaster treats a little boy (A:27)—as lessons whose validity he felt absolutely no inclination to question. In some of these undoubtable consolations, Ignatius is moved to do something; in others, he receives an interior illumination about God's presence in the world.

Let me give you an example of an undoubtable consolation moving him to action. Ignatius, who had decided to abstain from meat, woke up one morning to a vision of a dish of meat appearing before his eyes. It was accompanied, he said, by "a great movement of the will to eat it in the future," a movement so strong and clear that "he could not hesitate to make up his mind that he ought to eat meat." Even after his confessor encouraged him to scrutinize the movement, Ignatius says that "examine it as he would, he could never have any doubt about it" (A:27).

Now what are we to think of this? Does Ignatius believe he is describing something rare in the spiritual life? I do not believe so. In the first place, he does not focus on what he saw with his eyes or imagination. He underscores the clear movement of his will which, free of antecedent desire, simply and unequivocally moved toward eating meat. In my experience as a spiritual director, I have found that many people experience these clear movements of the will but unfortunately hesitate to trust them. Ignatius himself seems to think that these clear movements happen rather often. In a letter he wrote years later to a Sister Teresa Rejadell he says this: "It *often* happens that our Lord moves and urges the soul to this or that activity. He begins by laying open the soul, that is, by speaking interiorly to it without the din of words, lifting it up wholly to his divine love and ourselves to a sense of himself without any possibility of resistance on our part, even should we wish to resist."[21] Furthermore, the very fact that he gives rules in the *Exercises* for dealing with this kind of consolation while a retreatant is deliberating about what action to take (E:330,336) says that he expects that he or she will likely experience it.

In his autobiography, Ignatius goes on to describe other undoubtable consolations which illumined his mind both while he was at Manresa and afterwards. These movements brought profound understanding of many things—of how Jesus Christ was present in the Eucharist, of how God created light and the world, and of a great many other things, he says, concerning faith and learning, all accompanied by intense devotion and spiritual delight. What is happening here under what Ignatius calls "understanding" is not any new message from God which Ignatius suddenly understands. Other texts show that by "understanding" Ignatius means what we might call either a judgment or a validation of truth.[22] In other words, Ignatius did not experience an insight into *how* God creates or *how* Jesus is present in the Eucharist but rather what Newman calls a real assent to a known truth. In a mere notional assent, for example, we might make the judgment: "The idea that Jesus is present in the Eucharist is reliable; I am willing to stand by it." A real assent, in contrast, would assert: "It is true that Jesus is present; this is the reality of the Eucharist." In ordinary parlance, we often say "I realized" something or other. What is happening in consciousness is that a certain proposition makes so much sense of our experience that we find ourselves completely unable to raise a relevant question about its validity. I will come back to this criterion of the absence of relevant questions shortly.

Again, however, we should ask whether Ignatius believed that this undoubtable intellectual illumination was a rare occurrence.

In the same letter to Sister Teresa Rejadell, he says, "I will call your attention briefly to . . . lessons which our Lord *usually* gives." He describes one such "usual" lesson as "an interior consolation which casts out all uneasiness and draws one to a complete love of our Lord. In this consolation he enlightens some, and to others he reveals many secrets as a preparation for later visits.[23]

My point here is that these undoubtable consolations had as their chief purpose a confirmation of Ignatius' judgment—a judgment at times about God's will concerning particular activities and at times about God's real presence in the world, a confirmation mediated by an intense love for God. Ignatius discovered that human judgment, both judgments of value and judgments of fact, can be directly affected by God in such a way as to completely eliminate a certain kind of doubt. He accepted as a real and common possibility that a person can experience the complete elimination of questions about the value of one among several options. And where someone already holds a proposition about reality, that person can be stripped of all questions about the reality to which the proposition refers. Both kinds of judgments are accompanied by and probably in part constituted by an intense experience of love.

Ignatius did not experience an insight into how God creates or how Jesus is present in the Eucharist but rather what Newman calls a real assent to a known truth.

It is my belief that learning how to do this is essentially a matter of trusting the inbuilt norms of one's own intelligence. True, we need faith that God cares for us and a felt love for God, but we should complement that faith and love by an intellectual conversion that regularly monitors the presence of residual questions and knows that the absence of questions is ground enough for conviction. Although Ignatius did not write about the grounds for conviction, he certainly understood for himself what they are and how they ought to be employed if he was to be a useful instrument in the hands of God.

I mentioned earlier that Ignatius also gave guidelines for finding God's will in two other kinds of experiences. In one, a person experiences strong swings between consolation and desolation. In the other, a person is not moved by strong movements and so must rely more on reason to deliberate pros and cons.[24] In either case, Ignatius intends on finding the will of God and shows every confidence that anyone who wishes can do so. Much like the disciples whom Luke described in *Acts* as artlessly "casting lots" to find the replacement for Judas whom God has chosen (1:15-26), Ignatius takes the reality of God's will as the fundamental governing principle of the universe. It is this belief that God's will is not difficult to discover, and not his psychological genius for recognizing spirits, which kept Ignatius in the real world personally and gave him the practical horizon for working out rules for negotiating inner movements which would make sense to others.

Conclusion

We have seen five distinct steps in Ignatius' discovery of the elements and dynamics of the spiritual life. I have called this intellectual achievement "realism." For the sake of drawing our own lessons from his account, let me summarize what a fully-developed realism ought to consider.

1. The absolute prerequisite for realism is the habit of noticing. By the habit of noticing I mean a healthy curiosity about my own feelings and thoughts, unhampered by religious guilt or doctrinaire "shoulds" about religious obligations.

2. The essential breakthrough to realism is reached when I have the ability to deal with inner events as objectively as with outer events. This crucial intellectual juncture gives me a new meaning to the word "real."

3. Realism reaches its widest scope through a theology of history. My theology of history should take the Gospels as an account of real, historical work by God. It also should explain, whether in metaphor or not, how every person's desires and thoughts are connected to this history. Finally, it should direct my praxis towards shaping present history in cooperation with the movements in me that come from God.

4. Realism next gathers its artillery of categories from the fertile field of recognizable experience. In order to deal effectively with inner movements, I ought to understand the roles which feelings, judgments, insights and so on, play in the spiritual struggle. I should also test all other categories by seeing if they can be correlated with experienced events.

5. I can now work to change reality. With a realism that has

conceived a theology of history and has tested the key words used in talking about spiritual living, the door is open for me to discover patterns in the everyday experience of grace and malice, whether my own or the community's, and to engage the real world with a love guided by the light of a converted intelligence.

Notes

[1] *St. Ignatius' Own Story*, trans. W. Young (Chicago: Loyola University Press, 1956), ch. 1-3. References to the autobiography and to the *Spiritual Exercises* will be in the form (A: Young's paragraph number) and (E: paragraph number), respectively. For editions of the autobiography without paragraph numbers, for example, *The Autobiography of St. Ignatius: With Related Documents*, trans., J. O'Callaghan (New York: Harper & Row, 1974), use this legend: Ch. 1 = # 1-12; ch. 2 = #13-18; ch. 3 = #19-37.

[2] Young, *Ignatius' Own Story*, p. 4.

[3] The full title is "Rules for feeling and recognizing in some manner the different movements that are caused in the soul—the good, that they may be received; the evil, that they may be rejected." He calls the rules for the Second Week "Rules to the same effect with greater discernment of spirits," hence their more familiar title, "Rules for Discernment of Spirits."

[4] In a similar fashion, Ignatius recognized that very lofty and consoling thoughts were robbing him of sleep at night. "He looked into this matter a number of times and gave it some thought" and concluded that despite their content, their source was the evil spirit and therefore he would ignore them completely (A:26).

[5] J. O'Malley, "The Fourth Vow in Its Ignatian Context: A Historical Study," Studies in the Spirituality of Jesuits, 15/1 (Jan. 83), Part I: "St. Ignatius and Doctrine," pp. 8-14.

[6] J. de Guibert, *The Jesuits: Their Spiritual Doctrine and Practice* (Chicago: Loyola University Press, 1964), p. 118.

[7] Ignatius also introduces the parables of the Two Standards with an account of "the history" (E:137,150). I do not believe that this makes the "historical" focus of Scripture any less realistic. Rather, it makes the parable more realistic. Ignatius believes that the Two Standards represents an accurate account of what is actually going on throughout the world. Ignatius also introduces the more imaginary Three Classes of People meditation with the "history" of three couples who want to use 10,000 ducats well. It is fiction, but good fiction inasmuch as it says something about how actual people avoid letting "the desire of being better able to serve God our Lord [be] their motive" (E:155).

[8] Occurrences of "historia" in the *Exercises* are: 2(three times), 102, 111, 137, 150, 191, 201, 219. It is interesting to note that Ignatius never uses either the term "history" or the term "mystery" in the First Week.

The first prelude during the First Week is always "a mental representation of the place" (E:47), while in the rest of the retreat it is "call to mind the history" (E:102,111,191,219) leaving "mental representation of the place" as the second prelude. The reason for this difference can be found in the contrast between the graces of the First Week and the graces of the other three. During the First Week the retreatant asks for the graces of shame, confusion, sorrow, tears, revulsion, and fear on account of his or her own sins (E:48,55,63,65)—as if the only realistic understanding of sin is the inverse insight that sin is utterly without sense. During the Second Week, one asks repeatedly for "intimate knowledge" and "love" of our Lord (E:104). During the Third Week, one asks for sorrow, compassion, and shame (E:193) for the sake of Christ—"sorrow with Christ in sorrow, anguish with Christ in anguish, tears, and deep grief because of the great affliction Christ endures for me" (E:203)—not as a direct response to the absurdity of one's own sins. And during the Fourth Week the retreatant seeks to "rejoice intensely because of the great joy and glory of Christ our Lord" (E:221).

[9] There have been two meanings of "praxis" current in philosophy and theology—Marx's and Aristotle's. For Marx it meant the activity, particularly the economic activity, that shapes a person's consciousness. For Aristotle it meant the inner acts that precede making—doing rather than producing, conduct rather than product—and which are the source of external activity, even economic. I am using the term here in the far more astute Aristotelian sense. See B. Lonergan, "Theology and Praxis," in F.E. Crowe, ed., *A Third Collection: Papers by Bernard J.F. Lonergan*, SJ (New York: Paulist, 1985), p. 184.

[10] Principles and parables on desire in the *Exercises:* para. 23, 98, 146, 151, 155, 166, 167, 168.

[11] References to the need to monitor desire in the *Exercises:* para. 20, 73, 89, 130, 133, 174, 177, 185, 199, 339, 350.

[12] That desires are gifts from God: *Exercises*, para. 16. See also the many references to the "gift" of desires in his letters: W. Young, trans., *Letters of St. Ignatius of Loyola* (Chicago: Loyola University Press, 1959), pp. 19, 20, 43, 50, 92, 131, 153, 186, 222, 232, 314, 354, 368, 375, 378. Hereafter, Young, *Letters*.

[13] Both God and Satan have desires: *Exercises*, para. 234, 326, 327. In his letters, see Young, *Letters*, pp. 18-24 (June, 1536, letter to Teresa Rejadell), 131.

[14] Theory regarding thoughts: *Exercises*, para. 32, 346, 347.

[15] Practical advice regarding thoughts: ibid, para. 314, 315, 317, 329, 333, 334, 347, 351.

[16] How spirits use thoughts vs. affects: ibid, para. 314, 315, 317, 329. Also: "As a sequel to these *thoughts*, he was seized with a disgust of the life [of scruples] he was leading and a *desire* to be done with it. It was our Lord's way of awakening him from sleep" (A:25).

[17] The one clear exception is #50 referring to the angels who were

"changed from grace to malice"—an instance of what we would call "sanctifying grace."

[18] Ignatius has four other, more general descriptions of graces: the grace to amend my life (#61); the grace to be prompt and diligent to fulfill God's will (#91); the grace to be received under Christ's standard, in spiritual poverty, actual poverty, and receiving insults (#147); and the grace to imitate Christ (#248). He also has eight completely unspecified references to "grace": how solitude makes one "more disposed to receive graces and gifts" (#20); Communion helps preserve the soul in the increase of grace (#44); to amend, with the help of grace (#61, #243); to ask for only God's love and grace; these are enough (#234); to ask for the virtues or graces of which one has greater need (#257); see the graces and gifts by which the Apostles were raised above the Fathers of Old and New Testaments (#275); in desolation, the Lord withdraws intense graces (#320). While unspecified in these texts, the specified texts can give the perceptive director a very precise idea of the inner experience to which Ignatius is referring.

[19] Ignatius clearly prefers to focus on actual inner events rather than faculties. True, in the very first exercises, Ignatius has the retreatant apply the "three powers of the soul"—memory, intellect, and will—to various stories of sin. This triad certainly originates with Augustine, but whether or not Ignatius knew of it at Manresa, he clearly has the retreatant exercise these powers sheerly in order to experience the "graces" of the further movements specified usually in the second prelude of the various exercises.

[20] For persuasive arguments defending the normativity of this kind of consolation, see K. Rahner, "The Logic of Concrete Individual Knowledge in Ignatius Loyola," in *The Dynamic Element in the Church* (Montreal: Palm Publishers, 1964), pp. 84-170.

[21] Young, *Letters*, p. 22 (in the June, 1536, letter to Teresa Rejadell). Italics mine.

[22] "Falsehood and truth have of themselves a direct effect on the *understanding* and lead us to accept or reject a proposition even before we have reasoned about it" (ibid, p. 198). "For the will . . . draws the *understanding* after it and does not leave it free to *judge* correctly" (ibid, p. 202). Italics mine.

[23] Ibid, p. 21. Although it is not clear that doubt and resistance are impossible in the consolation he describes in this passage, at least he believes that a consolation illuminating one's judgment of reality can be frequent in a good soul. I encourage the reader not so much to check past experience as to notice in present experience that these movements occur probably more frequently than one might suspect.

[24] In the section entitled "Three Times for Making a Good Election" (E:175-178) Ignatius gives no rules for interpreting the undoubtable consolation, for the obvious reason that none is needed to settle doubt. In the case of a retreatant experiencing both consolation and desolation, he refers the director to the Rules for Recognizing Different Spirits. These

are appended to the end of the *Exercises*, I believe, because they are applicable not only for a retreatant seeking God's will but also for anyone negotiating the intellectual illuminations by which one sees God in all things during everyday life. In the case of a retreatant experiencing neither consolation nor desolation, Ignatius gives procedures within the text of the *Exercises* at that point, and repeats them almost verbatim in the Rules for Distributing Alms (E:337-344), probably because they do not apply more widely to seeing God in all things but only to finding God's will.

TAD DUNNE

Spiritual Integration
in Ignatius of Loyola

*I*n two previous articles, I have analyzed Ignatius of Loyola's spirituality for the purpose of understanding not so much what he learned but how he learned it.[1]

In the first article, I proposed that his keen sense of moderation in everyday practical matters was the fruit of a methodical extremism about interior religious movements. That is, he refused to give in to the suggestions of the evil spirits, even when the content of those suggestions appeared quite worthy of attention, with the surprising result that his everyday decisions showed consistent balance and moderation.

In the second article, I proposed that he learned how to ground this prudential spirituality on an intellectual realism. This realism gave Ignatius a standpoint from which he could be fiercely objective about the movements he experienced within himself. As he explored this inner world, he then saw the need to root the theological category of "grace" in recognizable experiences, and, in turn, to raise the recognizable experiences of "desire" and "thoughts" to the level of theological precision.

Now you and I learn about our spiritual life in many different ways—from our reading, our meditation, our spiritual direction, and our everyday trial-and-error experiences. The question is integration. How do we take one insight from prayer, another from some theology book, another from plain common sense, and decide which to follow? Ignatius seems to have achieved something on the level of method, on the basis of which he could integrate sometimes contradictory wisdoms coming from these different quarters. I think we can sketch out an answer if we review his life with the question, "How did Ignatius put it all together?"

In a nutshell, we could describe Ignatius's achievement as a spiritual integration of four different realms of meaning. These are: (1) the realm of everyday practicality; (2) the realm of religious experiences; (3) the realm of theological theories; and (4) the realm of an interior praxis which shapes the words he used in the other three realms.

In what follows, I would like to define in more general terms what I mean by "spiritual integration," and then explore how Ignatius integrated these four realms of meaning into a harmonious and balanced unity. Then we will look at Bernard Lonergan's contribution to understanding the fundamental struggles of the spiritual life.

Finally, we will return to Ignatius and explore the fundamental spiritual doctrine which his extraordinary methods taught him. I hope that his example and these updated reflections might give the reader a clearer idea of what personal spiritual integration might demand.

Spiritual Integration

"Spiritual integration"[2] is the capacity to draw effectively upon these four realms of meaning: everyday common sense, religious experience, theoretical reflection, and the praxis of philosophic interiority. Before exploring how these four might be integrated, we should look more closely at how each of these realms of meaning functions in itself.

Everyday common sense specializes in practical know-how and in giving life a dramatic flair. The common sense person gets along in the world not by some theoretical formula applicable in many situations but by knowing the ropes in each situation. It is *savoir faire* more than book-learning. He or she sizes up concrete situations quickly and learns what people are likely to accept and reject.

Theoretical reflection specializes in understanding how things are related to each other regardless of one's personal stake in the matter. The best theorists forbid any personal gain from interfering with their observations, hypotheses, and tests. Their aim is to state general laws that govern a wide spectrum of cases.

Religious experience is, first of all, just experience. Before it reaches the level of explicit knowledge, we feel as though we are being drawn by an invisible hand or being inflated with an unnamed spirit. Sometimes this experience directs us in practical decisions, and at other times it gives us a deeper appreciation of a truth than we've ever had before.

Finally, there is what I have called the *praxis of philosophic interiority*. By "interiority" I mean not just religious experiences but all possible experiences of consciousness—feelings, insights, deliberations, value judgments, doubts, questions, wonder, realizations and even love. By "philosophic praxis" I mean a reflection on these inner experiences with a view to giving precise and useful names to each of them and relating these names to one another in such a way as to give you or me, personally, a verifiable understanding of how interior processes generally work. This philosophic exercise gives us a model of subjectivity which we can use in the other three realms of meaning.[3]

As I have defined "spiritual integration," spiritually integrated men and women are able to move intelligently from one realm to the other. So although they may possess no more than average common sense, they do rely on theoretical perspectives to solve the psychological, technical, and social problems that arise between people of common sense. In other words, besides relying on common sense, they understand the usefulness of theory.

Second, the spiritually integrated experience a love in their hearts that will not quit. They have named that love "divine"; and they count on that love to illuminate their common sense values and their uses of theoretical reflection. This is how they rely on God to carry them through times of trouble and to spur them to gratitude for every gift.

Finally, and most importantly, the spiritually integrated will certainly use somewhat different language or categories for talking either practicality, theory, or religious experience. But they do not *think* in fundamentally different ways about how to keep their minds on track in each of these realms of meaning. While the objects they think and decide about require different languages and special procedures, they think about their own acts of thinking and choosing in basically the same way. That is, underneath the variety of methods used in each realm, they have one method for monitoring the authenticity of their own thinking and deciding.

By way of contrast, the spiritually *unintegrated* may be aware of these realms of meaning, but they do not move intelligently from one to the other. In most cases they make common sense their home base. Nearly all their reflections follow the common sense rules that all decisions must have a practical result and that all these results have to be immediately evident. Now and then they venture out from this home base and steal a theoretical insight from Psychology Today or Popular Science, but they usually pluck it out of its theoretical context and take it home to decorate the house. Now and then they experience a love for God that moves them beyond their sense of the everyday, but unless they can find a practical use for this new love, it withers. Now and then they sally forth into philosophy, although anything beyond what they find in Readers' Digest takes too long to read, and has no apparent consequences for the immediate future.

Ignatius

Many people think of Ignatius as one of the most practical-minded of all the saints. I would dispute this. I would call him an "extreme realist," which is something altogether different. He did not count on common sense above all else. Practicality was hardly his watchword. Uppermost in his mind was the will of God, and he would have been a hermit for the rest of his life had God so directed him. He was scrupulously concerned about the truth of his experiences, no matter where that truth might lead.[4]

As it happened, he was led first of all to understand that his inner experiences came from outside himself, and that there was an art to discerning whether his feelings and thoughts originated from God or from an evil spirit. By wrestling with his own understanding of his experiences, he gradually put together a picture of the human person which would serve him—and anyone who underwent his "spiritual exercises"—for a lifetime. By creating a consistent, verifiable and useful model of the human person, he was beginning the work of philosophic interiority.

There are other holy men and women who have had experiences remarkably similar to Ignatius's but whose understanding of those experiences were chiefly within other realms of meaning. John of the Cross, for example, hiked up the mountain of God and described the view from the top in terms at once splendidly poetic and solidly scholastic.[5] He moved comfortably in the realms of religious experience, common sense, Thomistic theory, and even poetry, if I may add poetry to the list of realms of meaning. But he did not seem to explore how thoughts and feelings work in a soul. Teresa of Avila kept a diary of her hike up that mountain, describing her experience as mounting through one mansion to another.[6] She, too, could move from religious experience to common sense and even to the realm of theory. (She preferred, it is said, the theoretical insights of a good theologian to the pious mutterings of a holy but unlearned priest.) Ignatius, by contrast, published no poetry, cautioned against too much theorizing about such issues as nature and grace, and left only the barest diary of his religious experiences. But by learning about the dynamics of the soul he crafted a method by which others could test the spirits as they were immersed in either common sense, theory, or religious experience. Ignatius, we could say, hiked up the mountain and saw the face of God, scrambled down again, calling to mind not so much *what* he learned but *how* he was taught, and then wrote a manual on how to *learn* to climb a mountain.

Many people think of Ignatius as one of the most practical-minded of all the saints. I would dispute this. I would call him an "extreme realist," which is altogether different.

Now Ignatius was not a philosopher. He did not try to explain how our inner processes determine what we make of ourselves and our worlds. So his spiritual integration did not reach the generality and completeness of a properly philosophical explanation. Instead, he invented three stories to depict the full range of a life shared with God: (1) "The Call of the Temporal King"; (2) "The Two Standards"; and (3) "The Contemplation to Obtain Love."[7] Taken together, these stories had the range and power which great epics and powerful dreams had formerly in Ignatius' life. They not only gave him a framework for understanding reality, they *excluded* other epics and dreams which competed for this hermeneutic honor. Ignatius included them in his *Spiritual Exercises* to give the retreatant the same tales to help direct his or her everyday actions.

For now, I want to focus mainly on his story of the Two Standards, and in particular on its power as a story to relate the realms of religious experience to the realm of common sense. (In my previous two articles I reviewed its analysis of the tactics of Lucifer and Christ as well as its universal range as a theology of history.) At the end, I will review a second story, his "Contemplation to Obtain Love," which deals less with method and more with content.[8]

What first strikes anyone reading the text of the Two Standards is the rich imagery Ignatius used to contrast the strategies of Satan and Christ. Satan is seated on a fiery throne, near Babylon, inspiring horror and terror. He scatters innumerable demons to absolutely every corner of life, so that no person or place is overlooked. He goads his demons to lay this trap: first they are to move people to desire riches, then to desire fame, and finally to self-sufficient pride. By contrast, Christ is standing in a lowly place in a great plain near Jerusalem. He handpicks disciples and sends them to every corner of the world, recommending that they help others by attracting them to want poverty, at least spiritual if not actual, then to want the humiliations which Christ suffered, so that they might gain the real prize, which is humility with Christ. Ignatius chose his words carefully: Lucifer inspires horror and terror; he scatters; he goads. Christ appears beautiful and attractive; he chooses; he recommends. Already, we are learning the "feel" of the difference between how these two forces touch our consciousness, a feel Ignatius fully intends to elicit in us. In other words, he uses imagery to teach us to identify and manage interior movements with a growing awareness of their connection to world process.

> *Ignatius learned that you cannot move from the realm of religious experience to the realm of common sense simply by deciding to do so. You must rely on the religious experience itself to move you.*

Besides these affective and imaginative components in the story of the Two Standards Ignatius also includes an action component—although with a brilliant nuance.[9] He does not expect the retreatant simply to choose Christ's standard and turn from Satan's, as if the exercise were some fundamentalist revival meeting. He is too skeptical about people's ability to commit themselves by sheer dint of effort. Instead he has the retreatant beg God for "the grace to be received under his standard, first in the highest spiritual poverty, . . . and even in actual poverty; secondly, in bearing insults and wrongs, thereby to imitate him better." In other words, the retreatant does not choose; he or she begs to be chosen. This begging prayer occurs more frequently than any other in the entire thirty day retreat—about forty times in all.[10] Ignatius learned that you cannot move from the realm of religious experience to the realm of common sense simply by deciding to do so. You must rely on the religious experience itself to move you. And you will be immensely helped by a fully dramatic understanding, with analytic, affective, and action dimensions, of how to negotiate this bridge between religious experience and the everyday world of practicalities.

In military parlance, we distinguish strategy and tactics, with strategy being the overall plan to defeat an enemy and tactics being the maneuvers made at close quarters with the enemy during the battle. The strategy which Ignatius outlined in his Two Standards would not help us very much if he had not added to the parable some directives on tactics. These he has provided in his rules for discerning spirits, his rules for scruples and in a letter to Teresa Rejadell. While we cannot go into them all here (although it takes only about twenty minutes to read them all), I would like to give some idea of their general drift.

Here is a collection of his descriptions of the tactics of the evil spirit.[11] The reason I give so many here is to convey some idea of how often and in how many familiar ways Ignatius saw the spirits of evil dragging down a soul. (I apologize for the sexist language, which, for a change, should offend men more than women):

> It is characteristic of the evil spirit to harass with anxiety, to afflict with sadness, to raise obstacles backed by fallacious reasonings that disturb the soul. In this way he seeks to prevent the soul from advancing [315].
>
> [The enemy of our human nature brings] . . . darkness of soul, turmoil of spirit, inclination to what is low and earthly, restlessness rising from many disturbances and temptations which lead to lack of faith, lack of hope, lack of love. The soul is completely heavy, tepid, sad and feeling separated from its Creator and Lord [317].
>
> [The enemy] . . . weakens the soul, or disquiets it; or by destroying the peace, tranquillity and quiet which it had before. . . . These things are a clear sign that the thoughts are proceeding from the evil spirit, the enemy of our progress and eternal salvation [333].
>
> [The enemy says,] "How can you continue a life . . . deprived of all satisfaction from friends, relatives, posses-

sions? How can you live so lonely a life, with no rest? You can save your soul in other ways and without such dangers" [Rej 7].

He tries to prevent a person from speaking of any of the blessings he or she has received. His purpose is to prevent us from producing fruit in others as well as in ourselves [Rej 9].

The enemy does not care whether he speaks the truth or whether he lies. His sole purpose is to overcome us [Rej 11].

He makes use of everything to vex us. . . . We find ourselves sad without knowing why. We cannot pray with devotion, nor contemplate, nor even speak or hear of the things of God with any interior taste or relish. . . . He thus works to bring us to a state of general discouragement. We can see what causes our great fear and weakness: it is a too-prolonged gaze at such times on our miseries [Rej 15].

When the enemy of our human nature tempts a just soul with his wiles and seductions, he earnestly desires that they be received secretly and kept a secret. . . . He knows that he cannot succeed in his evil undertaking once his evident deceits have been revealed [326].

The enemy of our human nature investigates from every side all our virtues. . . . Where he finds the defenses of eternal salvation weakest and most deficient, there he attacks and tries to take us by storm [327].

On the other side, look at these descriptions of what characterizes movements coming from God or the good spirits:

It is characteristic of the good spirit to give courage and strength, consolations, tears, inspirations and peace. This he does by making all easy, by removing all obstacles so that the soul goes forward in doing good [315].

In souls that are progressing to greater perfection the action of the good angel is delicate, gentle, delightful. It may be compared to a drop of water penetrating a sponge [335].

With these descriptions, it may seem relatively easy to know when we are being moved by the evil spirits and when by God. But it is not easy, and for two reasons.

First, unless a person has already understood the entire world process in terms of movements originating from good and evil spirits (or in terms of a struggle for authenticity), he or she will easily regard these experiences as sheerly accidental, just a mood one is in for the time being, just part of one's psychology, rather than encroachments upon one's person by spiritual beings with ulterior motives. Many Christians seem to believe that most of the things they do on a given day are neutral to God, as if God is interested only in preventing sins over here and in helping people over the humps of life over there. The power of Ignatius' saving tale of the Two Standards is that it presumes that every single thought, word, and action of ours is precious to God and bait for Satan.

Second, even for a person who does regard world process in these terms, there is a complexity in the tactics of the evil spirit that takes some measure of experience to recognize. As Robert Kennedy was fond of quoting, "Good judgment is usually the result of experience. And experience is frequently the result of bad judgment."[12] Let me quote again from the several places where Ignatius describes this devilish ploy.

> If a cause precedes, both the good angel and the evil spirit can give consolation to a soul, but for a different purpose. . . . The evil spirit consoles so that he might draw the soul to his own perverse intentions and wickedness [331].
>
> It is a mark of the evil spirit to assume the appearance of an angel of light. He begins by suggesting thoughts that are suited to a devout soul, and ends by suggesting his own [332].
>
> We can frequently be deceived because after a consolation or inspiration [from God], when the soul is still abiding in its joy, the enemy tries under the impetus of this joy to make us add to what we have received from God our Lord. His only purpose is to disturb and confuse us in everything. At other times he makes us lessen the import of the message we have received and confronts us with obstacles and difficulties, so as to prevent us from carrying out completely what had been made known to us. [And then Ignatius adds,] Right here there is more need of attention than anywhere else [Rej 16].

In other words, not all consolation can be trusted. Ignatius urges us to examine the whole course of consoling movements and, when we have been fooled, to discover exactly how so as to avoid that particular trap in the future. There is more to these rules, but this will give you the general idea. In practice, I have found that they are easier to apply to someone else than to myself; I can find help in them for myself mainly when I tell someone else what I am experiencing.

But, to repeat what I said earlier, the larger difficulty is believing seriously enough in the story of our spiritual struggle to want tactical rules such as these.

Lonergan and Spiritual Integration

Since the time of Ignatius, two revolutions in human thought have intervened which demand some kind of transformation of his praxis if it is to retain its power to guide spiritual living. There have been the revolutionary discoveries made about human consciousness, beginning with the cognitive critiques of Kant, and expanding with the existential reflections of Heidegger, Kierkegaard, Blondel, Marcel, and so forth, all of which completely turned the face of philosophy toward personal experience. Then there has been the Newtonian revolution in science that abandoned the search for certitude which characterized the Middle Ages and established instead an empirical method that produced verifiable explanations of experience. These two revolutions have merged to some extent, producing the empirical psychology of Freud and the empirical sociology of Durkheim.

Bernard Lonergan's great contribution to these two revolutions is to have brought Kant's question and Newton's method together into a full-blown empirical philosophy of consciousness. In order to see how an analysis of subjectivity gives an objective world view, it will help if I sketch out the structure of consciousness as Lonergan has articulated it.

In Lonergan's analysis, we transcend ourselves at five levels of consciousness.[13] First, whenever we attend to data. Second, when we get some insight into that data. Third, when we make a judgment that reality is really what we think it is. Fourth, when we commit ourselves to some action. And fifth, when we fall in love. For the sake of brevity, Lonergan calls these levels experience, understanding, judging, deciding, and loving.

As our consciousness moves through each of these five levels we not only experience ourselves in a different way, we also create the society and the culture in which we live. Indeed, these are the major processes within us by which the human dimensions of reality are created; there are no "structural difficulties" in a culture that are unconnected to these events in real men and women. It is very important to see this subjective pole of every objective situation. We can see, for example, that our awareness of problems and possibilities spring from experience, our technologies spring from understanding, our histories from judgments, our cultures from decisions and commitments and our communities from love. In other words, by understanding how these five levels of conscious events work to produce the everyday situations in which we live, we will also be able to question how they *fail* to work and how therefore human situations deteriorate.

Not to descend too much into the complexities within this five-level structure of consciousness, I think we can use it as a psychological framework for our own spiritual integration. In his explanation of what it means to be a person, Lonergan gives us not pre-packaged conclusions about how to act but words to help us understand the interior activities that shape our external histories. Like Ignatius giving us method to climb mountains, Lonergan provides us with a method for producing a continuous stream of good questions to ask ourselves about the quality of our choices, about the depth of our responses to people, and about how well the several loves of our lives fit together.

Lonergan provides us with a method for producing a continuous stream of good questions to ask ourselves about the quality of our choices, about the depth of our responses to people, and about how well the several loves of our lives fit together.

What are some of these questions? I would like to give you some examples that come to my mind, although with the caution that underlining such questions does practically no good at all. What counts is that each of us understands our own consciousness in such a way that these questions make sense and that we could easily raise them ourselves in a variety of forms.

The basic question, I believe, is "What am I doing here?" As I go about my business today, what is really going on in me and in my situations? This question can be teased out at the five levels of consciousness.

On the level of *experience* I ask myself: Am I attentive to my surroundings or am I shutting my eyes and stopping my ears for some reason? Do I actively notice my inner feelings and intuitions or do I fix my attention chiefly on the people, things and events outside of me?

On the level of *understanding* I ask: Am I asking why or how because I really wonder why or how or just because I want to be insightful and clever? That is, has my intellectual curiosity been honest or bluffing?

On the level of *judging*: Do I use my head ultimately to uncover the truth about myself and my world or merely to memorize, analyze and become a knowledgeable person? Am I interested, in other words, in all of reality or just in me and my situation?

On the level of *deciding*: Have I really put my heart into my choices or am I just being dutifully faithful to a job? Do I carry out my promises because I really believe it is worthwhile doing so, or only because I believe it's expected of me?

Finally, on the level of *loving*: Do I really love the people I claim to love, or do I have a secret love which I admit to no one? Does love of some person or persons dominate my life, or do I really love only success or sex or the bottle?

As I say, do not bother too much with these questions. Just as Ignatius's rules for discerning spirits do little good without a theology of history that uncovers the work of spirits everywhere, so these questions do little good without a complete realization that your own consciousness is indeed like this and that all human achievements are the results of this inner struggle.

The View from the Top

I said that I would return to Ignatius's other integrating story, the Contemplation to Obtain Love. It would be a mistake to overlook this because the very methodological power of a meditation like the Two Standards and an analysis of the structure of consciousness can blind us to what that method and structure lead us to, namely, the person and the purpose of God. We would be like a psychologist who learns all the tools of analysis but fails to fall in love. We would be like so many specialists today who know "how to" but not "for whom" nor "for what purpose." I think this will be more clear if I describe this contemplation. Here are a few excerpts:

> I will ponder with great affection how much God our Lord has done for me, and how much he has given me of what he possesses, and finally, how much, as far as he can, the same Lord desires to give himself to me [234].
>
> [I will marvel at] how God dwells . . . in the elements,

giving them existence; in the plants, giving them life; in the animals giving them sensation; in people giving them understanding. So he dwells in me, giving me existence, life, sensation, understanding; and makes a temple of me, since I am created in the likeness and image of the Divine Majesty [235].

[I will] consider how God works and labors for me in all creatures upon the face of the earth; that is, he conducts himself as one who labors [236].

[I will marvel how] all blessings and gifts descend from above. Thus my limited power comes from the supreme and infinite power above, and so, too, justice, goodness, mercy . . . as rays of light descend from the sun, and as the waters flow from their fountains, and so on [237].

Ignatius prefaces all these contemplations with two considerations which nudge the retreatant to the brink of action:

The first is that love ought to manifest itself in deeds rather than in words [231].

The second is that love consists in a mutual sharing . . . with the lover giving to and sharing with the beloved whatever he or she has or can attain; and . . . with the beloved doing the same for the lover [231].

So Ignatius's shrewd intellectual realism served a deeply personal desire: to welcome the blessings of life as gifts from God and to express his gratitude in action to God. Having seen that God gives his entire divine self to us through action, Ignatius's own strategies and tactics were dominated by a desire to offer to God dominion over every action of his soul. This was the sole reason why he began to wonder about the relationships between common sense, religious experience, and theoretical reflection—and why he articulated an intellectual realism to guide his steps from one realm to the other. In other words, his grateful love for God was the real driving force behind his own spiritual integration.

By speaking of love, I do not mean to step outside the context of philosophic interiority. Lonergan's analysis of the structure of consciousness makes very clear the relationship between what we love and how we spend our time today. What that relationship may be for you or me today may not be immediately evident, but the habit of wondering about this integration helps immensely to bring it about. This is because the upper levels are meant to integrate the lower levels. So, for example, when love runs smoothly on the fifth level, it is easier to make decisions on the fourth. When we make good decisions on the fourth, we tend to be more ready to face reality on the third, whether that reality is pleasant or not. When we are realists on the third level, we free our intelligences on the second to wonder why and how. And when we freely question experience like that, we find joy in being attentive on the first level.

This is not to say that consciousness does not also work from below upwards.[14] In every creative event, someone pays attention to possibilities, puts the data together through understanding, verifies the possibilities through judgment, executes the possibility through committee action, all for the sake of someone or something he or she loves.

But at the same time, there is a healing movement from above downwards by which we check on our progress and eliminate the problems, as far as we can. The act of raising questions about the integration of our spirit ought to be done from the top level of consciousness, that is, after we have remembered what or whom we love. From the standpoint of love, our commitments, our realism, our understanding and our attention fall into their real proper perspective. Unfortunately, secular psychology has conditioned us to start at the second level of consciousness and ask ourselves, "Now *why* did I do that?" or "*How* can I convince him to go with me?" Such questions are usually easier to resolve once we get in touch with the knowledge that comes through love and leave to the end the knowledge that comes through understanding.

Particularly in our prayer, it is important to start at the top, start with the actual loves of our life. When a presider at liturgy invites us to "be present" to God, many in the congregation start from the bottom, calling on their memory of what God looks like or acts like, then move up laboriously trying to understand, to stay in reality, to muster some feeling of commitment, as if they might finally reach a vision of God which will call forth floods of love. It is much quicker, however, to first remember the love which is in my heart these days. In other words, to be "present" to God by being present to the gift of being able to love which God gives me. From that vantage point, it is easy to move downwards and be present to my vocation, to the reality of God throughout the world, to the *whys* and *hows* that help me understand, and finally to the transformed eyes with which I look upon the world.

It must be emphasized that we experience strong resistance to this integration. It is everyone's experience and an abiding concern of Ignatius that something pulls us down. Call it a devil; we can call it whatever we want but we should not call it just fate or, what is worse, our own selves. The reason that the worldview of angels and devils has endured for centuries is that in every culture wise people seem to believe that they are neither the source of their own goodness nor the instigator of their own temptations. Life is a dialectic of desires, an ongoing tug of war between forces outside of us. The winners in this war are those who exercise their freedom to fight against the downward pull and cooperate with the upward pull.

Earlier I defined spiritual integration as the ability to move intelligently between the realms of common sense, religious experience, theoretical reflection, and philosophic interiority. It is the realm of philosophic interiority that provides questions such as these, enabling us to deal intelligently with the questions of how common sense, religious experience, and theoretical reflection go together in everyday life. So we can now define spiritual integration more precisely: It is the deliberate liberation of my attention by intelligence, of my intelligence by realism, of my realism by responsibility, and of my responsibility by love. The more deliberately we do this, of course, the more successful we eventually will be in moving between the realms of common sense, religious experience, and theory.

Having seen that God gives his entire divine self to us through action, Ignatius's own strategies and tactics were dominated by a desire to offer to God dominion over every action of his soul.

Although literate people today are able to think about their own spiritual integration in such psychological and philosophical terms, I would not want to drop the kind of symbolic integration offered by Ignatius in his Two Standards meditation. In spiritual direction, people easily talk about the good and evil spirits. Whatever the ontological status of "evil spirits" may be, the story of temptation provides a very simple way of talking about the movements in me whose origins lie outside of my control. The story also helps me maintain a high sense of interior vigilance about inner experience by depicting the origin of the detrimental movements as cunning spirits who intently desire to drag me down. Still less would I want to use this psychological praxis to replace the scriptural tale of Jesus obeying his own love and giving us a living example of how love is really the point of everything. While Lonergan's analysis of the structure of consciousness can give us valuable insight into what is going on within us, these stories give us the affective punch that moves the heart.

So, while I have been insisting that spiritual integration depends on an ability to move intelligently between common sense, religious experience, theory, and philosophic interiority, I cannot end without setting these intellectual and moral achievements within the largest context of all, which Ignatius gives in the Contemplation to Obtain Love. Let me close with one very telling quote:[15]

> Although others may think differently, it seems to me in the light of the Divine Goodness that *ingratitude* is the most abominable of sins and that it should be detested in the sight of our Creator and Lord by all of his creatures who are capable of enjoying his divine and everlasting glory. For it is a forgetting of the graces, benefits, and blessings received. As such it is the cause, beginning, and origin of all sins and misfortunes.

Notes

[1] See "Extremism In Ignatius Loyola" pp. 22-34 and "Realism in Ignatius Loyola" pp. 35-54.

[2] For a thorough explanation, see my *Lonergan and Spirituality: Towards a Spiritual Integration* (Chicago: Loyola University Press, 1985). In the present discussion, I am omitting the realms of art and scholarship.

[3] See his *Method in Theology* (New York: Herder and Herder, 1972), pp. 81-85.

[4] See *St. Ignatius' Own Story*, trans. W. Young (Chicago: Loyola University Press, 1956), para. 12, 99.

[5] See E. Allison Peers, translator and editor of *Living Flame of Love, Spiritual Canticle, Dark Night of the Soul* and *Ascent of Mount Carmel*. All Garden City, New York: Image Books, 1962, 1961, 1959, 1958, respectively. I have not analyzed John of the Cross's work at any depth, so there may be a case for saying that he did do some work in philosophic interiority, even though it may not have been expressed explicitly.

[6] She has four major works: *Life, Book of Foundations, Way of Perfection,* and *Interior Castle*. For an overview of the entire process of her spiritual growth see E. Allison Peers, ed./trans., *Interior Castle* (Garden City, New York: Image Books, 1961).

⁷ See his *Spiritual Exercises*, trans. L. Puhl (Westminster, Maryland: The Newman Press, 1959), para. 91-98, 230-237, and 136-147, respectively. Hereafter all references are to paragraph numbers. The expression "to obtain love" means to obtain a personal experience of love for God, not to obtain God's love for oneself. For this use of the word "obtain" (alcanzar) and its connection to such a grace, compare para. 11 (". . . labor to *obtain* what he seeks in the First Week"), 168 (". . . whoever desires to *obtain* this third kind of humility . . .").

⁸ I am omitting a treatment of "The Call of a Temporal King" because of space limitations. Two points are relevant to the present discussion: (1) Notice how, in para. 97, the retreatant identifies his or her own interiority as the primary battleground of the kingdom of Christ. In other words, the kingdom is first of all something a Christian *receives*, and only then something a Christian *preaches*. (2) In para. 98, the retreatant does *not* make the prayer recorded there. He or she listens to someone else make it. Ignatius expects that this procedure will more likely stir a person's desire (while waiting upon God to give the desire) than would a premature, idealistic offering of oneself.

⁹ If an allegory is an analogy for *understanding* the human condition through a story, a parable is an analogy for *provoking* a reaction through a story. In this sense, the Two Standards is a parable. We could also call it a "saving tale" in the sense used by Eric Voegelin, that is, a story of redemption that is at once universally relevant, of enduring interest, and provocative of action. See his "The Gospel and Culture," in D.C. Miller and D.Y. Hadidian, *Jesus and Man's Hope* (Pittsburgh: Pittsburgh Theological Seminary, 1971) Vol. 11, pp 59-101.

¹⁰ See para. 147, 148, 156, 159.

¹¹ Numbers in brackets refer to paragraph numbers in the *Spiritual Exercises*."Rej" references refer to Ignatius's letter of June 18, 1536, to Sr. Teresa Rejadell, with the numbers referring to paragraphs. See W. Young, trans., *Letters of Ignatius of Loyola* (Chicago: Loyola University Press, 1959), pp 18-24.

¹² From former Defense Secretary Robert A. Lovett, cited in R. Neustadt and E. May, *Thinking in Time* (New York: The Free Press, 1986), p. 11.

¹³ This analysis of Lonergan's occurs in many places. I recommend his "Healing and Creating in History" in F.E. Crowe, ed., *A Third Collection: Papers by Bernard J.F. Lonergan SJ* (New York: Paulist Press, 1985), pp. 100-109.

¹⁴ Ibid.

¹⁵ From his letter of 18 March 1542 to Fr. Simon Rodrigues; see Young, *Letters*, p. 55. Italics added.

DAVID L. FLEMING

Ignatian Exercises
and Conversion

conversion

For the past four hundred years *The Spiritual Exercises of St. Ignatius* has been the source book for a particular apostolic spirituality influential in the church. Traditionally, people involved in a retreat based on the dynamic of this manual were described as being involved in a conversion movement. With the contemporary interest in the conversion experience (for example, represented more speculatively in the works of theologian Bernard Lonergan, religion educationist James Fowler, and philosopher Walter Conn, and then more practically in the parish programs of the RCIA), I believe that we have the opportunity to gain fresh insight into various conversion movements present within the dynamic of the Ignatian Exercises.

Let me describe briefly what the main factors are with which we are dealing.

Ignatian Exercises

The phrase "Ignatian Exercises" has a fairly broad meaning which takes in both the full thirty-day retreat following the dynamic of the book *The Spiritual Exercises of St. Ignatius* and all the possible adaptations which are included in the Ignatian phrase, "to give some exercises."

Ignatius Loyola had strong restrictions on who should give the thirty-day *Exercises* as well as who would be apt candidates for such an experience. He took a very elitist attitude towards the use of the thirty-day retreat, observing both that there were not that many capable directors and that there were not that many people who would draw suffi-cient profit from this extended prayer experience. It was not a renewal tool for the masses or even for the majority of Christian people.

On the other hand, Ignatius seemed to be very free with encouragement and even expectation for candidates to the Society of Jesus, early on in their formation years, to experience the "giv-ing of some exercises" as part of their everyday ministry. Because Ignatius identified both in his *Exercises* book (in particular, *Sp Ex* §18) and in various other writings the giving of "some exercises" with the matter considered in the First Week, up until recently Jesuits particularly but also many others who have given retreats in the Ignatian manner have often felt "locked in" to giving exercises that lead to a "good confession." I believe that in the renewal of the *Exercises* which has taken place over the past twenty years or more—a renewal both in our understanding and in our presen-tation, we have become freer in

We need to question carefully how we deal with this integrated conversion dynamic of the full thirty-day Exercises when we are in the process of "giving some exercises." How do we break up the notion of conversion when we are giving just some exercises?

this adapting of the dynamic of the *Exercises* to particular indi-viduals and groups, beyond the idea of preparing them for a good confession. Even the First Week, then, is larger than a consider-ation of sin in our lives. And conversion means more than mak-ing a good confession.

I suspect that Ignatius's concern for the directors who are "giving some exercises" touches most pointedly on our under-standings of conversion. Ignatius is very aware of the conversion dynamic woven through the whole pattern of his *Spiritual Exercises.* One Ignatian Week builds upon a previous one. One Ignatian exercise builds upon the previous ones of the day or Week. Grace asked for and grace received continue always to be determining the movement of the retreat. Ignatius did not have the terminol-ogy of "stages," as in "stages of conversion," but his use of the word *Week* is similar and he certainly did have a sense of movement forward or upward and a building upon previous experience and grace given. We need to question carefully how we deal with this integrated conversion dynamic of the full thirty-day Exercises when we are in the process of "giving some exercises." How do we break up the notion of conversion when we are giving just some exercises?

The Conversion Process

As we have already noted, the process of conversion has caught the attention of psychologists, theologians, and religion educationists in our day. *Conversion* has deep roots in both Testaments of the Bible. The prophets, especially, speak out the call for conversion, and both John the Baptist and Jesus are presented in the openings of the Gospels making a call to conversion.

In both the Hebrew and in the Greek languages, the idea of conversion was captured in the simple notion of a "turning"— the secular word *turning* applied in a faith or religion context came to mean a turning from evil or less good and a turning to God or a greater good. To have a conversion is also commonly described as having a change of mind or a change of heart.

In recent analyses of the process of conversion, especially when applied to one's faith life or religious development, various aspects of the human response have been more carefully distinguished. If we borrow more from the Lonergan distinctions of conversion and apply these terms to a faith-life development, there is the possibility of considering conversion as intellectual (the way one sees or thinks about the whole of life as related to God) or the conversion as moral (the way one behaves as a child of God) or the conversion as affective (the way one is moved and responds in love to God and to others) or the conversion as religious (the way one reverences oneself, others, and the world in the light of a provident God). There can be a change, a shift, a turning, on any one level or any two of them at the same time, or perhaps even on all four levels at the same time. What we have become far more aware of today is the fact that conversion does not usually proceed apace on all four levels of intellectual, moral, affective, and religious. For example, since Vatican II a number of people may well need an intellectual conversion (that is, a new way of seeing and understanding their faith content in the light of the Council's spirit and approach), even though their moral and affective levels may be adequately functioning. Some have no affective response to their faith; they still observe Catholic practices, go to Mass on Sundays, maybe even read regularly the diocesan newspaper, but they have no feeling and no devotion in their practice of faith. An affective conversion is a real need in their Christian lives. Still others are leading a good enough life—intellectually, morally, and affectively—but they exercise no active religious life. Their faith does not effectively permeate their lives, particularly "in the marketplace. " They are in need of a conversion, designated by a specialized use of the word *religious*.

Conversion seems to put us into a spiraling conical movement that has us look at similar situations, but from a different level of life experience as well as from a new response to God's grace.

Furthermore, contemporary studies of the conversion process have tended to focus upon the individual. But through the emphasis given by Pope John Paul II in his encyclicals and by the United States bishops in their recent letters on peace and on the economy, we have become more conscious of the social dimension of conversion. This level of conversion has been less singled out, and so we do not yet have a common language or approach. Fr. J.J. Mueller SJ, in his little book called *What is Theology?* (Wilmington: Michael Glazier, Inc., 1988), makes a simple division of backward, forward, inward, and outward for the integral aspects of social conversion. In the social conversion movement, we must be aware of the past and past tradition (backward); so, too, we must reapply our values to contemporary situations (forward). Then we must acknowledge the change demanded of our own selves (inward) and the change we must live out with others (outward).

By our very word *process* applied to conversion, we acknowledge that conversion is not just a once-event in our lives. God continues to call and to challenge, and our attempt to respond demands a turning, a shift, a change of heart. We have a sense of being here before, but it is not quite the same. We use words like *deeper, higher,* or *richer* levels. So conversion is not like climbing some ladder, ever moving upward in a straight forward motion. Conversion seems to put us into a spiraling conical movement that has us look at similar situations, but from a different level of life experience as well as from a new response to God's grace.

Discernment

We have had more studies on discernment in recent years than in all previous eras of the church. Yet I suspect that there is greater misunderstanding and misuse of this term than ever before. I hesitate to add to our confusion, but I will be bold enough to offer what insight I think that I have on the subject in our present context. Again what follows are only general or foundational statements about discernment, but it is often here where we find confusion or false expectation.

Discernment is not an entrance into new knowledge; it is not a tapping into God's mind and getting the sure tip on what horse is going to win the next race. Discernment is not a promise of rightness over wrongness, of being correct over being incorrect, of not making a mistake, of not failing. In fact, by way of Christian paradox, we probably are letting ourselves in for more failure and dying by entering into the process of discernment. Why?

Discernment is always in terms of comparison study. To discern in the Ignatian tradition is to take the various knowledges which I have or which I can gather about a situation or a choice which is before me and to place them up against my own living and deciding as Jesus lived and decided. The comparison in decision making focuses on the question: Does this decision or action keep me where God is? Discernment is not asking God to bless my decision or action and be where I am, but rather my whole effort and attention is for me in all my decisions and actions to be where God is. For Jesus, that sometimes meant leaving a successful preaching mission to move on to other towns. For Jesus, it sometimes meant letting a close friend meet death, as in the case of Lazarus. For Jesus, it eventually meant allowing himself to be captured and crucified when prudence and common sense told him to escape—an escape which could be so clearly directed, at least by human insight, towards the good of his mission and the kingdom.

Discernment moves us beyond the Christian virtue of prudence. Because discernment takes the focus off me and my decision and fixes rather upon the relationship with God, it is always in the context of love which knows no bounds or excess. In a typical Christian paradox, we speak of a "discerning love." Martyrdom stands always as a prime example of discernment—a discernment flowing from the excess of love. It is discernment which calls forth the apostle and evangelizer—just as truly in past ages as in our own. Discernment, then, is always an integral part of Ignatian Exercises which stir us all to seek and find the will of God for our lives and action.

Stages of Conversion

There are a number of ways in which we could describe the various stages or levels of conversion in the *Exercises* of Ignatius. Just as naming or describing graces peculiar to each Week has been helpful in our understanding of the dynamic within the *Exercises*, so we seem to come to another rich way of understanding the movement through the idea of conversion. Rather than trying to describe in detail the conversion movement which is woven throughout the thirty-day retreat experience, I propose that we try to capture different kinds of experiences, but experiences which might be grouped within four descriptive expressions. These four descriptive expressions somewhat correspond to the movement of the Four Weeks and so they may be a part of any retreat in which we are "giving some exercises." In having a greater understanding of the built-in conversion dynamic reflected in these four descriptive expressions of our experiences in the *Exercises*, we hopefully can set forth more clearly the direction of the exercises which we are giving to the individual or to the group.

Movement from Self-focus to God-focus

In spiritual growth, just as in psychological growth, there is a necessary focusing on self-identity and value. In the catechetical question, "Who made me?" and its follow-up question, "Why did God make me?", we have a good example Of this priority focus. Even though the question is phrased in terms of the subject *God*, the emphasis is on me and my value and in what I do with my life. As I begin to grow in identity and value, I have the security to grow in intimacy and so to give myself in love.

Ignatius seemed to be able to touch into this basic kind of Christian catechesis in his consideration of the "Principle and Foundation" exercise (*Sp Ex* §23) and in the exercises of the First Week. The conversion movement of this time might be captured in the phrase "from self-focus to God-focus. " For the grace of this first movement is one of being caught up in the love of God and in God's saving action. My response is not to continue looking at the gift, but rather my focus is on the giver of the gift, the one who loves so much, even to death on a cross. And so the imagery of Christ on the cross in the Colloquy of the First Exercise (*Sp Ex* §53) deliberately draws my attention not to a mirror-image of myself, but to a God who loves so much. The questions which Ignatius proposes for the retreatant in this colloquy are about responses—not what am I getting, but what can I give. The most consistent grace-response of the Principle and Foundation and of the First Week is gratitude—"I give thanks."

We seem today to have a greater security need of focusing on our identity and value than the people of Ignatius's day.

We seem today to have a greater security need of focusing on our identity and value than the people of Ignatius's day. If it is true, I suspect that the causes are manifold—from the more common experience of broken and dysfunctional families, from the breakdown of neighborhood and parish social fabric, from our awareness of ecological disasters, and from our own potential for nuclear annihilation. Although the almost classical study of Bellah and others, called *Habits of the Heart* (Berkeley: University of California Press, 1985), has focused for us the dominating strain of individualism permeating our lives, it is my impression that people born after the Second World War—both lay and religious—have imbibed an individualism even more heightened in an affluent culture, eschewed by the assassinations of the 60s, the Vietnam disillusionment of the early 70s, and the continuing political scandals and vacuousness of more recent times. We seem so infected that even our attitude of approaching the scriptures, liturgy, and all other aspects of our faith life comes with a self-focus. If the scripture does not speak to me, don't bother with it. If Mass is not meaningful to me, forget it. As with any supermarket selection, I can pick and choose among the items connected with the practice of my Catholic faith for those that speak to me or appeal to me and have something to say to my life.

This is a situation calling for a conversion. The conversion, I believe, still has the same focus as that which Ignatius projected in the First Week. It is a movement from a self-focus to a God-focus. It may take a lot more careful development in the exercises we as retreat directors propose to help bring about this movement. As Ignatius tried to point out, this conversion movement is so basic to Christian living that people need to return to it over and over again. It was never meant to be a put-down to say that people could "at least" be given the exercises of the First Week. For Ignatius this was the basic conversion movement to which we all needed to return over and over. Yet *we* do not determine that it is the time to return to this consideration again; it is God who calls and graces us again with the newness of this conversion moment. Ignatius, for all his careful structuring of the *Exercises*, never let us forget that God is always the director of the movement. So in group retreats we must be especially conscious not to "pronounce" what the conversion moment is going to look like. We are always only preparing the ground; the conversion growth—its stage or level—is always God's action.

Movement from Self-determination to Discipleship

The Second Week within the full thirty-day experience of the *Exercises* has a complex movement, with the election process ordinarily seen as its centerpiece. In our consideration of giving some exercises, I will simplify the various movements of this week to one basic one—the idea of a movement from self-determination to discipleship.

For us to grow in our Christian vocation, it is necessary that we experience the conversion of a disciple. The Gospels are primarily the faith-stories of Jesus Christ, but as the same time they also present a picture of a disciple's call and gradual formation through the following of Jesus. Ignatius's focus on the gospel mysteries intends to put the retreatant back into the basic learning situation of the first disciples—listening, observing, and being as fully present as one can to a particular Gospel incident. This is the secret success of Ignatian contemplative prayer style.

In today's cultural milieu, there is a great emphasis on "pulling one's own strings" or being self-assertive. In its initial appearance, we may think that we have a spiritual variation on this theme found in Ignatius's "asking for what I want." To know what it is that I desire and to direct my prayer by means of desire remain essential building blocks for the Ignatian retreat. Yet Ignatius shrewdly inserts the prelude of desire (the second or third prelude which describes the grace to be asked for) within the context of the preparatory prayer which is always stated in terms of my intentions, actions, and operations of this day being focused on the praise and service of God. In addition, Ignatius places the retreatant in the gospel story situation in the previous prelude or preludes before the grace prelude in order to provide a context of "asking for what I want." So looked at more carefully, the grace prelude is not so much determining what *I* want as that I am *being shaped* in my desires of what I want in the light of following Jesus.

To follow Jesus does not come from my initiation, but from his call. I pray for a grace not to be deaf to that call in whatever ways it comes into my life. In the exercise "The Call of the King" (*Sp Ex* §§91-98), I can hear and watch a generous response to Jesus' call, but I cannot claim such generosity emanating from me. I come to know it as grace. Similarly, it is not my astute observation powers or my careful study habits which will allow me to come to know and understand Jesus and so be able to love him more. It remains a grace, for which I beg and wait.

Then there are the values which I hold dear, some perhaps from my family, some from my country and culture, some from my education and religious belief. As Ignatius capsulizes in the exercise called "The Two Standards" (*Sp Ex* §§136-148), Jesus challenges us with our value systems and invites us into his own. The challenge is so great that I first pray just for understanding, and then I pray that I might be received into his way of valuing life.

The conversion which marks this Second Week is tied into the word *disciple*. I am basically a learner, a follower when it comes to where Jesus is in my life. The value of self-determination must give way to my abiding role as a disciple—one always obedient, that is, always listening carefully to the Word of God, however it manifests itself in my life. Again this conversion is not a once-event in my life. To be a disciple of Jesus is to grow continuously in a following of service—a service the limits of which are determined by the call, and not first by me. Self-determination, even in our efforts to serve, can lead us on by excess or by defect. To stay true to the graced desires given by God is to know the continuing conversion of being disciple.

Movement from Sympathy to Compassion

Oftentimes we hear it said that the Third Week of the Ignatian Exercises is just a confirmation of what has been accomplished in the Second Week. I believe that this kind of an explanation misses the heart of the movement of the Third Week itself.

For the Third Week has its own conversion stage, one that I describe as the movement from sympathy to compassion.

Some years ago, the then Jesuit Superior General, Fr. Pedro Arrupe, coined a memorable phrase in an address he gave to the International Jesuit Alumni Association. He spoke about the call to be "men for others." In less sexist language, we might say "persons for others." It is a phrase which well captures the apostolic movement of the Second Week. "For others" expresses the generous idealism of the newly-won disciple. This kind of "do-gooder" idealism (and I am not using "do-gooder" in a demeaning way) necessarily inspires and challenges the convert. It ought to be a part of the enthusiasm of the follower of Jesus in his or her renewed apostolic call, after the manner of the exercise on "The Call of the King." I want my following of Jesus to make a difference for my world: it is to be a world which my Christian service role makes at once, in Father Arrupe's words, "more human and more divine."

Yet this generous ideal of being "for others" faces still another conversion call. It is the movement caught up in the expression of "being for" changing to a "being with." The grace for which I pray in the Third Week exercises is the grace of feeling anguish *with* Christ in anguish, sorrow *with* Christ in sorrow—in other words, the grace is the rich one of compassion. In the Second Week situation, I can have sympathy for a whole world—"poor world!"—and rush around trying to fix it, with God's grace. In the Third Week situation, I can only "be with" Jesus insofar as he lets me into his interiority of passion and death. I cannot change it, I cannot fix it; I feel useless, helpless, and I may want to escape from the situation which is so inevitable. The choicest blessing from God to me at this time is the grace of compassion.

A culture and a society which puts little value upon its aged people—in fact tries to hide them away in nursing homes and retirement centers—has little place for compassion. A society or culture which prefers to abort the possible Downs syndrome child has no place for compassion. A society or culture which wants only to fix the world to make it right has no place for compassion. This conversion movement is one of the most difficult calls for us to respond today. Our very sensitivity to justice issues almost puts us in conflict with the patient endurance of a Dorothy Day or a Mother Teresa. We do not easily accept that our *passion* for change must be embedded in a *compassion* for what is. We get on fire with "causes," and we can become violent, hateful, or despairing all too easily. There is so much in our makeup, in our training, and in our milieu that militates against our even being open to receiving what only God can give—the gift of compassion. Although each conversion moment demands a surrender and even a certain dying, surrender and dying is highlighted in this particular stage. For in our choice of life (the focus of any conversion) we now deliberately take on the suffering (what happens) which is part of life. It is an important moment of conversion, particularly in our acceptance of and service to the aged, to those afflicted with AIDS, and to anyone caught in the tragedies of human life. Perhaps, more importantly, this conversion is so special a gift because it is a graced moment in the acceptance of our own limitations—compassion with ourselves.

Movement from Living in Faith to Living in Realized Hope

The Fourth Week grace represents the last conversion moment which I will describe. As we are all aware, there is no "last moment" in the conversion process, except for the moment of death. And even if we might be able to say that there is a certain priority in time for the conversion moments which we have seen so far, remember that we are not talking about some kind of step-ladder progression. "What goes around comes around." We all will return over and over to the various kinds of conversion as exemplified in Ignatius's *Exercises*. But let us look more specifically now at the Fourth Week movement. I am describing this movement as one from living in faith to living in realized hope.

When we pray for the grace to enter into the joy of the risen Jesus, we seek to enter into a wholly new perspective on our world. The resurrection has happened; the victory has been realized in Jesus, the "firstborn from the dead." In our creed, we profess that we believe in the resurrection. So what does Ignatius intend by the grace we desire in this Week? Ignatius provides a context in which there is a movement from the faith which we all as Christians must have in the resurrection to a realized hope that the world has truly been affected. Like the dejected and confused apostles on that first Easter Sunday, we too face ourselves and our world with the same age-old problems—sickness, pettiness, failure, injustice, prejudice, disease, and war. What does the joy of Jesus mean to me? In what way can I enter into it effectively?

God's call and God's grace as always remain the source of this conversion moment. It is never something I can bring about or cause to happen. People do come naturally by dispositions that are more optimistic and pessimistic; again we are not referring to these natural psychological leanings. We are acknowledging a graced outlook upon life that truly affects my behavior in the whole of my life. In an oft-quoted line from the Jesuit poet, Gerard Manley Hopkins, our "world is charged with the grandeur of God." Ignatius's exercise, called "The Contemplation to Attain Love" (*Sp Ex* §§230-237), is not just a last minute addition or some grand finale to the Fourth Week. It is an integral outlook upon the world which flows naturally from the grace I seek in the exercises of the Fourth Week.

Is there such a thing as a true Christian optimism? I believe that it is radically necessitated by our Christian faith. But we as Christians do not easily live this optimism in any age. Perhaps it is even harder in our own time and culture than in previous ages because our knowledges and our communications bring before us all the tragedy and peril of human life. Yet God can still break through to call us to this very special moment of conversion, to make evident by the way we embody the living out of our Christian faith—a living that sparkles and shines forth its witness to a realized hope. Both St. Paul and St. Peter in their letters to the Christian churches use the imagery of how we are to shine like stars in the nighttime of our world. Shining like stars is to live as witnesses of a realized hope. It seems that Mother Teresa of Calcutta makes so profound an impression on our secular as well as on our Christian world because she exemplifies or embodies this "living in realized hope."

We do not easily accept that our passion for change must be embedded in a compassion for what is.

Conversion Levels

I mentioned earlier that with various writings on conversion, it has become common to distinguish levels of conversion—for example, as intellectual, moral, affective, and religious. I believe that in each of Ignatius's Weeks we can find the whole gamut of conversion levels in regard to our faith lives, with each retreatant responding to the way that God is leading him or her at this time.

Still, I am suggesting that we can see and expect a more likely priority of one movement among the conversion levels in each

Ignatian Week. Yet I must confess that I am suspicious when I do something like this because it all looks so neat and not messy the way life is. But for people who are familiar with studies on conversion influenced by Bernard Lonergan or James Fowler or Walter Conn, I will make some applications in hope that this may be helpful for your own further reflections. We have to hold on to the complexity of experiences of each of our various retreatants responding to the grace of God drawing and shaping each of them at this particular time in their life.

With these cautions mentioned, I will identify the First Week movement from self-focus to God-focus as entering us more likely into an intellectual conversion, a way of understanding ourselves and our world in relation to God. In the Second Week, I have identified a movement from self-determination to discipleship; that seems to me to describe more readily a moral conversion. We are being taught a whole new set of values in following our Master, the values expressed in the Beatitudes which sum up his own life. The Third Week, which I have described as a movement from sympathy to compassion, focuses more the affective conversion. And finally, the Fourth Week elicits in a special way the religious conversion which produces the mystical vision of a world totally alive in God.

Discernment and Social Conversion

I have not explicitly talked about discernment as I have attempted to describe the various individual stages of conversion in the *Exercises*. But from my introductory reflections, I hope that the comparison mode which is so central to Christian discernment has been readily evident as I describe the Christ-context of each Week. The Christ-centeredness of the *Exercises* from the first to the last exercise always faces us at the same time with the "kingdom to come." Christ and kingdom are inseparable. "Did you not know that I must be about my Father's business?" and "My meat and my drink is to do the will of my Father who sent me" are examples of Jesus' language of how his person and his mission are interlocked.

Strictly speaking, retreat directors do not need to "insert" a social dimension into their retreats. Jesus needs only to speak and to act through the mysteries of the Gospels. What retreat directors need to do is to shed light upon Jesus' message and meaning for our time. Directors have the responsibility to share the Ignatian guidelines for discernment so that people can gain understanding about their desires—perhaps on the one hand, to hide from taking action or, on the other, to prioritize foolishly new ways of serving in the face of their present commitments. The Rules for Discernment (*Sp Ex* §§313-336), which deal with excess or defect in loving God, paradoxically provide the balance in the rush of love involved in any conversion moment. Since discernment has to do with decision and action, especially as others are being affected, it is particularly in the area of social conversion that we find their application so central.

Conclusion

I hope that I have shown one way of viewing the Ignatian Exercises in terms of various conversion moments. In our more common giving of "some exercises," we need to be aware of the kind of conversion for which we might be preparing the ground. Retreat directors do "direct," and so there is the obligation upon a director to know how he or she is pointing the exercises which are being given to retreatants. We always still wait upon the Lord to see the grace given, but that does not excuse us from our own necessary preparation and presentation.

The very notion of conversion highlights the fact that Ignatian Exercises always involve people with Christ and with his mission. Conversion affects my relationships, and it affects my ways of acting—my behavior and my work. In our more heightened awareness of our Christian responsibility for our world, we as directors need more consciously to shed light for all who are "making some exercises" to see the connections between their personal conversion and their own efforts in the conversion of the world in which they live. "Thy kingdom come" must come alive both in their prayer and in their actions.

Two Key Transitions in Spiritual Growth

*B*oth in coming to understand our own spiritual development and (should we be engaged in spiritual direction) in
reflecting on where a directee of ours may presently be moving,
a sense of the various kinds of transition that often occur can be
a great help. I assume here that spiritual growth (changes, new
data) are to be expected, are even to be sought.

Quite a number of transitions are possible. One can move,
for example, from a life of mortal sin to a life of sanctifying
grace, from a rather legalistic reliance on external rules to a life
of personal choices; or, at the other end of the spectrum, one can
move from a devout life to a life of advanced mystical prayer. But
two other transitions deserve, I think, special attention today.

The two developments I have in mind are often at issue in
the Spiritual Exercises of St. Ignatius—one of them in the First
and Second Weeks taken as a whole, and the other in the unit
formed by the Third and Fourth Weeks. In his active spirituality
St. Ignatius may be said to have reshaped the "Three Ways"
(purgative, illuminative, unitive) into two spiritual transitions,
each of which reveals both a negative and a positive side.

This essay will attempt to describe and study these two
major movements that occur in many dedicated lives. After each
of them has been clarified, their relationship and especially their
differences will require comment.

The First Transition

Assuming, as St. Ignatius does at the start of his First Week

Rules for Discernment, that we are in touch with persons living a good Christian life, striving to get free of sinful ways and to grow into closer union with God, then this first important transition may be seen to move from relying mainly on getting emotional satisfaction to discerning spiritual consolations received from the Lord and felt in the heart.

This formulation makes a contrast between emotions and feelings (or felt knowing). Emotions in this usage refer to personal responses to objects in the external world around us (through our five senses) and to interpersonal events in our social setting. There is nothing wrong, of course, with emotional experiences. Emotions are often the main stuff of human life.

In their endless varieties they fill most of our daily hours. We wake up in one mood and at night perhaps we drift off to sleep in the grip of another. Between times we may be surprised by shifts and changes of emotion or brood over a lingering mystery of emotional confusion. Persons without emotional reactions are hard to bear. We might wonder if they suffer from some disorder. But perhaps their emotions are not warm and pleasant but of the cold, off-putting kind.

When we habitually demand to be satisfied emotionally, we become blocked against further spiritual growth.

Whatever their nature, we can be sure that our emotional responses provide the real texture of human life. In themselves they are part and parcel of God's creation. And like other creatures they may be put to good use or they may get us into trouble. Returning to the formula given above, what needs emphasis at this point is the habit of relying too much on emotional satisfactions.

When we habitually demand to be satisfied emotionally, we become blocked against further spiritual growth. We can become stuck right there. Without realizing the fact, we may be expecting God to deliver emotional satisfaction to us and we get angry when God fails to do so. We pray, in effect, a self-centered prayer, "my will be done on earth—not *Thine!*"

While nothing is wrong with emotions in themselves, we can put too much stock in them. Let us be honest, many of us do so a good part of the time. We come to rely almost entirely on our own emotional states. If they are satisfying, "God is good!" If not, "God has rejected me!"—or we imagine things are going wrong.

One of the major troubles of social life is to have others inflict their moods on us—because they tend to interpret the nature of reality in terms of current emotions. "The emotion that grips me now tells me who I am and what the world is doing to me."

Even if we can avoid inflicting our emotional state on others, we still often experience the world in accord with our emotional state at the moment. As the poet Pope tells us, "All looks yellow to the jaundiced eye"—and the world looks rosy through rose-colored glasses. Our emotions easily become a lens that colors our world—for the time they last. This is often how we are as we begin our spiritual journey. There is nothing very surprising about it.

And so a well-known stage of purification consists in getting free of emotional *demands*. First comes the step of noticing our emotional reactions, of naming them as they occur, and of refusing to identify our being with their continuance. In order to become liberated from their insistent claim upon us, we learn to do small penances.

In the past there has often been a danger of coming to despise our own emotions—an undesirable side-effect when struggling to gain freedom by willpower alone from these emotional claims. Without further treatment of that point, I merely note here the need to avoid puritanical efforts in this transition. We are dealing with spiritual growth, which is always initiated and brought about by divine grace. We do, of course, need to cooperate with such graces, and small penitential acts are forms of cooperation.

But our highly emotive personal responses are right and true in themselves. Even if emotional self-denial is necessary for a certain time, we will need to return to our emotions just as soon as we can get free of their tyranny. Then they may become, not only right and true, but beautiful and even holy. Emotional self-denial is only a temporary ploy within a larger movement of growth, not the main aim of the spiritual life.

An egotistical tendency (if it is present) to invest our sense of self mainly in our emotional satisfactions needs to be purified during the First Week exercises. That is, of course, a rather subjective way of approaching the areas of sinfulness that call for purification, but it seems appropriate here because I am focusing on interior transitions. The Rules for Discernment themselves lay heavy stress on the desolations to be expected in a person striving to move forward, and on the need to persevere in that intention despite the losses of emotional satisfaction that may be experienced.

Spiritual Feeling

In the more positive phases of the continuing transition, spiritual consolations arising from moments of union with Jesus the Lord may make their presence felt as one enters the Second Week of the Exercises. It is assumed at this point that exercitants have already heard the call of Christ to follow him and have responded (with varying degrees of enthusiasm) to that summons. And during the contemplations of the public life that follow, each one must learn how to discern true from false consolations.

An elementary principle to be noted here is that consolations of the Lord are not to be identified as "feeling good" and desolations as "feeling bad." Many today use the term "feeling" in a general sense that includes (or mainly denotes) what I have described above as emotions. That is a defensible usage, but in this essay I wish to separate the term "feelings" from the term "emotions" as already defined. I want to cast light on the rather different movements we may experience at a deeper, more interior level of our being.

In other words, I wish to define feeling (an enduring state) and feelings (momentary events or "touches") as personal responses that occur at our spiritual center in the core of our being, and not primarily in our social world. Humans may be said to enjoy a double-leveled awareness, one with outer and inner dimensions. In this discussion I am using emotions to refer to responses at the outer level, and feeling to refer to responses at the inner level.

Quite correctly, it should be insisted that outer and inner levels are continually interacting together. When a sudden event moves us wholly, it is often true that emotions and feelings are impossible to distinguish. Tears start from our eyes, our heart is fully engaged, we cry out with joy or sorrow, we even experience sensations in our body (waves of heat or cold, tingling of the spine, pressures in hands or feet, a burning forehead, and so on). Similar points may be made about calmer experiences as well.

In fact, it is normal for human beings to "sense" a two-way

intercourse between outer and inner events, between what occurs in the social world and simultaneously in the interior feeling. Our reflective capacity, which is not merely mental but also passionate, is precisely what makes our awareness human. Our consciousness is multidimensional. While we know and feel, we also know we are knowing and feeling. And when we respond emotionally, we are aware at the same time of various intuitions underlying our most emphatic emotions.

Even when we "forget our self" in some activity or other, that welcome effect is considered unusual—an exception to the rule, and never total. Besides, an egotistical self-awareness is not the only kind of selfhood we may experience. We may be full of self-doubt, for example, or eagerness, or mistrust, or calm happiness, and so on.

The Inner Self

All the same, what is transpiring in this first transition is precisely a development of interior selfhood. As certain modes of dominance by the outer self are overcome, we receive a new growth of inner self—a very important transition in anyone's life.

Today we may take it for granted that the "self" we are talking about, no matter how much trouble it may get us into, is a positive value in its own right, not to be identified with mere selfishness or false egotism. Only fairly recently did this new assumption gain acceptance.

For example, in *The Imitation of Christ* the term "self" was rarely used except in a pejorative sense, and it followed that one's main goal was to get free of it as much as possible. That view continued to be the dominant one until only a few decades ago. The shift that has taken place so recently has brought with it a new sense of the human subject, of selfhood as a valuable reality—however much it may need to be discovered, owned, purified, and developed.

A much stronger awareness of the "inner-self"—at least as a potential reality—has arisen among many members of our secular culture today. Often we know it first for negative reasons: we are hurt, we feel misunderstood, we are unable to communicate our special desires or intentions, we are judged wrongly or become unsure of what we really meant. It causes a great deal of confusion, anger, resentment, and so on. But at some point or other it may dawn on us that, despite the urgent need we may be feeling for much more growth and clarity, our inner self is a reality, valuable in and for its own simple being. We may begin to experience our own goodness as a fact. It need not, and cannot, be earned or proven. It is just "given."

Through faith I may know that my personal existence is received from God who does not choose to make me without loving me. My selfhood is real and my unique being is loved—even holy. That realization is such a remarkable event in anyone's life that it calls for prolonged attention and care during the earlier stages of spiritual growth.

Since I assume that the above reality is widely recognized and appreciated today, I wish to focus now upon the kind of transition involved in its realization. An individual coming through that key transition begins to experience things in a personal way that may be called heartfelt. They are spiritual feelings and illuminations in the inner self.

These consolations (or desolations) differ noticeably in quality from emotions experienced in the outer, social world. And the transition from relying mainly on emotions to relying mainly upon spiritual consolations (feeling) is a very significant "moment" in one's development.

Not a False but a True Self

This transition has been the main aim of novitiate programs in recent centuries, although in most cases the novitiate was directed toward the positive adoption of each congregation's way of life. In other words, a single spiritual "style" or mode of operation was proposed for every novice to imitate and put into practice, and what needed to be sacrificed in order to obtain this goal was the ordinary tendency to demand emotional satisfactions for oneself. The self in question was taken to be wholly "selfish" and needed to be "offered up."

Today a single spiritual lifestyle imposed on everyone alike has been replaced by "the charism of the founder/foundress" in a way that leaves room for the unique selfhood of each member to receive recognition and approval. As a result, the sense of self in question had to be clarified.

The false self, which needs to be purified, is one that demands emotional satisfactions and is upset when these are not forthcoming. But the true self, to be realized through penance and patient striving against desolations, is received as a gift from God and recognized in consolations consisting of spiritual feeling and preconceptual knowing (experiences of *sentir*).

A special way of following Christ, modeled in each congregation by the founder/foundress, will enable new members to undergo a radical purification of their conscious (or outer) self in the process of identifying their center of being in their heart's core. Members of vowed congregations who were trained in the older system have likely gone through an adjustment of this sort during recent decades. Each one will need to say how he or she has made the required adaptation, if indeed it has taken place, and what precisely was involved.

But in general it may be said with some confidence that this first transition, which is of primary importance in spiritual growth, has been clarified as the emergence of an inner self united with the Lord in discipleship. What prevents its growth is usually the habit of expecting or relying upon emotional satisfactions, a habit which must be changed if the desired transition is to take place.

Once it has been changed, and soon after the new inner self has grown accustomed to spiritual consolations, a reintegration of the whole person with her or his emotional responses should then commence. This process will involve the formation of new social habits on the basis of the inner self so recently received from the Lord as a true actuation of one's potential being.

The Second Transition

An expectation of further growth should not disappear from our purview for too long after the first transition has been completed. True enough, a directee who begins to enjoy true spiritual consolations does require considerable time (perhaps several years) to integrate them and create a new way of life on the basis of the inner self they bring alive. But the moment will inevitably come when remembering past graces will no longer suffice. As soon as signs of this new need begin to appear, the director (if not the directee) ought to recognize them. Such signs may point to the onset of a second, rather different transition.

What might signs of this new sort be like? In general, consolations of "the Second Week type" curiously do not seem to operate "as well as" ones of an earlier stage. In different contexts, we should notice, St. Ignatius employs the same word, "consolation," in somewhat different senses. In the First Week, for example, which deals with persons who seek to be more and more purified from their sins, the term simply means experiences leading to closer union with God. But in the Second Week it means experiences of persons bound in close discipleship to the Lord; because these apparent consolations may come from God or from the enemy, they need to be examined much more carefully. It is my contention here that the term is further varied in the Third and Fourth Weeks: if it gains in nuance by moving from the purgative to the illuminative way, we should not be surprised that it varies again in moving to the unitive way.

It is usually rather puzzling to find that "what used to make me happy no longer does so." Naturally enough, we normally expect things to continue as they were. But the fact of the matter is that we may change so significantly (because of our authentic spiritual growth) that what used to console us does not console us any more. Former ways, including ways of praying, that we had first discovered with some difficulty and later came to enjoy with a sense of real progress now seem to leave us cold. They no longer satisfy our hearts, but instead cause a certain malaise or uneasiness. It can be quite disconcerting.

What can have gone wrong? At first we may fasten on various explanations: we are not trying hard enough; we have grown complacent and lack humility; we should return to our former graces with renewed enthusiasm, and so on. But try as we will, the loss of taste, the lack of any real sense of meaning and value in our usual way of life, continues to bother us.

Of course, many different factors may be relevant in the case of each person. But I want to introduce the possibility of a new kind of transition as an important consideration in many cases. If indeed the divine Spirit is moving us to a new stage of growth, then we are obliged to give it some attention.

Unitive Experiences

Since what I will be describing has to do with the unitive way, let me begin by insisting that this traditional stage of spiritual development is not exceptional, not meant for only a very few persons, and not regularly accompanied by unusual mystical phenomena. Unitive graces are an ordinary occurrence in most devout lives, just as are those of the illuminative and purgative ways.

(Besides, concretely speaking, even after one has discerned unitive experiences, he or she is not usually separated for very long from renewed moments of purification and illumination. Perhaps one should stress the fact that occasional unitive graces do not mean one is "firmly established" in the unitive way—whatever that may mean.)

It is my conviction that the Third and Fourth Weeks of the Spiritual Exercises cannot be reduced to a "confirmation of Second Week graces." That may be legitimate in many cases, but the limitation ought to be spelled out rather than turned into a general rule.

One's interior meaning and value as a person created and saved by the Lord and called to his service will become much more surely "known" in consolations received when contemplating the Passion.

Let me be explicit: a limitation of Third and Fourth Week graces occurs quite legitimately when the individual person has for the first time received graces belonging to the first transition or when a notable deepening of that transition has been granted. In other words, the person's "inner self" has been realized or deepened in graces of union with Christ—and this is quite new for this individual. In that case (and it is a very important development) the Third and Fourth Weeks are likely to consist mainly of graces that confirm the key event that has so recently transformed the person involved.

The Passion of Jesus may be shared in many different ways—even by the same people at different times. I may cling to the cross in a sort of desperation if I am in serious danger of falling into mortal sin. Or during a crisis of decision making or of self-doubt I may dwell in the Garden of Gethsemane. Alternatively, I might find my personal illness or injuries transformed by a new way of sharing in the sufferings of Christ. Or I could accept obstacles thrown across my path, get free of resentments that have long bothered me, or deal more creatively with insults and humiliations that come my way by prayerfully participating in what the Lord endured in his Passion out of love for me.

This list could be much extended, but I simply wish to illustrate here the wide variety of possible experiences we may find. At least a mention may be made of special graces of union with the Passion, such as we may read about in St. Juliana or other spiritual writers. Some of these may be clarified in what follows, but my main concern is to speak about Third Week (and Fourth Week) graces in a way that might enable ordinary Christians seeking a closer union with the Lord to recognize the possible meaning of unitive experiences that may also have been given to them.

When the Passion of Christ "confirms" the first transition in the experience of a given directee, then that person's union with the Lord (so recently received or deepened) may be clarified and strengthened through worldly rejections and insults, even when these are taken in prayer to the limit situations of betrayal, imprisonment, violence, condemnation, and death. In other words, one's interior meaning and value as a person created and saved by the Lord and called to his service will become much more surely "known" in consolations received when contemplating the Passion.

The Resurrection contemplations, in similar fashion, may confirm the previous grace more positively through experiences of a new way of life operating out of spiritual feelings received in the depths of the inner self. Those "Second Week" consolations may become clarified and strengthened through experiences of union with the risen Lord. Such graces received during the Fourth Week are to be discerned, unless I am mistaken, as confirming the Second Week graces already obtained by the directee.

Limiting the Last Two Weeks

In short, in these cases (only), confirmation of the Election in the Passion and Resurrection contemplations may be taken as appropriate during the Third and Fourth Weeks. This means that the central grace of the Spiritual Exercises is seen to be one of intimate personal union with Jesus (most fully revealed in the Election). What I have called the "first transition" may be recognized as the main event for the individual person one is directing—even during the last two Weeks.

So frequently is this the case today that many directors tend to consider it the only true goal of the Third and Fourth Weeks. But if that is so, then their notion of the unitive way has become dangerously foreshortened. For all practical purposes, it has been subordinated to the purgative and illuminative ways.

But if the unitive way is truly a normal dimension in the growth of every devout Christian (as I believe it to be), then its omission from the Spiritual Exercises would be a limitation that raises serious questions. And to restrict unitive graces to a few exceptional persons would, in my opinion, be equally damaging.

There is secular evidence to give us pause today. When Maslow began to publish his findings on "peak experiences," he was under the impression that only a small number of persons had undergone this type of interior opening. But further research by himself and others produced widespread testimonies to similar events. Eventually he reached the conviction that peak experiences of one kind or another are universal, although ignored or repressed by a hardy few. While his concept of "peak experiences" is ambiguous and may refer to quite a wide range of phenomena, his evidence cannot be restricted to what I have named the first transition.

What I would like to call the second transition, then, would always assume the previous acquisition of first-transition graces. For example, if we suppose that a directee before making the Spiritual Exercises has already received profound graces of the Second Week type, what would likely occur during the first two Weeks? Usually one would expect the directee to receive confirmatory graces during those meditations and contemplations. But I would add that such prayer experiences might also be preparatory to more advanced graces possibly to be offered during Weeks Three and Four.

If a director is not open to this possibility, then the foreshortening of the Exercises, already mentioned, becomes all too likely. And if the more advanced graces of the second transition are actually given, such a director would not know what to make of them. The directee's experiences might easily be misunderstood and the director could fall into false discernments. I believe that this has in fact occurred far too often.

Challenges to a Good Way of Life

The reality of spiritual growth reveals how frequently believers find that God disallows their apparently excellent form of commitment to the divine service. "The rug is pulled out from under their feet," we could say. Let us assume, for the sake of argument here, that the way of life of a given directee is truly unselfish and generous. It has been discerned carefully under direction, and has in fact become fruitful in its apostolic outreach. Is it possible that God might call the individual to surrender, or move away from, this entirely good way of life?

Not only is it possible, it frequently takes place. A car accident, a heart attack, a financial loss, or social changes intervene to make our chosen course no longer viable. From many (limited) points of view, this makes no sense at all. But the point of view that matters is the divine one—where we are called to believe and trust without knowing why, without making our own merely "common sense views" the final criterion in our discernment.

This is what must have challenged Mary, the Mother of Jesus, on that first Holy Saturday. To her way of thinking, what could have been better than the life and teaching of Jesus? And yet its rejection in Israel was permitted by the divine mystery. Mary had to accept that baffling course of events, painful as it was in the extreme, without any "human" understanding of its value. We might say that God asked her to endure a spiritual death in her own heart corresponding exactly with the actual death of her Son.

Why is it necessary to "die" to our good interior self in order to "live" in the heights of the spirit? Whatever answers we attempt will necessarily dwell within the mystery of divine union.

If this line of thought is pushed a little further, of course, we may perceive that the Passion and Death of Jesus was itself most acutely a *spiritual* death for our Lord himself. Had he not set his heart upon the conversion of Israel whom he desired to gather under his wings as a hen gathers her chicks? But they would not have it so. Instead, he was compelled to accept the rejection of his teachings, and of himself with them, at the hands of those in Israel who were in positions of wealth, prestige, and power. Only a few remained his followers.

Jesus embraced this destiny out of love for all his people (including the very ones who were bent on his destruction). Not only did he accept the loss of what he had hoped to gain, but he did so with generosity of spirit. And so the Father raised him to a new role in the course of our history, a role that brought him into direct relation with every nation on earth. That spiritual death, which he so fully accepted, led to a new form of spiritual life for every people—even for ourselves.

This, of course, is the pattern set for all of us by our Lord in his paschal mystery. But it should be obvious that we do not reach the fuller modes of participation all at once. Only gradually over many years do the devout followers of Jesus find the path to a more complete union with the Lord in the mystery of divine purpose.

This does not mean that what we presently do will certainly be taken away during our course of active life (that remains a mystery of the future). It means only that, if we do move forward in union with the Lord, our basic attitude toward what we do and who we are will likely be tested in a more radical way. Even so, those who know us externally may not even notice the changes occurring deep within us.

But somehow, through threats of illness, accidents, or altered situations that touch each one of us deeply, experiences like those that came upon our Lady and the other disciples of our Lord—experiences, that is, of a spiritual death corresponding to the actual death embraced by Jesus out of love—will need to be encountered. And if we are graced by the divine love, we may pass through that "radicalization of the paschal mystery" so as to enter into a new kind of life in God—or at least into momentary tastes of it. This is what I mean by unitive graces.

The Root of the Matter

The term "radicalization" refers to the removal of more deeply rooted barriers to union with the Lord. Negative events similar to the ones mentioned above may occur in our lives, of course, without becoming the occasion of unitive graces. What is assumed here is that advanced graces of purification from sin have already been received, and that graces of intimate discipleship have also been conferred which have enabled well-discerned commitments to service of the Lord's kingdom in this world. It is only some years after a first transition has been made that certain negative events may trigger an experience of lost selfhood or lost capacity for going on—even though outwardly one still goes through the motions that resemble a normal life.

But why is it necessary to "die" to our good interior self in order to "live" in the heights of the spirit? Whatever answers we attempt will necessarily dwell within the mystery of divine union.

Does our chosen way of life in its underpinnings somehow tend to place a barrier between ourselves and God? If so, why should that be?

Does our most intimate sense of true selfhood always to some degree (because it remains unfinished) hinder us in our encounters with God? Does our entry into utter transcendence always call for a further surrender—and yet never actually deny the validity of our individual and communal being? (These are far from being new questions—they belong to a well-worn tradition.)

Sometimes our experiences of union seem to emphasize a oneness that obliterates awareness of distinct selfhood or to bring about a newness of love-identity in the Other that makes us easily forget our usual human longing for recognition as individuals. True. But these passing tastes and their remembered glories refer to unitive graces which at first can stun us with their breakthrough "difference."

By this I mean that the experiential qualities tend to capture too much attention at first—they are new to us, very fulfilling, and so sometimes a bit extravagant. Nonetheless, the substantial reality of a grace, once given, is never taken away by the Lord even though the experiential aspects are temporary. We remember the experiences, but we are still inwardly changed and even "put together" differently by the substantial character of those gifts.

The Way of the Cross

In the specific case of unitive graces, however, a prior experience of spiritual death points to another factor. There is no way to Easter, as we know, that does not pass through Calvary. In the terms already used above, this means that radical experiences of union with the risen Lord in the "heights of the spirit" are not possible for us until we have undergone a spiritual death "in the depths of the soul."

Perhaps this factor can be clarified by saying that we are not ready for unitive graces (of the Fourth Week type of consolation) until we have experienced the loss of interior consolations previously given us (Second Week spiritual feelings and illuminations). In terms of selfhood, we might say that we must die (not to any false self, but) to the good "inner self" given to us in the first transition. Only the loss of that very good gift can prepare us to receive a "higher self," spiritually communicated to us by the risen Christ in this second transition.

In consequence, the two transitions I have been describing are related in the Spiritual Exercises—and beyond them. The "spiritual death" that essentially prepares for the second transition is the experiential loss precisely of the grace already received in the first transition. There can be no second transition, then, if the first has not previously occurred.

We should note that the "second kind of humility" is certainly meant for use in the Election. The "third kind of humility," on the other hand, is intended to enable directees—should they actually receive that grace—to move forward into the second transition after their full acceptance of the first.

Concretely, of course, this conceptual clarity is muddied by many variations in practice: both transitions may be combined or crossmated, along with backward and forward movements, frequent delays and regressions, sudden spurts and more sudden withdrawals—endless "visions and revisions," as Eliot puts it. The actual circumstances do not often present ready-made examples for our mental laboratory.

All the same, our awareness of the "crucial" contrast between the second transition and the first may prove helpful. If the approach taken here is even approximately correct, then we may be assisted in discerning the special qualities of second-transition experiences, especially in their earlier phases (of the Third Week sort). And this may enable us to avoid false strictures on our own or others' responses to these movements of grace.

Qualities of the New Life

The first transition, then, moves an individual from relying mainly on emotional satisfactions to receiving spiritual consolations in the inner self. The second transition may be said to move one from a well-accepted habit of interior union with the Lord and a way of life based upon it to a new life received directly from the risen Christ and enabling experiences of a higher self.

It remains to suggest various qualities of the higher life that is enabled by unitive graces. First of all, although one's ordinary life, of course, continues, along with it (and not only behind it but also "in among" it) there is known to be a divine presence— ever so delicate and respectful of one's freedom. That factor may grow more powerful at certain times, but often it remains gentle, although unmistakable.

Another feature is a "higher" movement of the Spirit—rather unlike the heartwarming and compelling graces of the first transition (which are usually "deep" and "interior" in quality). It is the awareness of divine mystery operating everywhere, bringing about God's will despite all evidence to the contrary; it is a disposition to wait for God to reveal the divine will, to expect this and not to be surprised when it comes. It means not to speak until words are given, not to act until one "knows" how the Lord desires to act in the community.

These few features may be taken as examples of the higher life (often seen in the lives of the saints). In general, that nothing should prevent God from loving others through my life becomes the central desire of my existence, the main reason for continuing to live.

It need not, on the other hand, mean that the interior experiences of the inner self do not return and are not customary in one who has received unitive graces. It is just that one can no longer identify oneself with them. They are available at times and should be exercised. But they may also be taken away, and one is ready now to let them go. All this is possible because the risen Lord has made his divine presence felt by uplifting one to the level of his own activities in the church, in each person, and in every part of the world.

PETER G. VAN BREEMEN

examination

The Examination of Conscience

In the Ignatian tradition, which inspires many religious communities, the "examination of conscience" plays an important role. In the official documents of the Society of Jesus throughout the centuries its value is stressed time and again. Yet, in practice, it is usually the first form of prayer that is dropped. It is left out not just for lack of time, but even more because it is experienced as sterile. Notwithstanding a certain rediscovery and renewal during the last two decades, the examination of conscience is much discarded, and those who have trouble with it or have done away with it all together, find themselves, if not in very good, at least in very numerous company. However, the problem is not that the examination of conscience is useless, but that often the manner in which we tried to do it was ill-advised. There exist many misunderstandings and even caricatures, which, it seems to me, can all be traced back to two basic errors:

1. trying to examine ourselves according to general norms, while Ignatius starts from what is unique in *this* person, who is me;

2. judging our own conduct and our own person. burrowing into our own sinfulness, while Ignatius goes beyond that to discover how God reveals himself in what goes on inside me and in what happens around me.

It is not the object of this article, to offer a complete treatise on the examination of conscience; rather, it confines itself to these two difficulties. It wants to show a way out of these two cul-de-sacs.

It was George Aschenbrenner SJ in particular who with a liberating interpretation managed to rise above the moralism which had suffocated the "examen." It is significant that he did not give his article the title "Examen of Conscience," but that he called it "Consciousness Examen."[1] In less than a decade this article had become a classic. It has had a great influence in the English-speaking world. It led to the rediscovery of the examination of conscience, in spiritual literature as well as in everyday practice. Its success is partly due, I think, to the fact that the time for it was ripe and that it carried a high degree of self-evidence once it had been put into words.

Some fifteen years before Ashenbrenner's article, the German psychiatrist Albert Görres had published a still readable article on the examination of conscience according to Ignatius.[2] He sees the examination of conscience as the *Spiritual Exercises* in a nutshell and for daily use: "the examination of conscience is for the day and the hour what the *Spiritual Exercises* are for a lifetime." It is remarkable how he dealt already precisely with both difficulties mentioned above. Two quotations to illustrate this:

> 1. *Examen conseientiae* means: to examine the consciousness. Hence the "motiones animae." the movements of mind and heart with which a person meets reality, get special significance. Reflecting on one's own psychical experiences is, however, not a circling around the ego. On the contrary, it is distinctly theocentric, directed towards God: as he acts and reveals himself in these movements of mind and heart and as he wants to be found in these inner things and in all other things as well.
>
> 2. In the *Spiritual Exercises* (and from there in miniature in the examen) thankfulness, in the sense of comprehending and doing justice to reality, is applied to and practiced in the different areas of reality.

Feelings

The examination of conscience is not intended as a course in self-perfection but as a growth in finding God in all things. The accent is not on a psychological or moralistic self-analysis, but on the Spirit working in us and on the Lord who is telling us something. Its intention is to keep alive the faith-dimension of our existence—in other words, to direct our lives towards God more and more and to go on seeking God as the deepest Ground of our existence not only with our heads, but also with our hearts. The object is to trace our experiences back to their source, to stay in lasting contact with the Source, to keep in touch with the innermost part of ourselves as it lives before God's face. It is an effort to overcome estrangement and illusions. That requires discernment. It is an attempt to appreciate more fully reality and to let that reality bear fruit for God's kingdom. It is an exercise of prayer with the focus on God's great love for us and on how that great love is made manifest in the very concrete experiences of the past day or half day.

Our own experiences, therefore, play an important role—not in the sense of revolving around ourselves, but positively as directing us to God. The point is to discover—and that not solely with the intellect, but with the whole person—how God reveals himself in the movements of our hearts and minds and how God may be found in our inner experiences as well as in all things. This, however, presupposes that we observe those inner experiences. The overabundance of impressions, with which present-day society inundates us, does not make it easy really to get to our feelings and become aware of them. A hectic tempo of life, relentlessly pushing and urging us on, adds to that difficulty. A tightly controlled way of living one's faith can aggravate the situation even more through a strong inclination to shut out anything that is "unbecoming."

It is the same Albert Görres, who writes: "With theologians and religious the inability and the unwillingness to observe oneself without prejudice often reaches astonishing heights. They neither want nor allow themselves to know what they really feel. Since, however, an open and relaxed way of observing oneself—not as conscious reflection and self-knowledge, but primarily as a readiness to let the inner world speak—is at the same time the basis of our emotional contacts with our fellow-humans, each instance of self-estrangement and of warding off inward communication also interferes with the contacts we have with others. This is the reason why people's needs and problems are often so carelessly overlooked in sermons and pastoral care. The priest is incapable of having a real conversation because he has shut himself off from the psychological experience that the encounter with himself might bring him and because he does not allow his own deepest worries and problems to express themselves."[3]

Surprisingly relevant in this connection is a footnote placed in the title of the "Rules for the Discernment of Spirits" by Jan Philip Roothaan in his translation of the *Spiritual Exercises* [313]: "From the autograph it is worth noticing that these rules not merely serve to *discern* the movements of the soul, but also to *feel* and observe them. How numerous are those who do not even *feel* the soul's movements, that is to say who do not pay attention to them, who do not even observe them" (Roothaan's italics).[4]

Ignatius's great strength lies precisely in the fact that he was so attentive to his own feelings and experiences. The examination of conscience, then, is central, and recently we have been busy rediscovering this insight.

Listening to our feelings is an exercise in authenticity— in self-acceptance and in "being-oneself."

Feelings that are being repressed will do more harm than those one faces. Therefore, we should not hesitate to let them surface and at the same time not immediately begin to label them, let alone condemn them. Feelings are neither good nor bad, they are real. We cannot choose them. What we can do, after we have recognized and accepted them, is to choose what we are going to do with those feelings. Feelings are the driving force of life.

Listening to our feelings is an exercise in authenticity—in self-acceptance and in "being-oneself." Suppressing feelings is unreal; it is being dishonest, because certain feelings are present, and yet we do not want to admit that to ourselves. Suppressing feelings blocks and suffocates life. It is not until we become aware of what is going on within us, that we will be able to test these feelings, do something with them, choose for ourselves which direction these feelings will take us, give them the place they deserve, and perhaps trace them to their source. We then resemble a sailor who sails his own course in all winds. This process of interior clarification demands patience, trust, and attention. The examination of conscience wants to make room for that. Very simple questions can put us on our way. The main point, then, is not to stop at ourselves but to seek where God is at work and so make our response. For example: What moods, emotions, expectations, desires, feelings of resistance, restraint, and inhibition rose in me during the past half-day? Which ones got the upper-hand? How did I handle them? How do I feel physically: head, gut, heart? Which people did I try to come into closer contact with? What kind of people were they? With whom did I experience tension? Which things gave me joy? For what can I be thankful? What made me consciously think of Cod? In what do I recognize him *now*?

It is truly Ignatian to observe carefully and to find out which feelings make it easier for us to believe, hope, and love, and which lead to want of faith, hope, and love (see *Sp Ex* §316 and §317). In the terminology used by St. Paul the same question runs like this: Do they make the fruits of the Spirit grow or diminish— love, joy, peace, patience, kindness, goodness, faithfulness, gentleness, and modesty (Ga 5:22)? This is the compass by which Ignatius kept course, the yardstick by which he measured his choices. For this man, whose deepest desire was to seek, find, and do God's will, the feelings of his own God-centered heart were decisive. To this must be added that he presupposes a great deal of self-denial and a spirit of mortification.

At what frequency the examination of conscience should take place can be different for different people. Once a day, and then preferably before going to bed, is a good natural rhythm. In the *Spiritual Exercises* [25 and 26 as compared to 43] Ignatius speaks implicitly, and in the *Constitutions* [342 and 344] explicitly, of twice a day; sometimes he mentions the duration and that is always a quarter of an hour. This looks like another proof that Ignatius thought it very important that we should stay close to our own experiences and that in them we should discover God's nearness again and again. It is clearly his intention that through this twice daily exercise we should come to a permanent attitude that permeates all our day, as was the case in his own life to an exceptional degree.

Thankfulness

The examination of conscience has a long history going back to pagan antiquity. The Stoics, in particular, were very consistent in using it. Seneca writes about it in lyrical terms: "Is there anything more beautiful than this custom of examining the day in its entirety! How restful is the night that follows after such an examination of self! What quiet, deep, and liberating sleep is experienced, after the spirit was praised or reproved, after the spirit became its own spy and the secret censor of its own morals!

I use this precious means and each day I plead my case with myself as judge. When the light has been put out and my wife—already used to my way of acting—is silent, I review the whole day, examining and measuring my deeds and words; I hide nothing, I leave nothing out."[5]

Forms of examining one's conscience are also found in ancient India and in Islam. However, it was mainly from the Stoa and via the Desert Fathers that it was introduced into Christianity, where after the era of the persecutions, that is, after the peace of Constantine, it began to play a significant role. That role became increasingly larger, and in the Middle Ages the tradition had become widespread, especially among the Cistercians, the mendicant orders, and later also in the Devotio Moderna. It was through the movement of the Devotio Moderna that the examination of conscience was introduced to the laity.

Ignatius gives it first place when he describes the prayer forms of the *Spiritual Exercises:* "By the term 'Spiritual Exercises' is meant every method of examination of conscience, of meditation, of contemplation, of vocal and mental prayer, and of other spiritual activities that will be mentioned later" (1). In *Spiritual Exercise* 32 to 43 he gives a rather detailed description of the "General Examination of Conscience," and in 43 the method of five points well-known to us, namely, 1) giving thanks to God, 2) asking him to enlighten us, 3) calling ourselves to account, 4) asking God to forgive us, and 5) resolution to amend our life. In this he closely allies himself with the tradition before him. Yet, one can say that he brings out the aspect of thankfulness somewhat more than his predecessors did. In point of fact, he places the whole examination of conscience within the framework of thankfulness.

From Jesuit sources we also know that Ignatius considered thankfulness to be very important. For instance he begins a letter to Simao Rodriguez on 18 March 1542 as follows: "It appears to me in the light of divine goodness, with all due respect for a better judgment, that ingratitude is one of the most revolting sins, which in our Creator and Lord should be detested by those among his creatures who are able to rejoice in his divine and everlasting glory, because it means that one has forgotten the graces, benefits, and blessings received. And as such ingratitude is the cause, the beginning, and the origin of all sins. On the other hand the grateful acknowledgment of the blessings and gifts received is loved and esteemed, not only on earth but also in heaven."[6]

With this emphasis on thankfulness Ignatius places himself squarely in the Jewish-Christian tradition. In the Talmud we find this saying: "He who enjoys whatsoever in this world, without first saying a prayer of blessing and thanksgiving, is guilty of falsehood." This statement refers to the beginning of Psalm 24: "To God belongs the earth and all it holds." Only a "berakah" (blessing) gives a human being the right to use the goods of this world and without a blessing his use of them is unlawful. The Jewish tradition, therefore, has a great many "berakot," even for extremely profane matters. The psalms often speak of thankfulness, for example, "I thank God with all my heart, not one of his mercies I will forget" (Ps 103:2). "Let thanksgiving be your sacrifice to God. . . . Whoever makes thanksgiving his sacrifice honors me" (Ps 50:14 and 23).

Rabbi Abraham J. Heschel notes: "The profound and perpetual awareness of the wonder of being has become a part of religious consciousness of the Jew. Three times a day we pray: We thank Thee . . . for Thy miracles which are daily with us, for Thy continual marvels . . . Every evening we recite: He creates light and makes the dark. Twice a day we say: He is one. What is the meaning of such repetition? A scientific theory, once it is announced and accepted, does not have to be repeated twice a day. The insights of wonder must be constantly kept alive. Since there is a need for daily wonder, there is a need for daily worship." [7]

In the Christian tradition, too, thankfulness is fundamental. From of old, most of our prefaces are intoned with the forceful: "Father, it is our duty and our salvation, always and everywhere to give you thanks. . . " Our worship centers on and culminates in the Eucharist, a word that means thanksgiving.

Thankfulness can be defined as acknowledged dependence: a dependence to which we say "yes." Thankfulness recognizes that we are not the origin of our own lives nor of all that we need to exist. The opposite is pride. Acknowledging our dependence calls for a certain maturity. A *child* enjoys a gift without troubling itself about the origin of that gift; saying "thank you" has to be learned. The *adolescent* realizes where things come from, but finds it extremely difficult to acknowledge that dependence. An *adult* is aware of his or her dependence and is able to acknowledge and accept it with a thankful heart. That is why mature thankfulness leads to the right attitude towards the source of all good: to acknowledge God and to serve him. Ignatius likes to call it: the right "ordering of one's life" (*Sp Ex* §21). In the "Contemplation to attain the Love of God" at the end of the *Spiritual Exercises* he has the retreatant pray for "an intimate knowledge of the many blessings received, that filled with gratitude for all, I may in all things love and serve the Divine Majesty" [233]. This links up closely with the first point of the examination of conscience and creates the atmosphere in which it should take place.

Gratitude implies trust. Unless I trust a person I cannot be really thankful towards him or her. For thankfulness means that I allow somebody into my life. A real "present" renders the giver "present" in my life. That presupposes that the giver is really sincere and that his action is not a mere formality, *and* that the receiver receives and appreciates the present with serious attention. Carelessness on either side is fatal here.

Only in thankfulness do things get a chance to be fully themselves. A person who does not know how to be thankful diminishes reality and, we might say, flattens the world.

The believer can experience everything as a gift in which the Giver is present. Things, situations, people acquire a kind of fullness; they carry a richness within themselves, a reference to the goodness of the Giver; we discover that there is a mystery in all that exists, its "deepest Ground." On the other hand, one can also look upon things in a businesslike fashion, judging them by their utility and efficiency and leaving it at that. The way things function depends to a great extent on our attitude towards them. We can handle them with reverence and a sense of wonder, so that their inner secret is truly revealed and the Other in them recognized and reverenced. We can also deprive things of their depth, cut them loose from their roots, and reduce them to triviality. Only in thankfulness are things rightly appreciated, and they can stand out clearly. Only in thankfulness do things get a chance to be fully themselves. That is why one can say that being thankful is having a realistic attitude to life. It shows a sense of reality; it gives reality its rightful place. A person who does not know how to be thankful diminishes reality and, we might say, flattens the world.

We know that a process of mourning is needed to digest a loss. Similarly thankfulness is needed to digest what is positive, to discover the richness of what is received. Giving thanks completes the giving. Without thanks the giving has not fully taken place. Thankfulness gives life its depth and perspective; it makes reality transparent, clear, lucid. It is through thankfulness that humans and their world become more harmonious.

Thankfulness means tracing things back to their source from whom they come. Thankfulness lays open the entrance to the core of things. Only in that way can a human being be rooted in reality, confirmed in his or her existence. Ignatius used to call it: "finding God in all things."

Thankfulness really is finding the right connection between oneself and other persons and things. That is why it is a mature attitude. Thankfulness means on the one hand being conscious of one's own worth, and on the other hand being conscious of one's dependence. Thankfulness implies a healthy self-esteem, but at the same time it is altruistic, other-directed. Self-centeredness and egoism are the archenemies of every kind of thankfulness. One who is always after his or her own interests, whose attention is always centered on self, will never be a thankful person. Ungrateful is also the one who gets completely lost in the gift, while forgetting the giver. Thankfulness means that we do not see ourselves as the center of the universe; that we do not take things for granted, but as granted by God. Thankfulness heightens our awareness and makes it more transparent.

Thankfulness does not belittle, but rather lets things and people have their rightful place. People who are thankful do not belittle themselves either. The attitude of thankfulness and an inferiority complex do not go together. Anthony de Mello wrote in his book *Wellsprings:* "It is inconceivable that anybody could be grateful and unhappy."[8] Albert Görres says almost exactly the same: "One cannot be discontent and thankful at the same time."[9] When a person has a strongly developed sense of gratitude there is no need to worry about his or her spiritual health. Our Lady exemplifies this beautifully. Her Magnificat bears witness to her strong self-esteem ("Great things done to her"; "Each generation will call her blessed") and of a deep recognition of God. Thankfulness does not get locked into self-sufficiency and self-conceit, but rather acknowledges the Source transcending us.

Thankfulness requires a certain distance. The person for

whom the gift is everything forgets the giver. The one who is overly attached to something is not free enough to be truly grateful nor really to enjoy it. Nor is it possible for a person to be thankful for what has been thrust upon him or her. In this respect too, the quiet time of the examination of conscience can be liberating and fruitful—distancing oneself a while.

To recognize what is undervalued is therapeutical, and so thankfulness can be curative. Thankfulness is *salutary* as we pray and sing in the preface. To a person who is not thankful everything is burden and duty, coercion and fate, threat and disaster. Gratitude makes room and sets free. "Blessed are the pure of heart, for they shall see God" (Mt 5:8). The undivided heart, as it were, sees through everything and in that way discovers the depth, the deepest Ground in things. The pure heart is not greedy, is not enslaved, does not grab; it is not dissipated and bored; it looks beyond mere utility or self-advantage. To be like that makes it a great deal easier to live a thankful and prayerful life and to find God in it.

In the first chapter of St. Luke's gospel Mary sings her Magnificat, a song of thanksgiving. Immediately before that she spoke her "fiat."

Persons who dare not surrender themselves can never be thankful. Surrender and thankfulness interact and strengthen each other.

There is a close connection between the two. Persons who dare not surrender themselves can never be thankful. Surrender and thankfulness interact and strengthen each other. Such is our experience in the Eucharist, which is a celebration that comprises both gratitude and the gift of ourselves. Ultimately thankfulness means: loving in return with the same love with which one is loved. By being thankful for what we have received we are made ready for what must be done, without recklessness and without faint-heartedness. Thankfulness is not passivity; it is by no means noncommittal, never just a polite formula. Thankfulness transforms the gift received into a task to be done, and has, therefore, a "ready-to-work" attitude. It will teach us not only to work for God but to do God's work. In order to be able to distinguish working for God from doing God's work, Ignatius lets us listen to the voice of our heart in the biblical sense of the word.

Conclusion

With these reflections, by no means has everything been said about the examination of conscience. Those who listen attentively to their heart and try to live a life of gratitude are not going to find only beautiful and good things. There is also evil, around us and in us. The enemy (Mt 13:28) will go on to sow tares among the wheat. Against the background of thankfulness evil will stand out all the more clearly. Exactly where we, in deep felt gratitude for God's gifts, let the full light shine, the shadows cast by our own misuse of those gifts stand out in stark contrast. To that, too, we must pay attention; we need God's grace and the light of the Spirit to look that squarely in the face. Then there is also room for contrition, of the kind that sets free, for asking God and our fellow-humans for forgiveness, and for "the resolution to amend with the grace of God" (*Sp Ex* §43). This article does not go into that, in the hope that what has been said about listening to what our heart feels and about living in gratitude may help us to make room again for these traditional elements of the examination of conscience.

Notes

[1] Review for Religious Vol. 31, no. 1 (1972), pp. 14-21. Reprinted in David L. Fleming SJ (ed.), *Notes in the Spiritual Exercises of St. Ignatius of Loyola* (St. Louis: Review for Religious), pp. 175-185.

[2] "Über die Gewissensforschung nach der Weise des hl. Ignatius von Loyola," Geist und Leben 29 (1956), pp. 283-289.

[3] *Handbuch der Pastoraltheologie* II/1, Feiburg 1966, p. 303.

[4] Regensburg 1855, p. 304f, footnote 1.

[5] Seneca, De Ira III, 36, 2f.

[6] Monumenta Ignatiana, Series prima. I, p. 192.

[7] *God in Search of Man* (New York: 1955), p. 48f.

[8] Anand 1984, p. 26.

[9] "Gewissensforschung nach der Weise," p. 289.

Consciousness Examen:
Becoming God's Heart for the World

*T*o live contemplatively. Indeed, to become whom we contemplate: this is the invigorating experience, the hallmark enterprise and adventure that human existence is all about—that for which every human heart is longing. The magnetic appeal of the wholly beloved invites our hearts to a transformation which is never easy. But it is so intimately renewing as to be almost irresistible. It is the very heart of love. Lovers in their mutual contemplation are not always explicitly aware of this process of self-transformation into which they are being swept up. But certain challenging moments can starkly reveal the risky loss of self that is involved. And yet the very attractiveness of the beloved provides conviction and motivation to embrace this risk. In that magnetic moment, love seems an opportunity not to be missed. But love's opportunity and risk are also costly and lovers finally know this. Indeed, the cost involved in the contemplation of lovers strikes to the profound level of self-identity. But cost what it may, the beloved's attractiveness lures the lover on to surprisingly new depths.

The beloved in our reflection here is Christ Jesus, our God and Lord, our Brother and, finally, all our sisters and brothers, especially the most suffering ones across all time and space (see Mt 25:31-46). And contemplative transformation into this beloved is the fundamental process involved in, indeed it is, devotion to the Sacred Heart of Jesus Christ. It is also the process with which examination of conscience is concerned. And there we have at once the premise and the product of this reflection.

Both devotion to the Sacred Heart and examination of conscience have a long history in the Ignatian tradition. But they have rarely, if ever, been viewed in relationship to each other. In this article I will try to show how regular examination of conscience facilitates a transforming experience of one's own heart into the beloved of one's heart, the Sacred Heart of God in Jesus Christ. After a brief summary of the contemporary renewed understanding of the examen, I will make use especially of some of the graces prayed for in the First Week of the Spiritual Exercises, in order to describe the continuing conversion involved in a regular practice of examen. Finally, in support of the claim that the examen can convert our hearts into devotion to the Sacred Heart of God, I will describe a little of the apostolic power, the ardent love and thirst for justice, of such a growing and ongoing conversion. Ongoing: for we are never done with love.

In recent years there have been attempts, both within the Jesuit heritage and within the whole Church, to renew the understanding and practice of examination of conscience and of devotion to the Sacred Heart. Examination of conscience is now more often called consciousness examen or awareness examen.[1] In its renewed form the examen continues to bless and sensitize the hearts of many busy believers to the loving presence of God in all of daily life. And while much work has been done in developing a contemporary theological understanding of devotion to the Sacred Heart,[2] perhaps the actual practice of the devotion is not so widespread as that of consciousness examen, or at least is not widespread among those who frequently make use of consciousness examen. This article, finally, though its central point is to relate the two practices, is concerned more with the personal effects of regular examen than it is with the details of traditional or recent developments in devotion to the Sacred Heart.

Renewed Understanding of Examen

In the renewed understanding of the examen, two insights are key. First, a much more positive perspective has corrected a past view that often deteriorated into an overly negative, moralistic misunderstanding. Rather than highlighting the bad actions of a day, the examen gives primary concern to what is primary: God's revelation, a steadfast love in Christ Jesus always inviting and invigorating our consciousness. Formal examen sensitizes our hearts to the presence of this love in the ordinary details of every day. Whenever this love is recognized and responded to, our hearts simply must come alive with joy and gratitude. So gratitude is the major element in the actual time of examen-prayer, as it should also be in our daily lives of faith. And this gratefulness for the wonder of God's love stirs hearts to action. And so gratitude becomes the chief motive from which all ministry pours.

As the examen begins to make our hearts more aware of God's perduring love, we also begin to recognize how often and how easily we can be oblivious to that love, or how subtly, yet quite stubbornly, we can refuse response to love. This realization, when faced honestly and not rationalized away, can, whether rudely or quietly, awaken our hearts with healthy guilt, with sorrow and repentance. As this article will develop later, this experience of guilt and sorrow is anything but pleasant; yet, as an experience of God's love, it does purify us, it does transform us. And the effect of that can only be a bolder, freer, more wide ranging apostolic service. Mature faith and discipleship cannot happen without this painful transformation in the humiliating experience of guilt and sorrow. As the repentant sinner encounters God's forgiveness in Jesus, sorrow is transformed into hopeful, vigorous gratitude—and a burning zeal to serve God's loving justice in our world. In this way, thanksgiving—the central driving force in the heart of any mature disciple of Jesus Christ dominates the daily examen and fuels its impulse toward loving action.

> *As the examen begins to make our hearts more aware of God's perduring love, we also begin to recognize how often and how easily we can be oblivious to that love, or how subtly, yet quite stubbornly, we can refuse response to love.*

A second insight that renews our understanding of the examen is the importance of the *informal* examen, as distinguished from, though obviously not unrelated to, the *formal* examen.[3] The formal examen is a specific time and style of prayer. In a previous article I described the five traditional elements of such prayer.[4] Never meant as an end in itself, this formal practice of examen should gradually spill over and infiltrate itself, as a special faith-sensitivity, into a person's daily life. And so we come upon the informal examen: a way of living. The informal examen is more a matter of who we are and who we are becoming, whereas the formal examen is a specific prayer we regularly practice. Thus a regular practice of examen can lead to that self-transformation which makes possible a genuine faith-sensitivity of heart, a dynamic connaturality with the Beloved, which we are calling here informal examen. This dynamic development of formal examen into informal, into a pervasive faith-sensitivity of heart, is crucial—crucial both to a proper understanding of examen itself and to its role in the human heart's deeply desired experience of love: our becoming whom we contemplate.

Daily Conversion in Faith

Jesus' ministry erupts publicly among the people in a great sense of urgency: a wholly new revelation of God's love and the need for reform of mind and heart, if one is to recognize and respond to that love. It is so clear at the beginning of Mark and in the synagogue scene of chapter four in Luke. This radical personal conversion of faith is often described in the Scriptures as a matter of repentance. As a conversion that will cost a whole lifetime, it continually involves the risking and sacrificing of a temptingly attractive but false, illusory self while radically true and radiantly new creation is born in a person's daily response to the quiet urgency of God's love. But no experience of merely passing excitement will suffice for this.

Nor can such repentance and radical change of outlook ever be reduced simply to our own planning and control. A strategy of clear-sighted tactics and of fierce determination will always prove futile all by itself. In fact, if not properly motivated and accompanied by grace, it can actually corrupt the very adventure of faith into something unwholesome and unholy. Without a genuine experience of the wonder of God's love, the Gospel call, the call by grace and favor to radical change, cannot be heard, and healthy repentance cannot happen.[5] It is the attractive beauty and power of God's love which reveals the inadequacy and sinfulness of our condition and unloosens in our hearts a desire to be much more than what we now may be. It is in this way that the wonder of God's love reveals our sinfulness. And this profound truth, so capable of being misunderstood, is always the bedrock of mature spiritual life. God alone sees our sinfulness most clearly for what it truly is: a choice against love. And it is this God who calls us to intimacy in the beautiful revelation of Jesus come among us as forgiveness. Every detail of Jesus' life, most especially his dramatic experience on Calvary, stretches and stirs our hearts in hope for a new creation, a new life, a whole new self. But repentance, with its purifying pain and suffering, is the only way to this urgently longed-for newness.

An honest repentant acknowledgment of sinfulness in the face of such love is neither obvious nor easy, because it cuts our consciousness in humiliation. The guilt and shame and the embarrassment that come in the wake of such an acknowledgment sting and singe our consciousness. In the presence of such love, they make our spirits blush. The pain and hurt will, most often, and quite spontaneously, make us wary and seek to activate defense mechanisms such as the rationalizations of denial and the distractions, not of joy, but of pleasure. These are moments for careful discernment in the life of any believer. For the humiliating pain of acknowledged sin, as intended here, is not the result of some overly scrupulous conscience. Nor is it the unhealthy guilt of self-hatred. Rather it is the purifying consolation—not desolation, but consolation, however scourging—the consoling experience of God calling us to greater love and life and faith. Despite the pain, therefore, this repentant blush of heart is a grace not to be rejected. It is essential to any mature faith, to any measured zeal for God's world, to any discipleship that hopes to brave the road's full distance.

Healthy consoling guilt is always the result of an interpersonal love relationship. And it focuses the heart beyond the self, on the Beloved, in painful sorrow for the wound one's lack of love has caused.

The guilt that introduces our embarrassed, repentant response to God's great, tender love requires a brief description here. Much past experience of unhealthy guilt has understandably provoked the overreaction against, even to the point of a dangerous disregard of, all guilt as if all guilt were unhealthy. Though unhealthy guilt can surely plague and dishearten us, yet there is a guilt born of God. And it stings. But for the lover, it also signals the Beloved's presence, a very active presence, a redemptive consciousness, inviting greater intimacy in faith with God. Unhealthy guilt is always anxious, worried about self, in excessive fear of punishment, preoccupied with failure, at times verging on despair in the face of some unrealistic perfectionism. But healthy consoling guilt is always the result of an interpersonal love relationship. And it focuses the heart beyond the self, on the Beloved, in painful sorrow for the wound one's lack of love has caused. Healthy guilt does not despair, nor does it disrupt the deepest peace of the soul. The reason for this is that healthy guilt is always intimately and very positively related to encounter, a repentant sinner's encounter with God's forgiveness revealed and available now in a crucified Son's intransigent love.

In the Dying, a New Life

But in the tense struggle of this inner guilt, shame, and sorrow, we usually become aware of the risk and high stakes involved. A self, or some aspect of a self with which we have been enamored, perhaps for a long time, must be let go of. Something must die if the new is to be born. It is a mortifying experience, but, as it is not a mortification simply of our own making, neither can the outcome of it be clearly grasped in advance. It is a moment of perceived high risk. And the helplessness of such a moment, when we are on the verge of letting go of what used to be and are not yet in possession of what will be, can profoundly daunt and agitate our spirit. Furthermore, it is in no way simply our own power and ingenuity that will create a different future. In the helpless and sorrowful awareness of our sinfulness, it is only an act of trusting abandonment of self, sometimes done in the dark aloneness of faith, that will allow the Beloved to gift us with God's holiness, our only true human future. A process of conversion that has begun in love leads now to even greater love as a beloved God, in that faithful promise which is the risen Jesus, defies all darkness and rejects absurdity and pain as the final word, whether about this world or the next.

The heart of God revealed in Jesus excites our hearts with the invitation to a new and brighter future. But only a heart scoured clean in the humiliation of repentance can respond to that invitation. The issue is as profound as self-transformation and as hopeful as a wholly new creation. But without a mortified response to God's loving invitation and without a risky letting go of self, such a future remains simply tantalizing, cheap grace, illusion.

The forgiving love of God brings the process of repentance to a conclusion of lively gratitude, profound joy, and enthusiastic zeal for ministry. The sorrow of a forgiven sinner is not depressing, however painfully purifying. Neither is this sorrow obliterated by the joyous gratitude and zeal for service that realized forgiveness brings. Rather, the humility of a saved sinner, while not destructively focused on the past, never simply forgets the sorrowful memory of forgiven sin. One cannot help but wonder whether Peter in the maturity of his joy, during his after-breakfast walk with the risen Jesus, did not once again find his eyes well up with tears as three awkward questions burned his soul with his own lonely truth, but burned it precisely for the sake of fidelity, the journey in companionship, and, yes, for the great holiness of Peter that lay ahead (Jn 21:15-19).

As we gaze on God's forgiveness in Jesus crucified, besides a lively gratitude and profound joy, our heart knows the expansiveness of a great desire for God in Jesus— an apostolic desire to give ourselves as Jesus did in the ministry of God's forgiving justice.

The new self created in God's forgiveness is always strongly characterized by a profound, joyful thanksgiving for a deed neither deserved nor capable of accomplishment on one's own. This deed of forgiveness and the hope of a new and better future resonate strongly in the repentant sinner's heart, now riveted on the challenging beauty of God's forgiving love, found fleshed forever in Jesus on the cross. And so the whole dynamic of the First Week of the Spiritual Exercises propels a person to confrontation, to enlightenment and encouragement before this passionate experience of Jesus on Calvary. Having taken upon himself the sins of all, this Son, anguished in an olive grove over the agonizing prospect of a humiliating death, is able to renew that trusting abandonment of self which allows him to find once again, as always, not previous to, but in the very abandonment of dying, his dear Father. And his beloved Father blesses this anguished abandonment with a future of absolute fullness in resurrection. In the face of such enlivening abandonment on Jesus' part, we can find the graceful encouragement needed for that surrender of self which repentance always demands.

It is at this moment that the graces of fidelity and perseverance take root in the forgiven sinner's experience. And so Jesus' death into the future of resurrection stands faithfully, for all ages, as God's forgiveness. It gives graceful encouragement to all repentant sinners in this risky and humiliating process of self-transformation. The persevering faithfulness of this new creation, this new heart, will always depend on how profoundly, how pervasively transformed the repentant sinner is in the encounter with God's Word of forgiveness.

As we gaze on God's forgiveness in Jesus crucified, besides a lively gratitude and profound joy, our heart knows the expansiveness of a great desire for God in Jesus—an apostolic desire to give ourselves as Jesus did in the ministry of God's forgiving justice. This desire at the end of the First Week continues to expand as the attractiveness of God's love in Jesus is revealed through the remaining weeks of the Exercises. God's Spirit and kingdom revealed so compellingly in Jesus become our wholehearted desire. To live in daily imitation of Jesus, to serve as an apostle in whatever way God desires, becomes the very energy of our hearts. And yet, as the experience continues, this desire can stretch our hearts still further: we may be so transformed, we may, in such transformation, be so intimately identified with Jesus, that we become and, in the thoroughly real way the mysticism of baptism and Eucharist accomplish in us, we may *be* Jesus in and for our world. And so the joyous thanksgiving of a forgiven sinner, so much more than a mere devotional satisfaction, sets our hearts afire with such desire for new identity in Christ Jesus that we become mystical activists, heralds everywhere of the good news of God's transforming forgiveness.

This reflection offers the view that consciousness examen may play a role of special importance in facilitating such a process of radical conversion. The profundity and pervasiveness of the transformation spoken of will depend in large measure on a regular practice of examen. And rather than putting a clear conclusion to the process of radical conversion, the Exercises provide enlightening direction for the further and continual deepening of desire for this daily identification with Jesus. For this reason, as the formal Exercises conclude and move to become daily life, we are always left with an even greater need than before for regular examen, that we may continue the daily discernment of God's love converting us steadily into Christ Jesus our Lord.

Goal of Examen:
Devotion to the Sacred Heart of God in Jesus

Long after the retreat experience of the Exercises is finished, regular examen keeps our heart sensitive and responsive to the attractiveness of the Sacred Heart of God in Jesus. As we have already seen, thanksgiving and sorrow are the two chief affections in faith of the examen and the sorrow itself, as we have also seen, finds its fulfillment in thanksgiving. And so it is in and through its term of thanksgiving that regular examen mediates our conversion and growth into Christ Jesus. Through the basic thrust of the examen, each believer becomes a concrete embodiment here and now of the Sacred Heart of God in Jesus. Consciousness examen, therefore, by facilitating the transformation whereby a serious believer and disciple becomes devoted to the Sacred Heart, is profoundly related to that same devotion. For in this sense of the word, *devotion* refers to the fundamental shape and orientation of a believing heart to the Heart of God in Christ Jesus. And this sense of devotion cuts far beneath—it does not necessarily deny but rather must root—any specific, traditional devotional details and practices.

The transformation of self whereby our hearts radically become devotion to the Sacred Heart accomplishes some perceptible results in our lives. Growing integrity of heart, wholeheartedness, Ignatian magnanimity gradually centers, unites, and identifies our whole person and presence in the world. A white inner stillness, fanned to burning flame in God's own creative love, radiates an energy of recollection—a collectedness—that can meld our often fragmentary faith into the strong, live organism of a life decisively for God.

Such wholeheartedness first gives enlightenment, then courage, towards a fundamental desire and choice in the direction of the "heavenly" things of consolation and away from the "earthly" things of desolation. These desolate "earthly" things live in our flesh as the seven capital, selfish impulses toward sin that the Christian tradition has known so well for centuries; whereas the "heavenly" things of God's consoling love are the opposite impulses which also live in our consciousness where the

Spirit of Jesus invites and breathes their confirmation, their development in us, as virtues, as the very shape of our heart. In the interweaving complexity and tangle of our daily consciousness, we discover that the tempting experience of these capital impulses to sin is precisely the battlefield upon which the fidelity of our commitment and devotion to the virtuous heart of God in Christ is tested and strengthened. And so it is usually by standing strong against the tempting intensity of lust that the virtue of chastity grows. It is by decisively acknowledging and carefully standing against the violence of desolate rage that the tensile strength of nonviolent gentleness is forged. And so of all the personal and community motions of spirit that impel us towards or away from the justice of the Reign of God. The examen is daily involvement in this process of transforming the impulsive desolations of our consciousness into the deep, consoling devotion and virtue of God's Sacred Heart. Once again, as described earlier in this article, we notice that it is precisely in the dying that the new is born. And what is newly born through these mortifying struggles on the inner battlefield of our heart—the heart of each of us and the communal, societal heart of each group, each social structure—always affects apostolic presence in the world, always affects decisively actions for or against God's justice as revealed in the loving Heart of Jesus.

Finally, this conversion into the Sacred Heart of God in Jesus, this process of our becoming devotion to the Sacred Heart, does not displace our weakness with an arrogant sense of our own strength. No, just the opposite! Maturity in faith is always growth to grateful realization both of our weakness and of our dependence on God's love for everything. A steadfast belief in God's love does not replace human weakness. Rather, it helps us patiently to wait upon the Lord and recognize and celebrate God's love bringing strength into our weakness. For God's power is at its best in our weakness (see 2 Co 12:7-10). It is a power that is needed, for becoming whom we contemplate takes courage, even as it brings energy for it. It is high adventure, with a promised wage of persecution, to enter and be taken up into the affectivity of Jesus, God's counterculture heart for the world.

Consciousness examen, then, is not a way to greater, self-reliant strength. But as its daily practice transforms us into the Sacred Heart, we may become whom we contemplate and so stand in this world as living witnesses, agents of love, inviting others into God's Heart in Christ Jesus: "Come to me, all you who are weary and over-burdened, and I will give you rest! Put on my yoke and learn from me. For I am gentle and humble in heart and you will find rest for your souls, for my yoke is easy and my burden is light" (Mt 11:28-30).

And one more time we listen to the Beloved, becoming whom we contemplate: "This text is being fulfilled, today, even as you listen . . .

> 'The spirit of the Lord has been given to me, for he has anointed me. He has sent me to bring the good news to the poor, to proclaim liberty to captives and to the blind new sight, to set the downtrodden free, to proclaim the Lord's year of favor" (Lk 4:16-21).

Through a companionship with Jesus made intimate and tender, strong and apostolically peremptory, through days and years of fidelity to the examen of consciousness, and through the dynamic energy continually released in the experience of forgiven sinfulness, we may come to the apostolic gift which the fidelity of the friends of God can know. In becoming whom we contemplate, we may devoutly, reverently, boldly, and with his thirst for justice become, each of us and together, in the Holy Spirit, God's own heart for the world.

Notes

[1] George Aschenbrenner SJ, "Consciousness Examen," Review for Religious 31, no. 1 (January-February 1972): 14-21. See also the lengthy, very helpful article of David Keith Townsend SJ, "The Examen Re-Examined," CIS 18, 2 (1987): 11-64.

[2] Annice Callahan RSCJ, *Karl Rahner's Spirituality of the Pierced Heart: A Reinterpretation of Devotion to the Sacred Heart* (New York: University Press of America, 1985). This book contains references to the essential texts of Rahner on this subject.

[3] George Aschenbrenner SJ, "A Check on Our Availability: The Examen," Review for Religious 39, no. 3 (May-June 1980): 321-324.

[4] Op cit, Review for Religious 31 (1972): 14-21.

[5] See my article "Forgiveness," Sisters Today 45 (1973): 185-192.

attitude

The *Ought* of the Ignatian Quest

Each year, at the Academy Awards, separate envelopes are presented announcing the winner for best actress, best actor, best movie, best director, as well as a plethora of other categories. Just for the sake of imagination, what if you were to receive a special envelope with your name and the emblazoned heading "God's Will Inside"? Perhaps, you would skeptically think this is some ploy or joke. While the will of God is not communicated in such manner, how does one come to know God's plan? Are there any guideposts?

This article examines the faith journey of Ignatius Loyola to understand how he came to recognize God's will. Ignatius provides us with a pivotal question to assist our discovery of the divine intention, "What ought I do for Christ?" This principal question emerges from the praxis of Ignatius's *Autobiography*[1] and is placed at the beginning of the *Spiritual Exercises.*[2] Ignatius invites us to ponder its importance. By carefully reflecting on his own life experiences, Ignatius establishes a pragmatic method to decipher and to respond to God's plan.

The Question

Ignatius actually proposes three soul-searching questions that arise during the initial meditation of the *Spiritual Exercises*. The retreatant, imagining oneself before Christ on the cross, ponders these questions: "What have I done for Christ?" "What am I doing for Christ?" "What ought

I to do for Christ?"[3] The purpose of these queries is to create a process to stimulate the memory and prod the yearnings of the heart. Perhaps these were the principal questions for Ignatius which he hands on to the retreatant. The purpose of the first question, "What have I done for Christ?" activates one's sense of personal history. The retreatant reflects upon his or her Christian track record: What does this look like? To what degree has Christ been part of my life? In the context of prayer, the retreatant engages in an honest personal inventory.

The next question shifts to the present, "What am I doing for Christ?" The retreatant applies the same inquiring examination to more immediate patterns. What is the religious quality of my present life? What are my priorities? Where do I spend my time and energy? It is important to note the relational quality of Ignatius's questions. The focus is intentionally Christocentric—"for Christ." Ignatius is concerned with the retreatant's faith evolution.

Pilgrimage is the operative metaphor in understanding the process of how Ignatius grappled to know God's will.

In my opinion, the third question is the critical question of the *Exercises*. This final question is the overriding concern of Ignatius's spiritual journey: "What ought I to do for Christ?" This inquiry challenges the individual to seek a more committed discipleship with Christ. The retreatant, assessing talents and resources, earnestly asks "What is my unique Christian project?" "What is the specific service that I ought to be doing for Christ?" "What contribution ought I to make for Christ?"

Ignatius, who does not use words randomly, inserts the moral imperative of *ought* in this last question.[4] Ignatius avoids the less demanding questions like "What can I do for Christ?" or "What would I like to do for Christ?" or "What do I desire to do for Christ?" The choice of *ought* suggests a sense of answerable service and urgency between the retreatant and Christ. The question places Christ at the center of the retreatant's deliberations and choice-making decisions. An important shift has occurred; the personal ego of the retreatant has become subordinate to the reality of Christ.

The genius of Ignatius provides questions. He does not provide the envelope which contains the specific answer to what one "ought to do for Christ." This provocative challenge is found by paying consistent, prayerful, reflective attention to one's daily experiences.[5] With Ignatius's key question in mind, let us examine the method through which he came to discover what he ought to do for Christ.

Great Desires

The *Autobiography* is Ignatius's remembrance of his mid-life pilgrim years. Pilgrimage is the operative metaphor in understanding the process of how Ignatius grappled to know God's will. Ignatius's initial impulses to serve God never materialized. As a pilgrim in search of what he ought to do, he encountered setbacks, closed doors, even imprisonment. He had to revise his plans several times before he understood his unique mission. To Ignatius's credit, he kept searching for the will of God and assessing his experience. Seven episodes from the *Autobiography* illustrate how Ignatius gradually became aware of God's design.

The *Autobiography* begins with Ignatius being wounded on the battlefield of Pamplona. After a long convalescence at Loyola, where he was greatly inspired by reading the *Life of Christ*[6] and the *Lives of the Saints*,[7] Ignatius decided: "What he desired most of all to do, as soon as he was restored to health, was to go to Jerusalem undertaking all the disciplines and abstinences which a generous soul on fire with the love of God is wont to desire."[8]

As Ignatius starts to reform his life, two immediate goals emerge: 1) go to Jerusalem to associate with the holy places of Christ, 2) undertake discipline and abstinence. These resolves stem from a generous yet inexperienced person. Because of the severity of Ignatius's self-imposed penance and diet, these practices would later hamper his health and ministerial effectiveness. Ascetical ardor runs ahead of prudence. Also notice at this point that there is no mention of companions, *Spiritual Exercises*, engaging in spiritual conversation, advanced studies, ordination, special service to the pope, or the establishing of a new religious order. Such thoughts are not remotely found in the awareness of Ignatius during this stage of growth.

At this initial stage of conversion, he is an enthusiastic pilgrim in search of God and full of great desires. This, admittedly, is a significant switch in life goals. Previously his intent was to engage "in the exercise of arms, with a great and vain desire of winning glory" (1). Now we find Ignatius, without trace of martial bravado, preparing himself for the pilgrimage to Jerusalem.

Preparing for the Journey

How does Ignatius proceed to implement his new life goal? The process is incremental and deliberate, assessing information as his journey unfolds. His methodology is pragmatic, locating the will of God in the art of praxis.

After Ignatius has sufficiently recovered, he separates from his immediate culture and influences. He leaves Loyola and the ties of family. Seeking to be as free as possible, he settles debts and even rejects a last-minute offer of a new promising career from the Duke of Najera.

The monastery of Montserrat becomes Ignatius's first destination. On the way, he transforms his identity by exchanging his mule and fancy clothes for the simple attire of a pilgrim, a coarse garment, large hat, and staff. At Montserrat, Ignatius, who is desirous of becoming a worthy pilgrim, makes a detailed general confession and surrenders his sword and dagger after a night-long vigil before the statue of the Black Madonna.

The nearby town of Manresa becomes the site of his spiritual novitiate. There he engages in spiritual conversation and enters the cave of prayer where he begins to record the insights which will provide the foundation for the *Spiritual Exercises*. With each one of these steps, Ignatius strips himself of his attachments and previous lifestyle. He moves slowly, deliberately, always inching closer to his desired goal of Jerusalem.

Firm Determination

Upon arrival in the Holy City, Ignatius recalled, "It was his firm determination to remain in Jerusalem, perpetually visiting the holy places. But in addition to this devotion, he also proposed to be of help to souls" (45). Here we have a shift in what Ignatius perceives he is to do. The locus is still Jerusalem and its sites of devotion. However, Ignatius, instead of being preoccupied with penance, now desires to engage in spiritual conversation. This new habit, learned in Manresa and Barcelona, is included in his list of "firm determinations." Several questions emerge. Is God at all operative in this decision-making plan? Or is the pilgrim simply acting in a pious manner? How did Ignatius arrive at this set of "firm determinations"? Did he reason to this purpose? Did the religious environment of the Holy Land move him to such a decision? While the pilgrim does not reveal the process, he soon found out that he did not have the last word.

The Franciscan Guardian in charge of the Holy Land would not allow Ignatius to remain in the region because of local instabilities and lack of safety and food. Only under threat of excommunication did Ignatius concede to leave the Holy Land. Here a significant choice is made for Ignatius; he, too, has to conform to proper authority and limits.

What Ought I To Do Now?

This was a major altercation for the pilgrim. His determination was thwarted. The life plan, once obviously clear in his estimation, now had to be rethought. Eventually, Ignatius pursues a more careful seeking of God's volition. The *Autobiography* provides a key phrase that eventually becomes a fundamental question which is placed at the beginning of the *Spiritual Exercises*. "After the pilgrim understood that it was not God's will that he remain in Jerusalem, he kept thinking on what he ought to be doing" (50). This observation reveals a significant shift in Ignatius's awareness. For the first time, God's will takes precedence over his own desires and determinations. The pilgrim sees God's will as operative in the decision of a duly appointed authority, the Franciscan Guardian, and working through the reality of civil unrest. So while his initial intent of remaining in Jerusalem is canceled, Ignatius returns to his primary exploration.

Ignatius ponders in a new way, *quid agendum*. He is not led so much by impulse, holy desires, fervor, or firm determination. He reflects, weighs, and reassesses his goals. Not every holy activity, even performed in the Holy Land with good and noble intentions, is God's will.

The Student Years

Ignatius continues to investigate the direction he is to pursue next. "[F]inally (he) felt more inclined to study so as to be able to help souls. He then made up his mind to go to Barcelona . . ."

(50). Here we see Ignatius exploring his options and choosing the one that is more ministerially advantageous to his goal of "helping souls." Once the pilgrim finds a new path, he is ready to test the untried plan. Soon, Ignatius embarks on the road to studies at Barcelona, and eventually, to Alcala.

As the pilgrim grows in his spiritual identity and purpose, so does he mature in understanding the methodology about what he is to do. "While he was at Alcala, he worked at giving the *Spiritual Exercises* and in teaching Christian doctrine, and by this means brought forth fruit to God's glory, for there were many persons who acquired a deep knowledge and taste for spiritual things" (57). These two important activities—the *Spiritual Exercises* and catechesis—emerge as a constant means for Ignatius "to help souls." He is slowly coming in touch with his new mission: the directing of the *Exercises* and teaching Christian doctrine in order to promote God's glory. This insight alone took a process of five years.

At Salamanca, we find adjustments. The Inquisition prohibited Ignatius from defining mortal and venial sin because he had no academic degree. Since this decree hampered his apostolic ministry, he decides to move to the University of Paris to finish his studies. Ignatius comments: "Well, all through the time of his incarceration at Salamanca, he was never without the same desires of helping souls, and to study to this end and to gather together a few who felt as he did and hold those he had gathered. Once he had made up his mind to go to Paris, he agreed with them that they should wait for him where they were, while he would go and see whether there was some way in which they could all carry on their studies" (71).

Continual Discernment

For Ignatius, "helping souls" is his clear mission; study at Paris is now the means to this end. He also desires to bond with like-minded men who would form some sort of lay-ministry friendship. What is even more interesting is that Ignatius is now consulting with these companions as how to proceed in their move to Paris. The unity of the group also emerges as an important concern and value.

By the completion of the companions' study at Paris, "they had come to some decision as to what they were going to do. Their plan was to go to Venice and from there to Jerusalem, where they were to spend the rest of their lives for the good of souls. If they were refused permission to remain in Jerusalem, they would return to Rome, offer themselves to the Vicar of Christ, asking him to make use of them wherever he thought it would be more to God's glory and the good of souls" (85).

The path to find God's design for Ignatius and the companions has become more nuanced. They know that their mission is the service of the good of souls and the advancement of God's glory. The remaining questions are where and how. This ministry might be achieved at Jerusalem or through the guidance of the Vicar of Christ in Rome. Which doorway will open?

The Mission

The last chapter of the *Autobiography* concludes with Ignatius in Rome. The companions have chosen him as Superior General of the newly established Society of Jesus. Ignatius, now ordained, is in the process of writing its Constitutions.

Ignatius's quest to find God's will was circuitous. He accurately describes himself as a pilgrim in this journey. A thirty-year span stretches from his convalescent bed at Loyola to the completion of the Constitutions in 1550. It took him twenty years of wandering and study before he settled down in Rome to begin his major work and mission. Even though Ignatius was being illumined throughout these intervening years, his true finding of what he "ought to do" did not occur until he was fifty years old. It was then that he was able to focus his full energy on the formation of this new association of learned, priestly companions.

This quest for God was full of surprises. A hot-blooded Basque lost his self-preoccupation and became a mystic. A soldier of fame and personal glory became a Superior General of an order of priests whose purpose remains to live exclusively for the greater glory of God. An unschooled person became academically disciplined, holding a Master of Theology degree from the University of Paris. A once religiously excessive individual subject to extreme penances and scruples authored a classic text known for its insight, discernment, and balance.

The *Autobiography* and the *Exercises* reveal two sides of Ignatius seeking to find God's purpose. The *Exercises* present a systematic, abbreviated approach to the seeking of "what one ought to do for Christ?" Within the time frame of a thirty-day retreat, the

Exercises present a condensed spiritual wisdom that offers an integrated worldview. The different sections of the *Exercises*, from the First Principle and Foundation, the Rules for the Discernment of Spirits, the Three Ways in Making a Good and Correct Choice of a Way of Life,[9] to the Four Weeks of meditations that center on the life of Christ and culminate with the Contemplation of the Love of God are all designed to assist the retreatant to seek and respond generously to God's will.

The gift of the *Autobiography* is that it fills out the telegraphic quality of the *Exercises*. Here lessons are slowly learned; the process can be vague and murky. As previously noted, the main metaphor is pilgrimage, with no shortcuts. Ignatius reflects upon his life experience and assesses over and over again both goals and strategies to discover his mission. Just like the rest of us, Ignatius did not receive an envelope marked "God's will."

Ignatius reflects upon his life experience and assesses over and over again both goals and strategies to discover his mission. Just like the rest of us, Ignatius did not receive an envelope marked "God's will."

Central to both the *Exercises* and the *Autobiography* is the urgency of this quest to find out how best to serve God. Throughout the *Autobiography* and *Exercises* Ignatius addresses this fundamental moral question in different forms.

The Quest Today

As contemporary seekers of what we ought to do, we can learn many lessons from the path of Ignatius. This wisdom can certainly apply to those who are mentors in spiritual direction, retreat ministry, and formation work. First, Ignatius provides a clearly articulated question that orients a person in the service of Christ. The gift of one focused question can start people on their spiritual quest.

Next, from Ignatius's life experience, he demonstrates a process of testing each proposed plan and of making strategic accommodations along the way. Here, the overall orientation of the *Exercises* with its supporting network of guidelines, especially the Rules for the Discernment of Spirits, serves as a valuable resource.[10] For example, the Discernment Rules wisely caution the retreatant to monitor "various resolutions and plans," especially following the experience of fervent consolation. Ignatius advises that such resolutions "may come from our own reasoning on the relations of our concepts and on the consequences of our judgments, or they may come from the good or evil spirit. Hence, they must be carefully examined before they are given full approval and put into execution."[11]

As we reflect on the life of Ignatius, it is apparent that he asks much more than a general seeking of God's design, but an examination of every segment of the journey, the outcome of each step, and its ongoing development. Expect adjustments, altercations, and alterations! The will of God is more fluid than static. For those who pursue the spiritual path, the dispositions of attentive listening and adaptability are critical. Luke 11:9-10 reminds us as disciples of Jesus to ask, to seek, and to knock. Such an habitual attitude is standard equipment for the Christian journey. In many ways, to ask, to seek, and to knock is our regular ascetical exercise. The process of asking and seeking leads us to our daily bread, to the love of God, to the finding of our unique mission. In the spirit of Luke, the pilgrim Ignatius models for us the careful discerning process of responding to the invitations of the Divine intention.

Notes

[1] *St. Ignatius' Own Story as Told to Luis Gonzalez de Camara*. Translated by William J. Young SJ (Chicago: Loyola University Press, 1980). This is the English translation cited throughout this paper.

[2] *The Spiritual Exercises of St. Ignatius, A New Translation Based on Studies in the Language of the Autograph*. By Louis J. Puhl SJ (Chicago: Loyola University Press, 1951). This is the English translation cited throughout this paper.

[3] *Spiritual Exercises*, par. #53. References are cited by paragraph numbers standard in all modern editions. Ignatius places these three significant questions in the Colloquy section of the First Exercise of the retreat.

[4] "Pragmatism and the Glory: An American Reading of Ignatian Discernment" by William C. Spohn SJ, lecture given at Woodstock Theological Center, Georgetown University, 22 April 1991. I am indebted to William Spohn SJ for his insight into discernment as a moral activity. "[M]oral discernment, that is, the use of memory, imagination, emotion and intellect to discover what the appropriate action is."

[5] Spohn develops a pragmatic element essential to Ignatian discernment. "Discernment in the *Spiritual Exercises* does not end when the

retreatant has made the decision about what to do with his or her life. If this freedom increases over the months and years that follow the retreat, the life decision made in the retreat will be confirmed pragmatically."

[6] Ludoph of Saxony, a Carthusian monk, authored a four-volume classic on the *Life of Christ* which combined the main events of Christ's life and commentaries from the Fathers of the Church.

[7] Jacopo de Voragine, an Italian Dominican, wrote the *Legenda Aurea* which was translated into Spanish as the *Lives of the Saints* by Cistercian Gauberto Maria Vagad. Vagad's style was heroic, representing the saints as knights in the service of Christ the King.

[8] *St. Ignatius' Own Story*, sec. 9. In this particular edition, the text is divided into 101 sections. References hereafter are cited by section number only in the article.

[9] *Spiritual Exercises*, "Three Times When a Correct and Good Choice of a Way of Life May Be Made," par. #175-188. For Ignatius, the choice of a way of life must have two qualities. It must be correct as well as good; that is, aligned or ordered to the "praise, reverence, and service of God" as expressed in the First Principle.

[10] *A Commentary on Saint Ignatius' Rules for the Discernment of Spirits, A Guide to the Principles and Practice*. Jules J. Toner SJ (St. Louis: The Institute of Jesuit Sources, 1982). This valuable resource presents a thorough analysis of each discernment rule.

[11] *Spiritual Exercises*, par. #336. Excerpts taken from the eighth rule of the Rules For Discernment of Spirits, Second Week.

Stirred to Profound Gratitude

On 18 March 1542 (only two years after the papal approval of the Society of Jesus), Ignatius Loyola wrote to Simon Rodriguez, one of his first companions:

> It seems to me in the light of the Divine Goodness, although others may think differently, that ingratitude is the most abominable of sins and that it should be detested in the sight of our Creator and Lord by all of his creatures who are capable of enjoying his divine and everlasting glory. For it is a forgetting of the graces, benefits, and blessings received. As such it is the cause, beginning, and origin of all sins and misfortunes. On the contrary, the grateful acknowledgment of blessings and gifts received is loved and esteemed not only on earth but in heaven.[1]

These words of Ignatius reveal to us one of the key aspects of Ignatius's experience of God and his relationship to God and one of the central elements of Ignatian spirituality. At the heart of Ignatius's vision is the virtue of gratitude.

The importance of gratitude is not an idea developed in any depth in the secondary literature about Ignatius, nor does Ignatius discuss it at length in any of his own writings. One is a little hesitant to present as a central insight of Ignatian spirituality an idea that Ignatian scholars and even Ignatius himself rarely focus on and refer to only in passing. On the other hand, though the notion of gratitude is not developed at length by Ignatius or his interpreters, it is often presumed to be foundational to the religious experience of Ignatius and the early Jesuits. For instance, Pedro Ribadaneira, one of Ignatius's early companions, once wrote: "Among all the virtues that our Father [Ignatius] possessed was one by which he was especially distinguished: the virtue of gratitude. In that he was simply wonderful."[2] Hugo Rahner refers to "a characteristic which distinguished the noble heart of Ignatius from the very beginning of his conversion: a truly passionate gratitude."[3] Harvey Egan in his book on *Ignatius Loyola the Mystic* says that "Ignatius experienced mystically that gratitude and thanksgiving flowed from his authentic mystical life. To experience the mystery of the triune God in Christ rendered him gracefilled, grateful. He responded appropriately with thanksgiving. . . ."[4]

As for Ignatius himself, though the references to gratitude are limited, they do appear at key points in the *Spiritual Exercises* and in Ignatius's other spiritual writings, especially his *Spiritual Diary*. It is clear from the words of Ignatius in the letter to Simon Rodriguez and from other places in his writings that gratitude is central to his vision of God, the world, and the human person.

This article will explore the writings of Ignatius, including those with which most people are less familiar—his letters and his *Spiritual Diary*—and then reflect at the end on how gratitude can be seen as a unifying grace throughout Ignatian spirituality and Christian spirituality more broadly defined. These reflections are also submitted as part of a larger dialogue and discussion about the role of gratitude in Christians' moral and spiritual lives and in the history of Christian spirituality.

Before exploring the words of Ignatius, I would first suggest that Ignatius's passion for gratitude is rooted in two experiences: first, in Ignatius's own life experience as a beggar and, secondly, in his most profound mystical experience at the river Cardoner. From the time of his conversion, Ignatius lived as a beggar totally dependent on the support of others. As a pilgrim, as a student, and even as general of the Society of Jesus, Ignatius was aware of an enormous debt of gratitude to the women and men who gave generously to him and the early Jesuits. That sense of indebtedness is embodied in the *Constitutions of the Society* and in many of his letters to benefactors. Ignatius's most pervasive sense of gratitude, however, flowed from his experience while at Manresa in the year after his conversion. Ignatius relates in his *Autobiography* how, one day during the last few months of his stay at Manresa, he was blessed with a vision of God and creation that shaped his understanding of and feeling for the mysteries of the faith. He said that "he received such a lucidity in understanding that during the course of his entire life—now having passed his sixty-second year—if he were to gather all the helps he received from God and everything he knew, and add them together, he does not think they would add up to all that he received on that one occasion."[5] What Ignatius understood in a new way was how the world came from God and was returning to God. The two great acts of God are creation and the incarnation. This overwhelming sense of the giftedness of creation and redemption was at the heart of Ignatius's understanding of all of creation and human history and was the source of his passionate gratitude for all God's gifts. This vision is articulated in the key meditations of the *Spiritual Exercises*. Ignatius's gratitude, then, flowed from both his life experience and his mystical experience of God.

The Spiritual Exercises

The *Spiritual Exercises* is the book of Ignatius best known and certainly most influential in guiding the spiritual lives of innumerable retreatants over the last four hundred and fifty years. The *Spiritual Exercises* outlines and presents a series of activities—meditations, considerations, contemplations, methods of self-examination and prayer, and guidelines—for discerning God's will and making a decision.

The *Exercises* is a book for a director, a method to be adapted to the individual by the director for guiding another's prayer and discernment and facilitating a person's experience of God. It is also a record, the journal of Ignatius's own search for God, of his spiritual journey which is paradigmatic for other Christians' search for God. As a guide for others' journeys it is an important starting point for an exploration of gratitude in Ignatian spirituality.

What is the role of gratitude in the *Spiritual Exercises*? The explicit references are limited, but, on a deeper level, gratitude is central to the dynamic and movement of the *Exercises* and the retreatant's experience of God. This becomes most clear in the final grace prayed for in the *Exercises*, the grace that sums up the *Spiritual Exercises*, and the experience of thirty days of prayer and solitude. The final contemplation of the thirty-day retreat is entitled "Contemplation on the Love of God." It is a four-step reflection that invites the retreatant to recall all the gifts of God, how God dwells and labors in those gifts and finally how all those gifts come from God and lead us back to the giver of all gifts. It is a contemplation rooted in Ignatius's vision at the river Cardoner where he saw all things coming from God and returning to God.

What is most important, however, is the grace that is to be prayed for in this contemplation: "Here it will be to ask for an intimate knowledge of the many blessings received, that filled with gratitude for all, I may in all things love and serve the Divine Majesty" (§233).[6] It is the knowledge of the many blessings received that fills one with gratitude. That prayer is the culmination of the *Spiritual Exercises* and a summation of Ignatius's spirituality. Knowledge of God's gifts leads to gratitude which moves one to love and desire to serve God. Ignatius had noted at the beginning of this contemplation that love consists in a mutual sharing between persons. As George Ganss points out in commenting on this contemplation, "Love ordinarily arises from gratitude. The lover gives to the beloved and the beloved, recognizing the giver's goodness, experiences gratitude and increased love for the giver."[7] Out of this love and gratitude and a desire to serve, the retreatant is invited to say the Ignatian *Suscipe*, the prayer of total surrender and generosity. "Take, Lord, and receive all my liberty, my memory, my understanding, and my entire will, all that I have and possess. You have given all to me. To you, O Lord, I return it. All is yours, dispose of it wholly according to your will. Give me your love and your grace, for this is sufficient for me" (§234). This is the prayer of a grateful heart that recognizes all as gift to be shared.

Knowledge of God's gifts leads to gratitude which moves one to love and desire to serve God.

But gratitude is not only a grace experienced at the end of the *Exercises*. Throughout the *Exercises*, the retreatant experiences gratitude for God's gifts—for God's love in the Principle and Foundation, for God's mercy in the First Week, for God's call in Jesus in the Second Week, and for redemption gained through the death and resurrection in the Third and Fourth Weeks. In the Principle and Foundation, the retreatant reflects on the end for which he or she is created, the means to the end, and the need for indifference. The Principle and Foundation invites a person to a deeper experience of the love of God and the giftedness of creation. It calls forth a deep sense of gratitude for God's love and generosity. This gratitude for all the gifts of God, especially for the profound experience of God's unconditional love, can be a sign of a person's readiness to move into the First Week of the *Exercises*.

The First Week of the *Exercises* leads one to a further grace, that of knowing oneself as a loved sinner. It confronts one with a deep sense of sinfulness and of sorrow for sin, as well as a sense of God's unquestioned mercy. This experience of forgiveness calls forth gratitude in the retreatant. At the end of the second meditation of the First Week, Ignatius invites the person to "conclude with a colloquy, extolling the mercy of God our Lord, pouring out my thoughts to God, and giving thanks to God that up to this very moment God has granted me life. I will resolve with God's grace to amend for the future" (§61). At the end of the fifth meditation, on hell, there is a similar prayer of gratitude: "I will give thanks to God our Lord that God has not put an end to my life. . . . I shall also thank God for this, that up to this very moment God has shown himself so loving and merciful to me" (§71). By the end of the first week of the *Spiritual Exercises*, the gratitude for God's unconditional love manifested in creation has deepened and expanded into a gratitude for God's mercy, for the gift of unmerited forgiveness and salvation.

The remaining three Weeks of the *Exercises* can be dealt with more briefly. The only explicit reference to thanksgiving in these three Weeks is in the contemplation on the incarnation at the beginning of the Second Week. This contemplation, however, is presented as a model for all the contemplations of the life of Christ throughout the Second Week. Mary's response at the annunciation images the desired response to the gift of God becoming flesh in Jesus. "This will be to consider . . . how our Lady humbles herself and offers thanks to the Divine Majesty" (§108). It is obvious that Ignatius images a Christian response to the events of Christ's life, death, and resurrection as giving thanks for God's love in Jesus.[8]

Ignatius's explicit references to gratitude in the *Exercises*, then, are limited, but they reveal that gratitude is an important dynamic in the movement of the *Exercises* from grace to grace. One moves from an experience of gratitude for God's love to an experience of gratitude for forgiveness to an experience of gratitude for the call to labor at the side of Jesus and to share in the paschal mystery of dying and rising with Jesus. It is in reflecting on all these graces and gifts of God in the final contemplation that one is filled with gratitude and a renewed desire to love and serve God.

Before leaving the *Exercises*, there are two other references to gratitude that are important for understanding the mind of

Ignatius. They are not essential to the dynamic of the *Exercises*, but they are part of two spiritual exercises or practices that Ignatius encourages during the retreat and also in one's ongoing spiritual life after retreat. The first is the practice of review of meditation. Ignatius encourages the retreatant to spend a brief time after each period of prayer reviewing the graces of the prayer, the consolations and the desolations, the person's responses and resistances, as well as fidelity to the methods of prayer and dedication to the time of prayer. Ignatius directs: "I will consider for the space of a quarter of an hour how I succeeded in the meditation or contemplation. If poorly, I will seek the cause of the failure; and after I have found it, I will be sorry, so that I may do better in the future. If I have succeeded, I will give thanks to God our Lord, and the next time try to follow the same method" (§77). It is important after prayer to thank God for graces received and for the work of God within oneself. Gratitude deepens the graces and unites a person more closely to God as giver of all gifts.

It is important after prayer to thank God for graces received and for the work of God within oneself. Gratitude deepens the graces and unites a person more closely to God as giver of all gifts.

The second reference to gratitude comes at the beginning of the practice of examination of conscience that Ignatius proposes in the First Week of the *Exercises*. The first of five points of this method is "to give thanks to God our Lord for the favors received" (§43). One goes on to ask for the grace to know one's sins, to review them, to ask pardon, and to resolve to amend one's life. Ignatius, then, begins this time-honored spiritual practice with a moment of gratitude. Awareness of our sinfulness, sorrow, and purpose of amendment are all rooted in a sense of thanksgiving for God's gifts. This seems a confirmation of the previous reflection on gratitude as a grace flowing from the Principle and Foundation prior to beginning the First Week of the *Exercises*.

Contemporary spiritual writers have interpreted this practice of examen as a method of ongoing daily discernment that facilitates reflection on the movement of God and response or lack of response to that movement. It becomes a practice not so much of moral inventory as a sensitivity to how God has been at work in a person's life that day. The first point, then, becomes a grateful reflection on the gifts of God that day which invite to spiritual growth. This interpretation of the practice gives much more meaning to Ignatius's insistence on the essential role of this practice in Christians' spiritual lives. Again it emphasizes the importance of gratitude in Ignatius's spirituality.

The *Exercises* began as a journal of Ignatius's own experience of God at Manresa and became the instrument for leading many others on a similar spiritual journey. If gratitude is at the heart of the *Exercises*, it is at the heart of Ignatian spirituality.

The Spiritual Diary

In talking about the *Spiritual Diary*, Ganss says it "enables us to gaze most directly into the depths of Ignatius's heart in his intimate dealing with God. It also best reveals the sublimity of his mysticism."[9] The *Spiritual Diary* of Ignatius is the only remaining fragment of his spiritual diaries. The rest were destroyed. It is a daily journal of his graces and mystical experiences from 2 February 1544 to 27 February 1545. In the words of Adolf Haas in his study of the mysticism of Ignatius revealed in the *Diary*, "In the *Diary*, however, Ignatius lays completely bare the mystery of his intimacy with God. Consequently, no other document offers us a more penetrating insight into the magnificent world of faith that was the inner life of Ignatius."[10] The *Diary* was not intended for publication and so gives an unguarded record of his constant and profound mystical experiences and extraordinary gifts.

The *Diary* records Ignatius's graces as he discerned over a period of a year a question about the type of poverty that should be practiced in the newly formed Society of Jesus. It is a living example of how Ignatius used the principles and procedures for decision making that he had laid out in the *Spiritual Exercises*. What we find in the *Diary* is an extraordinary Trinitarian and Christ-centered mysticism and a mysticism of discernment. The theme of gratitude pervades the *Diary* and is the reason why Ignatius kept a diary of his experiences of God. According to Adolf Haas, "Ignatius thought of the recording of the graces he received above all as an act of personal thanksgiving" (p. 166).

The same explanation is given by Arturo Codina in his introduction to the first critical edition of the *Diary:* "This diary is a catalogue of the benefits received from God, which our Father Ignatius drew up because of his great gratitude to God and man. Ignatius did this not only to stamp them more firmly in his memory, but also to inflame his heart with an ever increasing love for such benefactors by a frequent rereading of them."[11] George Ganss reiterates this thought in his own introduction to the *Diary:* "Ignatius jotted down his experiences in the order in which they came, merely to keep alive his memory of them and his gratitude."[12]

It will help to give a few of the references to gratitude in the *Diary.* Ignatius says, "I could not bring myself to finish giving thanks to God our Lord, with great intensity, understanding, and tears, for so great a favor and so great a clarity I had received, just beyond explanation" (§21).[13] "Getting up and preparing for Mass, I gave thanks to his Divine Majesty, and offered him the oblation made, not without devotion and motion of tears" (§40). "After Mass, both in the chapel and later kneeling in my room, I wanted to thank God for such great graces. . . (§41). "Then I made the final confirmation to the Most Holy Trinity, in the presence of the whole heavenly court, giving thanks with great and intense affection, first to the Divine Persons, then to our Lady and to her Son, then to the angels, the holy fathers, the apostles and disciples, all the saints, and to all persons for the help they had given me in this matter" (§47).

There are about a dozen such explicit references to gratitude in the *Diary* so that a pattern is repeated as Ignatius seeks confirmation of a decision made. Ignatius first offers the decision to God, then asks for confirmation, and then gives thanks to God for the graces received. In the *Spiritual Exercises*, when Ignatius outlines the steps in a confirmation process, he makes no reference to the final act of thanksgiving. In the record of his own discernment in this concrete case, however, it seems that gratitude is an important means of closure on a decision (§§175-189).

Finally, the context of Ignatius's prayer and mystical experiences recorded in the *Diary* is important. Most of the mystical experiences he describes occurred during his prayer in the morning, which included the Eucharist. Harvey Egan remarks that "the *Spiritual Diary* attests that Ignatius's trinitarian and Christocentric mysticism developed almost exclusively in the atmosphere of the Mass. . . . The *Spiritual Diary* notes and associates almost every mystical grace he received with the Mass said that day."[14] It is not difficult to recognize the connection between Ignatius's sense of gratitude and the central role of the Eucharist in his mystical life.

The Constitutions of the Society of Jesus

It is clear from the *Spiritual Exercises* and Ignatius's *Spiritual Diary* that gratitude to God was a vital part of his relationship to God. But Ignatius's gratitude also extended to the many benefactors who supported him in his pilgrim and student years and who later supported the Society of Jesus. This gratitude is most clearly manifested in his letters and in the *Constitutions of the Society of Jesus*.

Ignatius was elected general of the Society of Jesus in 1541. One of his tasks was to expand the brief "Formula of the Institute" into a set of statutes or constitutions which could serve as the governing law of the Society. The "Formula of the Institute" had been written by Ignatius with the help of the early companions as a necessary step to obtaining papal approval for their new religious order in 1540. It is a statement of the basic structure and mission of the Society of Jesus. The *Constitutions*, on the other hand, is a detailed description of the organization and government of this order written by Ignatius between 1541 and his death in 1556.

The section of the *Constitutions* that deals most explicitly with gratitude is Part IV that discusses the colleges and universities of the Society. Ignatius begins this part of the *Constitutions* with a chapter on the gratitude owed to the founders and benefactors of the colleges. "It is highly proper for us to do something on our part in return for the devotion and generosity shown toward the Society by those whom the Divine Goodness employs as his ministers to found and endow its colleges" (§309).[15] Thus the human benefactors are seen as ministers of divine goodness. Gratitude is due to God but also to those who are instruments of God's goodness. This gratitude of Ignatius to God and benefactors was even more clearly stated in the original draft of the *Constitutions* of 1547. Ignatius wrote then: "Beginning with the gratitude so pleasing to God our Lord both towards the divine generosity, from which all good things come, and also towards his servants, through whose hands the good things come from above . . . it is our duty to take pains—in the same love and veneration towards our Creator and Lord—in some way to repay or respond to that pious reverence and love which these founders and benefactors show to us. . . ."[16]

The members of the Society are to express their gratitude first by spiritual works, celebrating Mass for the benefactors and offering other prayers, but Ignatius also legislates the practice of presenting a wax candle to the founder or a close relative each year on the anniversary of the Jesuits taking possession of the college. This was done, as Ignatius said, "as a sign of the gratitude due him [the founder] in our Lord" (*Cons.*, §312). Ignatius adds that "the same obligation of showing gratitude is incumbent in the Lord on [nonpriests] as well as on the priests" (§315). The brothers and scholastics are to offer prayers

Ignatius's gratitude also extended to the many benefactors who supported him in his pilgrim and student years and who later supported the Society of Jesus.

for the same intention for which the priests are celebrating Mass. Ignatius further remarks that the Society "is bound, by an obligation of charity and love, to show [to founders and benefactors and their dear ones] whatever service it can according to our humble profession, for the divine glory" (§318). Finally, Ignatius comments that founders and benefactors share in a special way in all the good works of the colleges and of the whole Society (§317). It is not surprising that Antonio de Aldama, in his commentary on the Constitutions, reflects that "Ignatius considers founders and benefactors only from the point of view of the gratitude that is due to them. Gratitude was one of his most characteristic virtues."[17]

The Letters

Finally, as evidence of the importance of gratitude for Ignatius, it is important to touch, if only briefly, on the letters of Ignatius. There are almost seven thousand letters and instructions of Ignatius gathered in twelve volumes of about eight hundred pages each. Without hoping to provide an exhaustive list of references to gratitude in seven thousand letters, a few examples can give some evidence of how often Ignatius wrote in a spirit of thanksgiving. First, recall his words to Simon Rodriguez speaking of ingratitude as "the most abominable of sins" because "it is a forgetting of the graces, benefits, and blessings received. . . . On the contrary, the grateful acknowledgment of blessings and gifts received is loved and esteemed not only on earth but also in heaven."[18] Further examples of this can be seen in the twenty-five letters that Ignatius addressed to benefactresses. Hugo Rahner has collected these letters and introduced them with some insightful reflections on the heart of Ignatius. Rahner remarks that "this correspondence brings Ignatius to life for us at his best: in his expression of gratitude." Rahner speaks of Ignatius's "imperishable gratitude" and almost "helpless gratitude."[19]

Two examples from these letters to benefactresses will suffice. To Donna Maria Frassoni del Gesso: "I have, indeed, not replied up to the present to Your Ladyship's letter of 10 December. I will do so now, thanking Your Ladyship for the great charity and devotion with which you help that work of God our Lord in Ferrara and for the good intention you have to help it for the future. I do not doubt that God our Lord will make you share in all the good that shall be done in it." To Dona Aldonza Gonzalez: "For all this I gave much thanks to God our Lord, of whose infinite and supreme goodness I hope that, through your holy desires, this work will in time come to be of great service."[20]

This same desire to give thanks also runs through many of Ignatius's letters to friends and spiritual directees and persons of prominence, as well as to fellow Jesuits. He wrote to his long-time benefactress and friend Isabel Roser in 1532: "I hope that God will not have to punish me for ingratitude, if in some way he makes me worthy of giving some praise and service to his Divine Majesty."[21] Later in the same letter, Ignatius prays that God will help him cancel his debt of gratitude to her. He adds, "Our Lord insists that we look to the giver, and love the giver more than the gift, and thus keep the giver ever before our eyes and in the most intimate thoughts of our heart."[22] Ignatius wrote with effusive gratitude in 1543 to John II, King of Portugal, "I find occasion to write this letter. I cannot help but rejoice in our Lord and give the Eternal Goodness infinite and ceaseless thanks when I reflect on how much, through the Lord's infinite and supreme goodness, the Lord does for us, unworthy as we are of any mention."[23] He wrote to the Jesuit Peter Canisius in 1546, "We give thanks to God for God's ineffable mercy and kindness with which God overwhelms us through the power of God's glorious name."[24]

To John of Avila, Ignatius writes to express his gratitude for the support he gave to the Society in Spain: "I made up my mind to write you for two reasons. The first is to give some sign of recognition and gratitude by way of the warmest thanks to God, and to your reverence in God's most holy name, for all that you have done for the glory of the Divine Majesty in behalf of us."[25] There are numerous other references in Ignatius's letters to his gratitude both to God and to benefactors. Even a cursory reading of the letters gives support to Hugo Rahner's comment that "when the time for gratitude came, there was no restraining him [Ignatius]."[26]

Final Reflection

The writings of Ignatius reveal gratitude as a central and recurring theme in spirituality and a distinctive element of his experience of God. Ignatius did not leave us systematic treatises or learned essays on spiritual topics. His writings have a more practical bent, from his handbook for directors that we know as the *Spiritual Exercises* to the *Constitutions of the Society of Jesus* to endless letters of spiritual advice and practical business to his own intimate diary of God's extraordinary workings in his soul. Much in Ignatius remains implicit and undeveloped and unarticulated. It seems clear, however, that gratitude is a clear and explicit theme and even passion in the writings of Ignatius. A further argument can be made that gratitude is a touchstone grace that reveals the very heart of Ignatius and his spirituality and mysticism. It takes nothing away from Ignatius to say that he did not fully realize or articulate just how central gratitude was to his vision of God and the human person. It is rather a compliment to the richness of his religious experience and to his own passion for service more than for systematic thinking to say that Ignatius's own conscious awareness could be enriched by reflection half a millennium later. What is on some levels implicit and nonthematic in his thought can be named and made explicit.

What is the foundation for saying that gratitude is at the heart of Ignatius's vision? First, at the heart of his experience of God is a profound experience of the giftedness of creation. It is rooted in his experience at the river Cardoner and it is embodied in the Principle and Foundation and above all in the final Contemplation on the Love of God. Ignatius saw everything as a gift from God, a gift to be received and shared. Hugo Rahner in his classic study of the theology of Ignatius refers to Ignatius's vision as a vision "from above."[27] All things come from God and return to God. It is this sense of giftedness that calls forth "helpless gratitude" in Ignatius. It is interesting that the only explicit reference to gratitude in Ignatius's *Autobiography* is immediately after his mystical experience at the river Cardoner. He remembers that "he went to kneel before a cross, which was near that place, to give thanks to God . . ." (§31). It is gratitude that kept him in touch with the giftedness of life and ultimately in touch with God, the giver of all gifts, and that deepened his relationship of total dependence and surrender to God. Ignatius not only saw everything as gift from God, he saw God dwelling and laboring in those gifts. He truly found God, the giver of all gifts, in all things. It was Ignatius's felt conviction that his own labor was labor with Christ laboring in the world. That conviction united him with God in contemplative oneness in the midst of activity.

Ignatian indifference or freedom flows from a sense of giftedness and gratitude. It is because everything is seen as gift that one can let go and trust in the fidelity of the giver. Gifts unrelated to a Giver become possessions, attachments, objects of unfreedom that are clung to. A grateful person is a free person because the grateful person holds everything in trust and never mistakes the gift for the giver. The temptation, of course, is to take things for granted, to claim things as one's own or as owed to one. When this happens a person is no longer surprised by life.

Ignatius's insistence on gratitude is related also to his commitment to poverty, to the desire to own and possess nothing, but to rely completely on God. Poverty of spirit and a desire for actual poverty flowed from Ignatius's experience of all things as gifts of God. Ignatius's *Spiritual Diary* highlights the importance of gratitude in his mystical experience of God. The *Diary*, in fact, is concerned with the confirmation of a decision about the poverty of the Society of Jesus. For Ignatius there is a strong ascetical link between gratitude and poverty. The awareness of all as gift freed Ignatius from attachment and the need to possess and accumulate, and his poverty reinforced his dependence on the benefactions of others and increased his gratitude for their generosity.

Gratitude also expands the heart and opens the person to the giftedness of all of reality. A profound experience of gratefulness is incompatible with pettiness and negativism and self-centeredness. Ignatius looked for generosity in one making the *Exercises*, not overly measured responses, but a willingness to risk all in following God. The final prayer of the *Exercises*, the *Suscipe*, is the prayer of a generous, expansive heart that has received all as gift and returns it freely, asking only for the ultimate gift of God's love and grace. Magnanimity, greatness of heart, a heart desirous to do more for God—these are all qualities identified with Ignatius. They are also qualities of a person filled with gratitude for the gifts of God.

Ignatius not only saw everything as gift from God, he saw God dwelling and laboring in those gifts.

Finally, Ignatian spirituality has always been recognized as action-centered. For Ignatius, love is shown in deeds as well as in words. Ignatius was driven by the desire to serve God and to discern and carry out God's will. Ignatian mysticism is not primarily a mysticism of loving union but a mysticism of service.[28] Again, gratitude is a source of that zeal to be of service. Gratitude opens a person's heart to ministry, to a desire to share the gift, to give in return. We recall the final grace prayed for in the *Exercises*, "Here it will be to ask for an intimate knowledge of the many blessings received, that filled with gratitude for all, I may in all things love and serve the Divine Majesty" (§233). Knowledge of gifts leads to gratitude which leads to love and desire to serve. George Ganss in his recent translation of the *Exercises* has caught the dynamic character of gratitude and its connection to service. His translation replaces Puhl's literal translation of "filled with gratitude" with "stirred to profound gratitude."[29] Gratitude impels one to service of the Divine Majesty. It stirs up a zeal to share the gifts received and to proclaim the good news that God desires to gift all people with a share in the life of God.

As mentioned earlier, Ignatius insisted on the twice-daily practice of examen of conscience, the first step of which is to give thanks for all God's gifts and benefits. Certainly the examen was part of the honest self-discipline and self-examination that characterized Ignatius, but it may be that Ignatius also was convinced, even if only subconsciously, that if a person stops twice a day to give thanks to God, that person will grow in the freedom, greatness of heart, and desire to serve that characterize the true disciple of Christ. In this regard, Ignatius has much to teach Christians about their relationship with God and the importance of gratitude in growing in that relationship. For that, it seems only appropriate to be grateful.

Notes

[1] *Letters of St. Ignatius of Loyola*, trans. William J. Young SJ (Chicago: Loyola University Press, 1959), p. 55.

[2] Quoted in Hugo Rahner SJ, *St. Ignatius Loyola: Letters to Women*, trans. Kathleen Pond and S.A.H. Weetman (New York: Herder and Herder, 1960), p. 169.

[3] H. Rahner, *St. Ignatius . . . to Women*, p. 169.

[4] Harvey Egan SJ, *Ignatius Loyola the Mystic* (Wilmington: Michael Glazier, 1987), p. 114.

[5] *A Pilgrim's Journey: The Autobiography of St. Ignatius Loyola*, trans. Joseph Tylenda SJ (Wilmington: Michael Glazier, 1985), §30.

[6] *Spiritual Exercises* citations are from *The Spiritual Exercises of St. Ignatius*, trans. Louis J. Puhl SJ (Chicago: Loyola University Press, 1951).

[7] George E. Ganss SJ, ed., *Ignatius of Loyola* (New York: Paulist Press, 1991), p. 418, n. 109.

[8] See Ganss, *Ignatius*, p. 419, n. 112.

[9] Ganss, *Ignatius*, p. 229.

[10] Adolf Haas SJ, "The Mysticism of St. Ignatius according to His *Spiritual Diary*," in *Ignatius of Loyola: His Personality and Spiritual Heritage, 1556-1956*, ed. Friedrich Wulf SJ (St. Louis: Institute of Jesuit Sources, 1977), p. 165.

[11] Quoted in Haas, "Mysticism," p. 166, n. 5.

[12] Ganss, *Ignatius*, p. 232.

[13] *Spiritual Diary* citations are from Antonio T. de Nicolas. *Powers of Imagining: Ignatius de Loyola* (Albany: State University of New York Press, 1986).

[14] Egan, *Ignatius*, p. 113.

[15] *Constitutions* citations are from St. Ignatius of Loyola, *The Constitutions of the Society of Jesus*, trans. George E. Ganss SJ (St. Louis: Institute of Jesuit Sources, 1970).

[16] Quoted in H. Rahner, *St. Ignatius . . . to Women*, p. 171.

[17] Antonio M. de Aldama, *An Introductory Commentary on the Constitutions* (St. Louis: Institute of Jesuit Sources, 1989), p. 150.

[18] *Letters*, trans. Young, p. 55.

[19] H. Rahner, *St. Ignatius . . . to Women*, p. 170.

[20] H. Rahner, *St. Ignatius . . . to Women*, pp. 191 and 241.

[21] *Letters*, trans. Young, p. 9.

[22] *Letters*, trans. Young, p. 10.

[23] *Letters*, trans. Young, p. 65.

[24] *Letters*, trans. Young, p. 97.

[25] *Letters*, trans. Young, p. 182.

[26] H. Rahner, *St. Ignatius . . . to Women*, p. 170.

[27] See Hugo Rahner SJ, *Ignatius the Theologian*, trans. Michael Barry (San Francisco: Ignatius Press, 1990), pp. 3-10.

[28] See Joseph de Guibert SJ, *The Jesuits: Their Spiritual Doctrine and Practice*, trans. William J. Young SJ (St. Louis: Institute of Jesuit Sources, 1986), p. 50.

[29] Ganss, *Ignatius*, p. 176.

The Development of Christian Identity through the *Spiritual Exercises* of St. Ignatius

movement

To write a short paper on the *Spiritual Exercises* seems impossible as the literature is voluminous, expanding over four hundred years, and expertise abounds. My intent, however, is to be neither encyclopedic in scope nor historical in interpretation. Rather, I will present the structure, content, and psycho-spiritual process from the particular perspective of the graced development of self-identity in the directee who experiences the *Spiritual Exercises*.

The *Exercises*, a short guidebook which evolved from the experiences of Ignatius and his colleagues, has five main parts, namely, the "Principle and Foundation," and four distinct phases, called Weeks. Each part builds on the process of its predecessor. In order to use these experiences today in the spirit and intent of Ignatius, it is essential that guides know experientially the primary focus of each stage. Only then can accurate adaptation be made for twentieth-century culture.

Before approaching the text head on, it is important to consider the role of God's grace as it is understood today. Ignatius has us pray for "graces" which sound on the surface like packages of holiness which we order through a divine UPS to be opened and used as necessary. Although that sense of grace as commodity has been prevalent, and while it is true that grace is for our beneficial use, theologians today present grace as God's ongoing "self-communication." Karl Rahner is the foremost teacher of the viewpoint that "the entire purpose of creation is that God might be grace for us, to God's glory."[2] God's self-communication always shapes us and our life whether we know it or not. It is our "original redemptive grace," implicit in all we are and do. We make it explicit as we enter into or reject the life, death, and resurrection of Jesus.[3]

My personal sense of this self-communication of God is that of basic love-energy empowering me to enter and live Christ's life. I am given the energy to speak my unique word, myself's language, to shape my share of creation. Through grace, God authorizes me into living. Referring to his life, Jesus says for and with me, "I have the power to lay it down, and I have the power to take it up again. This command I received from my Father" (Jn 10:18).[4]

The guide is to be primarily a support person and a point of balance, who can adapt the exercises to best enable the directee to hear the word of God for her.

The significance of hearing clearly my unique "God's self-word" is obvious: From this graced sense of identity flows my ongoing sense of direction in life. As I learn through loving attentiveness, that is, discipleship, to hear more fully, so I can choose more accurately how and when to pick up or lay down the specific, concrete aspects of my life. In Ignatian terms, this basic God orientation, my inner ear tuned to God, is "essential consolation." To turn off God with a deaf ear is "desolation." To learn the nuances of these states in daily life, to compare them with our basic identity, and to apply our learnings to our choices is discernment. In the *Spiritual Exercises* Ignatius gives us a method to be used with an individual and her guide, whereby her God-given identity may be heard and her direction discerned.

Ignatius begins with some twenty suggestions, called "Annotations," in which he characterizes the guide and the directee. The guide is to be primarily a support person and a point of balance, who can adapt the exercises to best enable the directee to hear the word of God for her. The guide strives to build trust between the directee and God [2, 6-10, 14, 15, 18, 19]. The directee is to be primarily a courageous and generous person who desires to be ever more freely available to God and God's purposes. The directee is responsible to the guide to discuss faithfully the movements, content, of her prayer so as to follow the lead of the Spirit [3-5, 11-13, 16, 17, 20]. Guide and directee are to work together with mutual respect and openness toward the goal of inner freedom from "any tendency that is disordered" [21, 22]. Ultimately our desires and God's desires will be identified in one accord.

The exercises which Ignatius gives are a series of meditations for the First Week and contemplations for the following three Weeks. The centerpiece is a set of exercises which facilitate a specific commitment to the person and work of Christ. In each phase, the directee is asked to place herself reverently before God and ask for what she desires [48]. Her desire will flow from the material supplied for prayer. Then she is asked to share her prayerful observations in a "colloquy" with Christ. This is not a formal speech, but

> The colloquy is made, properly speaking, as one friend speaks to another, . . . now asking some grace, now blaming oneself for some misdeed, now communicating one's affairs, and asking advice in them [54].

Ignatius gives specific direction to each week with the specified graces. Repetitions of significant points in the meditations and colloquies intensify the process [62]. Clearly, friendship with the persons of the Trinity is a prerequisite for such colloquial speech. Friendship may not be a given in our awareness of God or we may have drifted away from this intimacy. It may be necessary to devote time to develop these conditions, summarized by Ignatius in the "Principle and Foundation," through Scripture or some other individually oriented method. The essential point is that we know ourselves accepted by God and acceptable to ourselves.[5]

For myself, a long and turbulent process culminated in a touchstone experience in which I watched three streams tumble over rocks to form one wide swift stream, the Gyssinge river in Sweden, and found the mirror image experienced interiorly of myself coming together as one. I felt "just like myself," expansive and relaxed: I am who I am. I am intrinsically good. The river became the inner flow of energy and gracious life (Journal, June 1985).

Having come into myself as is, I was better disposed for the exercises of the First Week. This phase, along with the Principle and Foundation, is the critical phase of the *Exercises*. Without its fruits, we cannot effectively continue on to the remaining phases.

Ignatius provides measures for people not ready to continue. The *Exercises* are not for everyone [18]. In the First Week, we begin to focus on those "rocks" which break up our flow and threaten our movement to God. Unless we recognize them, we cannot navigate through them, nor will we ever come to see their ruggedness as part of the whole picture. Our focus will reveal these rocks to be the surface evidence of a deeper geological fault within ourselves and within our society and culture. Sin is personal, interpersonal, and social; each builds on the others.[6]

Ignatius carefully structures the First Week into five meditations which move us from a generalized awareness of sin as basic to human history into a sense of specific personal sinfulness, and finally to a desire to oppose the serious contamination by sin of our world. Although meditation tends to be intellectual, the affective intensity of this process is indicated in the graces requested and the nature of the colloquies. We are to pray for two main graces: first, "to ask for shame and confusion at myself . . ." [48] and, following, "to beg a great and intense sorrow and tears for my sins" [55]. We are to speak in colloquy with Christ imaged before us on the cross which he chooses for love of us [53]:

> . . . how from Creator he is come to making himself man, and from life eternal is come to temporal death, and so to die for my sins.
> Likewise, looking at myself, what I have done for Christ, what I am doing for Christ, what I ought to do for Christ.

The purpose of the colloquies is to solidify our focus on Christ crucified as the one who saves us from the traps, the Scylla and Charybdis, from which we have little power to escape or navigate. We are asked to image and experience our own hells (fifth meditation) so that we desire greatly to stay close to Christ, the mercy of God. The reliance on Christ, our power and energy, is essential [65-72].

The terms "shame and confusion" need some explanation, especially for women who are shamed and told they are crazy often enough in our society. My reaction to the text was "My God, I have felt this way much of my life. Why do I pray for these feelings now?" (7/16/85). It would have been helpful to have some explanation of current understandings of Ignatius's intent here. The sense is not that of failure to live up to tyrannical "shoulds" which paralyze or anger people. Aschenbrenner and Gray stress the sense of embarrassment at failing a dear friend to whom one is closely related. My own word is "chagrin" at recognizing the reality of my attitudes and consequent actions. This sense becomes a stimulant to growthful response.

Similarly, "confusion" refers not to interior muddiness, but more to a sense of surprise, dissonance, and wonder that God has actually taken care of us and kept us alive while we have been so destructive to ourselves and others. The movement here is away from morbid introspection onto the ongoing love of God for us and creation. The central point, as I experienced it, is to share the vantage point of Christ crucified toward attitudes and decisions. "Come next to me," he says; "be like me." His voice is both calm and urgent, a marked contrast to my own anxious demands to prove and rescue myself. His is the voice of acceptance for us as beloved sinners. In accepting ourselves as we are accepted, we have moved close to the goal of Week One. Yet the process is really never finished as new obstacles are thrown up from our inner fault. We have, however, learned how to navigate more effectively.[7]

The story of Bartimaeus (Mk 10:46-52) had been a catalyst for my psycho-spiritual growth over the past year, so I was not surprised when it surfaced again toward the end of my First Week (8/8/85). It summed up the elements of this week and provided a transition to Week Two. Thus, there is an awareness of Christ present as a source of mercy coupled with an awareness of one's own need. There is the element of community support [60]. There is the urging of Christ, "What do you desire?" which draws forth the articulation of a specific need, "I want to see." Christ heals in response to the individual's faith and thus the person is empowered to "start to follow him up the road."

Ignatius suggested a consideration to effect this transition in which he asks us to listen to Christ, the king, who calls us to serve with him and share his conditions. Considering all that has gone before, we would not wish to be stingy in our response [91-100]. Considerable discussion has been generated about the nature of this reflection.[8] The consensus seems to be that it is transitional and not of ultimate importance for our society where kings and kingdoms seem archaic and patriarchal. For Ignatius, the lord-vassal relationship was the cement of the feudal world and expressed best the covenanted relationship he wished to develop between the retreatant and Christ.

For our purpose, it is sufficient to note the shift in focus from identification as beloved sinner to coming to see oneself as disciple-in-process. With self-acceptance, the energy formerly needed to protect the egocentric self is freed to be directed into the service of Christ. The sense of love in relationship is strong and moves outward in the desire to make it visible and tangible (11/13/85). The action of the Spirit, working through the process of Weeks Two, Three and Four, ideally will develop the identification with Christ to the point where Christ and self are one,". . . the life I live now is not my own; Christ is living in me" (Ga 2:20). It is unlikely that this would be fulfilled in an eight or thirty-day retreat; rather it is the developmental process of one's life.

Having desired to serve with Christ, even to grow into his likeness, it is natural to wish to know him better, more interiorly. This movement marks the beginning of Week Two [104]. Since we normally grow in friendship by spending time with our friends, Ignatius suggests a new method of prayer to help us. While we continue with the graces and the colloquies, now we are encouraged to use not only our intellects, but also our imaginations and all our senses, to enter more fully into specific events of Jesus' life and ministry just as if we were historically present. We are "to reflect on myself in order to draw some profit" [114] and to share our awarenesses with whoever draws us in the story, usually Jesus, Mary, or God as Abba [199]. This form is maintained through this and the following weeks while the subjects are changed according to the needs of the retreatant and the theme of the week [119, 18].

The scenes may seem at first like pictures in an album, but soon the Spirit of Christ present works interiorly to reshape us into growing disciples. This work is encouraged by repetitions of those points where we experienced some knowledge, consolation, or desolation [118]. This repetition may involve a short passage over two or three sessions or it may involve a major repetition, over several weeks, for example, in the Nineteenth Annotation retreat. Sufficient time must be allowed for growth to occur as qualities emerge which need attention in a disciple.

While awkward at first, I grew accustomed to trusting my own inner suggestions and directions, which is essential to the movement of the retreat. The method became less of a method and more of a natural inner movement. Often, the content of the prayer became simpler, more absorbing, sometimes painful and sometimes delightful. I learned by feel, so to speak, when "all the profit" was drawn: nothing more was happening and there was a sense of staleness. This was different from nothing happening because I did not welcome what threatened to emerge. Then there was an inner pressure and a sense of myself with averted gaze.

This developing sensitivity to our inner promptings enables us to hear the voice of Christ, our leader. As we are led, we begin to wonder about the direction of our lives. This is a natural movement which Ignatius, a man of apostolic action, promoted through a series of exercises designed to concretize our decisions on service. Ignatius begins these exercises at the point where we are contemplating the time when Jesus, age twelve, decided to leave his parents briefly to "be about my Father's business" [135]. Perhaps we too need to make a break and move directly into some more invested "spirited" action for compassionate justice in our world.

Ignatius signals this break by changing the form from contemplation to meditation. This shift, jarring to some perhaps, helps us recognize the seriousness needed for reflection. The meditations are named "Two Standards" [136-148], "Three Types of Persons" [149-156], and "Three Kinds of Humility" [164-168]. While all three are significant for the disciple, Ignatius centers our attention on the "Two Standards" by its central location, by the length of time, four periods, to be spent on it, and by the nature of the content.[9] We request the grace to know the "deceits of the bad chief (Lucifer) and to guard against them"; and "for knowledge of the true life which the supreme and true Captain shows and the grace to imitate him" [139]. We pray for knowledge upon which to base our future discernment as we witness and serve. We seek insight into what Ignatius perceives as a cosmic struggle over the continuance of our humanity in its goodness and freedom. Although we know that Christ has won, the opposition is unrelenting as it seeks to enslave us in personal and societal evil. Ignatius describes the classic view of sin: riches lead to a desire for honor and culminate in pride [142]. Christ is seen with the three traditional remedies: poverty, contempt for the world, and humility [146].

We have come to see this as a very masculine understanding of sin. It is important to recognize that for women sinfulness may take the form of passivity and self-abnegation, fostered, if not actively encouraged, by the demand by church authorities and other patriarchs for "bearing your cross," self-denial, and humility. In this way women have become the victim battered by the image of the cross.[10] Women need to understand the importance of having a self before they seek to transcend it. We need to hear "I AM" strongly in ourselves to recognize Christ joining his "I AM" to ours. Then we are equipped with the interior strength to join forces with our male colleagues to work toward the establishment of a new heaven and a new earth. In practice, I found this happening for myself as I moved from the stance of "I will. . . .; you will . . ." to "How will we. . . ?" Where evil seeks to dominate and isolate, God seeks to foster community and mutuality.

Praying with the three exercises fosters our desire to know and do God's will which emerges as our inner desire. This emergence happens in the context of our continuing contemplation of the ministry of Christ. We check our emerging notions against our inner sense of self, our Christ-self as we experience it now. We can say, "This fits; go with it" or "This is not the way. Stop." Options may be surprising, or not clear-cut; the point is to seek an inner sense of balance, equanimity, and trust in God's care.

It is important to recognize that for women sinfulness may take the form of passivity and self-abnegation, fostered, if not actively encouraged, by the demand by church authorities and other patriarchs for "bearing your cross," self-denial, and humility.

External norms become less important as personal growth and insight develop. Ignatius formulated his insights drawn from his experience into rules for discernment as helps for guides and directees. Ignatius distinguishes between beginners in the prayer life and more mature pray-ers. Beginners tend to face more clear-cut, good/bad decisions, while others who have lived longer and are more finely tuned to God often deal with good, better, best decisions. Since we are not equally mature in all aspects of our lives, we sometimes find ourselves operating in both groups, though not at the same time.

Jesus' life provides an example. At age twelve, he decided to begin the process of interiorizing his Abba's business as he matured into adulthood. Hearing an inner call, he left Nazareth to be baptized by John and was "sent by the Spirit" into the desert with no external supports to face his demons and angels, his desolation and consolation. Satan tempts Jesus in his core identity: "If you are the son of God . . ." (Mt 4:6). Jesus' authority is exactly in that he knows who he is and has no need to prove it. He seems comfortable with himself and relaxed in his strength. His power is revealed in the nature of his anger with Satan. "Enough! Away with you. You will not challenge God further" (Mt 4:10). Jesus is empowered to anger, not out of self-defense, but by the love of God. Lucifer could not withstand this assertive power and left, while angels came to wait upon Jesus.

"Angels," those consoling messengers from God, we may see as the interior movements which cause us to burn with love for our Creator and all of creation and which bring tears in response to the gracious gifts of God, whether of insight or sorrow for our sins. Most importantly, for the long haul, consolations are "every increase of hope, faith, and charity and all interior joy which leaves us in quiet, peaceful love of God" [316]. Each increase strengthens us in our ability to say to evil "Enough! Go away" and continue on our way to God.

Desolation, on the other hand, is just the opposite for beginners [317-322]. Demonic elements cause us inner darkness, turmoil, self-doubt, fearfulness, boredom, laziness, whatever moves us away from God. Whatever is self-defeating is suspect. For example, contrast the self-talk, "I don't care. It's not very important anyhow. I can't do it" with "Let's see what we can do about that. Yes, I've done pretty well and I'd like to try." The former sucks me into inactivity and loss of worth, while the latter energizes me into meaningful activity. Ignatius stresses that it is important to contradict these voices, to fight back and not change our minds if our choice was well made initially. Desolation is not permanent, so be patient. God allows these feelings to attack us for our own learning and strengthening. Even desolations can become worthwhile to the disgust of Wormwood and his uncle Screwtape.[11]

Desolation *per se* is not characteristic of the life of mature pray-ers. Rather, as was seen with the example of Christ in the desert, evil comes as Lucifer, an "angel of light." Notice that Lucifer proposed a worthwhile project to Christ. "Turn these stones into bread since you are hungry. You could feed other hungry people as well." Good people will reject overt evils, but are susceptible to good-sounding ideas. As Screwtape advises his not too bright nephew, Wormwood, ". . . it will be impossible to *remove* spirituality from his life, we must *corrupt* it." There is rejoicing in hell over one spoilt saint.[12]

Ongoing discernment becomes critical for our personal and professional growth. Major choices are involved, but the testing of our small, daily, habit-building choices is more significant. The shades of difference and the implications for the future tend to be more nuanced. We become better acquainted with the insidious influence of evil by evaluating daily our thoughts, feelings, and behaviors. Where we were drawn away from God we look for the "serpent's tail" which is the critical moment where evil became apparent. What was our "self-talk," our environment? How can we intervene and strategize for change?[13]

Thus, through practice, we are schooled to the discernment of our ranging moods and ideas to listen for God. We learn to cope with the ungodly in us so that even desolations can lead us to God. Our feelings tend toward more equilibrium as we are more founded in God. Ignatius describes this experience as being like "a drop of water which enters into a sponge" while, if evil comes, it is like water falling on rocks or an intruder breaking into our home [335].

The opposite is true for persons headed for evil. They probably do not cope at all and are subject to the rule of their impulses and compulsions. Thus the evil spirit works quietly, at home, while goodness must intervene distinctly, with teeth, so to speak, to gain attention and cause enough disturbance and remorse to bring about change [314].

As we discern our choices, it is important that we refer them to God for confirmation. Is this really where God wishes us to go as far as we can tell now? If we have put on the mind and heart of Christ so far, we will follow him into the core of discipleship, his passion, death and resurrection. As the crucifixion indicates, success by human measures is not necessarily a sign of confirmation. Rather, a realistic sense of the difficulties involved, combined with an underlying sense of trust and peace with God, is a much healthier indicator. Time will reveal whether the decision leads the person into God or into egocentricity.[14] In my journal, I wrote "I will keep moving with *yes* as long as I keep my eyes and ears on him (Jesus). Otherwise, I sink into self-doubt and/or ego idolatry" (March 1986).

As we pray for the grace of confirmation, we also pray for the graces specific to Week Three, the passion and death of Jesus. The first is reminiscent of Week One, to receive "grief, feeling and confusion because for my sins the Lord is going to the Passion [193]. The second reflects the increasing identification with Jesus, "to share Christ's grief, anguish, tears and interior pain for all he suffered for me" [203]. Ignatius asks us to consider "how the Divinity hides Itself" [196] and "what I ought to do and suffer for Him" [197]. This may be very hard, just as it was for the disillusioned disciples, and, like them, we may be tempted to desert Jesus [195, 206]. We are to share everything in our colloquies, whether we are bored, distracted, or becoming compassionate for his people whom we meet in our community. We may experience a mixture of feelings such as when we visit someone who is seriously ill in the hospital. We do not enjoy feeling powerless.[15]

Alexander Lefrank distinguishes two stages for the inner process of this phase.[16] They may emerge together and become mixed as they involve the choice made by the directee upon which she focuses her identification with Christ. The first stage deals with the choice itself as the person is assailed by doubts. Is it really correct? Perhaps I am arrogant to consider this? Am I doing it right? Varying degrees of anxiety, confusion, doubt and darkness mark this stage. Assuming that the choice was correctly reached, and that these questions were appropriately dealt with at that time, these thoughts can be seen as self-defeating and evil. They need to be handed over to God. Loyalty, trust, and steadfast love are the requisite qualities for discipleship. Support and confidence from the guide and friends are really important when uncertainty prevails.

Stage two involves interiorly sharing the mental suffering experienced by Christ whereby doubts, despair, and hopelessness may arise about the entire enterprise of the *Exercises*, of discipleship generally, and of one's own existence. "I am crazy and weird to be doing this. I'm not any good for the people I serve and they don't want me around." Whereas, when these thoughts and feelings occurred in the past, there was some reassurance in prayer; now in this stage God seems gone or very quiet. Like Jesus, we may feel abandoned and reassurance from other people sounds hollow and false. It is about as comforting as sour wine on a sponge. In fact, the identity of the person with Christ is now so complete that the dying of Christ happens within and is unseen, but felt. There is little control over either of these two stages. The choice is to deny or accept the ramifications of allegiance to Christ. Say *yes* or *no* to Love. "No greater love exists than this, that a friend would lay down her life for another" (Jn 15:13).

These profound graces may be received within the Third Week in varying degrees, depending on our level of maturity. Or, we may experience more fully the graces characteristic of earlier phases. All are valuable and will be given in their own time as the inner process lives out its own dynamic as it moves to completion.[17] The value of focusing on the humanity of Jesus is that it encourages the emergence of issues of human weakness and limitation for the directee. These need acceptance to be useful for ministry.

The value of focusing on the humanity of Jesus is that it encourages the emergence of issues of human weakness and limitation for the directee. These need acceptance to be useful for ministry.

I found this to be true of my own experience in this phase and since. There was quite a mixture of issues and movements. When I desired to believe in him, where others jeered and mocked, I was privileged to be with him in this spirit in the persons of two women I met at this time. Barbara was twenty-six and had been repeatedly victimized sexually by her stepfather since she was a teen. She had returned home to care for her dying mother and was attacked again by this man three days after her mother's death. She collapsed mentally, and I was struck by her suffering as the "betrayal of innocence" as incest has so truly been described. Josie was sitting in the Shelter House when I noticed her face—sad, lonely, and drawn. She sat holding herself. I found out she was from another state and had gotten trapped into a situation of sexual bondage, rape, and severe physical abuse. We spent many hours together over the days, not really doing much, until she could move on. I knew I had met Christ in her woundedness.

Perennial personal issues reemerged when I thought they had been settled. By taking my time I learned a good deal about myself and gained more quietness and peace in my prayer and daily life. Upon reflection, I would sum up my experience of prayer in this phase as being somewhat like that of Jesus in the Garden. He encountered his fears and losses; people did not respond as he hoped. He could have chosen to quit and have a long life doing something less risky. But that would not have been honest and would have invalidated, made worthless, all he had said and done so far. All the pain and joy would be for nothing. So we sat, apart, in the same darkness. What we came to share was the sense of being deeply loved by God. There was no exaltation in our choices, just quiet acceptance before moving on. This scene has become more typical from the Third Week onwards.

Another theme typifying my process at this point was how extensively Jesus accepted, loved, and went out of his way to provide for his friends, his mother, even the criminal dying next to him during his passion. He warned Peter and the apostles that their faith would be shaken, but that he would be raised up and go ahead of them to Galilee (Mt 16:31-32). He had evidently made special plans prior to the Passover so they could all be together before he died (Mt 26:17-18). He promised the criminal that they would be together in Paradise (Lk 23:39-43) and created community for Mary and the disciples as he was dying (Jn 19:25-27). For myself, in his death I found my old wounds healed and a sense of newness struggling to emerge (3/21/86).

These graced awarenesses gave me a deeper sense of "God with us" in pain, hurt, and betrayal although we may not know just how this "being with" is. I experience a strengthened confidence in myself as capable of dealing with the realities of life. The concurrence of woundedness and strength, dying and new life, points out a fact of the process of the Third and Fourth Weeks. Though separated, they occur together. Dying and resurrection are parts of the same movement.

The transition to Fourth Week is by now a matter entirely for the grace of God who will give us whatever we need for our developing identity with Christ.[18] Ignatius leads us to encounter the Risen Christ through the experiences of the first disciples as Christ appeared to them. The grace we pray for is to "rejoice and be glad intensely at so great glory and joy of Christ our Lord" [221]. In particular, we are to note how, in contrast to the Passion where Divinity hid itself, in the Resurrection Divinity is revealed by its effects [223]. Related to this revelation, we note how Christ serves as consoler and we "compare how friends are accustomed to console friends" [224].

The grace desired is not one of great emotional fervor, but

rather in continuity with Ignatius's description of "water filling the sponge." We wait for and savor the gift by watching Jesus enjoy his new way of existence in his body. Slowly, his joy, confidence, and vigor penetrate us more and more fully. The intensity is in the degree to which we incorporate the truth that suffering and joy, death and life, are juxtaposed in one life. The author of John's gospel expressed this reality in Chapter 17: "Now is my hour come" (vs. I) when the glory of witness and service are revealed in the passion and death of Jesus.

Two Scripture passages strongly affected my Fourth-Week experiences which were basically extensions of the Third-Week process. Ephesians 3:16-21, especially "May he strengthen you inwardly through the working of his Spirit . . . whose power now at work in us can do immeasurably more than we ask or imagine . . . " became a motif of my prayer and reflection. The inner sense of strength which emerged in Week Three became fairly consistent as I took on several challenging tasks.

The nature of this inner power became clearer as I prayed with the appearance of Jesus to Thomas over a period of about two weeks. The first phase of my awareness was a piercing sense of the great humility of Christ as he came to his disciples. He simply stands before them without shame for his wounds, with no fear of being rejected, no authoritarianism as Lord of the Universe, no defenses. He comes with gentle confidence and persistent desire that we believe; he will do whatever it takes to get us to believe. The second phase of my awareness, avoided at first, was to identify myself with Thomas. I recognized that my demands for "hands-on" security were obstacles to my being with God and to my potential for service. To live in faith and live without "being right" (and therefore acceptable), no matter what the possible outcome may be, is the way to go on in daily life. I wrote, "Perhaps my emptiness will become your fullness. The invitation is to trust or to die. . . . Die to fear over and over. Rise to trust. You are with me; you go before me" (4/26/86).

Within a few days I noticed that praying the *Exercises* as a structure seemed to be fading. I had no idea if this was good or bad. The Scripture had no focus while the same themes of previous days continued to be lived out. It does not surprise me that my first reaction to the ascension was resistance, avoidance, and fearful insecurity. "You're leaving me; yet I don't want to confine you." There was another two weeks of struggle, mourning, grief and finally listening and trusting. Christ's words to his disciples (Jn 14:25-31) helped me to see myself as blessed to go forth to witness and serve. Perhaps it was not merely coincidental that my retreat ended as my first class, HD 690, at St. Mary's began.

I will conclude this account of God's grace acting through the *Spiritual Exercises* by marking the significance of its open-endedness. Although the Contemplation to Attain Divine Love [230-237] did not seem essential to my personal experience, it did serve the purpose of a review and stimulus to gratitude. One thing that did strike me again was Ignatius's great love for creation and humanity as the work and home of God. We are in the matrix of the Principle and Foundation, come around to the beginning, but not at the same starting place nor as the same people.

We have seen a development of our personal identity as it becomes reconciled to its humanity and ceases to play Caesar and is subsequently transformed into the body of Christ. To some degree we have put on Christ, not through our labors which merely dispose us for this gift of grace, but through the work of the Spirit who lives in us for this purpose. It is appropriate to finish with the Scripture which pushed me into this journey into God some years ago by opening my eyes to who I am becoming. "All of us, gazing in the Lord's glory with unveiled faces, are being transformed from glory to glory into his very image by the Lord who is the Spirit" (2 Co 3:18).

Notes

[1] David Fleming SJ, *The Spiritual Exercises of St. Ignatius. A Literal Translation and a Contemporary Reading*, St. Louis: The Institute of Jesuit Sources, 1978.

[2] Brian O. McDermott, *What are they saying about the Grace of Christ?* New York: Paulist, 1984, p. 8.

[3] Ibid, p. 10.

[4] Brian O. McDermott, p. 55, defines "Abba-Father" as "absolutely near" rather than a divine male patriarch.

[5] Ibid, ch. 2.

[6] See Ruth Burrows, *Guidelines for Mystical Prayer*, Denville, New Jersey: Dimension Books, 1980, pp. 15-86. Peter McVerry, "Sin: The Social, National and International Aspects," The Way, Supplement 48, Autumn 1983, pp. 39-49. Enneagram Workshop: Discussion of Primary Obstacles to Grace.

[7] Maurice Giuliani, "The Exercises in Daily Life," *Progressio*, Supplements 18-19, November 1981, p. 60.

[8] The Way, Supplement 18, Spring 1973. This entire issue deals with the "Call of the King."

[9] Richard F. Copeland, "A Directory for the Second and Third Weeks," The Way, Supplement 46, Spring 1983, pp. 29-37.

[10] Carolyn Osiek, *Beyond Anger*, New York: Paulist, 1986, ch. 3 and 4, begins to reclaim the spirituality of the cross for women. Joann Wolski Conn, *Women's Spirituality*, New York: Paulist, 1986, joins feminist experience with the rules of discernment.

[11] C.S. Lewis, *Screwtape Letters*, New York: Macmillan, 1960. Mary C. Coelho, "Understanding Consolation and Desolation," See pp. 44 Jan/Feb 1985. Thomas H. Green, *Weeds Among the Wheat*, Notre Dame: Ave Maria Press, 1984.

[12] C.S. Lewis, p. 116.

[13] George Aschenbrenner, "Consciousness Examen," Review for Religious 31, no. 1 (January-February 1972): 14-21.

[14] Richard Copeland, A Directory for the Second and Third Weeks: Contemplating Christ's Earthly Life, "Directory," The Way, Supplement 46, Spring 1983, pp. 4344. John Veltri, Orientations 11, Canada: Loyola House, 1981, p. 110, B38-B42. Alexander Lefrank, pp. 109- 114.

[15] John Veltri, 11, A 25. Jean Laplace, *An Experience of Life in the Spirit*, Chicago: Franciscan Herald Press, 1977, p. 157.

[16] Alexander Lefrank, "Freedom for Service," *Progressio*, Supplement 3, April 1974, Rome: World Federation of Christian Life Communities, pp. 109-112.

[17] Richard Copeland, p. 51. Veltri, II, pp. 106-107.

[18] Alexander Lefrank, "Freedom for Service," *Progressio*, Supplement 3, April 1974, Rome: World Federation of Christian Life Communities, pp. 123-125.

The Spirituality of Surrender

*L*osing, whether it is losing a friendly bet, an important argument, or a business contract, is a difficult pill to swallow. We detest losing. The same is true for any diehard sports fan who endures a hometown rout. We walk away replaying the game, blaming the unfair referees, or creating strategies that "would have" favorably altered the score.

When the defeat entails greater stakes, there is higher resistance to a surrender. To address a serious problem like addiction is personally painful. Implicit in such reality is a pervasive sense of failure. One has lost control over life's direction. The only way to regain control is to surrender what has not worked and seek a new way. This process is replete with difficulty.

This article will examine the spirituality of surrender as a means of coming home to God.[1] Surrendering to God will be looked at in three ways. The first involves an understanding of how surrender is operative in twelve-step recovery programs like Alcoholics Anonymous. The second involves a look at the life of Ignatius of Loyola and the surrender components of the final prayer of the *Spiritual Exercises*, the "Suscipe," or "Take and Receive." The third considers Jesus' act of surrender on the cross in Luke 23:46. Each of these three different "ways" of surrendering involves putting our ultimate identity and confidence in God.

Let Go, Let God

At Alcoholics Anonymous meetings or twelve-step recovery retreats, the expression "Let go, let God" is often used. These four important words constitute the core spirituality of A.A. and similar recovery programs that have adapted the twelve steps to their particular addiction. "Let go, let God" is an invitation to surrender one's unmanageable life to God.

"Let go, let God" is a gentle conversion reminder, a kind of mantra, which assists us both to admit the addiction and to hand it over along with its various forms of compulsions to God. The long form of the prayer would be something like "Let go of alcohol (or whatever the specific substance or nonsubstance addiction might be) and let the hand and grace of God guide my life."

The prayer is not magic. Saying "Let go, let God" does not instantaneously bring about recovery. Its first purpose is to assist the recovering addict to keep to the daily partnership task of surrendering the addiction to God. The second purpose of "Let go, let God" is to be a prayer of liberation, to call on the greater power of God to help one escape from destructive lifestyle patterns. In this way the creative resources of the individual and the action of God are focused on together. The prayer also serves to silence those addiction-related inner-committee tapes and voices of doubt, loneliness, fear, and caustic shame that can interfere with a person's slow recovery. These, too, need to be handed over to God.

"Let go, let God" is an invitation to surrender one's unmanageable life to God.

I have the greatest admiration for all who enter the surrender process of a twelve-step program. For many, it is the difference between death and life, the difference between barely existing as a human and participating in community, between dysfunctionalism and experiencing the serenity that only God gives with amazing grace.

The first three steps of Anonymous programs set up this "Let go, let God" dynamic. The language of the twelve steps is straightforward and simple. This is part of their wisdom and wide appeal. The steps make sense to a lot of people. Since A.A. began in 1935 at Akron, Ohio, Anonymous recovery programs have multiplied to treat various forms of addiction.[2] These include Narcotics Anonymous, Overeaters Anonymous, Gamblers Anonymous, Emotions Anonymous, Workaholics Anonymous, Sexaholics Anonymous, Al-Anon, and Adult Children of Alcoholics.

Let us examine these first three steps.

1. We admitted we were powerless over alcohol [or the other specific addiction], that our lives had become unmanageable.[3]

The first step is crucial. You admit you have a serious problem. There is no denial of the fact. The blunt reality is your life is out of control, in fact, unmanageable. Furthermore, you are powerless to do anything about it.

At Anonymous meetings, this first step is handled in an upfront manner. When members speak, they state their first name and their addictiveness: "I'm John. I'm an alcoholic." "I'm Susan. I'm a recovering overeater." In formal religion we might refer to this acknowledgment as group confession. In recovery programs it is simply admitting what can no longer be denied. Step one is an honest, vulnerable beginning place. Owning and naming the unmanageable addiction is essential to the surrendering process. When one is aware of a specific uncontrollable disease, one can effectively pray "Let go."

But to whom does one surrender? Steps two and three look at the second part of the mantra: "Let God." God is the significant associate in restoring harmony. To appreciate the spirituality of the twelve steps, it is important to reflect that the existence and action of God are mentioned seven times in the twelve steps. The particular addiction is only mentioned once, and that is in the first step. The activity of surrendering one's addiction and life to God becomes the spirituality cornerstone of the remaining steps.

2. We came to believe that a Power greater than ourselves could restore us to sanity.[4]

Step two admits the need of an outside corrective authority, a Higher Power, to bring about a stability in one's life. This is the first glimpse of light that invites God in as the restorer of sanity.

There are two other important spirituality elements operative in the second step: (1) the belief that a Higher Wisdom exists and (2) a disposition of humility on the part of the believer. These two qualities counterculturally work against the arrogance of the ego that craves to cling to the addiction. Step two indicates that the recovery process entails an attentive listening to a new Teacher, which means that the addict has to take on the attitude of learner. There is a major shift in trust: from addiction to God.

3. We made a decision to turn our will and our lives over to the care of God *as we understood him*.[5]

Step three is where the capitulation actually occurs. First, a concrete decision to surrender has to be made. Second, this decision is total. It includes the will making conscious choices, and it affects one's entire being and journey. Third, the whole person is placed in the care of God according to the individual's faith background.

The spirituality of "Let go, let God" is a conversion process. Conversion of its nature has two basic movements: the surrendering of the compulsion, shame, and destructive addictive patterns which reduce freedom; the turning to the care of God and the Holy Spirit to be one's permanent resource of wisdom and identity.

Matthew 11:28-30 speaks of a "letting go, letting God" process: "Come to me, all you who labor and are overburdened, and I will give you rest. Shoulder my yoke and learn from me, for I am gentle and humble in heart, and you will find rest for your souls. Yes, my yoke is easy and my burden light."[6] These three verses contain the confirmation signs that accompany a true surrender. A learning will occur, the process will be gentle and humble. Rest will be experienced. A new relationship arises, a companionship with the Master, which will be nonaddictive, easy, and light.

The Surrender of Ignatius of Loyola

Another way of surrendering one's life to God comes from the spirituality of Ignatius's surrender as expressed in his prayer the "Suscipe," or "Take and Receive." On his pilgrim journey Ignatius was called to surrender on several notable occasions. The first was during the defense of the city of Pamplona, Spain. In 1521 Ignatius, wounded by cannon shrapnel, reviewed the illusions of his life as sober death approached. But he did not die. His long convalescence became a conversion process. He gradually yielded up his stubborn self-preoccupation, bravado, and ambition and began to discover a new self in God.[7]

The spirituality record of Ignatius's surrender to God is found in his classic work, the *Spiritual Exercises*. Today, 450 years after its first published edition, it is still considered a significant theological work noted for its integration of Scripture, guidelines for discernment, sense of mission, and themes of justice. The *Exercises'* developmental stages of growth in discipleship and intimacy enable a person to come home to God.

The last prayer of the *Exercises* is called the "Suscipe" or "Take and Receive." I invite you to spend some time contemplating the components of this prayer. What is Ignatius, the once vain soldier-at-arms, now a mystic, asking us to do?

Take, Lord, and receive
all my liberty,
my memory,
my understanding,
and my entire will--
all that I have and call my own.
You have given it all to me.
To you, Lord, I return it.
Everything is yours;
do with it what you will.
Give me only your love and your grace.
That is enough for me.[8]

The "Suscipe" is a deceptively profound prayer. It invites us to acknowledge the primacy of God in our totality; it answers the humbling question "What aspect of our being is not a gift of God?" In the light of this answer, Ignatius invites us to surrender all to God. The last part of the prayer is a seeking of the purer gifts: "Give me only your love and grace. That is enough for me." Ignatius does not compromise in the process of "letting go of self and letting God in."

I recall a forceful experience in praying the "Suscipe." It happened fifteen years ago during a retreat. I attempted to pray and could not. I realized I had not surrendered anything, certainly not my liberty, memory, understanding, and will to anyone, much less to God. I told my director that I could not pray this prayer at all. As a consequence, I seriously questioned remaining a Jesuit. The director gave sage advice. He invited me to return to the chapel and pray the "Suscipe" with my own words in my own way.

I prayed, "Lord, I give you my sins which I know so well, those many areas of my life where I am not obedient, poor, and chaste. I give you my pride, my negativity, my hatred and vindictiveness, my compulsive rebellion and addictiveness to self. I am overly familiar with these dark recesses. And I truly need to surrender these to you. Send forth your Holy Spirit to guide, anoint, and heal with a love that I am most in need of, your grace."

Like an ambush, the opportunity to surrender can appear at unlikely moments. Do not let the occasion pass by. The benefit of letting God in always outweighs whatever is surrendered.

Jesus on the Cross

We turn to the spirituality of Jesus and the particular way he has taught us to surrender. He, too, had to face a special moment of surrender. His prayer in Luke 23:46 is a powerful expression of letting go: "Father, into your hands I commit my spirit."[9] Here on the cross Jesus is still the master teacher. He models for us how to pray and hand over our daily experiences and our life to God. Notice the key elements: (1) The prayer is addressed to the Father; (2) Jesus urges us to surrender, to commend, to let go; (3) Jesus specifies what is to be handed over. He gives what little is left, his spirit and last breath.

In the daily minor or major surrenders of our own pilgrimage, we can pray in the spirituality of either the twelve steps, Ignatius, or Jesus. Specify in the "Let go, let God" mantra and the "Suscipe" whatever needs to be named and yielded: "Let go of addiction and manipulation. Let God in." "Take, Lord, my dishonesty, my hurts, my doubts and sinfulness." God can handle and work with these blighted areas quite well.

Adapt the prayer of Jesus to your immediate concerns: "Father, into your hands I commit my grief, my sense of failure, my disappointment, my pettiness and vulnerability. . . ." Commend these regions of brokenness to the higher compassion and understanding of God.

It is clear that not only our joys but also our sorrows must be offered to God. Our ability to be powerless allows God to meet us and tenderly heal us on our journey, embracing us as we truly are. Moreover, the art of surrendering involves a lifelong process. Some days we succeed better than others. If we postpone learning the spirituality of surrender, we will face it unprepared at death, when the surrender is sudden. Perhaps we can learn to surrender to the care, to the heart, of God *in advance*.

Notes

[1] For more information on this topic, see Gerald G. May, *Addiction and Grace* (San Francisco: HarperCollins, 1991), pp. 162-181.

[2] Ernest Kurtz, *Not-God: A History of Alcoholics Anonymous* (Center City, Minn.: Hazeldon, 1991), pp. 37-57.

[3] Anonymous, *Twelve Steps and Twelve Traditions* (New York: Alcoholics Anonymous World Services, 1952), p. 21.

[4] Ibid, p. 25.

[5] Ibid, p. 34.

[6] *The New Jerusalem Bible* (New York: Doubleday, 1985).

[7] *St. Ignatius' Own Story*, trans. William J. Young SJ (Chicago: Henry Regnery Co., 1956), pp. 7-27.

[8] David L. Fleming SJ, *The Spiritual Exercises of St. Ignatius: A Literal Translation and a Contemporary Reading* (St. Louis: Institute of Jesuit Sources, 1980), p. 141.

[9] *The New Jerusalem Bible*.

God's Human Face Revealed:
A Retreat in Wales

I had been living and working in Amman, Jordan, for eight years when in 1989 I began reading *The Journeying Self,* by Diarmuid McGann. Becoming deeply involved with it, I came across these words: "The journey of faith begins at the Lord's invitation. He finds us in our places of marginal existence, where we hunger for liberation." I did not go further than that for several months, but those lines I read over and over again. I could wrest no personal meaning from them, and yet somehow they riveted me. At the same time I was picking my way through a book by Karl Rahner. Being no scholar, "picking" is how I cope with Rahner, and yet I am hugely attracted by him. Of the many sentences I jotted down knowing that I would return to them, here are a few:

> In contemplation the pray-er is intent on hearing an utterance of God never given before. . . .
> We need the courage to believe that God will say something permanent. It will happen when God is ready.
> God places me in complete freedom. He deals with me leaving intact my autonomy and self-direction. God is Love and in the face of that—I decide.

There were many more, and while I went about my life in community and my teaching duties, these thoughts floated in and out of my mind whenever my interior screen was empty, setting up such a longing that I knew I would need to respond sooner or later.

Remote Preparation—I Go to Anjara

The time to plan my annual retreat came round. I thought of Jerusalem, where I had made retreats before, but I had little heart for going there because of the heavy military presence at the time. Though Jordan itself has no retreat facilities, I knew that Father Joseph Na'maat, a diocesan priest in the north of Jordan, had spare rooms in a separate building which anyone was welcome to use on a self-catering basis. He said if I came during July I would have the entire building to myself. With typical Jordanian courtesy he also told me that his house and his table would be mine anytime I felt lonely. Josephine, his housekeeper, would, he assured me, keep an eye on things and make sure I was all right. The fee was so small it was a joke.

I waved to Father Joseph each morning after Mass and that was the excitement over for the day.

So eight days on my own loomed. How would I work it out? I went along the shelves of our library and found Rahner's *Eight Day Retreat* and a paperback copy of the Ignatian *Exercises*. From my room I picked up my Bible and missal and that was all. I think the journey of faith McGann discusses began for me that day. I felt quite naked going off with what seemed so little in the way of resources.

Anjara is a village in the northern Jordanian countryside. Feeling at home in the Arab world and having enough Arabic to do my own shopping, talk with people, and get by generally, I had no fears along those lines. On my arrival I was given a warm welcome by Father Joseph and the redoubtable Josephine. Then, after being shown "my" building and handed the keys, I heard the oft-repeated words "If it gets too lonely, you know where we are!"

That first evening I worked out a program for the eight days, allotting time for the breviary, rosary, and Scripture reading. I then marked out three separate hours daily for prayer, leaving time for rest and recreation which, during the eight days, would take the form of walks, sitting on the roof in the sun absorbing the view, and wandering in my host's extensive orchard followed by his floppy old dog.

Knowing nothing previously about the *Exercises*, I soon abandoned the paperback because it made no sense to me. I stuck to the Bible and the missal and continued to read over the sentences from McGann and Rahner which had so affected me. For the full eight days I spoke to no one, except the dog. I waved to Father Joseph each morning after Mass and that was the excitement over for the day. Through the grace of God, I remained faithful to all to which I had committed myself.

On my final evening Josephine came to bring me over to supper and, like the hedgerow and byways folk of the gospel, I was compelled to attend. If you have never experienced an Arab supper or indeed Arab hospitality, you have missed one of life's lovelier moments. We sat on the verandah eating, talking, and—I must admit—drinking slightly too much of Father Joseph's homemade wine. The sun slowly sank behind the brown hills. Lamps were lit, creating a soft pool of light in the velvet darkness, and the night insects began their concert. We sat on. Eventually, however, and with real reluctance I rose, to a duet from Father Joseph and Josephine of "So soon?" I went to bed that night heavy with good food and wine and quite drunk—no, not from wine, but from the heady smell of honeysuckle and jasmine coupled with the heart-swell that comes from having spent a long summer evening with friends.

The following day I returned to Amman knowing that I must do the long retreat. This is where the invitation mentioned by McGann and previously so dimly perceived was pointing. What a Franciscan was doing being so convinced that a Jesuit approach to life and prayer was the right one, I cannot say. But convinced I was.

To Wales

I set about obtaining permissions for the following year and began to look for a place. Almost everyone I spoke to suggested looking for a Jesuit-run center, saying this would be right for what I had in mind. But I prefer retreat houses run by women: they are cozier, and I like my creature comforts. After a few blanks I got a positive answer from a small guest-cum-retreat house, Coleg y Groes, in North Wales. Yes, they could take me. Yes, one of them could direct me. Yes, they were in the heart of the country, and to all my other questions yes . . . yes . . . yes. I booked, hesitant to share with some of my more conservative friends that all was not as they might expect. I would be alone without the support of a group; I would be directed by a deacon, not a priest;

worse still, an Anglican deacon; worse again, a *woman* Anglican deacon! What would Ignatius have said?

In August 1990 I returned to England, and in July 1991 I traveled to Wales. Arriving in time for supper, I found the small 18th-century house nestled behind the Anglican parish church in the village of Corwen. My room was very nice, with the promise of quiet. My quick eye noticed the electric kettle, tea bags, and coffee. It all augured well.

I Meet My Directress

Margaret, who was to direct me, suggested I join the other guests for supper that first evening; after that I would dine alone. Supper was served in a delightful low-beamed room with a huge fireplace cut from Welsh stone. Flowers were in the deeply set window alcoves, and the whole place exuded security and good living. I began, however, to get the sinking feeling that comes from having made a big decision and then seeing the signs going wrong.

> *I began to get the sinking feeling that comes from having made a big decision and then seeing the signs going wrong.*

To my Roman mind the conversation became so Anglican, centered on the ordination of women. Most of the women present, and indeed Margaret herself, were ordained deacons. It was the last thing I wanted to get involved in. Intermingled with that were fairly long dissertations on the three resident cats. I drained my coffee cup as I tried to quell the rising panic within me. Relief came when Margaret suggested we go to my room for a first talk. In five minutes my fears evaporated. I knew instinctively that in her I was on to a winner.

That night I slept well, waking totally refreshed. I made coffee, and one glance at the Welsh weather put me into warm trousers and a thick sweater. In the still sleeping village I found the small Catholic church. Inside, in a back pew, was a very still figure. I knelt down near the door, ready to escape if this man were not the sort I ought to seek out for company. After some minutes he looked up and said "Welcome." This was Father Joseph (I seemed destined to be mixed up with Josephs and Josephines). In answer to my question he said that so seldom did anyone come for daily Mass that we could arrange it any time suited to the two of us. Father became a true friend to me during my thirty days. He watched over me with such care and was always available for counsel or confession. That first morning he arranged for me to have a key to the church so that I could come and go at will. He knew Margaret and felt I was safe in her hands.

The Thirty Days Begin

And so the routine for the thirty days began. Margaret suggested that for the first three days I just browse over my own favorite passages of Scripture, go for walks, and take on an atmosphere of quiet. That first morning I took my Bible and went out. I sat overlooking a sweeping green valley and read slowly through some of my favorites: "Widen the spaces of your tent . ." (Is 55:2); "Behold the Bridegroom is coming . . ." (Mt 25:7); "May He give you the power . . . to grow strong . . . ." (Ep 3:16-21). And through it all I wondered just what I was doing, alone in Wales, on the threshold of this experience.

Those first three days went in very gently. Sleep, walks, quiet reading, and three one-hour prayer periods a day. The kettle, tea, and coffee played their part. On the fourth day we started in earnest into the pattern of the retreat. We moved into four one hour periods of prayer a day. Each "day" would begin at 5 p.m. The four "weeks" were to be flexible as regards length.

Margaret spent considerable time giving me the background to the Exercises. As she spoke, words from Robert Gleeson's introduction to Anthony Mottola's translation of the *Exercises* came back to me: "Ignatius intended to stay in Manresa for a few days. These days stretched into ten months with results that are still reverberating around the world." Yes, I thought, even to Corwen.

Something of Margaret's own love for Ignatius overflowed into me. Here was no mere competent guide, but rather one who was imbued with the spirit of Ignatius. I felt very secure, but realized Margaret was no soft touch as she explained the conditions: no reading, other than that prescribed; no music, news, correspondence, conversation, and so forth. She spoke of the necessity of being utterly faithful to the full one-hour prayer periods, and she warned me off interior conversation which could easily become the little foxes destroying the vineyard. When she had finished, my snug feeling of security had drastically slipped, to be replaced by a sense of vulnerable nakedness. Thus stripped I entered the first "week" of the retreat.

The First Week (Seven Days)

Sin, in its hideousness, was the focus of this first week. Powerful meditations on words previously heard but never fully absorbed came back to influence my prayer. The First Principle and Foundation offered at the beginning of this week presented such a challenge that it almost unseated me. Could I, in complete sincerity, make such a prayer? Part of my background reading said, "This law which I enjoin on you this day is not beyond your strength" (Dt 30:11-14). These words stood, like a kind mother, beside the demands of the First Principle and Foundation, urging me to compliance. Yet I hesitated.

I moved on into the sin of Adam and Eve; the Angels; the Prodigal Son—all meditated on against a background of Philippians 2:1-11, Baruch 1:13-22 and 63, and Ephesians 1:13-14 and all deepening in me an appreciation of the heinousness of sin. Karl Rahner says (I quote from memory), "I need to see sin, not so much as an offence against God, but rather as a rebuff against Jesus personally," and "I see him wasting there on the cross—for us—and seeing him in such plight, I make my decision." It is difficult to take a detached view of sin with words like that running round one's mind.

As the first week was coming to a close, the next commitment point was drawing near, the Kingdom meditation with its inbuilt self-offering; and yet I had still not made the First Principle and Foundation my own. I felt discouraged. If I could not personalize the sentiments of the First Principle and Foundation, was there any point in going on? I told Margaret of my difficulty. She suggested rewriting it in language I would feel at home with. And that proved to be the answer. It was the stiff, masculine language that was getting in the way. After rewriting it in my own words, I could accept what Deuteronomy had been trying to tell me.

On the seventh evening Margaret said that tomorrow would be a repose day. She explained what this meant: one prayer period this evening, a good night's sleep, then, after morning Mass, out for the day; on my return in the evening, one more prayer period before she came to see me. She gave me a few ideas as to where

I could go. I chose Llangollen: it seemed a place where I could continue to be quiet while doing something different.

The Kingdom Meditation— and Some Sort of Disturbance

The meditation given me for the eve of the repose day was the Kingdom, so after supper, and with my inner eye on my day out, I settled down to this period of reflective prayer—and it all went wrong. The whole hour tumbled around in a confusion of despondency and misery. I saw myself as a hypocrite and a fool and felt sick with disappointment and embarrassment. I was not being called as Rahner suggested; this was all totally beyond me regardless of Deuteronomy; there was nothing here for me. Some of us are destined for mediocrity; I was obviously one such. Illusion would get me nowhere, and getting nowhere was costing a lot of money and time.

Leaving my room, I went out into the garden. The moon was riding high, swiftly brushing aside the small clouds which, busy about their own affairs, were trotting along in the opposite direction. Shadows flitted about the garden, and somewhere nearby an owl hooted. Further away a dog was barking, but it soon trailed off into a lazy yawn—his heart just was not in it. And here, under the canopy of deep sky, my thought slowly came together and clarified; I began to see what was going on. I returned to my room and found my crucifix and holding it firmly commanded, in the name and power of the crucified and resurrected Christ, everything not of God to depart. I repeated the command twice. The result: "The storm abated and there was a great calm" (Mk 4:39). Without further ado I made my Kingdom offering as given by Ignatius, went to bed, and slept.

The First Repose Day

A glorious day of sunshine and Welsh mountains. A ride on the Railway Enthusiasts' railway from Llangollen along the mountainside to Deeside Halt; a leisurely walk by the canal where later I sat and ate my sandwiches while watching boys—up to the age of forty plus—playing with their boats. Full of fresh air and peace, I returned to Corwen on an early evening bus. Each turn in the road presented a different scene to delight the heart, and I found myself silently singing the word of St. Francis's Canticle of the Sun: "All praise be yours, my Lord, through all that you have made . . . and first for Brother Sun . . . how beautiful he is! How radiant! . . . and Brothers Wind and Air . . . and all the weathers' moods. . . ." It seemed so appropriate. (Something I discovered during these thirty days was that Francis and Ignatius have much in common.)

After supper Margaret came, and I told her of the previous night's upset. She said it was to be expected and then referred me to the description of discernment of spirits in the *Exercises*, where it was all clearly set out. The important thing, she said, was that I had made the Kingdom offering. Much was gained and nothing at all lost.

The Second Week (Eleven Days)

And so into the second week. I traveled far in that week. Journeying with Jesus through his life in the given meditations, I became aware of another journey I was making, toward a deeper commitment—and yet my previous fear of *full* commitment reared up again and again. The demand was too clear, too total, too final. There was no space for maneuver. I stalled badly and frequently during that week. Margaret advised me to use the First Principle and Foundation offering and also the Kingdom offering as ways into the given meditations. She also gave me some salutary advice: "Don't try to give today what properly belongs to tomorrow." "The grace for the future is not yet being offered." I remembered similar advice given me in the past. As a young sister I had made a group retreat under a Carmelite friar. In one of his talks he said that many people fail to advance because they quail before what they fear may be asked of them if they say an unreserved yes. They forget that God is totally to be trusted and would never take unfair advantage of a generous yes. A superior, at a later date, took up the same theme with me (it seems I have had this lack-of-trust problem forever!) and said: "The Lord is total courtesy. He doesn't grab. He looks at what you have and asks 'May I take this?' If you refuse, he will not insist—for the time being anyway." Um—for the time being.

The Two Standards and the Three Classes of Men

These meditations caused the same problem that the First

Principle and Foundation and the Kingdom had caused; as I saw it, all called for total and irrevocable commitment. Again I had to remind myself of what Margaret had said and what the Carmelite friar and my own superior had said when I was just knee high in my religious life. I spent long hours begging the grace of trust. I tried to reset my focus and not waste precious time looking at abstract problems and missing the grace of reality. I turned to St. Francis at this stage and found his presence a great comfort.

On the twentieth day, after lots of struggle but also tremendous peaks of joy and achievement, Margaret suggested I spend one day drawing the experience of the entire two weeks together and then summarize it in a truthful prayer of offering. As I set about doing this, I found it amazing how I could look back along the road I had traveled and see so clearly the efforts, frustrations, joys, hopes, gains, losses, and desires and the loneliness and—running in and out of it all like a flame in dry grass—the fear. And yet somehow it all came together with a marvelous coherence: everything fitted. I could see, with a rare clarity, that God was with me. I had moved. I had definitely moved. I had moved light years from where I had been two weeks previously. For better or for worse, *I had moved.* The agonizing lack of trust, the fears, the anxieties were all part of this pattern of walking. The Lord had supplied where I had been weak. Together we had made it through these two weeks. He had blessed me beyond all imagining and had accepted my desire as though it were something of substance. I was content.

On the twenty-second day, a repose day, I went to Ruthin and presume I had a relaxed day, but I have no memory of it. Without the brief note in my journal saying I had been there, I would not know I had. What that says about me I have no idea.

The Third Week (Five Days)

Margaret moved me into the last earthly days of Jesus. Over the next days, spread over five one-hour meditation periods, which included a midnight hour, I contemplated the Lord at the Last Supper, Gethsemane, and Calvary and right through to the postresurrection period. Having visited the Holy Land many times while living in the Middle East, I found it very easy to situate these meditations, but somehow the depths eluded me.

On the twenty-fourth day Margaret suggested that I spend four of my five one-hour prayer periods reading through the four different accounts of the Passion. Anyone who has done this in one day will know it does not come easy. Physically it is draining to read something of that nature and length with concentration. By the evening it had quite taken me over, and after supper I went for a long walk, but somehow I could not shake off (was I even meant to?) the felt heaviness of trudging the Calvary road four times.

Another Disturbance

During the night I woke in the grip of a strange tension, feeling physically cold and frightened. I have never been especially brave, but I am not given to irrational fear, and this sense of menace was wholly irrational; yet it made me feel that, if I did not give up this retreat, it would break me. For several minutes I did nothing beyond switching on the light and allowing the fear to swamp me. Fear of what? I could put no name to it. Then I remembered Margaret's words, based on those of Ignatius: "It is common for the evil spirit to cause sadness, fear, discouragement, and acute anxiety and to place all sorts of obstacles in the way of right reason. The good spirit gives courage, strength, inspiration, light, and peace so that right reason will prevail. Learn to distinguish." Once again I reached for my crucifix and holy water and followed my previous routine. All returned to normal, but it took some time.

The twenty-sixth day I spent quietly looking back over the entire Passion. It proved to be a very hard day. It is not easy to stay with someone in agony while knowing you are part responsible.

On the twenty-seventh day, another repose day, I went to Lake Bala. It was a beautiful day, but too hot. Tourists and picnickers were all over the place—not helpful. I found the Catholic church, a small converted stable. It was very peaceful, and I stayed quietly there for some time before boarding the bus for the ride home through heart-lifting scenery.

The Fourth Week—Coming to the End

I was now coming to the end of this whole experience, and Margaret suggested moving back from five to four periods of prayer, omitting the night one. She also brought me a tape recorder and some classical-music tapes. Winning some grand prize could not have brought me more joy. I was ecstatic.

On the twenty-eighth day I meditated on John 20:11-18, Mary

Magdalen's encounter with Jesus in the garden, with Isaiah 30:18-26 and 35:1-10 as background. I also used Luke 24:13-35, the Emmaus story, with Psalm 62 as background. I became quite filled with the quiet. Jesus' sufferings were over. His pain was finished. I was able to walk calmly in the garden with Mary Magdalen—you see, *I* knew the answer to her question. The Emmaus road also was peaceful. Again I had the advantage: *I* knew who he was. All this was leading me quite naturally into the Contemplation to Attain Divine Love. From the twenty-ninth day onward I used this contemplation for one period each day, the other three periods covering postresurrection Scripture. I continued my daily walks in the serene countryside, which for me became Galilee, where Jesus said he would meet his friends again and where I myself have walked many times.

A Final Disturbance

One meditation, on the thirtieth day, was given over to the events that include Jesus cooking breakfast for his hungry disciples. As I moved further into the scene, it all changed and became blasphemous; but I did not recognize it as such. My discerning powers were, it seemed, in suspension. During Mass the following morning I became aware that something had been very wrong with that meditation. I looked back at it and saw immediately the gross irreverence of the scenes which had been presented to my view. I was aghast and marveled that I had not realized at the time what was going on. I went hotfoot to Father Joseph after Mass and poured out my sorry story. He took it all very calmly—as confessors are apt to do—and explained how the devil will use every possible means to stop a person pursuing a course that has as its aim a closer union with God. Margaret, of course, said the same thing. The experience left me with a profound disgust of the one who works such evil things.

The Final Days

The thirty-first and final day arrived. I drew together the elements of the four key meditations—the Kingdom, the Two Standards, the Three Classes of Men, the Three Modes of Humility. I then moved them into a prayer of offering that I tried to make utterly truthful and realistic for me.

Later that day I had a final few words with Father Joseph and returned the keys of the church. Back at the house I had a last talk with Margaret and my retreat was over. The following day I left Corwen and—via Wrexham, Chester, Crewe, Euston, and Plaistow, changing train or bus at each one—I arrived home in London.

Eighteen Months Later

Days have built on days, and a year and a half has passed since my long retreat. By now it should have gone the way of all the others. It has not done so. Father Joseph's words during our final talk, "You will never be the same again, this experience has changed you," have stayed with me; I know them to be true. That retreat has changed many things. It has set sin in its right context, one which makes scant distinction between small and big offenses. It has cleared away any number of secondary purposes and underlined the one purpose for which I was born. It has filled my storerooms with kindling, that I may not perish when my winter fires burn low. It has increased my recovery rate, so that sin and repentance are almost simultaneous. It has brought a staying power I never thought to possess; a strength to stay with prayer even when, apparently, there is nothing in it to stay for. It has brought an acceptance that I am as I am and, as far as performance goes, the future will not be much different; progress will still be wobbly, with backward steps, with fears and sin. But this acceptance of my situation has brought a new dependence; I know I will make it through to the end if I cling like a limpet to Christ. There is, quite simply, no other way.

The Human Face of God

But overriding and underpinning all this is the greatest change of all. I am aware that, through all the contemplations of that month, even those during which I was distracted, irritated, fidgety, or just plain bored, God was working. He was working as one whose work it is to take an old manuscript, mosaic, or fresco and restore it to its original beauty; he was etching and bringing into relief, for me personally, the lines of his own human face. I can no longer think of God without, at the same time, seeing Christ; I see him, in some small measure, as Francis of Assisi saw him in great, in the people, however seemingly insignificant, and in the events, however trivial, that form the fabric of my everyday life. This new vision is the greatest grace to accompany me into these, the afterdays.

The word "Wales" will never again mean for me just a geographical place, but rather will set a pause for remembering: remembering that revelation did not end with the Apocalypse; remembering how God revealed his face to me in Wales; remembering how something of beauty was planted within me and has, in spite of me, continued to grow. My life has become permanently divided into "before Wales" and "after Wales." And it all started way back in Jordan, where I "hungered for liberation" and knew myself "intent on hearing an utterance of God never given before" (in the words of McGann and Rahner) and felt strongly impelled, Franciscan and all that I am, to take up the invitation to an Ignatian experience. That, and so much more, is what my long retreat was all about.

prayer

Christian Zen-cum-Ignatian Meditation

Or

What You Always Wanted to Know
About Being a Mystic
But Were Afraid to Ask

People of the ancient world strove in many ways to communicate with whoever they believed to be out there, with whoever made the world and somehow controlled their lives and destinies. They offered in sacrifice choice things: grain or wine poured out, sheep or oxen slaughtered then immolated with fire. The smoke, they thought, would rise before the gods with a pleasing odor. They played flutes, used prayer wheels. painted their bodies, stamped their feet, and babbled. They hoped to get the gods' attention, to bring down favors from them.

Human nature has not changed with the New Dispensation, nor have the ways men and women try to pray, except these are now purified and made gentle by revelation. Christ invited us to intimacy with his Father, and we respond by lifting our hearts to him: in the Eucharist (above all, the true and ultimate sacrifice), in vocal prayer (such as the Rosary), and in private prayer. We address God with words often chosen from the Psalms or given us by Christ himself or by his saints. These same words, as we use them, enrich our hearts and minds with wisdom.

But there are problems with using words in prayer—even God's words. Over time we tend to multiply them and to load onto them our own intellectual and emotional baggage, allowing our selfishness to co-opt their meaning. So in some prayers we might even want to dispense with words, to use body language only, which can sometimes be for us clearer, deeper, more powerful than spoken words. This, I think, is the prayer Christ meant when he said, "When you pray, go into your room and shut the door and pray to your Father who is in secret." In such private and largely nonvocal prayer we offer God ourselves in our silent presence, and God responds to us, creatively, in our lives.

This kind of prayer goes under a variety of descriptive names: meditation, contemplation, and mental prayer. There is a long history of it in the church, going back to her earliest years, but it flourished especially in Europe in the fourteenth through the sixteenth centuries with a succession of great spiritual directors. St. Ignatius Loyola taught his followers in his Spiritual Exercises to meditate upon structured concepts and upon chiseled images—both anchored in powerful words—to explore the destructiveness of their sins, to accept forgiveness for them, and then, centering their lives in Christ, to redirect them to God in service of the church. But he reserved a choice place at the end of these Exercises for his largely wordless, though still rich in imagery, Contemplation for Obtaining Divine Love. Others led their followers to shun in their meditations activities of both the intelligence and the imagination and, instead, to go beneath these, down to the marrow of the soul, to encounter the Father in that secret "room" they felt Jesus was speaking of.

Zen has been used for decades by Christian contemplatives who came under the influence of ascetics of the East.

Zen as practiced by Christians is, in many ways, like this latter form of prayer. It is not new, for it has been used for decades by Christian contemplatives who came under the influence of ascetics of the East. Although in recent years Zen has experienced in the West a growth in popularity, many devout people, unfortunately, have misconceptions of it, bringing mistrust.

Zen masters themselves often give little help in understanding their elusive discipline. When one puts questions to them about it, they often smile and remain silent. I believe this is because they see Zen not as a doctrine but as an activity—and thus an experience—so simple and immediate that, when one attempts to conceptualize it, he only obscures it, as when one tries to define the experience of love or of life. But I feel once people see what Zen is not—certainly not a rival to Christian spirituality—they may wish to try to do Zen themselves and thus to experience the extraordinary benefits claimed to derive from it.

Let us consider first—lacking a better term—traditional Zen. Rather than enter the question of the historical origins of it, let it suffice to say it has been practiced for more than 1400 years. Concerning the question of its place of origin—whether India, Tibet, China, or Japan—let us concede simply that it developed in the East, probably in a pantheistic culture. But this should not influence Zen's practical value to us as a mode of meditation any more than the lack of faith of a philosopher should keep us from benefiting from his thinking. After all, a key foundation of scholastic philosophy and theology is a series of clear concepts St. Thomas found in the writings of the pagan Aristotle that first came to Europe through the works of Islamic thinkers. Of greater importance for our purpose are the reasons Zen developed into the form it ultimately took. These we hope we can intuit as we consider the practice of Zen itself; from these, perhaps, we can gain an insight into why Zen has been found by Christian contemplatives of former times and today to be useful in their prayer life.

To do Zen one follows a series of seven conventions. So that our efforts remain not an exercise in looking only but translate into a creative experience, let the gentle reader observe successively these conventions as we set them forth:

1. Having chosen carefully the place for our meditation—as free as possible from distractions, harsh lights, sounds, and drafts—we assume the Zen position, as shown in the illustration on this page. In this position we join our hands and bow from the waist in the traditional oriental gesture of courtesy which here means, "Now I begin my meditation." A similar bow at the end will mean, "Now I end my meditation." If we must stand to attend to something—best disconnect the telephone beforehand— or we have an itch or a cramp we simply cannot ignore, we bow as we break off meditating, then again as we resume it. This puts parentheses around each session of our meditation, separating it from interruptions coming from us and from our world around us.

2. We try to keep our backs as erect as comfortably possible:

the base of the spine is the key. We do not worry if at first it tires quickly. After a couple of weeks of daily meditation, it will surprise us by its new toughness, even during longer sessions of Zen.

3. Our legs should be crossed as well as possible, but comfortably, making allowances for bad knees and general decrepitude. We strive to keep faithful to the time we agree with ourselves to meditate daily. Twenty-minute sessions are good to begin with. As we go longer, circulatory pain in our legs can force us to take a break. For this, we bow, stand, join hands before us, pace the room for two minutes; then, taking again the Zen position, we bow, and resume meditating.

4. Our hands and wrists should rest comfortably on the insides of our thighs—left four fingers on top of right four fingers, the fingers underneath press up dynamically against those above, while the tips of the thumbs touch together ever so lightly and delicately. Here we aim to combine a relaxed and stable dynamism of our fingers with an alert delicacy in the touch of our thumbs.

5. Our head should be erect, tilted slightly forward comfortably, and with chin in. Our tongue should rest relaxed in the base of our mouth, and we avoid all nervous movement of tongue and jaw. Lips should be relaxed and slightly parted to permit exhaling through the mouth.

6. Our eyes should remain half closed and out of focus. If we close our eyes, we will go to sleep; if we focus them on anything, that thing will become a distraction.

7. Our breathing should be not from the chest but from the diaphragm. We loosen our belts, allowing our lower abdomen full freedom to expand and contract. We inhale, knowing the air we take in through our nostrils will heal and give peace, and the air we exhale through our mouth will carry out those things that rob us of peace. This breathing is indeed the key to both traditional and Christian Zen because, once we are in observance of these conventions, the conscious listening to the sound of our breathing becomes the central continuous deliberate activity during the entire time we are meditating. We strive to make this breathing more and more regular, more deeply from the diaphragm. We seek to become increasingly absorbed in reposefully listening to and centering ourselves in its sound. As we descend deeper into this centering, the thoughts, desires, and images that our mind naturally generates will diminish to nil. If some persist, we do not fight against them, but, by continuously

renewing this reposeful centering, we ignore them. If they continue aggressively, it is probably because we are not observing certain of the conventions above. Perhaps our hands have slipped away from the position of dynamism and delicacy, or we are permitting nervous activity in our mouth. But most often the reason will be found in our breathing being not from the diaphragm, or our not centering ourselves in its sound. Striving meticulously to maintain these conventions, in spite of the turmoil our daily lives may be subjected to at the time, and striving, as well, to pass the whole period with a minimum of surrenders to needs to scratch or to shift our body's members, make for steady progress over the months, over the years. Indeed this striving for perfection in every detail—in posture and in centering in our breathing—becomes the daily bread and butter of Zen meditation.

Even the pain we will feel in our legs after thirty or so minutes of continuous meditation can be turned to our advantage. As this pain grows, we seek to enter it, to center within it, and, as it were, to find in it a certain rest. Thus our concentration upon our breathing will become more complete and more central, and foreign thoughts will be more completely excluded.

The above conventions are, curiously, the essentials of Zen as it has developed over the past millennium. Being in essence nonverbal, nonconceptual, and nonimaginative, Zen does not lend itself to being systematized. To those practicing Zen, it is the experience that matters, whereas the conflicting ways one tries to describe or analyze this experience are to them secondary at best.

But for us Westerners, who look for reasons to be persuaded, let us ask what we are doing when we do Zen, and why. Simply stated, following these conventions meticulously permits us a maximum control of both our physical and mental activities, and from this we are able to suspend them partially. Thus, during meditation, the Zen position encompasses and brings under control in appropriate ways every member and organ of our body—even our heart—which, we will find, will beat slower as we descend deeper into the centering. While consciously listening to the sound of our breathing itself, we can make it more regular, more from the diaphragm, and it will further become the key to controlling and emptying the activities of our mind: memory, intelligence, will, and imagination, including especially emotions.

Thus, in doing Zen we strive to make each session of meditation both as dynamic and as empty as possible. As far as I know there is no better way than this to disengage our physical and mental powers over an extended period of time while still continuing awake and alert. Anyone attempting to observe self-imposed silence and recollection during a conventional retreat knows how recalcitrant our bodies and our minds are to this kind of discipline. Not even in sleep itself, which we now know is filled with both physical and mental activity, is there such a diminishment of these as there is in Zen meditation.

Zen does not lend itself to being systematized.

This partial suspension of our bodily and mental activities for a set period of time daily is the objective of Zen, and from this derive its singular benefits. As we strive for this disengagement, and achieve it in a growing degree, we are actually inducing our physical and mental powers into a daily, deep repose. Not only are each member of our bodies, but also the thoughts of our hearts, put to rest during our meditation: our conflicting values competing for dominance; our desires, inordinate or not; our ambitions and passionate longings; and our memories, both joyful and painful, with ruminations of past grievances. Thus we turn over, to our own mysterious powers of healing within us, our bodies, minds, and hearts; and from this daily repose and renewing of the whole person, a peace is given.

We speak, of course, of daily meditation—not over weeks, but over months, over years. If we do Zen faithfully, we will become aware of certain gifts that mysteriously enter our lives. We are surprised by new insights that fall out of nowhere into our minds, perhaps not during the time of meditation, but at other times during the day or night. We acquire a deeper understanding of our own best values, of how to bring to bear our nobler motivations. We acquire a deeper understanding of our own weaknesses, and we see ways which perhaps we did not see before to put to rest inordinate desires. We become less afflicted by painful images of griefs or disappointments; and we are less obsessed by regrets, by personal defeats and shames. Even memories of hurts from deep in our childhood, of which we are perhaps only barely aware but which still send poisonous tentacles up into our present relationships, can be uncovered and healed. We are mystified by how our own recuperative powers can now work within us. Just as, for example, when one morning we awake and realize happily that at last we are healed of a drawn-out bout with the flu, so in practicing Zen we might one day realize that now—but not before—we are able to turn with sincere affection toward a friend who has deeply hurt us. In short, what we experience in ourselves is a self-rehabilitating human being, perhaps with long-immobilized personal gifts now renewed. From this, then, our own creative energies can emerge unencumbered, with a new freedom. This healing will often spread to others around us in our family, in our community and work place, even when they are not aware we meditate.

As described thus far, traditional Zen is not intrinsically a religious action; it is, thus, neither theistic nor atheistic. Hence the curious smiles coming from Zen masters when one asks if, as practitioners of Zen, they believe in God.

Somewhere further on in this direction lies the experience of enlightenment. Zen masters describe enlightenment as a perception totally beyond reason, beyond imagining; intuitive, yet at the core of our life itself. All of Zen teaching, they add, is but an effort to take the disciple beyond concepts and images that stand for reality, and put him or her in intimate contact with that reality itself. It is in vain, they maintain, to pursue intellectually this stage, since all ratiocination on this point is useless, futile, and confusing. Thomas Merton calls this "the Zen fact" and compares it to an alarm clock. When it goes off, the sleeper 1) does not hear and just keeps on sleeping; or 2) making a misguided response, in effect turns the alarm off, permitting him to go back to sleep; or 3) he jumps out of bed with a shout of astonishment that it is so late. Zen is the alarm clock, it merely enables us to wake up and become aware. It teaches nothing. It points. Merton continues: "But we in the West, in ego-centered practicality and . . . manipulation of everything, always pass from one thing to another, from cause to effect, from the first to the next to the last and then back to the first. Everything always points to something else and hence we never stop anywhere because we cannot; as soon as we pause, the escalator reaches the end of the ride and we have to get off and find another one. Nothing is allowed just to be and to mean itself; everything has to signify something else. Zen is designed to frustrate the mind thinking in such terms. 'The Zen fact,' whatever it may be, always lands across our road like a fallen tree beyond which we cannot pass. Nor are such 'facts' lacking in Christianity—the

Cross for example . . . which gives Christians a radically new consciousness."

The way some Zen masters describe enlightenment, as an experience of the unity of all being, reflects the monistic, cosmotheistic, philosophical climate of Zen's origins; and it can be disconcerting to a Christian. Yet, if one takes seriously one of the central teachings of Zen itself—namely, that it is the experience and not the concept of it that matters—then one may judge pantheistic doctrine as the above to be not central to Zen. Indeed such might be for us the "misguidance" that prompts us to turn off the alarm clock, to go back to sleep and miss the experience. The "fact" of Zen is simply the experience that puts us in touch with this ultimate personal reality itself, and that, I believe, must at last come down to be our own individual living soul—the concrete reality, not a concept of it. We cannot think our way to our soul's living presence, or analyze or visualize it; but in doing Zen we are brought to the experience of the soul's availing itself of space to renew itself, and then of its mysterious healing powers in renewing our body, mind, and heart.

Being in Zen an apprentice of only some twenty-five years, a full-blown experience of enlightenment, with its sudden flash of intuition, is still unknown to me. Nor do I seek it as such; as Christian, I try to keep my heart open to whatever grace the Lord sends and to whatever form he wants it to take.

But before we dismiss Zen and turn off the alarm clock, I suggest we take seriously stated opinions of respected specialists, not only of such as Thomas Merton or Dom Aelred Graham, but also of Dr. John C. H. Wu, an eminent jurist and diplomat, a Chinese convert to Catholicism, and a scholar, who is able to write of Zen not from hearsay or study alone, but from within. He is not afraid to write that he brought Zen and Confucianism with him into Christianity. Looking further back, I have been assured by Carmelites who are specialists in both their tradition of contemplation and in Christian Zen that these two traditions are essentially the same: what Teresa of Avila, in her own inimitable way, and what John of the Cross—and what Meister Eckhart 200 years before them—practiced, perhaps unknown to them, was essentially Christian Zen.

But what is Christian Zen, which we will now call centering prayer, and how is it prayer if traditional Zen is not? Will an attempt to use Zen in prayer, contrary to what Zen masters maintain—that one cannot accommodate true Zen to any ulterior pur-pose—render it ineffectual? To answer, let me offer an analogy. Consider a ballet apprentice who works daily on her technique. She may give little thought to what ballet grammar—the body language she is learning—might be saying or to whom; she metic-ulously strives only to perfect every move, every step of it. For the present, the immediate benefits of her efforts—pride in pleasing a respected teacher, satisfaction in mastering an art—are suffi-cient reasons for striving for self-discipline; and she grows daily in poise and beauty. But one day a certain impresario discovers her and offers her a part in a new production. Now she has two things she lacked before: a role, a *dramatis persona* to live within, and an envisioned audience. These give form and finality to her efforts. Just as this ballerina can adapt her previously acquired skills to this new orientation, so also, as many Christian contemplatives have found, the skills and the strengths of traditional Zen, with little change in its dynamics, can be fitted into the larger synthesis of Christian prayer.

Neither our ballerina above, nor a person doing Zen medi-tations daily, acts without a certain basic desire, or even a pas-sion, which drives their actions, enabling them to keep a daily commitment. One must first wish to do what is necessary to become, to be—whether in ballet, in Zen, or in Christian prayer. Satisfaction found therein will, in turn, sustain and nourish the motivation.

When the prophet Samuel was a small boy sleeping in the temple, he was awakened repeatedly by a voice calling, "Samuel, Samuel!" Each time he got up and went to his master, the elderly priest Eli, and asked what he wanted. Each time Eli replied, "I didn't call, my son; go and lie down again." Again Samuel heard the voice calling, and again he went to the old priest. But this time Eli, perceiving it was the Lord calling, instructed him, "The next time he calls, you must respond, 'Speak, Lord, for your ser-vant is listening.'" Whether that night Samuel really heard the voice of God, or whether he heard only, as he had many times before, the wind blowing through the porticos of the temple, his listening and then giving response is the same. It is the reality from which the call came that makes the difference between an obedient child and the prophet-to-be. We must listen continu-ously to the voice of the Lord who speaks to us when and how he chooses.

If we find traditional Zen apt for putting us in contact with the healing and peace-giving powers of our human spirit within, how much more will we find centering prayer apt for opening our beings to the Spirit of God within us, to surrendering ourselves to this Healer, this Comforter? It will be this Spirit's voice we listen for within the sound of our breathing, as she leads us into that silence within, where, using utterances beyond human words, with ineffable groaning, she cries, "Abba, Father!" Far from taking from Zen its dignity, this carries it to its fulfillment. What a grace it is that Christian contemplatives discovered Zen and were able to enrich Christian asceticism with it.

We must listen continuously to the voice of the Lord who speaks to us when and how he chooses.

The Christ-centered dynamics of the Ignatian Spiritual Exercises, especially when renewed yearly, give peace and build motivations to service, but they were not meant to be used daily over a long period of time when they can become exhausting. Centering prayer, on the other hand, not in contrast to the Exercises but ancillary to them, offers spiritual repose. Many of Ignatius's instructions can be applied with profit to Zen meditation: making preparation before meditation by spiritual reading and acts of self-denial; cultivating honesty and sincerity in evaluating our efforts at praying; making from time to time reviews of moments of joy or of sadness; and, with the retreat master's help, using carefully Ignatius's instructions on the discernment of spirits.

In sessions of centering prayer, unlike in other forms of meditation, one does not pray the words of any pious text, nor even of Holy Scripture. Words, whether we want them to or not, will bloom into images, and images invite concepts which multiply, and thus we are on the way to taking our bodies and minds out of that total surrender to the Spirit, the true mode of centering prayer. Rather, we should see each session of this prayer as that time when the Bridegroom is present before us, looking into our eyes, speaking into our hearts, so we put aside during this quality time his love-letters from times past, no matter how treasured they are. With no more than a bow of adoration and a word to greet him by name, such as, "Jesus, have mercy on me, a sinner," we surrender ourselves with total passivity to his Spirit within us, who will shape our minds and hearts according to his holy will. In this action of the Spirit, one is reminded of a great, silent, moving body of water, imperceptibly and with ease, carrying all obstacles before it. We will look forward to this daily prayer as the best moment of our day, and find in it an anchor for the rest of our lives.

Let me mention now one special blessing I have received through centering prayer. When I was a very small child, I once heard my older brothers, one six, the other seven years old, talking about how hell is "for ever and ever—for eternity, which never, ever ends." My mind became beset with fearful images of this eternity, like "the void of infinity" that so terrified Pascal. These were most acute when I was ill, which I often was, with high fever, and with accompanying nightmares. During these I often dreamed I was looking up and saw the ceiling above me (and all reality with it) recede up and up and up, for ever and ever. My sight was forced to go with it, on and on, and I could never, ever make it stop; and that was eternity. And I felt desperately alone and forsaken. I could not turn off the nightmare, until my screams brought my father or mother who would awake me and comfort me. This terror remained with me even into later life.

When I discovered Zen meditation, which then became for me centering prayer, I took up the custom, after meditating and during the brief prickly feeling as my legs recovered circulation, of lying back on the rug and looking straight up at the ceiling, never forgetting that this was the way I had so fearfully felt I was looking into the face of eternity. But over the years, gradually, imperceptibly, the terror departed. In its place has grown a trust in God's mercy and, even, flashes—ever so brief and fleeting—of joy in looking forward to my death, which now is approaching apace. These graces I consider among the most precious of my life.

Remembering how the ancients strove to get the gods' attention, we know we have already the Father's attention in his son, Jesus, who taught us to pray to his father by offering, not perishable gifts of animals slaughtered or wine or grain poured out, but one infinitely more desirable: our total selves. This same Jesus promised, moreover, "whatever you ask the Father in my name, he will give it to you." Jesus must have meant precisely that, unless we ask for something that is not good for us, then he will give us something else—something far better for us. Centering prayer, as an ancilla to the Spiritual Exercises, more than any other prayer method I know, enables us to put ourselves into this total trusting frame of mind, not stating what we think we want, or need, or when, but silently taking Jesus at his word and waiting. The Father, who knows our needs far better than we do, will respond; and why wouldn't he, since Jesus said he would?

Ignatian and Monastic Contemplation

*T*he religious life in its present identity-seeking state lends itself to theorizing and speculation of mixed value for the concrete people involved. And I am in the process of adding to this body of writing! My issue is this. Articles appear and reappear on different styles, charisms, categories of religious life, and the lifestyle or spirituality appropriate to each. The subject is important and can be very interesting. Concretely, though, what is the religious life about? What is its heart? Where is it going ? I believe that if one reflects on a very central insight of two major currents in the religious life—currents which writers tend to oppose or contrast with each other—one finds some very thought-provoking results.

One central theme of the *Spiritual Exercises* of Ignatius of Loyola—Exercises which were *the* formative spiritual experience for the prospective or young Jesuit—was the importance of coming to "find God in all things."[1] Ignatian spirituality is said to be one of service rather than of nuptial union,[2] with a strong accent on mortification and abnegation rather than on prolonged prayer. (Ignatius was wont to say that a quarter of an hour's prayer was sufficient to unite the mortified person to God and that without this mortification an hour would not suffice.[3]) Nonetheless, one falsifies the perspective if, in emphasizing service, one forgets the above goal of the Exercises.

Clearly, here one should return to Scripture. If it is God in whom we live, move, and are;[4] if it is the purpose of the Incarnation to divinize the human person, making Jesus the Firstborn of many brothers and sisters,[5] it is important to come to see the world and people much as he did. De Guibert stresses the trinitarian and eucharistic nature of Ignatian spirituality, seeing as a central intuition Ignatius's vision at La Storta where he saw himself placed "with Christ." This position was the heart of the apostolic service that was to follow, and the service has no meaning without it—one could even say, without a certain consciousness of this "position."

In other words, then, the Jesuit vocation *is* characterized by a call to apostolic service and generosity. But the soul or inner life of this call is a growing awareness of God's love working in and through all things and preceding, underlying, any human action of any worth.

At first glance, and judging by externals, one could hardly imagine anything more different from the Jesuit stress on apostolic service than the monastic, with its emphasis on the priority of the Work of God (*Opus Dei*), normally within the monastery. But let us look deeper.

The term "Opus Dei" has come, in recent centuries, to be taken as a reference to the Divine Office. This was not its original meaning. The monastic life was originally seen as a call to pray always, to live one's life in, for, and with God, and it was this *life*—all of it—that was the Work of God.[6] This "monastic" attitude and spirituality became characteristic of whole centuries in the Christian East and West, and can still be found, for example, in the nineteenth-century tale of the Pilgrim,[7] as well as contemporary writers like Paul Evdokimov[8]—an indication of how deeply this original "monastic" insight became important even to "lay" life. Is not "pray always" addressed to everyone? This exhortation which sent people into the deserts of Scete sent the nineteenth-century Pilgrim, too, on his journey. Is the Pilgrim Everyman?

One might say not. Most people cannot leave everything to seek and obey the instructions of a starets. Few people are called to the desert. The monastic life with its rhythm of prayer and work, Office and closeness to nature, silence and listening, seems

The monastic life was originally seen as a call to pray always, to live one's life in, for, and with God, and it was this life—all of it—that was the Work of God.

a very special call. And, to return to our original question, it seems an orientation wholly different from the Ignatian, with the latter's dedication to apostolic service. Again, however, let us look deeper.

The monk or nun works, normally, within the monastery, in a way that is meant to further the life of prayer, the Work of God. That is to say that the work is lived in a certain quiet, an attitude of listening, a respect for the rhythms of nature and of the human person seeking to hear and obey God. This day-long Opus Dei—this turning of all of life into praise and prayer—is the apostolic service par excellence of the monastic life—even where some monastic communities do have other apostolic work as well. The essential is the inner orientation which makes all life prayer, which unites the person living it to God in Christ. Reflection on this fact needs to go in two directions—comparison with Ignatian thought and, again, with "lay" life.

If the inner horizon of the Jesuit's service is God's love acting in all things, and if all of life, here, is service of God; if, on the other hand, for the monk or nun the aim is that everything becomes Opus Dei, one can only wonder if, at the summit of the mountain, all paths do not end at the same place. One can also wonder if this end is not meant to be part of the journey as well. Is accenting the differences of means so very helpful? Does not each individual, rather, have to find those means that further this single end—learning from his or her spiritual tradition, of course, as each vocation is a call to live a certain charism, but with the one and only end firmly in mind? Apostolic service without this "soul" becomes salt without savor, as the monastic rhythm of life without it becomes mere routine.

But there is more. Benedict, following the centuries before him, considered the monastic life to be "lay," simply Christian living. (This is why I use the term in quotation marks.) And indeed, most religious are "lay" in that they are not in orders. The religious life per se is not priestly. The ordinary "lay" life of many people—notably those in less high-powered professions— has much in common with daily life in a monastic house. That is to say, until recently it had. A rhythm of daily manual labor— cooking, sewing, cleaning or farming, chopping wood, building— is something many a housewife or househusband, builder or other worker, as well as many a monastic knows. This rhythm can serve prayer. Zen tradition, like the Western monastic, points out endlessly the importance of the ordinary in our lives. But the question is how one does this "ordinary." Now life has become pressurized for most people. Home tasks are fit in on the outer fringes of jobs or a profession. Life becomes a frenzied race to make money (often needed) without respect for body, mind, nature, quiet—as for many a religious it can become an equally frenzied race to serve. Maybe a look at the top of the mountain can encourage all of us to set our sights a bit differently—a bit more counter-culturally as well. The Ignatian call to service was meant to require a total generosity and abnegation. But where these were present, service was seen as profoundly uniting with God— and as performed in this perspective. Monastic prayer and work, and all the factors of the rhythmed day and life, rather than being seen as a very special and esoteric mode of existence can, on the contrary, suggest another kind of discipline aimed at orienting the whole day, with its simple or complex tasks, to the life-giving presence of God. Some of this discipline fits anyone's day.

The Ignatian call to service was meant to require a total generosity and abnegation. But where these were present, service was seen as profoundly uniting with God—and as performed in this perspective.

Both these perspectives contain a single lesson—that the essential remains the orientation to God, even the conscious orientation to God. Both contain a corollary of equal importance. This orientation is lived in a human body and psyche; by human persons who only at their peril cut themselves off from contact with the natural world and the laws of their being. The misuse of our body, psyche, and the world around us that shows in workaholism (as much an addiction as alcoholism), tension, strain, burnout, inability or unreadiness to deal with psychological, emotional, simply human needs—all these and so much else in so many lives speak of the loss of touch with essential rhythms. The East would speak of being out of Tao. Both Ignatian and monastic asceticism speak—albeit in very different ways—of the "instrument" (perhaps best imagined as a musical instrument) that needs to be tuned to the touch of God. Misuse of the instrument is not asceticism, service, or generosity. It is quite simply lack of discernment—a key virtue to the desert as well as the Ignatian tradition.

Christianity is a single call lived out in as many ways as there are people. There are families of thought, traditions, texts, and history. But basically there is one call to personal relationship with the living God. If this is not central, all else is straw. And where it is honored, apostolic fecundity and contemplative union grow together. I believe that where we center on life—in discernment—more than on theory, the call comes clear. But one needs the courage to go to the heart of the call and let the rest go—or go into its proper place. I believe this is the one lesson both traditions teach—along with so many others, each an insight into the ways of God. In the concreteness of our lives God speaks. The invitation is to the purity of heart that sees God—that is, purity of *heart* and so, of love.

Notes

[1] *The Spiritual Exercises of St. Ignatius—a Literal Translation and a Contemporary Reading*, David L. Fleming SJ, (St. Louis: The Institute of Jesuit Sources, 1978), pp. 138-143.

[2] Joseph de Guibert SJ, *La Spiritualité de la Compagnie de Jesus—Esquisse Historique*, (Rome: Institutum Historicum S.I., 1953), pp. 38-39.

[3] Quoted in de Guibert, op cit, p. 75.

[4] Ac 17:28.

[5] Rm 8:29.

[6] See Irenée Hausherr SJ, "Opus Dei," *Orientalia Christiana Periodica* 13 (1947), passim.

[7] *The Way of a Pilgrim and The Pilgrim Continues His Way*, Helen Bacovin trans., (Garden City: Doubleday & Co., Image Books, 1978).

[8] See, for example, Paul Evdokimov, *The Struggle with God*, (Glen Rock, New Jersey: Paulist Press, 1966), pp. 11-131.

The Path of Contemplation–I

*T*he rarest thing in this world is joy. Yet it is joy and joy only which can renew the world, heal it of its nameless ills, and make it what it is truly meant to be, a living word of the Father. What stops joy is grief: the grief we have when we see beauty ruined, innocence despoiled, hopes betrayed, and all that we hold dear cast aside for naught. These things happen not in the abstract but in our own lives, in the lives of our communities and families, and in the world we live. To come to joy we have to walk through the paths of our grief which have so molded us that the source of our perceptions is our pain. We often see only through our hurt. To walk through the paths of our grief, we have first to acknowledge each hurt in our lives. This is painful because we have to admit that we are severely damaged people. Then we have to hold each hurt and to live with it in the daily round of our lives until we can know it. Only then can we name that hurt, as it is, without lies or drama or false humility. We can only do so if we do it lovingly—as a mother holds a bruised child. Then, only then, we have to let it go free, at which time it becomes a door through which the mercy of God enters into this world. All this must be learned.

The path to joy leads through grief. Yet the fruit of contemplation is joy. "Why do we need to walk this particular path?" one may ask. "Surely there are other paths to joy!" This does not seem to to be either the common experience of humanity or, indeed, the pattern proposed by the major religious traditions. Certainly it has not been the way Christ lived in the world as that life is portrayed in Philippians 2:5-11. Christ enters into the condition of suffering humanity to raise us to the joy of the resurrection. As the Eucharistic preface for the Easter season tells us, the joy of the resurrection renews the whole world. That resurrection did not occur until after the life, crucifixion, and death of Jesus.

His path is our path. If we truly seek to follow him, to help him in the work of bringing the world back to the Father, we must follow his path. That path is made available to us through contemplation, and we already have the material we need to work with and to open to transformation. It is ourselves.

First, we need to ask ourselves: What is it which stops us from being joyful? To get an answer we need to examine ourselves, to listen to our lives. Already we have taken the first three steps on the path to contemplation. In spending time with this dialogue, we have declared, concretely, our willingness to walk some way along the path. We cannot walk this path unwillingly. God does not force himself on anyone. He lets us free. It is our fears and compulsions and anxieties which stop us from being free. The second step we have made in walking with God is in bringing ourselves, bringing that history which is unique to every one of us. Within that history we find our personal path to contemplation. Thirdly, we walk this path with a deliberate purpose: to be with God, in whom is the fullness of life. We do not walk this path for the world's approval, nor for the transitory security of fortifying the defenses of our ego, and certainly not to maintain, even unconsciously, the forces of destruction which can enter our world through us. We walk this path ultimately to be a special presence of God in whatever situation we find ourselves.

Often we start something even before we know it, and so when we consciously decide to walk the path of contemplation, we do not have to make a new beginning, but merely to walk the path we are already walking on. What we have to do is walk it more attentively, more in tune with the forces of life which surround us on so many levels. We are here to walk that path with faithfulness, with integrity, with creativity, with love. There is a pattern in our lives which moves to contemplation; it is a pattern of attentiveness, faith, humility, creativity. If we follow that path, we learn to move with God, and we learn what that means for each of us concretely.

The first step is being attentive. We often think that we are attentive, that we know what is going on in our lives and in the lives of those around us. This is often simply not true. Freud has an interesting thing to say about "repression." In "Remembering,

Repeating, and Working-Through" (1914) he has an insight which is applicable to the spiritual life. "The patient does not *remember* anything of what he has forgotten and repressed, but *acts* it out. He reproduces it not as a memory but as an action; he *repeats* it, without, of course, knowing that he is repeating it." Repression makes us inattentive. Repression is different from suppression, in which we know something or feel something and use all our abilities to keep it from happening. Normally we are quite attentive to what we suppress, for example, our sexual desires or our anger. But what we repress we are not attentive to at all. The thing that stops us from getting in contact with what we repress is *fear*. So if we want to find out what limits our attention, we need to look at how we fear. One normally thinks of fear as an enemy—and in a way it is—but our fears usually signal the way we must move.

We need to think of fear as a door beyond which is a group of children—aspects of ourselves— who have never grown up and instead have become wild, autistic. Their wildness, their withdrawal from what is human, is because they have never been acknowledged, never been known for what they are, never been loved. A hurt is a desire that has never grown to love, and so it plays according to its own rules. It becomes wild. We defend ourselves from hurt through fear. On a spiritual level, on the path of contemplation, hurts are dimensions of our lives that have never known love, have never spent time with God. Those hurts are repressed, yet they affect our lives because they come out in the way we act. Think of the person in a religious community, or a family, who is so organized that other people have become an intolerable burden to her. What has stopped her from being flexible, what lack of love has let her believe that concepts are more important than people? And yet she is usually quite convinced that she witnesses, in the face of crumbling community standards, a fidelity to the highest values of life. Consider the effect she has

Often we start something even before we know it, and so when we consciously decide to walk the path of contemplation, we do not have to make a new beginning, but merely to walk the path we are already walking on.

on community with her anger and her passive aggression and her unspoken sense of judgment. Or consider the member of the community who is always unhappy, always complaining, or the one who is always tired. Often their reasons for their behavior are quite valid, but they are truths maintained without love, and truths without love are lies.

The positions of these *personas* we have just considered emerge from their strengths. We hide from our fears behind our strengths, and our strengths may be either positive or negative. Our strengths affirm us: the good teacher, the good administrator, the willing subject, the politically committed religious. What our strengths do *not* do is let us enter into the areas of darkness in our lives which need to spend time with God. In contemplation those areas of darkness meet God much as the wily Jacob meets God at Peniel, wrestles with him in the dark, and is renamed and is transformed into Israel, the father of nations (Gn 32:22-32).

That fight with God is named "contemplation." The word itself comes from the Latin *contemplari*, to observe carefully; and the Latin word itself comes from two words: *com* an intensive, and *templum* the open space marked out by augurs in the Near East to observe the stars and thus discern the fate of things. Roman augurs who wanted to tell what the gods wanted also opened a space, usually in birds' entrails, and looked carefully to see what the signs present in that opened space meant.

It is useful to reflect on this Latin word for a bit because the *templum*, the open space, became where the gods appeared: the temple. We have to create that open space in which God appears, and that space is covered up by our strengths and hidden by our fears, overlooked in our daily life. To get to that open space where we can experience God, we have to examine our fears, for we experience God through his saving work in his overcoming of our fears. We experience God when he transforms us, when he heals our hurts and our fears have no more power over us.

How do we examine our fears? It is of little use merely to have an intellectual knowledge of our fears. That is rather like going to the doctor with a pain in your stomach and being told you have something with a long Latin-sounding name. Merely knowing the name does not stop the pain. Knowing your fears goes deeper than having the names for them. To know your fears you have to live with them, rather than shut them out of the house you live in, though of course they surround your house. You cannot ignore your fears. You have to spend time with them. "Contemplation" is to spend time with. Indeed the root *temp*, to stretch or to extend, gives us the Latin *tempus, temporis*, a span of time, and the intensive form *con* intensifies that sense of time so that it moves from *chronos* to *kairos*, from ordinary time to revelatory time.

How can we spend time with our fears so that that time can become revelatory? Imagine we are put in a fearful situation. We go to the dentist. We sit in that chair, it tilts back, a bright light shines in our face at something we cannot see. What we do see is that long needle moving just out of our sight. We are helpless and are filled, already, with previous memories of being injected. What do we do? We scrunch up our faces, close our eyes, grip our hands. We try our best to disassociate ourselves from that area of pain. We lose our sense of calm and we become inattentive to how minimal the pain really is because we become focused on rejecting or denying it. Ironically enough, the psychologists tell us that this kind of effort to avoid pain actually increases our subjective experience of pain (*Journal of Behavioral Medicine* vol. 10, 139-144; also *Psychology Today*, August 1987, p. 54). Fears maintain themselves through panic. When we panic we become blinded to everything else but our fear, which then controls us totally. In this way panic limits our attentiveness by limiting our freedom and thus limits our possibilities of being fully human.

To spend time with our fear we have to see the way in which fears walk through our lives, how they affect our relationships, our work, our self-image, our hopes; they affect the way we look at our past, our communities, our expectations of ourselves and others, the way we play, our sense of humor, even the way we keep our rooms. Our fears touch everything we do, and often it is our fears that do things and not we ourselves because we have no freedom in them. It is our fears which cause us to maintain our sins. Here sin is not to be seen as the opposition to the "thou-shalt-nots" but rather as the lack of creativity, the inability to be loving, or intelligent, or even aware. Those times when we have been such when we look at our history reveal to us our fear. Of course the question arises: Is not even the way in which we look at our history touched by our fear? That may be so, but the way we look at our history is also touched by our drive to transcendence, and so there is a gray area in the story of our lives which makes us uncomfortable and which becomes the scene of our discovery of God. We go out into that gray area when we start contemplation.

When we look at the word "contemplation" we discover that the root *temp*, to stretch, also provides the basis for the word "temptation." When we set out to do God's will, to be a manifestation of *his* time in the world, we come into the gray areas of our lives, the places of our temptations. Contemplation leads to temptation. Jesus, after he is baptized in the Jordan, goes out to the wilderness—a place where he is without his strengths, a place where he encounters his fears—to discover God's will. There he is tempted as he attempts to spend time with God. His temptations urge him to be less than who he is. Our temptations urge us to be less than who we are. Our fears make us less than who we are.

Like Christ we are to be words of God; we are to be the signs of his presence in the world; we are to witness through joy to his transforming presence. The areas in our lives where we do not experience joy are areas mastered by fear. That fear can be transformed only if we spend time with it. We have to become the open spaces in which God becomes more present to the world. That openness can happen when we present our fear to the Father and remain with it in contemplation until he transforms it. God can enter our world only in what we call human time; it is one of the mysteries of the Incarnation that he chooses to do this. Actually it is the manifestation of his faith in us, his hope in us, his love for us, that he abandons himself to our time.

The first step in contemplation is to hold our fears up to the Father, rather than hide from him, as did Adam and Eve in the garden. In the time we give him, he is present to our fears. He transforms us, and the grace we ask for as we walk into the gray areas of our lives is to know and to be present to those fears. Of course we can do that only if he is present with us, so in coming to be present to our fears we also come to be present to him in new and surprising ways.

Looking at Our Fears

There are two ways of being present to our fears. We could look at them and wonder how we can be so stupid, and then make plans to be a perfectionist, to make sure that those mistakes never happen again or, if they do, never become known. If anyone learned about them, we would excuse them as part of a bigger plan which only we know about. I think certain aspects of governments' foreign policy operate on these principles. That way of looking at our fear keeps us in our fear and we are not transformed. The other way of looking at our fear is to experience the amazement that no one has pushed us down the stairs or slipped some ground glass into our coffee, or that we have not destroyed ourselves. That amazement leads us to ask why. What is it that has kept us alive? The more we ponder about it, the more we are filled with a sense of wonder—which gives us no answer. That wonder, that sense of amazement, is our first awareness of the presence of God in the space we have created by looking at our fears.

Like Christ we are to be words of God; we are to be the signs of his presence in the world; we are to witness through joy to his transforming presence.

That sense of wonder is dynamic. It reaches out. It touches the things we took for granted or ignored. We look at things and get lost in them. Why? Because everything becomes unknowable according to the old rules by which we have ruled our lives and looked at things. What was previously insignificant now moves into significance: the light on a magazine cover, the pattern of voices singing out of key, the way your skin smells when you have just got up in the morning. All becomes something you notice. It is rather like children who watch the world with open eyes. Have you ever noticed the way young children stare at you? It is without shame or without guile. And have you ever noticed the way in which you can stare back at young children? They do not turn away from a gaze. The eyes in icons do the same thing. They are filled with a sense of wonder. They gaze at you without judgment or suggestion, and that openness encourages you to be open, to gaze back. To gaze at something is different from looking at something. When we look *at* something, we are usually looking *for* something: an explanation, a distraction, the exercise of curiosity or power. Gazing at something provides none of these. To gaze, or the more rustic word to gawk, comes from the root *ga*, to rejoice, and we have from it the Latin word *gaudete*, rejoice.

To be attentive is to rejoice in the presence of something. When we are present in prayer, we are attentive and become aware of the dimensions, the forces, the powers, the presences which constitute the space in which we find our identity. In the gazing which contemplation allows, that space reveals itself to us. The patience we learn in contemplation is the time of that space. That time is not our time, is not determined by *chronos*, yet it is available to us and so is in time. The gazing we attend to in contemplation gives contemplation its freedom, and in turn we discover that we gain freedom at the same time. When our fears trap us, we become restless and obsessed; when we look at our fears, we need to look at them not from our needs. We do not need at this time to say: I have to find out my fears, I have to face them, I have to haul them out kicking and screaming into the open, I have to bash them on their heads until they are quite still, and then I have to lay them out on the ground and line them up like dead rabbits at a shoot, so that everyone will know what a good and spiritual person I am.

If we are afraid of our fears, imagine how much more our fears are afraid of us. If we kill our fears, we become inhuman. What we need to do is transform our fears, and we can only transform them if we gaze at them in wonder, and we can only do so if we see them in the context of God's love for us. It is rather like floating in a deep lake. If we relax we are all right; we can enjoy the sun on our bodies, the cool water on our faces, the laziness of our limbs. But as soon as we start to worry about how deep the lake is, how far we are from shore, what bad swimmers we are, what if we catch a cramp—as soon as we start to panic, we lose our sense of wonder, our sense of enjoyment of life. Suddenly everything is the enemy.

Often as we relax into attentiveness, the gazing which is the beginning of contemplation, we are overtaken by a sense of panic. In this is the beginnings of discernment. The good spirit leads us to relax, the bad spirit to panic.

Our path to contemplation is found by following the good spirit. Yet we can use what happens to us when we panic. We can ask ourselves what it is that makes us panic. That thing is a fear. And we can also ask ourselves: How did we get into that state of panic? How was the good we began with transformed into panic? From that we can get some insight into the way in which our fear controls us—not the general way, but the specific way. In this we are being attentive to ourselves and are beginning to understand our fear and how it works on us, the way in which it moves to take away our freedom. Note at this time we are not trying to discover the source of our fear or the private name we have for it; we are just trying to find out how it works, how it limits our attentiveness and stops us on our personal path to contemplation.

How does fear stop our contemplation? Maybe a small story may show you what I mean. Imagine yourself as a child again, out on one of those overnight camping trips. Supper is over; you have gorged yourself on hot dogs which you have burned over the campfire, have had lots of pop and potato chips. Now that night has fallen and you have changed into your pajamas, you sit around the campfire and tell ghost stories until late at night, until you are almost asleep. You stumble into the tent, curl up into the sleeping bag, and soon are out like a light. Suddenly you wake up. All that pop you drank and the excitement of the day is having its effect. You have to go to the bathroom. But it is dark all around, you are in a strange place, there are strange creatures outside, bears, wolves, coyotes, snakes, ghosts even.

You wonder if you can wait it out until morning; you try to find a comfortable position to get back to sleep. Nothing works. You toss and turn. You even contemplate wetting the bed. After all, it is not the first time you have done that. But you do not want to sleep in the damp which so soon gets cold. Besides, you know in the morning you will have to face the mockery of your friends. Finally you can take it no more. You stumble out of the tent. Even the campfire has died out. You cannot see a thing. You stumble to a tree and wait there. Every sound is horrible, you sense the presence of terrible creatures ready to devour you all around. And nothing comes. Every second seems like an eternity. All you can do is wait.

But, as you wait, your eyes become accustomed to the dark. You see the camp just behind you; you are astonished by how bright and how close the stars seem; you recognize the tree you are next to; you suddenly discover the cool wind, certainly cooler than in the tent. You suddenly discover that you are smiling to yourself. This is not so bad, you think. It is exciting and quiet and, as you think that, you discover that you are going and you are flooded with a sense of relief. You sigh and finish. You finish, but you hesitate to go back to the tent. You have a secret. The night is no big deal. You shiver, turn, go back to the tent, slip into your bag, stretch, and go back to sleep. When you wake up in the morning, you wonder where you are and then it suddenly all comes back to you: the night, your fears, your secret. You feel you are a different person in some way, no longer a baby. You tell no one about it. It is your secret.

We all face nights, and there are depths of night. There is physical night; then there is the night we enter into when we attempt anything new; there are nights that come upon us when we leave behind the securities of one way of living as we change jobs, communities, modes of living, even this life for another.

Our fears are doors to the night. In overcoming our fears we discover that living is more filled with wonder than we had previously imagined. Our fears stop us from seeing things as they are, and because they are so spontaneous they stop us from being free. Our fears not only stop us, they also stop the people around us, from being free. You know the effect one fearful person has within a community or a family. The old proverb sums this up: One bad apple spoils the barrel. Fears are signs of arrested development. They stop us from growing to be who we are, and each of our fears stops our community, be it family or residence or parish, from being fully alive and thus from being a kingdom of God.

Often we resent our fears and often we resent the fears of others and the impositions and restraints those fears have on us. As children we are often forced to accept the fears of our parents; as members of society, common social fears shape our consciousness and we, if we are religious and members of a community, absorb fears which make our witness ineffectual and our sense of joy shallow. This is, of course, one way to understand original sin and to suggest why—to get back to originating grace, the grace which gives us a second birth as children of God—we have to move in contemplation along the path of grief.

There is grief because our original nature, as the Zen Buddhists would have it, is clouded by illusion; illusion shapes our perceptions. To change our perceptions, to see God and live, means we have to get rid of our illusions.

We do not lose all our illusions at once. That takes time. Fear creates illusions, the beasts and awful creatures of the night which lie in wait for us outside our tents of childhood. The process of seeing truly, of contemplating, is to see with the eyes of God, and to see with the eyes of God is to see with the heart of God in whom all is held, including us as we truly are. The way God sees us is as time. Time is more than the patience of God. Time is the eye with which God sees us and the eye with which we see God.

Only in time can we spend time with God. Only in time and with time and through time can we be contemplative.

But, you may ask, what does this mean? It means that contemplation is not at the end of a journey. Contemplation is the journey itself. The path is contemplation. One cannot arrive at contemplation. The saints in heaven, as they contemplate God forever, fall freely lost in wonder and joy. Here, in this existence, contemplation is the time we spend coming to terms with our fears which create illusions, false ways of seeing. In contemplation one sinks through layers and layers of self to a deeper sense of self in which the self becomes less and less selfish. One does this in an inner stillness which allows us to be attentive. Often, as we sink into contemplation, the disturbances we encounter, the fears, are nameless; they are experienced primarily on as feeling. This is because the values we have become have been refined to spontaneity. To be sure, we may engage, if we want to, in the exploration of the education which has led us to become those values. Contemplation, however, is not psychoanalysis; it is more than just that. The analysis that we need, most of all, is to discern the right path. The basic antitheses on the level of feeling at this stage of contemplation are wonder and panic. The bad spirit creates panic; the good spirit encourages wonder. The inner senses of the spirit gaze on the fear, resting closer and closer. There is pain, but the pain comes as one holds the fear. The self shrinks away from the pain, but in contemplation comes back to it because it is the nature of grace to seek out what is lost and what is hurt in order to heal it and bring it to light.

In contemplation one becomes attentive to pain. It is not that one likes pain, as if one were a masochist. The contemplative does not love pain, but realizes that the pain is healing because it is felt only when the hurt covered with the scab of fear is touched by the love of the Father.

In contemplation one embraces the fear finally even though it hurts. It hurts like hell, literally, for hell is a collection of hurts. One attends to the hurt like a servant, like a suffering servant. Hurt is the lack of love. In the attentiveness of contemplation, that lack of love meets love. If we think that, of our own accord, we can satisfy this lack of love, we are mistaken. This lack of love can be satisfied only by the source of love, and that is why in contemplation we become only an open space, a temple, in which God can appear and the hurt can gain sanctuary.

When that hurt becomes human, its pain disappears. Whether pain ever disappears totally, until the end of time, I do not know. It is not just ourselves, as individuals, who have to be healed; there are the people we are connected to, and the ones they are connected to, and the ones they are connected to, until at last we stretch back and forth from the beginning of time to the end of time, and then there is all creation groaning in an act of birth. In contemplation we stretch. The etymologies of "contemplation" that we discussed are rooted in *temp*. Its original meaning is to stretch, and from *temp* we get not only "temple," "attempt," and "temptation," but also "tapestry." In contemplation as we stretch, go beyond the barriers of our ego maintained by fear, and sink into time, we discover ourselves not as individuals—which is an abstraction and illusion—but as tapestry in which all of creation is woven. In weaving, the temple is the device for keeping the warp taut on the loom. Contemplation stretches us and keeps us taut in our vocation.

The Danger of Clarity

We live in a constructed world. As we grow we are educated into values which cover everything from when and how we go to the bathroom to our attitudes about ourselves, others, and God. Even the language we think in and the words we use, the signs we share to communicate, are constructs. We often think that because our feelings are spontaneous they are natural. Yet even our feelings, our acts of perception, are taught. Feelings, emotions, are just values refined to spontaneity. We are constructs, the world we live in is constructed, and that construct which is our world, our cosmos, everything, is called *creation*.

We get our sense of identity, our sense of direction, our sense of vocation, even our desire for happiness, from these constructs. One cannot stress too much the radical importance of those forms which give our life meaning. One needs only to think of the sense of dislocation one feels when one goes to a different place or to a new job or when someone close to one dies. There is a gap, an emptiness, that is scary and frightening. At least we have been conditioned to think of that emptiness (if we think of it as emptiness) as scary.

The relationship between fear and the constructs by which we attune ourselves to our experiences needs to be examined.

What we need to do is to get in contact with what it means to live in a constructed world. This will take some work, and it is work, as John's gospel tells us: Our work is to believe in God. Fear keeps us in an unhealthy relationship with creation. Fear makes us seek security and, in security, we grasp at creation, at this constructed world of ours, as if it could provide the security we need. The peace of the world is not the peace of contemplation. The Gospel of Luke has Christ saying: "Do you think I have come to give peace on earth? No, I tell you, but rather division; for henceforth in one house there will be five divided, three against two and two against three; they will be divided, father against son and son against father, mother against daughter and daughter against her mother, mother-in-law against daughter-in-law and daughter-in-law against her mother-in-law" (Lk 12:51-53). Similarly, in John's gospel, Jesus tells his disciples, "Peace I bequeath to you, my own peace I give you; a peace the world cannot give, this is my gift to you" (Jn 14:27).

The next few steps on the path to contemplation involve coming to correct terms with the construct of creation. If we have spent time with our fears, rather than hiding from them or allowing them to hide from us, we have already moved out of the familiar routines of our lives, and already we are in a different place. We are in a different world. If we look at the lives of those who have walked the path of contemplation, we discover that at the beginning there is always a withdrawal from the normal, the habitual, or the commonplace. Teresa of Avila says in her *Autobiography:* "The Lord became desirous of preparing me for that state of life which was best for me. He sent me a serious illness." The same thing occurs with Francis of Assisi and Ignatius of Loyola. In fact, St. Ignatius in his *Spiritual Exercises* insists on this withdrawal if the soul desires "to approach and be united with its Creator and Lord".(no. 20)

The effect of this dislocation is to realize the limitations of the myth which gives our life meaning. To take away the supports of meaning throws the questing soul onto itself and more specifically onto a critical examination of the myth through which we structure experience into meaning. Despite the anxiety such dislocation might cause, we grow to realize that we can and do survive without it. The night does not devour us. If the first door to contemplation is fear, the second door is clarity. Clarity I take to mean the ways in which we understand things. I have two friends who are Freudians, and I am always amazed how they seek to understand the world according to Freud. Or one can think of those people in religious communities who transpose their anger onto the arena of social justice and who see the world just in terms of politics and economics, in terms of oppressor and oppressed. Some people construct their world out of anger, others out of pleasure, some out of knowledge, yet others out of pain.

The way to understand the trap of clarity is to look at the way ideology entraps. Ideology gives clarity. An ideology presents clear and definite norms of behavior, establishes appropriate responses to counterpositions, offers a security in the midst of complexity, and situates the human in a system which effectively controls life. The trap of clarity substitutes a worldview for reality. The person striving for holiness who submits to a worldview instead of living a faithful relationship with God translates dogmas into logical propositions instead of reading them as signifying in a particular historical moment the loving compassion of a community of believers. When one lives according to a worldview instead of in a living relationship with the Father, one has, to be sure, the ease of living life according to social norms, but those norms also cause pain and oppression. They make us less than we are. We become like those scribes and Pharisees whom Christ condemns because "for the sake of . . . tradition [they] make void the word of God" (Mt 15:6).

We need to ask ourselves what are the myths which inform our lives. Myths are not, in themselves, evil. It is when they seek to displace reality that they trap us. So we need to ask a further question: How do we hold the myths we use and which shape us? Religious generally take vows of poverty, chastity, and obedience. Does our obedience make us irresponsible? Does chastity make us sexless, unloving, and unlovable? Does poverty make us misers? If they do, then we do not hold our vows as contemplatives; we hold them as prisons. We are trapped in clarity.

Why do we hold onto what traps us? It is because we have not yet learned to trust the Void, which is the way God comes to us as we walk through the second door of contemplation. The path of contemplation does not ask us to be stupid, naive, or ignorant. What we discover as we walk that path are the limits to our intelligence, the inability of the ways in which we understand the world to deal with everything we experience. Often our inattentiveness, manifested in the things we overlook, comes because we do not know what to do with what we would see or discover. And if we cannot make sense of the world, how can we deal with it? Yet we are not called to make sense of the world. The only one who can make sense of the world is God, and we are not God.

The myths we use to function in the world are *broken* myths. They cannot cover everything. Our legal system is biased towards the rich; our educational system towards the average; our medical system towards efficiency; our religious systems towards the establishment. But there are many who do not benefit from these systems: the ignored, the abandoned, the alienated, the outcasts, the marginalized.

Fear keeps us in an unhealthy relationship with creation. Fear makes us seek security and, in security, we grasp at creation, at this constructed world of ours, as if it could provide the security we need.

The present world we live in does not have much use for God as a living reality. It finds the dead God who can be used to justify dead systems more manageable. And that is why the path of contemplation is so difficult—because to walk that path one has to come to the edge of the myths which give our lives meaning and look down into the nothingness which surrounds them. It is only in contemplation, when we spend time in this nothingness, that that nothingness is really the mystery we call God.

But to name that nothingness, that mystery, as God, really does not help us at this particular point of our journey. It is to substitute one sound for another, for it is rather like telling a person learning the alphabet about semantics, or a person who knows addition and subtraction about probability-chaos theories, or a child who is hurt about love. It is just a word, a sound, another theory. The last thing the soul questing for God wants is another theory. What it wants is the experience of God, and that experience of God can only be found by living with God, living—spiritually—out of nothingness rather than out of myths, institutions, worldviews, conventional social norms.

To live in that radical insecurity is painful because one not only loses a way, one loses even the name of the way, one loses all sense of direction. It is to be in the dark, lost. It is as if one waking up from a dream discovers that one is in a foreign country on a street corner stark naked without money and not understanding the language. What is one to do? It is a time of enormous discouragement and depression, but what happens in that long time of pain is that one's vision and one's heart become purified. At this time the temptation to return to inadequate myths—like a dog to its vomit—is very strong. If one returns again and again, one discovers that they do not satisfy. One is restless in them, rather like wearing tight clothes, even though they might be fashionable. Finally one just has to take them off, go out into the darkness, and complain bitterly to God that he is not there. It is not that God is not there; he is there. The complaining comes from our perspective which does not let us see him. It is not as if he could appear otherwise, because for him to do that, for him to appear in ways we can understand at this stage, is for him to appear as sin.

We can only wait in that darkness until our perspective changes, until our attitudes change, until we come to the *lived* awareness of how conditional our existence is. We discover that we can take nothing for granted, neither our lives nor the things we hold most dear: our friends, our health, our vocation, our sanity even. Even our understanding of how the love of God should manifest itself changes, for if we hold love to be the affirmation of our selfishness—there to be warm and affirming, peaceful, non-judgmental, happy and simple—what we discover is that this presence of God is cruel and painful; it teases us with a desire that it never satisfies. In our quest to satisfy that desire, we are stripped to basic desires, past even our dependency upon our sexuality to define ourselves. As we are stripped we are stripped to the rawness of our sexuality, stripped past shame, and however we entertain those temptations, fall into them or not, we discover that even they do not satisfy the hunger we have.

We have a hunger for what we do not know. That hunger not only takes away the myths by which we know; it also takes away even the desire for knowledge, for knowledge is now seen to be ineffectual against our need. At this stage even the wisdom of the wise does not help.

As can be expected, it is also a time of vocation crisis, for with the terrible clarity of the hunger, and its lack of compassion, we can at this stage see the falseness, the inadequacies, the errors, and the compromises of the communities to which we have committed our lives. We wonder if this is our path, but at this stage we have no other path to go down. One has to tell people at this stage: No reason to stay is no reason to go. The desire for flight is enormous. Anything, even the sense of movement, to give one the satisfaction of at least attempting to satisfy that hunger, invites, only to frustrate, that intolerable urge.

Nothing helps. We just have to stay there in prayer. In this stage on the path of contemplation, nothing seems to be happening. We cannot spend time in prayer the way we can spend an hour knitting or reading or watching TV or gardening. We become conscious of time in prayer. Contemplation becomes an intensification of time; time seems to stretch on and on filled with temptations and distractions, but with no ease or satisfaction.

This particular stage of contemplation spills over into our daily life and, actually, is a sign of the weaving together of our life which has been previously fragmented and compartmentalized by fear. At this stage our call is to fidelity, to be faithful to that hunger, that purifying process. It is the opposite to clarity where the self sees and understands reality in terms of myths, institutions, and conventions, where we can get an answer for almost anything. The opposite of that clarity is faith in which we say yes to the unknown. When we step out of a particular fear and are not trapped by it, we tend to see things more clearly. Often we use that clarity to attack those who are trapped in that fear—the way reformed cigarette smokers are the most aggressive antismokers. We move on then from one trap to the next. We learn to move out of that trap through contemplation.

Contemplation moves us from being attentive to things to being lost in wonderment at what is present to us to a deeper wondering, a wondering about ourselves, a wondering about our path. That wonder shows us to be in mystery where answers do not occur on any other level but the mysterious. Our entry now into the mysterious—in the act of contemplation—is through fidelity to our hunger. In that darkness we learn to use our spiritual senses.

The Path of Contemplation–II

*I*n the preface to his novel *The Fratricides*, Nikos Kazantzakis has placed this poem:

God speaks:
He who seeks me, finds me.
He who finds me, knows me.
He who knows me, loves me.
He who loves me, him I love.
He whom I love, I kill.

Passing through Death

The journey towards God in contemplation leads towards death, and so we face death constantly on the path of contemplation. Here one refers not only to physical death, but also to the deaths of the various levels of the self. If in contemplation we discover that we live various deaths, through contemplation we move to resurrections beyond those deaths. When we move to give up fear, we face a form of death, we become outsiders. We no longer participate in the common sense, the myths, of the world we live in which keep us socialized through fear. When we give up clarity, we also die the death of finding the meaning for things. One becomes a sacred fool. Yes, no, maybe, all become equally valid answers to almost any question. Someone asks you: What does so and so mean? You answer: Well, it depends. And it does depend on the perspective you want to take, or not take. When you say "Well, it depends," often you are treated as if you are silly.

As we move through life we are called to face many deaths: the deaths of family and friends, the deaths of apostolates, the deaths even of certain self-representations of church.

At whatever level of self is engaged in the act of contemplation, one goes through those stages of coming to terms with death that Kubler-Ross has written about: denial, bargaining, anger, depression, resignation. Of course, there are stages beyond resignation. Beyond passive acceptance, there is active acceptance, and beyond acceptance there is creativity—or what we would call resurrection.

As one moves from level to level of contemplation, one goes through stages of death to creativity. Each death opens greater and greater areas of freedom and exposes us to subtler and subtler temptations. If, in this description of the path of contemplation, I am concentrating on the temptations and on the pain involved, it is because these things cause greater confusion than the peace and joy and the sense of life which accompany freedom. When directing someone on retreat, one often asks that old question: Well, how is it going? The person answers, "Great, I am feeling peaceful and happy." One asks, "Do you want to talk about it?" The person usually says, "No, not really." The person looks at you with that air of kindness which says: What is there to talk about? This is what I have come on retreat for, isn't it . . . to have experiences of bliss, peace, contentment? Then there is a little silence and the retreatant gets up and says, "Well, see you tomorrow . . . or whenever." After the person leaves, one wonders about that bliss. Where is it coming from? Where is it carrying that person?

St. Ignatius, in his rules for discernment, says that those in consolation should prepare for ensuing desolation (*Sp Ex* §323 and §324). It is a different case for those who come in desolation. They usually want to know how to get out of it. They do not want that experience. They understand it as a clear sign that God is not with them because they understand God in terms of sweetness and light.

The path of contemplation is not to give anyone experiences. If experiences come, they come. We all have experiences. Everything is an experience. The path to contemplation is how to make more and more full the time we find ourselves in God's time. It is how to see God in everything, how to see everything in God, how to see everything as God sees everything.

The path to contemplation is not just to see God more clearly, or how to feel his presence more passionately; it is also to see the world as he sees the world. So when we struggle to move from a perspective of ideology to one of faith, this involves not only changing or correcting or expanding our notions of God; it also involves changing or correcting or expanding our attitudes and our notions of the world. To see the world with the human eyes of faith is to accept, first of all, the limitations of the world. It is not to put false expectations onto the world, even when the world solicits those expectations. If, for instance, we were to read in one of the major newspapers the arts-and-entertainment section every Sunday, we would soon discover dozens of movies and plays touted as "The year's best!" "The Best of the Decade!" "One of the Most Significant of the Century!" even. If we were to go to only a handful of these, only those which have won major awards, we would soon realize how disappointing most of them are. And, oddly enough, the good ones seldom get that kind of attention or award. Or consider the things we buy or do to be happy. Often they cause us more grief than pleasure, except the dubious pleasure of knowing that we are conforming to someone else's myths about what will make us happy.

The world, creation, we ourselves, are not God; and to put on others or ourselves expectations that are godlike is to court disaster, or at least depression, because such expectations are impossible. What we learn on the level of faith, through the pain of purifying our vision, is a new evaluation of ourselves, our communities, our works, and our God.

To be faithful is to have only one God. To be faithful is to allow oneself to be possessed by God and only by God. To be faithful is not to possess God as if he were a divine puppet we could manipulate to show our power or as if he were a teddy bear we could hug every time we want to be comforted. To be possessed by God is to die many deaths; it is to engage in a passion that nothing in the world can stop—neither pleasure nor humiliation, good health nor bad, approval nor disapproval.

If we were to think of Christ on the cross, his hunger and desire to remain faithful to the Father in the face of the unknowingness of death, the mockery, the humiliation, and the sense of abandonment, we would see that what he has done is commit himself radically to the Void. Even the concept "God" is inadequate to comfort him in the face of the Void. He cries, echoing the psalmist, "My God, my God, why have you forsaken me" (Mt 27:46), and gives up his spirit. He lives towards, and past, a death his vocation calls him to, and the one our vocation also calls us to.

In giving up his spirit to what we call here the Void, or Father, is the dissolution of self, the dissolution of those forces or energies which make up our ego by being directed *in*. In living death what constitutes our self is radically directed *out*. Every movement in our lives which effects this change of direction is a death.

Our deaths do not come until we are ready for them along the path of contemplation. As we become what God wants us to become, cocreators of the universe, the deaths we face, learn to accept, and live out of are the deaths we deal with in purgatory. Purgatory is nothing other than the path of contemplation when we are immersed in a love which burns our selfishness away. For those who are interpenetrated by the fires of love and do not recognize it, that is hell. The path of contemplation makes us realize the gift of pain, especially spiritual pain. In this life pain means that we are on the way. For one who believes, pain ends only when everything and everyone are united by being aspects of Christ to the Father. In the meantime we suffer from our own blindness, the blindness of others, and the hate which stems from that blindness, until all are converted, redeemed, and made one with the Father.

In living death what constitutes our self is radically directed out. Every movement in our lives which effects this change of direction is a death.

If we were to ask ourselves why go through this pain, these deaths, a purely selfish answer would be that no one will get to heaven, the fullness of life, until everyone gets to heaven. Heaven, the fullness of life, will always be incomplete if our worst enemy is not there, transformed, filled with the glory and the love of God. And if our worst enemy is not in heaven, we are not there either because a part of us is still possessed by hate rather than love, apathy rather than concern. That hate in ourselves and in our worst enemy is precisely that which is not heaven. Because we are perverse creatures—in fact, Jeremiah says that there is nothing so perverse as the heart of man—we might think: Well, I can give up a little piece of heaven to see some of the people I hate in hell. It serves them right, and I do not mind paying that little price. After all, I am with enough friends and, in a crunch anyway, I can get by with just one friend.

That pearl of little price! When we have just one fragment of hate, in truth we do not have even one friend. Hate is selfish, it wants no friends, and it will work and work on us until we are absolutely alone. The path to contemplation is the way to make friends with ourselves, with others, and with God.

But, like Mary at the Annunciation, we can ask: How is that possible? Fears, on one hand, are easy to recognize, to pray over, to deal with. But how does one deal with clarity—to use it against itself—as a friend? We can ask ourselves: What do I not understand? To make a list of all the things that we do not understand—things that make us angry or fearful or that we dismiss as unimportant: stock-car races, why so and so behaves in such and such a way, why we are not more liked or appreciated, why the winters are so long, why we are happy or unhappy about certain things in ourselves, in others, in God, in the church, in the world—is to bring these things to attention. We bring them to light to wonder about, but we are doing something more important. We are confessing our limitations, our inability to have all the answers. We are acknowledging our ignorance, our weakness, our brokenness, our inability to discern in detail the evolving plan of creation in which we are involved.

To confess is not just to acknowledge; it is to bear witness to. We admit to ourselves that we are not God. Now this can be a very liberating moment, and an exciting one, because we are giving up the pretense of having it all together. What destroys us is not our brokenness; it is the illusions and pretenses we use to hide that brokenness from ourselves and others. What those illusions do is cover our wounds so that they fester and eat into the very bones of our lives, rather than leave them open to the healing love of the Father. To live our brokenness openly is to manifest in our lives the scandal of the Cross—and the scandal of the Father's love. To live out of one's brokenness maintains one's fidelity.

Fidelity, then, is not merely an intellectual assent to dogma. It is not a mere recitation of the creeds and the constitutions of our religious orders. It is a way of bearing ourselves; it is the attitude we take to the myths of the world. The work of the faithful ones is the refusal to live out of those myths and the determination to point out their deceptions. To do this is not to create another myth, but instead it is to live toward the calling that we are: manifestations of the mystery of God's presence in the world.

At this stage along the path, contemplation is the presence of mystery to mystery.

If we can wait faithfully in the darkness, following the path our hunger takes us, what gets transformed in ourselves is the notion of time. We discover a vital life after the deaths we endure. We discover that we can live without answers and so we can live differently in time. Time becomes not the stretch given us to do things, but—every moment of it—an entry into the mystery of God's presence. Time becomes the encounter with wonder. This allows us to put things in perspective: the humble mending of a shirt is as important as organizing a community or running a school or a hospital. Everything, then, allows us a chance to encounter God.

At this stage contemplation is not letting our mind go blank or tuning in to our alpha waves; it is going beyond the borders of our mind. It is not being enticed by the mind to try to enter more fully into the mystery of God through some systematic exposition that creates just another intellectual construct. The mystery of God is the source of the mind, and the heart, and all of their products. By sinking into that mystery which the mystics describe as "void," "nothingness," "darkness," we can for the first time enjoy the mind because if we persevere in fidelity mind becomes tamed again and ordered again. Its products, then, are not to justify itself but to build up the kingdom of God.

Living Death Decisively

If we can enter into our deaths and stay with the agony—however it may manifest itself to us as pain, boredom, exhaustion, or something else—in time we discover life in that death. Life has been there all along, for Christ has been there before us, waiting for us as the Father waited for him. If we can live through our deaths in patience and humility, we discover a new face of Christ and a new face of the Father.

Yet it is one thing to be aware of the ultimate context within which the insights into life are to be had and quite another to have to make concrete and appropriate decisions based on our awareness of that context. We all know that our values are to be eschatological, but how to live eschatologically in our daily life is quite a different matter.

The temptations against which a person on this stage of the

path has to contend with are either to dismiss any decision as insignificant when faced with the void or to regard any decision as so crucial that one is faced with scruples. Both are blocks on the path to transcendence because both deny the Incarnation, the fact that God does speak in the world so that it is possible to do his will in time. The last four words are important. Because he has chosen time to manifest himself in time, time is important, and because his word is incarnated in time it is *his* time. And though his word may be misunderstood, abused, or manipulated by his creatures, yet God's speech is time.

The question of discernment is the question of using time properly, and one can use time properly only if one understands time properly. Time presents the invitation to transcendence. It is the word of God calling, inviting, disposing, leading us. To ignore time is to ignore God's invitation, and so is to ignore God. Therefore one cannot do nothing; one cannot be apathetic or other-worldly and live a spiritual life. On the other hand, one cannot live a spiritual life and work out of one's fears or ideologies or selfishness. The question is, of course, what is to be done, what do we have to do now?

We need to ask this question because the path to contemplation leads to action. In fact, contemplation comes to its fruit in action. The contemplative is active in the world as God is active in the world, and so contemplation is neither quietism nor being worldly. The temptation that comes at this stage of the path emerges from trying to decide what is the right thing to do.

It would be easy to say, "Everything." Everything and anything done in freedom is the right thing to do, and that is true. But often one is not free. One is—or should be—aware of just how much a sinner one is; and that awareness of just how much one's compulsions, known and unknown, enter into what one does makes the contemplative who does want to do the work of God hesitate. What is to be done? What is the right thing to do?

There is, at this stage, a clear need for what St. Ignatius calls the discernment of spirits because in dying one is tugged by many different forces. The underlying pull is often between pride and humility, between maintaining one's illusory ego at the present or more pleasant levels of existence and entering the void and becoming an integral part of the creativity of God in time. What causes the tension is the growing awareness of the void opening within oneself. It is only when one accepts the void within oneself and within the lived spaces of one's life that one can move to that further level of intimacy with God. What is of concern here is the difficulties encountered in living the void in a concrete manner. The forces of the ego, of *self*-preservation, engage in a life-and-death struggle not to accept the reality of the self as void because it sees it literally as death.

Prayer opens us up to death. We learn to face death in prayer and to face that sense of being totally dependent upon life beyond our control. At this stage, in effect, we live that prayer in our lives, and it is here we discover the meaning of the beatitudes for us: what it means to be poor in spirit, to be meek, to mourn, to hunger, to thirst for justice, to be, in spite of the burdens we bear, merciful, clean of heart, peacemakers, and to suffer, truly, persecution for the sake of heaven. To live the beatitudes is to acknowledge death. Yet it is not to seek death, which would be an instance of pride since martyrs are made not by human will but through God's dispensation. We do not have to seek death. What contemplation does is uncover the death, and the resurrection, we already are.

Prayer opens us up to death. We learn to face death in prayer and to face that sense of being totally dependent upon life beyond our control.

If we want to discern, we need to do it out of death, out of our awareness of the void that is at the center of us. If we can live consciously with the void that centers us—for it never goes away—we discover that through it we are connected to the Father because it is the spirit of the Incarnation given to us. Christ on the cross opens to the void and discovers in his humanity the redemptive love of the Father.

Often when we consider these things we become scared, or skeptical. We think that we have neither the courage nor the special skills to walk the path of contemplation. In truth, each of us is called to walk that path, and in walking it we discover that we have whatever is necessary to walk it. This is how contemplation changes our self-image and thus opens our imaginations to greater dimensions of wonder and our lives to greater freedom and love.

Contemplation allows us to live our lives spiritually. Whatever happens to us, we live our lives. Often in practice we tend to live our lives as professionals, as teachers, administrators, whatever. We tend to invest this professional status with the emotional expectations appropriate to the spiritual life, and on that professional level things do not make spiritual sense and we become frustrated. It is as though, in spite of our calling, we were trying the most secular forms of satisfaction first and trying to apply those forms of satisfaction even to our understanding of our religious life. Think of the guilt we sometimes feel when we remember we are told to love our neighbor, a member of our community, and we know emotionally just how much we cordially hate that person. To live one's life merely at the emotional or professional level is to trap oneself in a diminished self-image. We are saved not by how we feel or by what roles we assume in the marketplace, but only by the Father's love for us. It is rather frightening to come to understand how helpless we are to save ourselves. Contemplation, in opening us up to the void, gives us the humility to live our lives spiritually. Within that humility we discover the passion, the courage, and the humor to make decisions and live our lives in accordance with God's will.

Humility overcomes scruples and apathy. For the person with scruples, God's will is completely caught up in a dead tradition. It is as though God's plan for creation were a predeterminded blueprint that one must discover and apply with rigid fidelity. If one holds this, then one holds that the Father predetermined his Son's death, and what we worship then is a selfish God enmeshed in an abstract justice. This is the God of institutions. If we worship such a God, that act denies both God's freedom and our own, keeps us spiritually undeveloped, stops us from making adult decisions, and thus stops us from being responsible. To be scrupulous is to deny one's responsibility, and to be responsible is to respond to God's invitation to be free. Our institutions, our constitutions, our vows, our relationships with superiors are valid only if they bring us, and themselves, to freedom.

The decisions we make on the path we are walking are of value only if they bring us and the people and the occupations we work with to freedom. It is an illusion to think only of personal freedom, for freedom involves everyone, not just ourselves; and so when we make decisions that claim to be responsible, we need to make them with a concrete context in mind and indeed with every factor and person making up that context. The decisions must bring all in that context to freedom.

Freedom is a very frightening thing, for it calls us to be supportive to what is reasonable and to withdraw our support from what is not. No one within himself or herself has that kind of energy, and often we sacrifice the freedom we are called to for security. Our energy to make and endure responsible decisions comes from the passion we discover within ourselves when we move to an intimacy with the Father. When we open ourselves to the hunger to be one with the Father, we are carried and sustained by that hunger. When that hunger we have meets the hunger the Father has for us, we enter into a context of love which is the presence of the Holy Spirit. We share then in the spirit of holiness.

When one loves somebody, one knows what that person is thinking and feeling because one thinks and feels just as that person does. The same heart is shared, the same approach to life. When people are in love, there is an incredible simplicity between them, an incredible openness to each other, an incredible playfulness and ease. When you are in love with someone, whatever that person does is all right, and whatever you do is all right for that other person. When St. Augustine tells us, "Love and do what you will," he is speaking about this level of responsiveness which is available to us all as we open ourselves up to the void.

That is why—when you discover that the void in yourself is the door through which God enters your life; when, instead of hiding from that void or hiding that void from yourself, you learn to accept it, live with it, cherish it, seek it out in all the areas of life—you start becoming more and more intimate with God, and then it does not matter what you do or what God does. Then the decisions and the doing are not important. What is important is being with God. It is rather like going on a holiday with a friend. It really does not matter what you do; you can do everything or nothing. What is important is the time you spend together. Contemplation, here, is shared time. One's time is God's time, and no other time is as interesting, as nourishing, or as alive as that time.

To be contemplative, to be alive in the void, is to extend the range of one's emotions and the depth of one's emotions because every aspect of one's life is touched by God. Nothing is withered up and nothing repressed. You may say, "But surely in the contemplative life one's sexuality is repressed." It is not. One's prayer becomes so emotional as to satisfy in a most delicate and strong way the generative instinct each of us has, and we discover that our sexuality is a part of everything else that we are. It is not cut off and put in the freezer. In that sexuality which moves towards integration, we discover the sense of joy, of belonging, of sharing all we are. Similarly, despite what people might say about poverty, we discover that we have sufficient, in fact more than enough, for our needs. In the state of contemplative love, we discover that obedience never becomes elaborate power plays or passive-aggressive games. We discover that it is no big deal to do this or that. We discover that God can be found here or there or anywhere.

This enthusiasm for the void is not naiveté or idealism, nor is it unrealistic about what sharing God's time with him, or God's sharing our time with us, can do. Contemplation does transform, and that transformation becomes the beginning of ever deeper, more all-encompassing transformations. The path to contemplation never ends, one never gets bored. There is in contemplation no dead end, no final death, and one discovers that what looks like death from the outside, when approached and reached out to, is really a door to fuller life. When St. Francis embraces the leprous old woman in rags—this is the way he describes Lady Poverty—she becomes beautiful.

The temptation we have to see through in discernment is to stop before death. If we stop before we go through the doors of death, we end up not glorifying the power of God through the resurrection, but fostering inadequate notions of ourselves hemmed in by fear, and so we do not give the Father the freedom to be in the world. Difficult times are not difficult if God is with us, and God is with us in every stage and in every aspect of our lives. Our difficulty is that our fears stop us from recognizing his presence, and so we often mistake something else for him.

In contemplation we do not choose death, we choose the Father. There is a subtle spiritual pride that invites us to choose death at times, to say yes to the things we know can destroy us and most likely will. We want the world and God to see what good religious we are. Or sometimes our reasons are much more blatant. We figure we need a change or that we should be more up the corporate religious ladder than we are, and so we say yes to a job or we ambition it. Of course, superiors and administrators are usually quite glad, and even relieved, that we accept to do this or that thing. So we walk into death and soon become mauled, disillusioned, burnt out, cynical. The glamour, the acknowledgment we sought in order to satisfy ourselves cannot support us, and we cannot support ourselves. We get destroyed or addicted.

What went wrong? What went wrong is that our eyes were fixed on the job rather than on the Father, and so we set off on a path that little by little carried us to our deaths and our deaths only. I am not suggesting that we should not take difficult jobs, but I am suggesting that we should take those jobs only when they involve oneness with the Father. This, of course, should be true not only for difficult jobs but even for any job, even flossing our teeth.

There is in contemplation no dead end, no final death, and one discovers that what looks like death from the outside, when approached and reached out to, is really a door to fuller life.

People often ask: How is one one with the Father? When they are asked what *they* think about it, they usually describe being one with the Father in terms of high mysticism, raptures, ecstasies, visions, transports, voices, miracles, healings. What they want is rather like Harlequin romances for religious, as if God were a drug that induced a high. Often those people have to be asked: What is it like being with a best friend? Then they tell a different story of ease and laughter, simple sharing, being relaxed with, puttering around. It is the same with God. In fact, that is God *there.* I am not denying raptures, visions, and ecstasies. But those things are enormously humbling—for we are given those things at times because we are so autistic, so fearful, so dreadfully lost and confused that we have need of being shown that we are loved; and even then it takes ages before we can find out what they really signify, if we ever really do. Love actually is the most dreadfully ordinary of things, and because it can do everything the most dreadfully extraordinary (1 Co 13).

At this stage of contemplation, when we move into the commonplace, the practical, and the actual, we move into the world to transform it, not to make it more psychedelic with heightened awareness. We move into the world to make it more peaceful, more relaxed, more simple, more joyful, more of a home. On the level of discernment, contemplation moves to make the world a home so that all can discover the true God in his true time. If it all seems ordinary, it is because we learn in contemplation to use time as God uses time, not to bring it to an end, for God's time is a "world without end," but to make it richer and more available for all.

Contemplation and Creativity

Contemplation comes to its fruit in action. In contemplation we start off looking for God, then we continue by looking at God, and we end up looking with the eyes of God. We look as God looks. And what does God look at? God looks at the world, and he shows us how to look at the world. But as God contemplates the world, he is not distant from it. He spends his time in the world. He does this as love. As God lives in this world lovingly, so too as we become more and more contemplative we too live in this world lovingly. We live lovingly in this world by making it more human, a home, the place where community is nourished. Anything that builds up community builds up the kingdom of God: washing dishes, putting an obnoxious person in his or her place, not hogging the only car in the house. The ordinary and extraordinary things that make life flow rather than remain stagnant build up community.

Community starts with the people we live with. It does not start with the people we share an address with because community is more than just an institution. Community is the one we share our values with, the ones with whom we share what is valuable to us. If we ask ourselves who has the same values that we have, the same insights, the same sense of joy, the same vision, the same pain; if we ask who are those with whom we "resonate" and if we truly seek an answer, that answer might surprise us. My answer includes a fourteenth-century Zen monk, a Hassidic mystic called Zusia who has this marvelous insight that suffering is the clothes of grace, a friend of mine from novitiate days who is now a lawyer in Nova Scotia with three children and a fox farm, and my drinking buddies from graduate-school days, among others. Community extends through time and through space—sometimes in simple ways as in the community of saints, sometimes in more complex ways as we discover the presence of dead friends and relatives in the way we speak or move or deal with situations. What happens in contemplation as we become more peaceful ourselves is that we become a home in which many, living and dead, can become present to this world *here*. In this context the "many rooms" of the heavenly mansion Jesus promises makes sense.

Contemplation leads to an awareness of community beyond a timetable. Community is the awareness of love-as-time, for we become aware of the strands of our lives interwoven with the strands of others' lives. When we contemplate what rises from the depths, what comes to us from the void is the presence of other lives in our present life. As in true community they support, give direction and comfort. They share time with us—like the breaking of bread together, the sharing of a meal with each other. That is why the Eucharist is so important. In it all the acts of contemplation are made actively present.

In the Eucharist God is made present, life is shared, a bonding with others occurs, sins are forgiven, the gifts of the Spirit are shared, and there is created in our time an open space for the world to enter and become humanized. In contemplation the same things occur. This is the last stage of contemplation—before we move again to deeper levels of fear, deeper openings to wonder, and the whole process begins again, spiraling out until everything and everyone is involved and all past, present, and future are aflame with God's love. I believe this, and I believe that no one will be himself or herself until this happens. The path of contemplation opens us out to all of creation and reality and opens all of creation and reality to God. That opening out and the interweaving of our lives create community that allows us to be more alive and to risk more.

It is a tremendous gift to be on the right path and a bigger gift to be aware that one is on the right path, but it is *awesome* to encounter others on the same path, and then more and more. It does not matter what sex or age they are, what job they do, or where they are from. There is a living bond which makes much possible.

The path to contemplation ties us, by making us members of a community, into a tradition. A tradition is not something static, nor handed down like Mother's silver with the stern admonition "This is the way things are done," continuing the false myth "This is the only way things can be done." That is not tradition, that is ritual custom. Tradition is alive and ongoing and capable of welcoming disparate elements in its development. Often people trapped by fear try to keep tradition alive by freezing it to make it secure. Yet if we truly walk the path of contemplation, we belong to a tradition which carries on the saving work of Christ who was raised to life, a tradition that the prophets carried on before him and that the saints, mystics, martyrs, and holy men and women continue on after him until the fullness of the Second Coming.

All of these share one thing in common. They are creative. The path to contemplation leads to creativity, the highest form of action. To be creative—and this is different from exercising power—extends over all activities: cooking and sewing, being a nurse or teacher or administrator, giving or receiving spiritual direction. It is only secondarily to be innovative, for the root of creativity is not originality—which is a Romantic reinterpretation of that activity. To understand creativity we need to look at the original creator, God as Father and as Mother. To be creative is to give life, to allow life to be lived most fully.

When contemplation moves us to creativity, we ask ourselves how. When we forgive ourselves and when we forgive others, we give ourselves and others the time, the space, the encouragement to be healed and to live openly without guilt. When we do that, we bring people back to life; we raise them from the dead to a new life. Often when we say we are sorry we just mean: Can we be civil to each other again, without too much tension? But to reduce forgiveness to a social convention does not give life because the space then opened is just a social space. To forgive we have to open a spiritual space, and to do that we have to hold the pain we ourselves have and the pain the other person, the institution, or the culture gives us *together* with the pain that causes the other person, institution, community, or culture to hurt us. We cannot do it alone, and so we need the support of the community we find as we walk the path of contemplation. What we create we create out of brokenness, alienation, disease. We create, as T.S. Eliot puts it, "with shabby equipment always breaking down." What a good artist or musician does is create openings, spaces through which we can see life, live it, enjoy it, and share it. When we move in contemplation, we move to the same activity in the world.

To be creative is to move beyond the clichés of religious life. It is always interesting to observe the ways in which different religious communities live in a postmodern culture with the same problems of overwork, lack of vocations, financial difficulties, and aging members. Some of these communities are life-giving, others are deadly. What causes the difference? In the ones which are alive, there is a self-sacrificing love which is echoed in 2

Corinthians 6:4-10. The communities with life are not afraid to talk about their spiritual life and the pains of their lives. They share the pains and the joys of their lives. They celebrate what they have and they celebrate who they are.

One of the biggest blocks on the path of contemplation is the lack of celebration, a fear to celebrate joy, to enjoy parties, to go out to dinner, to entertain, to spend relaxed and relaxing time with those others whose path we cross. There is a peculiar repression in religious life that rejects anything fun or enjoyable. The rationale varies: it is against poverty, religious do not behave this way, we do not have the time, I'm too tired. There is a very strong and perverse myth that insists that the proper witness to God's love excludes fun. When did you last hear someone laugh in a church service? Why is it considered inappropriate? That creeping fear spreads itself across relationships and denies them for the sake of "a witness to chastity" even though we are emotional and sexual and social human beings. That same fear suggests "in the name of obedience" that we do not take responsibility for our lives and for maintaining life in our communities because that is the superior's job. This fear under the guise of poverty encourages parsimony. This false myth makes us walking dead, zombies for Christ.

To forgive we have to open a spiritual space, and to do that we have to hold the pain we ourselves have and the pain the other person, the institution, or the culture gives us together with the pain that causes the other person, institution, community, or culture to hurt us.

What is lost is humor, a delight in our absurdity and in the absurdity of the world. Everything becomes heavy and serious. The freedom we attain in contemplation allows us to delight in our lives in the way God as Father and Mother delights in our lives, the way that a parent delights when a child is enjoying itself. This delight in life allows our existence in time to be play, and contemplation becomes play—for play is the highest form of creativity.

It is always interesting to ask the question in spiritual direction: Do you ever play with God? It is also interesting to ask: Whom do you play with? Do you ever play? When is the last time you played? Serious people do not play, and we do not play with serious people; we also do not play with silly people. We can only truly play with people with a sense of humor. How can we ever enjoy God, delight in the mystery God seduces us with, risk ourselves in him, or even understand him as the one we can play with, if we are always serious?

Such seriousness damages us, others, and everything we do. It builds up such resentment that it distorts us so that we cannot function normally. There is a story about a spiritual director a few years ago who on an eight-day retreat met a sister who was so angry she had to do a retreat that she said she hated the director, hated her superiors, hated God, and even hated herself for being there. Now this director, who was slightly crazy himself took one look at her, got up from his chair, went over to his wallet, pulled out some money, and gave it to her saying, "Sister, for at least once in your life try to have a pleasant day." The story goes that the sister took the money, went downtown, bought ice-cream cones, went shopping, had a nice little lunch, went off to a show, came back, and had, apparently, a good retreat after that. In fact, the story comes from her. What did she discover with her day? Quite simply that God likes fun too. The God she started to discover that day is one who does not hurt and who does not delight in anyone's suffering, but is rather the one who heals our hurts and whose salvific work is best witnessed to by our laughter.

Laughter cannot be forced; joy breaks down barriers; play occurs when people re-create, without competition, envy, jealousy, or anger. When we trust God we can trust ourselves in God, and when we can trust ourselves with God we can relax, we can recreate, and then we can *recreate* into something joyful what has been broken and damaged, what has been dead.

Contemplation makes us witnesses to the true face of God because as we delight in him we learn to delight in our lives. Our life then, and because of contemplation, does not become a grind, a task, or a distraction from boredom; it becomes an adventure, a holiday—even though at times it may be difficult or riddled with anxiety.

In that joy, and because we can trust, we explore further and further what it means to be alive. We go down deeper and we expand. As we do this we uncover new hurts that have to be healed, new forms of repression that have to be dismantled, new invitations to power that have to be refused, and newer and newer ways of being creative and thereby making this world, our culture, our institutions, and our communities more alive. As they say in the sequel to *Star Trek*, the journey continues.

It is a journey into joy, for in it and through it the dead rise and share its life. As the Easter Preface has it, "The joy of the resurrection renews the whole world."

Conclusion

Walking the path of contemplation makes us see reality with spiritual eyes. Contemplation does not give us two worlds, the practical world in which we wash our underwear and dislike broccoli and a spiritual world to which we withdraw to escape. Contemplation makes the washing of underwear a spiritual act. It opens levels of awareness on the level of the commonplace. We have only one world, and it is in this world that God spends time with us. Insofar as we share the passion Christ has for the Father and the passion the Father has for the world and insofar as we share their Spirit, the places we live in will be touched by the healing and transforming presence of God.

Through contemplation we become the living words of God in our world, and we are sent by that vocation to become the continuing presence of Christ not only in our apostolate and in the places we live but in everything we do. If we *have* to *tell* people about God, let us tell them about what he has done for us, about what we have personally experienced: the transformation of our fears, the freedom from the prisons of false myths, the passion of our hunger and where it has led us. That is, if we have to speak to people about God. But let people, the ones we encounter, know about God through the lives we lead: by our willingness to bear the pain of forgiving, by our joy in the humblest of tasks, by our laughter even in the darkest moments.

What we have been given is not given only for us. It is given to be shared. Only in that sharing do we experience what it means to be church, and if we are truly church then we can transform the institutions we now have and thereby create those open spaces—those temples and sanctuaries—in which God, who promises to be ever with us, can dwell and in which others who are now lost and alienated and searching can dwell and fulfill themselves creatively.

The path to contemplation never ends. Christ himself is in agony until the world is brought back to the Father. The saints and the martyrs in their contemplative states share our joys and struggles on earth just as we share, through contemplation, their joys and passion in heaven. We, those whom God shares his time with, as we go farther and farther on that path to contemplation, will find ourselves called to hold different fears up to his love, allow more and more of the constrictive scaffoldings we have relied on to drop away, enter into deeper and deeper deaths, become more and more simple, and discover ways beyond present telling of being creative in the situations in which we will find ourselves.

The path of contemplation does not only lead to life. The path to contemplation is life. Let us celebrate life.

Jesus, The Human Face of God

To have seen me is to have seen the Father (Jn 14:9). With this startling claim, the Jesus of John's gospel challenges us to a faith-experience which answered the longing of devout persons throughout human history—the contemplative longing to see the face of God. Moses begged for a glimpse of God's glory and was told he could not see God's face and live (Ex 33:10-23). The psalmists also express this yearning with their desire to be in God's presence in the temple:

> My soul thirsts for you. . . . When shall I come and behold the face of God? (Ps 42:2).
> I long to gaze on you in the sanctuary (Ps 63:2).

For Saint Paul, as for the evangelist John, Jesus is now the temple where the face of God can be experienced:

> For it is the God who said, "Let light shine out of darkness," who has shone in our hearts to give the light of the knowledge of the glory of God in the face of Christ (2 Co 4:6).

More than any human hunger to see God, however, the Judeo-Christian tradition presents a God who longs to reveal the divine presence and personality to humans. Our God desires to be known by us much more than we desire to know God:

> The ox knows its owner and the ass its master's crib, Israel knows nothing; my people understand nothing (Is 1:3).
> I will give them a heart to know that I am the Lord, and they shall be my people, and I will be their God (Jr 24:7).

This divine desire to communicate personally with humanity finds its fulfillment in the Incarnation. The Word becomes flesh—is spoken in our vernacular, for our understanding of who and how God is. The invisible face becomes visible in the human body of Jesus—a body we are not merely to see, but to become:

> And we all, with unveiled faces beholding the glory of the Lord, are being changed into his likeness from one degree of glory to another (2 Co 3:18).

With this in mind, we need to be aware that, as we contemplate Jesus, we are looking at more than Jesus. Jesus is always the revelation of God, as well as revelation of who we, created in God's image, are to become. The gospels are meant to challenge our faith—to stretch the stays of our tents, our too limited, narrow, and often pagan image and understanding of God and church—so that God can transform our understanding and behavior with the truth. There are many contemporary events in which we can hear echoes of this call for interior stretching:

> This place is too small for me; give me more space to live in (Is 49:20).

In the novel on which last year's popular film, *The Color Purple*, was based, author Alice Walker puts in the mouth of the woman, Shug, as she challenges Celie to change her image of God, what we might hear as a divine reminder that we all have to continually grow in our understanding and imagining of what God is like.

> She say, "Celie, tell the truth, have you ever found God in church? I never did. I just found a bunch of folks hoping for him to show. Any God I ever felt in church I brought in with me. And I think all the other folks did too. They came to church to *share* God not find God."
>
> "Some folks didn't have him to share," I said. "They the ones didn't speak to me while I was there struggling with my big belly and Mr._____ children."
>
> "Right," she say.
>
> Then she say: "Tell me what your God look like, Celie."
>
> "Aw naw," I say. I'm too shame. Nobody ever ast me this before, so I'm sort of took by surprise. Besides, when I think about it, it don't seem quite right. But it all I got. I decided to stick up for him, just to see what Shug say.
>
> "Okay," I say. "He big and old and tall and graybearded and white. He wear white robes and go barefooted. . . ."

Unfortunately, much of Shug's delightful account that follows in the novel about her own growth in discovering God was omitted in the film.

The Second Vatican Council also called us to remember and take part in this growth of understanding in its *Decree on Revelation:*

> This tradition which comes from the apostles developed in the church with the help of the Holy Spirit. For there is a growth in the understanding of the realities and the words which have been handed down. This happens through the contemplation and study made by believers, who treasure these things in their hearts (see Lk 2:19, 51) (*Dei Verbum* 2:8).

Jesus himself suggests this process in John's gospel:

> . . . it is for your own good that I am going because unless I go, the Advocate will not come to you; but if I do go, I will send him to you (16:7).

> I still have many things to say to you but they would be too much for you now. But when the Spirit of Truth comes he will lead you to the complete truth. . . (16:12-13).

> This Advocate, the Holy Spirit, whom the Father will send in my name, will teach you everything and remind you of all I have said to you (14:25-26).

Thus, this developing understanding of the meaning and message of Jesus grows through the contemplation of how each gospel paints a unique portrait, as it were, of the face of Jesus and through him of the face of God. We must, as John the Baptist bids us, "look" at the Lamb of God and respond to Jesus' invitation to "come and see" how he lives by spending some personal time with him in prayer (see Jn 1:35-39). Only then will we gradually come to "know the Father" and experience the eternal life God offers (see Jn 17:3).

Turning to the gospels, it is clear that Jesus challenged and changed the popular and religious images of God prevalent in the culture of his day. This counter-culture stance cost him his life. Jesus' values and lifestyle sharply distinguished his view of authority from that of the pagan state:

> A dispute arose also between them about which should be considered the greatest, but he said to them, "Among pagans it is the kings who lord it over them and those who have authority over them are given the title Benefactor. This must not happen with you. No; the greatest among you must behave as if he were the youngest, the leader, as if he were the one who serves" (Lk 22:24-26).

Consistent with the liberating action of God in Israel's history,

Jesus claims he has come not to control peoples' lives by force or privileged position, but to call them to choose, freely, a life of collaborative service. Involving his disciples in feeding the multitudes (Mk 6:35, 44) and the servants when the water was to be changed into wine (Jn 2:1-11) are but two "signs" of Jesus' desire to involve humanity in the work and mystery of redemption as his collaborators. Jesus did not want slaves for followers; he wanted friends (Jn 15:15). He was willing to risk possible rejection, misunderstanding, and limitation of his work that such involvement would risk, as well as the vulnerability to human interaction and honest communication such intimate relationships would demand. He chose to be *with* people, rather than over people, and in that choice, he reveals much about God's agelong desire and effort to be Emmanuel.

This is the God who preferred "backpacking" with his people rather than abiding in some temple which would have exalted and confined his presence, as Yahweh's response to David shows:

> Are you the man to build me a house to dwell in? I have never stayed in a house from the day I brought the Israelites out of Egypt until today, but have always led a wanderer's life in a tent. In all my journeying with the whole people of Israel, did I say to anyone of the judges of Israel, . . . "Why have you not built me a house of cedar?" (2 Sm 7:5-7).

Jesus was also a counter-culture force against the religious system of pharisaic Judaism with its tendency to make a caricature of the God of revelation. Their legalism had turned salvation into something to be earned by human effort, through the fulfillment of rigidly prescribed external observances. Fidelity to their interpretation and cultic additions to the Law became a measuring rod dividing the "clean" from the "unclean"—with its fearfilled threat of divine judgment.

By contrast, Jesus preached the "good news" of the kingdom: that salvation was *gift* from a gracious God who showered his grace down freely like rain on the just and unjust, and who, like a patient farmer, let wheat and weeds grow up together, knowing his good planting would survive the struggle and in time be harvested home to his barn (see Mt 5:45 and 13:24-30).

Jesus called this good and gracious God, *Abba*, his familiar and intimate name for the Father he saw as life-giver. Jesus showed the face of this God in his nonjudgmental association with the poor, the outcasts, and the marginal, whose company he preferred to the self-righteous. He showed the face of this God in his compassion for the sinners who humbly depended on God's goodness for salvation, not proudly claiming their own. In his actions, as well as his teachings, Jesus revealed that the God who consistently chose to be *with* his people preferred collaboration over domination, liberty over legalism, equality over discrimination and a relationship motivated by friendship rather than fear. Those who clung to their man-made image of God were unable and unwilling to accept this revelation of God from Jesus:

> Besides, the Father who sent me bears witness to me himself. You have never heard his voice, you have never seen his shape, and his word finds no home in you because you do not believe in the one he has sent. You study the Scriptures, believing that in them you have eternal life; now these same Scriptures testify to me, and yet you refuse to come to me for life! (Jn 5:37-39).

Each year in the Lenten season, it is especially appropriate to contemplate the face of the suffering Jesus. It is in his passion and resurrection that Jesus reveals the depth of the saving love of God. Contemporary theologians give meaningful expression to the growing understanding of the mystery of Jesus that is developing in the church of our time. Books such as Monica Hellwig's *Jesus, the Compassion of God: New Perspectives on the Tradition of Christianity* (Michael Glazier Publishers, 1983) and Walter Kasper's *The God of Jesus Christ* (Crossroad, 1984) are among the many which show a shift in attitude regarding God's role in the suffering and death of Jesus.

This developing understanding of the meaning and message of Jesus grows through the contemplation of how each gospel paints a unique portrait, of the face of Jesus and through him of the face of God.

Many Christians have been formed to believe in a God who willed or caused the death of Jesus, by putting the price tag of the cross on humanity's redemption. This mis-formed faith is often the result of a misinterpretation of the Scriptures, especially the words of Jesus during his anguish in the garden of Gethsemane:

> Abba, Father, everything is possible for you. Take this cup
> away from me. But let it be as you, not I, would have it (Mk
> 14:36).

In what sense is everything possible for God? In what way
did God will this cup for Jesus?

It is very clear from the gospels' account that Jesus died
because of the malicious will of human beings, not that of God.
Human sinfulness—greed, dishonesty, cowardice, and the sacrifice
of the innocent to protect the position of those in power—put
Jesus on the cross. Jesus arrived at the cross because he was faithful to himself and to the mission as servant-Messiah he believed
was God's will for him. John's gospel describes this will of God
very well:

> God so loved the world that he gave his only Son so that
> everyone who believes in him may not be lost but may have
> eternal life (3:16).

The will of God is always to give life, not death.

Whereas Jesus arrived at the cross because he was faithful,
he remained there because God was faithful. God had given Jesus
to humanity; God didn't take back that gift by removing Jesus
from humanity's choice of the cross. God would have had to
manipulate human freedom to do so. Unlike the pagan gods, that
isn't the style of this *Abba*. The "everything" possible to this God
didn't include that option. Or rather, this God wouldn't have chosen that option. So this faithful, life-giving God didn't save Jesus
from dying; God saved him from death. God's ultimate gift to
Jesus and to humanity is the life-giving act of resurrection.

What do we *see* of God as we look at the face of the suffering
Jesus? We see a God willing to endure the death of the one most
beloved to him; we see a God willing to suffer death to give us life.
The words of the Gospel describe well the extent of this love:

> There is no greater love than to lay down one's life for one's
> friends (Jn 15:13).

God's great desire to befriend humanity finds its ultimate
expression here on Calvary:

> To have seen me is to have seen the Father (Jn 14:9).

As with his great prophets through the centuries—Moses,
Isaiah, Jeremiah—God is faithful to his promise to be *with* his
servant in the sufferings fidelity to his mission will inevitably

bring. God is with Jesus on the cross. The human experience of Jesus' faith and love also find ultimate expression here. He trusted God would save him, not knowing how.

Father, into your hands I commit my spirit (Lk 23:46).

All the Scripture texts put into the mouth (and thereby the mind and heart) of Jesus during the passion by the evangelists, when read in their full context (Ps 22, 31, 110; Is 53) are expressions of hope and trust in God's victory, not despair of God's help.

To see this God, who is faithful to Jesus, not by manipulating the human reality of the cross by removing it, but by saving him from its power to ultimately destroy him, is to see a God who will also be *with* us in all the daily dyings in our lives.

Each year as we celebrate the Paschal Mystery in the seasons of Lent and Eastertide, we are reminded that in baptism we have passed through death to risen life with Jesus. We are called to profess our faith once again in the mystery of the redemptive love of a God who loves us too much to lose us, and whose "yes" to life always transcends and transforms our "no." Good Friday is not the last word; Easter is.

We are called to live this faith by putting into practice the counter-cultural values and message of Jesus of honest and loving, collaborative concern for the good and freedom of all peoples. This will involve the ongoing struggle against hypocrisy, oppression, and social injustice wherever these occur. By doing so we continue the prophetic work of Jesus to witness to the life-giving will of God for humanity. Now it is in his risen body, in the mystery of the church, that Jesus continues to reveal the human face of God. The victorian poet, Gerard Manley Hopkins SJ, describes this mystery well:

. . . for Christ plays in ten thousand places,
lovely in limbs, and lovely in eyes not his,
To the Father through the features of men's faces.

An Ignatian Contemplation
on the Baptism of Our Lord

*B*aptism has once again become an integral part of the Christian experience. Instead of simply an individual event between God and the baptized, the sacrament once more celebrates a person's entrance into the community of believers. Moreover, with the renewal and expansion of the understanding of ministry, it is baptism that now offers the foundation for the call to mission and service for every member of the People of God.

Even with all these rich theological and liturgical developments, I have still found it difficult to make any vital connection between them and my own baptism. In part, I simply have no sentiments or recollections to explore or deepen. Like many other pre-Conciliar born, I was rushed to the local parish on the Sunday following my birth to save me from a sudden case of limbo. Nor does my mother have any spiritual remembrances of my baptism to share with me, since on that day she was still in the hospital recuperating from my worldly entrance. Thus until very recently the experiential and spiritual sense of my own baptism remained in a limbo of its own.

The meaning and power of my own baptism finally came alive, however, as I shared Jesus' experience of his own baptism during several periods of prayer on my recent thirty-day retreat. The thrust of contemporary spirituality reminds us to pay close attention to our human experience—whether in prayer, in ministry, or in the rest of life—and to ask what the Lord might be saying or how he might be inviting. Often these moments become actual revelations of God's living Word for us—either individually or collectively. Through these experiences we realize the Gospel no longer as a onetime event in the past but as always happening— and now most immediately to us.

From this perspective of the ongoing Gospel I share the fruits of a very transforming experience of the baptism of our Lord. Though admittedly the very personal encounter of one individual, maybe my experience will contribute to our collective efforts to reclaim the experiential and spiritual roots of our baptismal call to community and ministry with God's people.

I entitled this article "An Ignatian Contemplation . . ." to highlight a very definite approach to praying the Scriptures. Instead of methodically plodding through the Gospel, I contemplated, that is, I watched attentively and receptively the scene of our Lord's baptism, letting it touch my mind and heart. I began by reading through the scripture text (Mt 3:13-17) several times, then I put down my Bible, closed my eyes, and let the event come alive before the inner eye of my imagination.

Following Ignatius's instructions in the *Spiritual Exercises* [1, 14], I then took my place in the scene, so that I would be experiencing the baptism as an engaged participant and not as a disinterested spectator. Paying attention to the persons, their words, and their actions, I contemplated the event as if it were happening now for the first time.

On the banks of the Jordan, Jesus steps out from the crowd and presents himself to his cousin John for baptism. His voice filled with emotion, John protests saying, "I should be baptized by you, yet you come to me!" But Jesus responds very straightforwardly. "Let it be for now." Then in a very powerful moment of the contemplation, I hear Jesus go on to explain himself, "I'm no different from the rest of the people gathered here. We're all struggling to gain our human freedom and wholeness. With all the fear and unfreedoms we carry around from growing up plus all the pressures and demands on us today, it's a wonder we're not more wounded than we are."

For Jesus, this very heartfelt experience becomes his baptism into a deep identification and solidarity with the rest of the human family united together in the struggle to become more human and free. Jesus' words to John then cannot be taken as some sort of pious self-effacement. Rather, our brother Jesus is experiencing his baptism as a deep, deep bondedness with the human family gathered at the healing waters of rebirth and wholeness.

As I continue to contemplate the baptism unfolding before

me, I am drawn to even closer physical proximity with Jesus by the magnetism of his human compassion and tenderness. At the same time I begin to feel close again to several friends from whom I have parted company because of certain decisions on their part that hurt me very deeply. Along with this new feeling of closeness comes the realization that despite the pain and darkness that have separated us, there exists a deeper bond of solidarity in the human struggle that binds us together. We are no different from each other or from the rest of the people on the face of the earth.

In one way or another we are each carrying around within us parts of our wounded child and of our stressed adult. The shadow of our fuller human potential and psychic wholeness always seems to lie just beyond our reach. With this realization a lot of the bite to my pain and anger subsides and I hear myself saying very serenely, "In our choices and endeavors, we really do try to give as much as we can at the moment. Sometimes our responses aren't adequate or all that the situation might call for or that we or others might hope for. Because we will always be carrying around our wounded and unfinished selves, we at times end up creating pain and darkness—for others as well as for ourselves—despite our best and freest possible intentions at that moment. I am no different from the rest of mortals. We are all in our own way longing and struggling for our human freedom and wholeness as daughters and sons of the living God." These intense feelings of solidarity with my friends that accompany these reflections free me to let go of a lot more of the pain and misunderstanding in our relationship. And almost immediately these people actually appear on the banks of the Jordan and, ecstatic and teary-eyed, we embrace one another.

By this time Jesus and John are sitting off to the side talking intently to one another. I am savoring the wonderful feelings of reconciliation and the pure joy of this moment when all of a sudden my attention switches. Several close friends for whom I had initially been either teacher, spiritual director, or mentor become present to me. These new feelings of solidarity in the human struggle now bring a different sort of bondedness with them. Any leftover images of being in some way "the expert" or "the helper" or simply the one who is a couple of steps ahead of the others seem to disappear forever. I am just acutely aware of how similar our journeys and struggles have been at such a profound level. A marvelous celebration of deep friendship and belonging to each other takes place as they, too, appear on the banks of the Jordan and I jump up to embrace them.

This first moment of the baptism climaxes as I join hands with my friends who have come to the Jordan. Together with Jesus and John we dance in circles and zigzag chains across the sands. Then we run into the water to splash and frolic like little children and truly we are, because so many of the hurts and wounds of growing up and of adult life are being healed. This wonderful moment comes to a close when with ecstatic reverence we take turns baptizing one another in these life-giving waters of human compassion and solidarity.

Because the baptism has become not only Jesus' but mine as well, I feel myself being drawn into that same solidarity with God. I simply rest in this deep sense of belonging to God.

The second major moment of the baptism begins as Jesus steps out of the water. This time the heavens open and a voice proclaims, "This is My Son, the Beloved, on whom My favor rests." Along with his sense of profound solidarity with the human family, Jesus now experiences most intensely his deep, deep solidarity with God.

Because the baptism has become not only Jesus' but mine as well, I feel myself being drawn into that same solidarity with God. I now hear a voice from the heavens addressed to me, "You, too, are My son, the beloved, on whom My favor rests." Initially, I simply rest in this deep sense of belonging to God.

Though still feeling very much the earthen vessel, chipped and broken in so many ways, I receive nonetheless a strong assurance in the prayer that I will have whatever I need by way of resources for my personal journey and for my ministry. With God's favor there will be enough of hope, courage, and justice, of human and psychic energy, and of whatever else needed for today with more to come tomorrow. The Lord has spoken. . . . Rather than end a prayer that is really only beginning to unfold, I simply thank the Lord from the depths of my spirit for sharing the baptism with me both in contemplation and in life.

This Ignatian contemplation of the baptism of our Lord invites several brief comments. First of all, we realize that the foundations for a renewed understanding of Christian baptism do not come so much from our own sacramental initiation as from sharing the experience of baptism with Jesus. Like the Lord, we are baptized into covenantal solidarity with both our brothers and sisters and with our gracious God.

From this perspective, baptism loses much of its static notion as simply a once-in-a-lifetime event. Especially for adults being baptized or reclaiming their baptismal call, as we did in this contemplation, the celebration of baptism becomes a dynamic initiation into a lifelong process that continues to open up new levels of human and divine solidarity as our Christian existence unfolds day by day.

This sacred bondedness with the human family confronts the blatant barriers and subtle alienation that separate us from each other. Baptism invites us to embrace the human family—both near and far—as "my people" and not just God's people. Our experience is meant to mirror that of Jesus: "I am no different from anybody else." The heart of the matter remains this recognition that we are all struggling with varying degrees of success for our human freedom and wholeness—two of the gateways to encountering the divine in ourselves. Here, too, our experience follows the pattern of Jesus in discovering his own divinity. In facing the forces that would shrink, wound, or destroy these most precious gifts of God to us, we plumb the depths of our human resources and discover the wellsprings of the divine energy in us as well.

Second, this baptism into human solidarity against the enemies of our humanity celebrates our entrance as adults into the Christian community. We now recognize and claim for our own this community both broken and healed yet always struggling for greater wholeness.

Third, this very sacred experience of human solidarity becomes the foundational stance for each Christian's involvement in ministry as part of our baptismal commitment. It is only from a vital sense of bondedness to each other that we can enter into the joys and struggles of one another without pretense or feigned empathy. By the Lord's design we are in this human struggle *together.* Baptism then celebrates our call to be companions to one another and to all our brothers and sisters in the unfolding of the kingdom of God in our time.

Fourth, the divine bondedness solidifies as we hear the voice from heaven address us with the same love and promise offered to

Jesus: "You are My beloved on whom My favor rests." This proclamation then nurtures our heartfelt sense of belonging utterly to God. Moreover, this divine connectedness touches all the dimensions of who we are, so that we begin to look and feel more and more with the eyes and heart of our gracious God on ourselves, others, and our world.

In the face of our human wounds and inadequacies, this sense of divine favor sustains Christian perseverance and empowerment for life and ministry. We can be stretched to the limits of our understanding and of our physical and psychic energies, yet we now know deep down that no matter what comes God's favor will sustain us this day and there will be more of what we need tomorrow. From the Lord we need only ask with Ignatius in the *Suscipe* of the Spiritual Exercises: "Give me only Your love and Your grace; that is enough for me" [234].

For those hungry to deepen their commitment to Christian community and ministry, an Ignatian contemplation of the baptism may be the occasion to nourish those desires as they share this moment with Jesus as though it were happening for the first time. We never know whom or what we might meet on the banks of the Jordan!

Ruminating on the Two Standards

D uring the month of June, 1537, Ignatius of Loyola and
six of his nine friends in the Lord received Holy Orders
in Venice.[1] Instead of celebrating their first Masses immediately,
however, the newly-ordained companions felt a need to give themselves to a period of intense preparation for that event. Partly
from a sense of unworthiness, partly from a desire for a desert
experience after half a year of unremitting work in the hospitals
of Venice, they decided to withdraw into solitude for three
months, devoting themselves to prayer and begging for their daily
needs. During the first forty days, following the example of Jesus,
they would strictly adhere to their solitude, after which they would
also engage in preaching and other apostolic work. With this
intent they went off in groups of two or three to different lonely
places, but remained within the territory of the Republic of Venice
since they were still hoping to sail to the Holy Land. Favre joined
Ignatius and Laynez, now priests like himself, as they settled into
an old, derelict, windowless monastery on the outskirts of Vicenza,
in a place called Vivarolo. In late September all the companions
reassembled in Vicenza and four of them, not including Ignatius,
celebrated their first Mass. Soon they again scattered, this time to
engage in pastoral work in the university cities of Italy. Ignatius,
Favre, and Laynez set out for Rome.

This period spent in northern Italy signaled for Ignatius a
return, or revival, of the consolations and mystical graces which
had been muted during the years of study in Paris. In his
Autobiography we read:

> During the time he was at Vicenza he had many spiritual
> visions and ordinary consolations (quite the contrary of
> what he had experienced in Paris). Especially when he began

to prepare for the priesthood at Venice and when he was preparing to say Mass and in all his journeys he had great supernatural visitations like those he used to have when he was at Manresa.[2]

Vivarolo could be described as a second Manresa. Certainly there was a newness about the experiences of Ignatius in 1537, but there was also a continuity with what had happened on the banks of the River Cardoner fifteen years before. It is this continuity that Hugo Rahner stresses as he writes about Vivarolo:

> It will be no mistake to see the content of the mystical graces in Inigo's soul to consist primarily in the colloquy that he gives in the meditation on the Two Standards. The prayer to our Lady that she obtain for the one praying that he be received under the standard of the poor but divine King, the prayer to Jesus that he obtain this grace from the Father, the prayer to the Father to grant this grace: all this in its unusually deep dogmatical structure suggests clearly its mystical origin in the vision of Manresa.[3]

These reflections, clearly in harmony with the *Autobiography* itself, help one to enter into the mind and heart of Ignatius as he made that fateful journey to Rome. He was still consciously preparing for his first Mass (which he wished to postpone for a year), and so his Romeward movement was in this sense a prolongation of the three months of solitude he had undertaken with his companions. Even more significant, however, was the continuity between his prayer at Vivarolo and his prayer on the journey. This consisted of desires and deep longing to be received under the standard of Christ, to be placed with him, especially now as Ignatius the priest.

And so, at the last stop before Rome, while at prayer in an abandoned chapel, Ignatius received another mystical grace which was for him a definitive answer to his prayer. In the terse language of the *Autobiography* he tells us:

> Divided into three or four groups, the pilgrim with Favre and Laynez, they went to Rome. On this journey he was visited very specially by God. After he became a priest he had decided to spend a year without saying Mass, preparing himself and begging our Lady to deign to place him with her Son. One day, while still a few miles from Rome, he was praying in a church and experienced such a change in his soul and saw so clearly that God the Father had placed him with his Son Christ that his mind could not doubt that God the Father had indeed placed him with his Son.[4]

This personal account of what happened can be elaborated by examining the testimonies of other early Jesuit writers who all regarded the La Storta experience as crucial, not only for Ignatius but for the Society of Jesus. The most authentic of these descriptions is that of Laynez who was with Ignatius at the time, and to whom Ignatius narrated what he had experienced.

> As we were coming along the road from Sienna here to Rome, it happened that our father received many spiritual consolations, principally from the most holy Eucharist. For Master Peter Favre and I celebrated holy Mass each day. He did not celebrate, but received holy communion. Then he told me that it seemed to him as if God the Father had imprinted the following words in his heart: *Ego ero vobis Romae propitius.*[5] Since our father did not know what these words might mean, he remarked: "I do not know what will happen to us; perhaps we will be crucified in Rome." Then, another time, he said, it appeared to him as if he saw Christ with the cross on his shoulder, and next to him the eternal Father who said to him: "I want you to take this man as your servant"; and Jesus thus took him and said: "I want you to serve us." After this he had a great devotion to the most holy Name and wanted the brotherhood to be called the Society of Jesus.[6]

In this more vivid and more detailed account of Laynez we discover some of the elements contained within the experience of being placed with the Son, and in particular note the corporate dimension and apostolic thrust which point and lead to the eventual founding of the Society of Jesus.

Spiritual Theology

We have been ruminating on the Two Standards, not so much as an integral part of the *Spiritual Exercises*, but as a constitutive component in the experience of Ignatius at Vivarolo and La Storta. Against this background we might now look at the theology of the Two Standards. It is clear that we are dealing primarily with spiritual or mystical theology, the theology of a lived Christian experience of God. In the *Spiritual Exercises*, Ignatius does not set out to teach dogmatic or moral theology. Undoubtedly he has certain dogmatic and moral presuppositions, and he expects to find these shared by the exercitant; and he is willing to foster through the Exercises *el sentido verdadero que en la Iglesia militante debemos tener.*[7] This might be described as just assent to Catholic orthodoxy, yet the word *sentido* not only denotes intellectual assent but also a correlative affective response. Ignatius is pointing to a way of the exercitant experiencing himself or herself as related to God through being a member of the (Catholic) Christian community or family, with a sensitive, appreciative awareness and feeling for that family's way of life and tradition. There is a holistic way of belonging to the church, an experiential way of coming close to Christ within the continuing incarnational mystery that is the church, and this Ignatius presupposes. Within such a context we can see how each particular exercise proposed by Ignatius is a way of facilitating in the exercitant the reception of a particular experiential grace, specified each time in the *id quod volo*[8] and (often in an expanded form) in the colloquy.

Ignatius is pointing to a way of the exercitant experiencing himself or herself as related to God through being a member of the (Catholic) Christian community or family, with a sensitive, appreciative awareness and feeling for that family's way of life and tradition.

If this is true of the *Exercises* in general, it is certainly true of the Two Standards. This exercise is aimed at facilitating the reception of a particular grace which Ignatius himself experienced with varying nuances at Manresa, at Vivarolo, and which culminated in the vision of La Storta when he "saw so clearly that God the Father had placed him with his Son Christ that his mind could not doubt that God the Father had indeed placed him with his Son." Everything in the exercise is geared to that grace and can also be seen as a kind of commentary on the experience of being placed with Christ, or of moving towards being placed with Christ. The writing of the exercise itself, of course, predates La Storta, but just as the La Storta experience deepened, confirmed, and in some way made definitive the grace for Ignatius (and for the emerging Society of Jesus), so, too, does it clarify for us both the purpose of the exercise and the spiritual theology of Ignatius which arose out of his experience of being placed with Christ. Spiritual theology, although it must be rooted in the faith tradition of the church, even if not precisely in dogmatic theology, has as its explicit focus the description and interpretation of Christian experience. Since such experience is the human response to unseen realities, it can be elusive in itself, and intractable in its conceptualization and verbalization. For this reason Jesus often used the parabolic and mythic form of communication as more flexible and evocative than that of direct, objective statement. Similarly in the Two Standards, Ignatius keeps pointing towards, hinting at, suggesting certain kinds of religious experience through the parabolic and mythic presentation of Satan and Christ.

Imagine you see the chief of all the enemy in the vast plain about Babylon, seated on a great throne of fire and smoke, his appearance inspiring horror and terror. Consider Christ our Lord, standing in a lowly place in a great plain about the region of Jerusalem, his appearance beautiful and attractive.[9]

What these two leaders think, plan, say and do is meant to resonate within the exercitant, drawing attention to certain kinds of experience which are perhaps already happening, or which the exercise itself may provoke. Through all of this Ignatius is hoping to stimulate the desire for, and open the person to the central grace of being placed with Christ.

Unlike dogmatic theology, where one can understand what one has not necessarily experienced, spiritual theology demands that one have some experience of what is being described, some awareness of the presence of that unseen reality which pervasively influences human lives. In the Two Standards, Ignatius is helping the exercitant to differentiate (discern). He says that the way towards being placed with Christ involves the experience of opposing inner movements (both attractions and revulsions), and that these movements need to be noticed, examined, sifted, weighed. He also teaches that such movements are not necessarily towards or away from that unseen world immediately in itself, but are often towards or away from the seen and tangible realities of this world. They thus include our attitudes towards, and relationships with the material world, other human persons, and ourselves. They are therefore often mysterious only in their ultimate interpretation and meaning. This interaction between the seen and the unseen, the world of matter and the world of spirit, is something that Ignatius takes for granted, points to in his imagery, but expounds only insofar as that helps the exercitant to enter into the fullness of God's plan and to illuminate that experience as shared with the director.

Myth and Reality

This ruminating brings to mind an occasion when I was listening to the liturgical readings on the feast of the Jesuit brother, St. Alphonsus Rodriguez. It seemed to me that what was being proclaimed was the myth and the reality of the Two Standards. In the Pauline reading, Christian experience was being described in mythic terms:

> Finally, grow strong in the Lord, with the strength of his power. Put God's armor on so as to be able to resist the devil's tactics. For it is not against human enemies that we have to struggle, but against the Sovereignties and the Powers who originate the darkness in this world, the spiritual army of evil in the heavens. That is why you must rely on God's armor, or you will not be able to put up any resistance when the worst happens, or have enough resources to hold your ground. So stand your ground, with truth buckled round your waist, and integrity for a breastplate, wearing for shoes on your feet the eagerness to spread the gospel of peace and always carrying the shield of faith so that you can use it to put out the burning arrows of the evil one. And then you must accept salvation from God to be your helmet and receive the word of God from the Spirit to use as a sword (Ep 6:10-17).

This vivid, imaginative, powerful description of the cosmic conflict between God and the devil, between the forces of good and evil, had about it the ring of truth even allowing for, or maybe because of, its skillful rhetorical presentation. Yet it also sounded somewhat incongruous to me as I pictured Alphonsus, a widower and former merchant, fulfilling with quiet perseverance the duties of doorkeeper, and the other simple tasks, for the last forty-six of his eighty-four years of life, when he was attached to the Jesuit college at Palma in Majorca. Could his daily routine of opening the door for the community and visitors, of accompanying the priests as they went to visit the sick in the town, really be part of such an awesome scenario? It was almost with a sense of relief that I heard the gospel passage read.

> Jesus then told the guests a parable, because he had noticed how they picked the places of honor. He said this, "When someone invites you to a wedding feast, do not take your seat in the place of honor: a more distinguished person than you may have been invited, and the person who invited you both may come and say: "Give up your place to this man." And then, to your embarrassment, you would have to go and take the lowest place. No: when you are a guest, make your

way to the lowest place and sit there, so that, when your host comes, he may say: "My friend, move up higher." In that way, everyone with you at the table will see you honored. For everyone who exalts himself will be humbled and the man who humbles himself will be exalted" (Lk 14:7-11).

That passage sounded so much more appropriate for Alphonsus, so much more "real." It spoke of a humility which showed itself in simple choices and actions. I could imagine the courtesy and reverence with which Alphonsus greeted callers to · the college, the deference which he paid to the members of his community. His commitment as a Christian and as a religious was incarnated, and could only become evident, in the most ordinary of human circumstances and experiences. All the references in Ephesians to Sovereignties and Powers, and to the battle-gear of ancient times, appeared less applicable to the life of this brother than the amusing though pointed parable of Jesus about the man who refrained from trying to upstage his neighbors at a dinner-party.

And yet, when one reads the *Autobiography* of Alphonsus, one sees that not only is he himself perfectly at home in that world of myth, but that he interprets his own experiences in mythic terms which for him adequately, and even literally, convey the "real."

> He [God] gave the demons permission to persecute him. Since the permission was very liberal, the testing and suffering they gave him were very great. . . . To all appearances it was as if there were no God for him, only demons. . . . Then, as the evil spirits had planned to come at midnight, so he felt them come at that hour with great turmoil and disturbance; the great army of hell, in the middle of the night, as they had agreed. Some seized hold of him and others embraced him under evil forms in order to incite him to evil, nor was he able to avoid them. Here he was consumed with sadness and almost dead and strangled with rage, that they were holding him. Here he was quite encompassed with sinful matter. Here, if he wanted to look for any consolation to give him relief, he did not find it.[10]

It is as if we were reading about Antony or some other of the Desert Fathers. But just as in the two liturgical readings of his feast, Alphonsus's account of his battling with demons is balanced by the down-to-earth ordinariness and humanness of comments such as this (related to the need for religious to practice custody of the eyes when going about the town):

But even though they go about with this recollection and modesty, that does not stop them from seeing someone who greets them passing by, for they have to treat such people with courtesy and good breeding.[11]

What, then, is the relationship between Alphonsus's experience of demonic temptation and his cultured social attitudes? Or between Paul's celestial warfare and the human foibles gently mocked by Jesus? Or, in terms of the Two Standards, between Ignatius's mythic presentation of Christ and Satan, and the human choices which he indicates: riches, honor, pride on the one hand; poverty, contempt, humility on the other? If one were to demythologize Alphonsus or Paul or Ignatius, would such an apparent simplification strengthen or weaken, clarify, or obscure the truth?

Answers to such questions depend on one's understanding of myth. If people comprehend and communicate aspects of reality through myth because, at their stage of human development, they are unable to do so otherwise, then it is at least theoretically possible that a later generation may outgrow such a limitation and succeed in comprehending and communicating in a superior mode. But if there are areas of human experience which by their very nature can only be comprehended and communicated through myth, then the most that a later generation can do is to substitute its own myth for the earlier one, and in so doing to become truly creative. In either hypothesis myth does not exist merely because people are ignorant or ill-informed or pre-scientific. It exists because of a deeply-rooted sense of the ambiguity, paradox, and mystery of life. By acknowledging all of this, myth seeks to discover ultimate meaning and purpose in the most commonplace of human experiences. Without it, much of reality would lie outside the range of understanding and so not form part of the cumulative wisdom of humankind. The challenge is to pursue truth both in the creative images and symbols of myth as well as in the language of logical thought and the categories of the human and natural sciences.

Good and Evil Spirits

Such ruminations in turn prompt a variety of other questions. The most obvious one in a Christian context concerns the existence of spirits as created, personal beings: angels and demons, and

in particular Satan. This does not rank among the major theological issues of our day, and Christians adopt a wide range of
positions regarding it. Some deny the very existence of spirits,
explaining their presence in the tradition as creative projections
of inner religious experience. Others affirm the existence of spirits, but hold that what is said about them in Scripture and other
sources is in large part mythic, because too obviously anthropo-
morphic. This is a limited form of agnosticism in relation to the
nature and activities of spirits. More commonly, perhaps, there
seems to be a broader agnosticism which could be articulated as
follows: Created personal spirits may or may not exist, but one
cannot be certain. Still less can one be sure of their role if they do
exist. In any case the matter is hardly relevant to our present-day
concerns.

The denial of the existence of spirits, as well as this broader
agnosticism, are both strongly challenged when faced with the
interpretation of the Christian tradition given by Karl Rahner in
the theological encyclopedia, *Sacramentum Mundi:*

> *i. On Angels*
> Angels exist, but are merely creatures. The profession of
> faith of Lateran IV and the teaching on creation of Vatican
> I affirm the creation of spiritual beings, angels, in addition
> to men. . . . It cannot be said that the conciliar statements
> only mean that if there are such personal spiritual princi-
> palities and powers, they like everything else are creatures
> of the one, absolute God, though this, the ultimate import
> of the affirmation, is what is finally decisive.[12]
>
> *ii. On Demons*
> In view of the created and non-human character of these
> various spiritual, personal principalities and powers, all that
> is affirmed of the natural essence of the angels must be
> ascribed to them, too. In accordance with the teaching of
> faith regarding their existence, we must maintain with equal
> certainty the plurality of such non-human demonical pow-
> ers.[13]
>
> *iii. On the Devil; Satan*
> The devil . . . is not to be regarded as a mere mythological
> personification of evil in the world; the existence of the
> devil cannot be denied.[14]

In Rahner's view, therefore, it would seem that the scope for
agnosticism is limited by the certain teaching of the tradition, as
is the scope for myth.

Applying this to the Two Standards, the mythic element in

the presentation of Satan and other spirits is restricted in somewhat the same way, although not as precisely, as the mythic element in the presentation of Christ, who is the historical Jesus of Nazareth and the contemporary Risen Lord. Where room for myth legitimately exists is in the description of how human persons experience the presence and activity of good and evil spirits' and this is exactly how Ignatius uses it. This modern problematic, of course, would have been somewhat puzzling for Ignatius. The existence of an invisible world, inhabited by spirits both good and bad, was part of the cultural imagination as well as the faith of sixteenth-century Europe, and was unquestioned by Catholics or Reformers. Inevitably it was among the presuppositions of the *Spiritual Exercises.*

Such presuppositions concerning spirits cannot be taken for granted today, and even where they do exist they are likely to be less prominent in a person's hierarchy of truths, and equally importantly, to be held with far less emotional intensity than in the time of Ignatius. Given the more agnostic or skeptical attitude of men and women living in our "post-Christian" western world, certain practical, pastoral issues arise for those in the ministry of spiritual direction. One such is posed by Jules Toner who, although holding to his own belief in the reality of personal good and evil spirits, yet asks: "Should good or evil created spirits be taken into consideration or left aside when discerning spirits?"[15] His answer is worth quoting at some length.

> Regarding [this] question, we should keep in mind that leaving good and evil spirits out of account in discernment of spirits does not necessarily imply a denial of their existence or of their influence on human lives. One may decide to omit them from consideration because of uncertainty. Or one may believe with certainty in their existence and influence and in the value of recognizing their influence if we could, but remain so dubious of being able to discover when and in what way they are involved that it seems useless to try. Or again one may think that in any case this problem concerning the existence and influence of the good and evil spirits is not worth bothering about; for, one may think, whatever the solution reached, it will be of little or no significance for the ultimate practical purpose of discerning spirits. The ultimate purpose is to open ourselves to be led and guided by the Holy Spirit and to reject any influence contrary to his, whatever the source of that influence may be. To do this, it seems enough to recognize: (1) the signs of the Holy Spirit prompting us, whether with or without

the mediation of a good angel; (2) the signs of whatever force is opposed to him, without need to discern whether this force includes the promptings of a personal evil spirit or not; and (3) the naturally good promptings of our own hearts which, like all else in the universe, are under God's providence but are not what is meant by movements of the Spirit. For some persons, believing that a temptation or spiritual desolation is prompted by an evil spirit serves to call forth greater resistance (without unhealthy fear), more enthusiasm to conquer the movement. But that is not to say that such belief is necessary in order to respond well and to use the Ignatian rules as guides in doing so. For others, it may be that facing the sinfulness within ourselves is helped by leaving aside the possible influence of an evil spirit. Or for still others, because of certain emotional conditions, their focusing attention on the influence of the evil spirits would have unhealthy consequences. And so on.[16]

Toner's approach, so faithfully Ignatian in its willingness to adapt to the personality and beliefs of the person discerning, is widely accepted by spiritual directors today. But some nagging doubts remain. For example, if Satan does exist, can one say that the religious experience of a person who denies or even abstracts from that existence, is as deep as that of a person for whom Satan is a personal spirit working towards his/her destruction? If the truth about our universe is that it is the scene of a cosmic war in which we cannot but play a part, does a person who does not accept, or leaves out of account, the existence of good and evil spirits enter as fully into the truth as one who consciously experiences his or her own life as immersed in that conflict? In demythologizing spirits, even for tactical reasons in pastoral situations, do we risk eliminating not only anthropomorphisms and other sources of possible distortion and error, but part of the reality itself which revelation has attempted to communicate? There are no easy answers. Perhaps the culturally conditioned theological climate of today is not overly sympathetic to the questions themselves. But that will not prevent some of us at least from continuing to ruminate on the Two Standards—and related matters.

Notes

[1] Favre, Jay and Brôet were already priests, Salmerón only received orders up to the diaconate, not yet being twenty-two years of age.

[2] *The Autobiography of St Ignatius Loyola*, translated by Joseph F. O'Callaghan (New York, 1974), p. 88. Other editions, paragraph 95.

[3] Hugo Rahner, *The Vision of St. Ignatius in the Chapel of La Storta* (Rome, 1975), p. 38.

[4] *Autobiography*, trans. O'Callaghan, p. 89. Other editions, par. 96.

[5] *Translation:* I will be favorable to you [plural] in Rome.

[6] *Monumenta Historica Societatis Jesu, Fontes Narrativi*, II, p 133. Quoted in Rahner, *Vision*, pp. 61-62.

[7] *Translation:* The true affective understanding which we ought to have in the church militant.

[8] *Translation:* That which I desire. See the second or third prelude in every Ignatian exercise .

[9] *The Spiritual Exercises of St Ignatius*, translated by Louis J. Puhl (Chicago, 1951), nn. 140, 144.

[10] *St. Alphonsus Rodriguez: Autobiography*, translated by William Yeomans (London, 1964), pp. 43-45.

[11] Ibid, p. 62.

[12] Karl Rahner, in *Sacramentum Mundi* (New York & London, 1968), vol. I, p. 34.

[13] Ibid, vol. II, p. 72.

[14] Ibid, vol. II, p. 73.

[15] Jules J. Toner, *A Commentary on Saint Ignatius' Rules for the Discernment of Spirits* (St. Louis, 1982), p. 34.

[16] Ibid, pp. 34-35.

Directing the Third Week

I have been crucified with Christ; it is no longer I who live, but Christ who lives in me; and the life I now live in the flesh I live by faith in the Son of God, who loved me and gave himself for me (Ga 2:20).

Without a doubt, the Third Week of the *Spiritual Exercises* of St. Ignatius extends an invitation to a most intimate and personal experience of the very core of Jesus' being. Retreatants' encounters with Jesus can be so stark, so simple, so sacred, so profound, that any attempt even to verbalize the experiences may seem to be a violation of the sacred.

That is, unless there are difficulties; for the Third Week can also be extraordinarily difficult. Having had so many expectations and aspirations stirred during the Second Week, it is not uncommon for retreatants to find themselves unable to let go, unable to make the shift to the Third Week without considerable frustration. They may, like the apostle Peter, simply not want Jesus to suffer; they may be wedded to memories of Second Week consolations; they may be incapable of facing the reality of negativity, opposition, suffering, and death. In any event, the director's task is to aid retreatants in discerning the meaning of their experience; and directors will be more or less helpful to the extent that they themselves have appropriated the dynamics of the Third Week.

Compartmentalizing Jesus

Many of us, both as retreatants and as directors, tend to compartmentalize the historical Jesus by focusing on little vignettes from his life during our praying of the *Exercises*.[1] We focus so precisely on the mystery at hand that the person of Jesus and the concrete historical context of his life are often overlooked. We lose perspective, for we fail to appreciate the overall dynamics of Jesus' life. This is a particular problem in the Third Week, where Jesus' life can be neglected as we focus on his death, as though his death had been unconnected to all that preceded it.

St. Ignatius provided us with several ways to avoid this tendency to compartmentalize Jesus' life. One way was his suggestion that retreatants not read ahead [127]; instead they are urged to recall frequently the events of Jesus' life from the Incarnation to the present mystery [130]. This also applies to the Third Week, when the retreatant is urged to recall throughout the day all of Jesus' labors, from his birth to the then current mystery [206]. This should not, of course, be conceived of as a simple listing of the various events over and over again. Rather, the retreatant is invited to forge connections among these events, to understand them, to see the unity underlying all of Jesus' life.

Another way to avoid the tendency to compartmentalize Jesus' life is to see his life and death in very personal terms, in relational terms, and thus in historical terms. In the Third Week, Ignatius stressed that Jesus suffered for my sins, for me, which is to say that his death was not simply a brute political fact, nor even an unfortunate example of what happens to good people throughout the world. Neither did Ignatius depict Jesus' death as having been first and foremost a religious event, an event of cosmic expiation or redemption. No; Ignatius was at pains to underscore the fact that the crucifixion did not simply happen to Jesus. Rather, Jesus himself elected to die. This made it personal; and our struggling to come to grips with Jesus' decision brings his life and death together.

All too often, however, retreatants can go through the Third Week without really trying to understand why Jesus made this most crucial of decisions. They remain bystanders, passive observers; they see and react without appreciating the meaning of his death, a meaning which had, of course, everything to do with how he lived his life, the concrete decisions he made, the people whose cause he took as his own. Understanding why Jesus willed his death requires that we know Jesus intimately, that we have at least begun to appropriate his life—his convictions, hopes, dreams, concerns, regrets—especially during the Second Week. Hence, the depth of the Third Week encounter with Jesus depends on the depth in which the retreatant encountered Jesus in the Second Week; and this, in turn, depends on how well the director and retreatant integrated Ignatius's emphasis on Jesus' own decision making, how they dealt with the constant theme of suffering and hardship which surprisingly runs through the whole Second Week, especially in the Triple Colloquy. To share Jesus' Passion requires that we share his passions, passions which were evidenced throughout his life, passions which were epitomized in his decisions, passions whose inner coherence led to his decision to risk his life.

The challenge to all retreatants is simply to stay with the person of Jesus, to be as close to him and to his experience as possible; for union with Jesus is the only consolation of the Third Week; nothing else consoles.

This may seem to be in some contrast to Ignatius's own directives. In (162) Ignatius suggested that the director could shorten the Second Week by omitting some of the assigned mysteries, thus suggesting that the content of the mysteries may not be all that crucial. As Ignatius said, there will be greater time for more complete meditations of all the mysteries outside the *Exercises*. This is, of course, true; for there is no way to exhaust or even adequately to consider the whole of Jesus' life in a few weeks. But this does not mean that the content is unimportant. What it does seem to suggest, however, is that, for Ignatius's purposes in the *Exercises*, an intimate knowledge of the overall dynamic and purpose of Jesus' life from the point of view of decision—beginning with the decision by the Trinity through to Jesus' decision to die—is what is required.

This very Ignatian emphasis on Jesus' having chosen to die was not simply concocted to bring the topic of election cleverly into Christ's life. Hardly, for it more than does justice to the Gospel accounts, wherein Jesus is depicted as having freely decided to go to Jerusalem. He could easily have run away, but he chose not to. Jesus actually *elected* to die for his disciples, out of loyalty to his Father and to his disciples. He could have taken Peter's advice and not gone to Jerusalem; and judging by the strength of his "Get behind me, Satan" reply to Peter's suggestion, he must have been sorely tempted to do exactly that. But he would have thereby risked everything he had preached, everything he had taught; and he would have had to spend the rest of his life running away from Jerusalem, from himself, and from the disciples whom he would have let down horribly. His decision to go to Jerusalem was a consistent decision, one which, in a sense, he had been making each time he took an unpopular prophetic, or even a simply compassionate, stand. He chose to go to Jerusalem, because in a profound sense he had to go to Jerusalem. As he himself purportedly said, it really would not have been right for a prophet to die outside of Jerusalem, to restrict his proclamation of God's reign to the safe periphery of Jewish cultural, economic, and political life. Quite simply, the life he lived, the people whose cause he took up, the disciples he had drawn—these were worth dying for; and no one would have followed him had he acted otherwise.

Not everyone would approach Jesus' decision in exactly the same way. But unless retreatants reach some appreciation of why Jesus knowingly and willingly died for his friends, for the poor on whose behalf he proclaimed the good news—that is, unless they have had some awareness of the central element of Jesus' own freedom and his election (and its probable costs) during their praying of the Second Week material, there is a risk that the Passion will be perceived as nothing more than an obscene and revolting event. The crucial unitive thrust of the Third Week will be lost to them, only to be replaced by what are often lopsided theologies of suffering, redemption, and satisfaction.

Staying with Jesus

Many retreatants will feel revulsion at Jesus' suffering, and rightly so. Some may understandably close their eyes and hearts to the obscenity and find the going rough. Some will pray through the Third Week with much dryness, perhaps feeling something of the aridity Jesus himself must have felt. But, at some point, most will respond with love to the very vulnerable, very weak, very loving person behind the revolting obscenity and the excruciating pain. Some may even taste the Johannine flavor of victory in the cross, while others will wait for the Fourth Week. Whatever the case, the challenge to all retreatants is simply to stay with the person of Jesus, to be as close to him and to his experience as possible; for union with Jesus is the only consolation of the Third Week; nothing else consoles.

For all that, staying with Jesus, as Ignatius insisted, and as we well know, is not at all easy. Only a consummate sadist could enjoy the Third Week experience. In fact, the apostles remain prime examples of just how difficult it must have been and how demanding it still is to stay with Jesus through his Passion. Staying quietly with Jesus at the foot of the cross is an extraordinary *labor* of love which requires "great effort," as Ignatius said. Even more strongly, Ignatius expected us to have to "force ourselves" out of love to feel what we "want to feel"; it actually takes some courage. Though the Third Week calls forth great desire and great love, both of these must actually be chosen; and the choice must be deliberate enough for us to maintain our prayer and to labor through the points despite the abhorrence we naturally have of the violent suffering of someone we love.

Directors may decide to reiterate this aspect very pointedly with particular retreatants. Many retreatants get unduly frustrated with themselves for not being able to respond spontaneously to Jesus' Passion; they may even go through powerful bouts of actual desolation, as they torment themselves for initially having to work so hard to feel anything at all. Perhaps because of the great contemporary stress on the connection between spontaneity and authenticity, many people refuse to admit that we ever need to choose to love, choose to feel compassion, choose to feel sorrow. Ignatius's "choosing with the will" seems to them to be unnatural, forced, simply unauthentic. Thus some directors may profitably decide to stress the "striving" which was emphasized by Ignatius in the six points of the first exercise of the Third Week [194-197].

That being said, some retreatants will feel absolutely numb during much of the Passion. Yet this is far from being an inhuman or unsympathetic response. In fact, feeling anesthetized, deadened. paralyzed, tired. frustrated, edgy, angry, depressed—all of these may well be signs that a retreatant is actually very present to the reality of the Passion, even to Jesus' own experience. Encouragement to stay with Jesus is perhaps all they can be given and all they really need.

Given this variety of responses to the Third Week material, directors may want to temper their own expectations for their retreatants' prayer—so great is a director's desire that his or her retreatant have a "powerful" experience during this pivotal Week. We should remind ourselves that the Third Week can be a very quiet Week, with very subtle movements of mind and heart. "Great striving" does not necessarily mean that retreatants ought to feel correspondingly great and incredibly intense emotions; neither does it mean that they ought to feel drawn to monumental expressions of the most profound love imaginable while contemplating the Passion. In fact, if retreatants are being frequently overwhelmed by their own emotions, a sensitive director might well suspect that something is amiss. Though this goes well beyond the hard data, and though each retreatant's experience is his or her own, still it is more than arguably the case that Jesus would not have particularly needed spectacular, effusive expressions of love during his Passion. After all, was it not enough to stay awake in prayer with him? Again, the theme of presence, simply being with Jesus, comes to the fore; and many retreatants are content to let their eyes meet Jesus' once or twice, gratified to have an opportunity to let their presence convey a wordless "I love you." Despite some retreatants' desires to emote extraordinarily, these "quieter" responses, especially in a Western cultural context, often indicate a profound attending to the person of Jesus and to the reality of the Passion.

Suffering with Christ

All too often Christians respond to the cross with great emotion because they feel so badly for Jesus. We tend to react to Jesus the way we would react were we to witness a horrible accident: We turn inward; we become super-conscious of ourselves and of our own feelings. Again, this is all very natural; and Ignatius actually suggested that in the Third Week retreatants ought to feel sorrow and grief *for* Jesus and ought to avoid joyful thoughts [206]. But it is not so clear that this is what Ignatius had in mind for the prayer time itself. Ignatius wanted us to focus during the actual prayer periods on Jesus' suffering, not on how bad we feel. Consider the second prelude of the first exercise of the First Week:

> [48] The second prelude is to ask God our Lord for what I want and desire. The petition ought to correspond to the subject matter; which is to say, if the contemplation were on

the resurrection. I would ask for joy with Christ rejoicing; *if on the Passion, I would ask for pains, tears, and torment with Christ tormented.*[2]

We are not to ask for pain, tears, and torment simply because we feel so bad about Jesus' Passion. No: we ask for these "gifts" chiefly because we feel so close to Jesus, who is himself experiencing anguish. We want to get right inside his very person, desiring that intimate knowledge of Jesus for which we have persistently begged for days and days. We are called to "*com*-passion," feeling *with* Jesus, rather than only *for* Jesus. Thus in the Third Week we are called neither to imitate Jesus' suffering nor to suffer in his place, but most precisely to union with Jesus in his suffering.

Confirmation of an Election

Though this is not all that explicit in the text of the *Exercises*, it stands to reason that an election made in the Second Week be confirmed to some degree during the Third and Fourth Weeks, and indeed in subsequent weeks as well. The *Official Directory* of 1599 states that "the Third Week steadies and confirms the election now made.[3] It would be a mistake, however, to make confirmation itself the major goal of the Third Week. Jesus must always remain the focus of prayer, no matter which Week the retreatant is in, and regardless of whether a formal election has been made.

It is intriguing to note that Ignatius did not himself mention confirmation in the text of the Third or Fourth Weeks; nor did he propose any "confirmation exercises" for the Third or Fourth Weeks other than having the retreatants reflect on what they ought to do and suffer for Christ [197]. This suggests that praying the Third and Fourth Weeks *as they are* is itself the confirmation exercise.

How is confirmation discerned then? First, perhaps a cautionary word about less-than-helpful approaches to confirmation may be in order. After having taken personal responsibility for an election in the Second Week, some retreatants are surprisingly ready to relinquish much of their personal responsibility and to turn to an external authority to corroborate, authorize, or even to change their election. And yet, confirmation is hardly a disempowerment of that sort. Confirmation is not saying to the Lord, "Jesus, now you tell me what you want me to do." Not to put words in his mouth, but would not Jesus be likely to respond,

"No. You tell me what *you* want'"? Confirmation is not getting a divine second opinion. Still, in the election material of the Second Week [183, 188], Ignatius did ask the retreatant to offer God his or her choice expressly for confirmation; and this confirmation, like everything else in the *Exercises*, is discerned on the basis of the movements of spirits.

Some retreatants are understandably preoccupied with their election, and instead of discerning spirits per se, they ask Jesus while he is on the cross to confirm their election. This is actually very common and is the spontaneous strategy many retreatants use to seek confirmation. This natural impulse may be a holdover from the First Week colloquy with Jesus on the cross, though with one important twist: Rather than ask themselves what they have done, are doing, and ought to do for Christ, they ask Christ what they ought to do. Actually, the sixth point for the Third Week exercises explicitly suggests that the retreatants ask *themselves* what they ought to do and suffer for Christ [197].

Some retreatants are understandably preoccupied with their election, and instead of discerning spirits per se, they ask Jesus while he is on the cross to confirm their election.

No matter what a director says ahead of time, odds are that many retreatants would probably go ahead and simply ask Jesus to verify or authorize their elections for them. In one sense, there is often little harm in their trying, but directors should know that this is hardly a discernment of spirits and it hardly constitutes confirmation in any Ignatian sense. Sometimes this confusion can even get in the way of the retreatants' attending to Jesus during prayer, for their attention is drawn away from Jesus to themselves, and the perspective of freedom in Christ needed for any authentic discernment is lost.

Though it is often preferable that retreatants discover the truth of these principles experientially, suggestions by the director on how to approach confirmation can nonetheless be very helpful. For instance, directors might suggest that their retreatants "wear their election" throughout the Third Week, that is, that the retreatants prepare for their contemplations quite consciously as "the person who made and is making this particular choice." At the same time, a little nudge to remain focused on Jesus, rather than on themselves, never hurts.

Confirmation of the Election-Maker

While the most obvious approach to confirmation is, as one might expect, to seek to have this or that particular decision confirmed (and this is quite proper for the Second Week), an approach more suited to the Third Week is to have myself as "the election-maker, or elector, who has made this particular election" confirmed. This distinction can be especially significant for elections focusing on vocation or state of life questions, when it is pivotally important that retreatants be able to accompany Jesus through his Passion with their elections very much a part of them. Directors need to urge retreatants to bring themselves to the Passion in such a way that their elections are truly constitutive of their being loyal disciples to the end. Thus *the retreatant* is confirmed in intimacy with Jesus, confirmed as a loved-disciple. The election itself is then confirmed inasmuch as the election was a part of the retreatant's apostolic identity.

An argument can be made that this approach corresponds to the outlines of Jesus' own experience. After Jesus decided to leave home and decided to be baptized, he was confirmed by God (in prayer, if we follow Luke's account). The experience was one of approval, of affirmation; and there was no directive given, no confirmation of decision apart from the very real confirmation of Jesus' whole person as being "beloved" by God.

The same can be said for the Transfiguration experience. Whatever the historical grounds for the accounts of the Transfiguration, it is tantalizing to note that the Transfiguration is placed in the context of the prophecies of the Passion, in the midst of Jesus' decision to go to Jerusalem. The baptismal experience is relived, and Jesus is again confirmed. This time it is a confirmation of his history, a confirmation that he had not gone off track, that he had discerned God's promptings authentically, that he had remained true to the trajectory of his life since his baptism. Again, rather than a confirmation of a particular decision or an election considered somehow apart from the person, the confirmation received was a confirmation of the person: Jesus was confirmed again as the "beloved" in the context of his life.

The possibility of recognizing this type of confirmation in our own lives depends, of course, on our belief that an inauthentic or simply wrong election will occasion some tension or incongruence in our relationship with the Lord, as well as in our relationships with ourselves—that is, there will be some detectable movement or pattern of desolation. This insight is really what makes the discernment of spirits possible in the first place. Often, we say that an election is confirmed inasmuch as the election is experienced as "consoling," as contributing to a pattern of consolation which evidences some increase and concretization of faith, hope, and love. But here we are suggesting that confirmation can be discerned when the election-maker experiences consolation and affirmation precisely as one who has made an election. This may, for instance, happen when a retreatant realizes that he or she must take responsibility for the election, and, in so doing, experiences even greater intimacy with the Lord, who likewise took responsibility for his life and actions.

Retreatants may experience their own freedom to such an extent that they have the distinct impression that the Lord would be equally happy with any of the options they are considering.

When dealing with very mature retreatants, it is to be expected that their elections will be marked by a striking degree of freedom. During the Second Week and particularly during the election exercises, these retreatants may experience their own freedom to such an extent that they have the distinct impression that the Lord would be equally happy with any of the options they are considering. The affirmation is so complete that the Lord seems more than willing to go along with their election, whatever it is. It is as though the Lord wanted nothing other than that they make a good and responsible election. This is a very special experience, one often marked by a profound joy juxtaposed to an almost overwhelming sense of awe at the depth of personal freedom and responsibility: joy at being accepted and loved; amazement at the Lord's deliberated solidarity with, and trust of, the retreatant; and awe (and perhaps some fear) as the retreatant realizes just how total a response is called for by such a gift of radical freedom. Again, it should be clear that the only confirmation which makes sense in this context would be that which continues to affirm the retreatant as a loved and approved election-maker in the context of a realistic discipleship. This often occurs simply enough when a retreatant expresses his or her radical freedom by staying with Jesus, wanting nothing other than to remain at the foot of the cross.

The Interview

In speaking to retreatants about their prayer review, rather than directly ask about their election (often thereby insinuating that they should somehow be praying quite precisely on their election), it might be better instead to ask them to pay particular attention to the quality of their time with Jesus. Was there any tension? Did they feel any irking concerns? Did they feel distant or alienated from Jesus? They ought to be especially sensitive to, and curious about, any tension, reluctance, diffidence, hesitancy, heaviness they may notice. If they determine that they have been authentic in their prayer, that their desires come from the core of their being, then this openness is itself a good indication of a pattern of consolation and confirmation.

If, on the other hand. a retreatant's election is truly weighing down on him or her, the retreatant can be encouraged to speak it out during the colloquies, to look at his or her motives, to ask whether the heaviness is actually a realistic response to a genuine invitation to follow the way of the cross with Jesus [199]. If the retreatant is being called to the cross, the confirmation may be discerned, not so much in a Second or Fourth Week experience of joy as in the depth and quality of a reluctant-but-real "yes" emanating from the heart, one which quite appropriately is more a response to Jesus than to the election at hand.

Some retreatants may have a difficult time recognizing a confirmation on the level of their desire, largely because they have incredibly unrealistic expectations of themselves; they feel that they should *want* to embrace the cross with all their minds, hearts, and strength; that they should experience joy at the prospect; that this joy should vanquish all their resistance, all their reluctance. Once again, a gentle nudge to keep focused on Jesus, on his very reluctant "yes" to suffering, may help. They could be asked whether there is anything wrong with saying "yes" as Jesus said "yes." There is no shortage of instances where a reluctant-but-real "yes" authentically issued from the very depths of a person in a way that a very enthusiastic "yes" could never have.

All of this is to suggest that confirmation and consolation are not equivalent to "enthusiasm." Reality remains the best test of consolation; deception, the clearest sign of desolation. A visceral reaction to the reality of suffering entailed in a particular course of action is to be considered a very real type of consolation, discomfiting though it may be. Confirmation has everything to do with reality, and it requires an openness to bear (or share) the real cost of the election, an openness which is called forth by the compelling example of Jesus' own election. If this type of frank realization of the all-too-real possibility of suffering continues throughout the Third Week and constitutes a solid pattern which does not take the retreatant away from the Lord, then the person is probably in a pattern of consolation; and there are solid grounds for considering the election confirmed.

A retreatant may think that her very good election seems foolish, or insignificant, or even useless in front of the cross, given the radicalness of the Lord's own love.

One interesting deception for which directors are advised to remain on the lookout is the habit some people have of psyching themselves out of a confirmation by misinterpreting their responses in the Third Week. For instance, a retreatant may think that her very good election seems foolish, or insignificant, or even useless in front of the cross, given the radicalness of the Lord's own love. She may seem open to bearing the cost of a difficult election, but she does not see how her election is going to be very costly at all. In situations like this, directors can do little else than continue to draw their retreatants gently back to Jesus. It might help to ask the retreatants whether, for instance, they experience Jesus as being dismissive of them and their election. It might also help to point out how the retreatants' attention has subtly but unmistakably shifted to themselves. This, of course, is a classic case of deception under the guise of good: "This election wasn't good enough. I'm capable of something more radical. I want to do something more radical." So the election is dropped.

What if the election is not at all front and center during the Third Week? Does that mean the election cannot be considered confirmed? On the contrary. If a retreatant has authentically experienced consolation during the Third Week, and if no desires conflicting with the election emerged, then the retreatant has been confirmed, election and all, as long as the election really was authentic and corresponded to desires which could be said to be constitutive of his or her person. The same could be said of a retreatant who experiences consolation without previous or proportionate cause. If the retreatant has made an election and has appropriated that election, an openness to the Lord's presence and activity would be expected, and so consolation without proportionate cause should be considered a powerful confirmation. Just as the Third Week exercises are themselves the confirmation exercises, so the experiences of the Third Week are the data for the discernment of the confirmation. All of this, of course, places an emphasis on the quality of the prior week's discernment process, for unless both the director and retreatant determine and embrace the actual roots of the desires which led to the election, the election will not have been appropriated enough to enable an accurate discernment of spirits in the Third Week.

There will also be occasions when retreatants discover that, far from identifying themselves with their election, they had not really made an election after all. They may have tried to make an election merely because they thought their directors expected it of them, or because they wanted to have some—say, any—resolution made by the end of their retreat, perhaps thinking that a retreat without a resolution is not a real retreat. In these cases, if the prayer of the Third Week seems authentic, and the election simply no longer seems to be all that important, the retreatant might do best to put the matter of the election on the back-burner, to be picked up with his or her ongoing director after the *Exercises* are over.

Vulnerability in the Third Week

A few words about vulnerability in the Third Week may be in order here. Jesus was exquisitely vulnerable and his love was most palpable throughout his Passion. Because the fruit of this week is an intimate union with this vulnerable Jesus, some people will be upset to discover that they respond sexually to Jesus or are beset with sexual temptations which seem to come out of nowhere. Intense physical vulnerability can often call forth a desire to be equally vulnerable, to be physically vulnerable, even to be sexually vulnerable; and this can happen to both men and women of any and all sexual proclivities. Perhaps the best thing to do when a retreatant seems bothered by all this is first to suggest that the real danger is to become worried or turned-in on oneself. As with other temptations, an analysis of the sequence of images or thoughts preceding and following the temptation may sometimes help [333-334]. Some directors in particular cases prefer to advise their retreatants of this possibility ahead of time, presuming that this is the type of thing which some retreatants might not easily confide to their director.

Rather than simply ignore the sexual dimension, it is important to be aware that the sexual response may well signal a breakthrough for some on the level of intimacy, a very physical but passing sign that they were responding totally to Jesus, that they have been disarmingly open and spontaneous. It could be a potentially painful mistake for either the retreatant or director to think uncritically that some huge sexual issue had to be faced right in the middle of the Third Week. At the same time, a block may well surface which will indeed have to be dealt with either during or after the retreat.

How to Give the Third Week Exercises

The first exercise of the Third Week gives the general pattern for all the Third Week exercises, except that the grace prayed for in the first exercise is transitional and is only to be used for that single exercise:

> [193] The third prelude is to ask for what I desire: Here it will be grief, intense feelings, and confusion, because our Lord is entering his Passion for my sins.

The first exercise and the first grace focus on Jesus' election to suffer: the retreatant considers "what he (Jesus) decides to suffer" [195], and why he decides to suffer specifically "for me." It cannot be stressed too much that Jesus actually preferred to suffer, which is to say. he quite particularly chose the path of suffering after he had considered the other possibilities. Retreatants who have made difficult elections may begin to feel confirmed (perhaps even very powerfully) as they see and feel the difficult but loving election which Jesus made.

The grace to be prayed for throughout the rest of the Third Week is the grace of the second exercise:

> [203] The third prelude is to ask for what I desire. In the Passion, it is proper to ask for sorrow with Christ in sorrow, to be broken with Christ broken, for tears and deep grief because of the great pain Christ endured for me.

This second grace is used for the rest of the Third Week. It is instructive to note that in contrast to the first grace of the Third Week [193], where Christ is said to be going to his Passion *for my sins*, here Christ undergoes his suffering *for me*. This shift is probably not accidental. for it corresponds to Ignatius's intention that the Third Week be experienced very personally.

The preludes change for each mystery: The first is the story of the mystery, the second is to visualize the place(s), while the third is the grace, which changes as noted above. It sometimes needs to be stressed that the points of the first exercise are used *throughout the whole Week*. They are as follows:

> *First Point* [194]. I see the persons at the meal and, reflecting on myself, I try to draw something from it all [194].
>
> *Second Point* I listen to the conversations, and similarly try to draw something.
>
> *Third Point* I see what the persons are doing, and draw something.
>
> *Fourth Point* [195]. I consider what Christ our Lord suffers in his humanity, or wills to suffer, depending on the passage being contemplated; and I begin with great effort to force myself to grieve, to be sad, and to weep. I will similarly work at the points which follow.

Note how explicit is Ignatius's expectation that we will need to stir up our own emotions; we must actually choose to grieve, to be sad, to weep.

> *Fifth Point* [196] I consider how the divinity hides itself, which is to say, how the divinity could destroy its enemies, but does not do so, leaving, instead, the most sacred humanity to suffer so cruelly.

Though this is a bit complicated Christologically, it is nonetheless important. Our theological tradition holds that there is only one divine will, one shared by the Father, Son, and Spirit:

it also holds that Jesus has (not just *had!*) a separate human will. Even though it is true that Ignatius wanted to stress the voluntary aspect of Jesus' death via this point, it would not be out of place for us to consider that God (the divine will, the divinity) could have saved Jesus, but chose not to. This, perhaps more orthodox, theological point was in fact central to Jesus' own struggle with God's seeming abandoning of him on the cross; and it should strike us as well. We should remind ourselves throughout the Passion that Jesus was in the same boat as are all other human beings—no special treatment was accorded—and his suffering was the result of God's presumably deliberate choice not to save him from that suffering.

> *Sixth Point* [197] I consider that Christ suffers all this for my sins. and so forth. I also consider what I ought to do and suffer for him.

Here, the election may be brought to the fore, though some retreatants may prefer to focus on a more immediate response to Jesus, that is, an outpouring of desire to be united with Jesus in his suffering. Indeed. the more immediate response may be what Ignatius had in mind.

To close, either a single colloquy is made to Jesus, or the triple colloquy is used. This same option obtains for all the colloquies of the Third Week.

The Mysteries

Ignatius has his own emphases when he outlined the mysteries for the Third Week; however, he was also careful not to leave very much out from the Passion accounts of each of the four gospels. The result is a series of woven accounts, not patterned on one gospel in particular. Because of the "pearl-stringing" some directors depart from the precise points given by Ignatius and instead focus their retreatants' attention on one gospel at a time. Others let the retreatants go through Ignatius's points with their Scripture in hand, letting the retreatants raise and resolve any problems which Ignatius's text and the retreatants' own reading of Scripture might provoke.

There are advantages to the latter approach. For instance, in his rendering of the Last Supper [289], Ignatius wrote that Judas was going to sell the Lord. Some retreatants find that this emphasis, while appropriately dramatic, does not really address what must have been a very ambiguous and troubling decision for Judas. Or, to take another example, Ignatius referred to the Last Supper as "the greatest sign of his love" [289, pt. 3]. Was it the greatest sign? How so? What were Jesus' intentions? What are we to make of Jesus' desire to unite himself to his disciples? What was going through Jesus' mind as he offered the bread and wine? Was his desire, his prayer, heard and answered? All of this is to suggest that struggling with Ignatius's text can often trigger a profound reappraisal of the scriptural passages themselves; and this is no small help in entering into prayer.

Theological Problems

Some retreatants may get into a theological mess with any talk of Jesus' having died "for me." Similar problems may have cropped up earlier, but they often come to the surface powerfully during the Third Week. A retreatant may say to herself, for instance, that Jesus did not even know her, so how could he possibly have been conscious of having died for her? She is right, of course. Jesus did not know her, could not possibly have known her, if he was truly "human like us in all things, but sin" and if his two natures were and remain unmingled. Or, if the retreatant has studied formal theology, she might object that Jesus did not intend to redeem anyone, that this was the theological meaning given to the cross by the early Church from the perspective of the Resurrection. Though these difficulties are often construed to be distractions, such theological questions should rarely be dismissed outright. Indeed, the director will often have to engage the retreatant theologically.

Some directors, however, have an aversion to bringing theology into retreats. Some forget that we love with our minds, that our minds and hearts are one and the same, even though our language almost always divides them. With our greater sensitivity to directing those we sometimes characterize as "thinking types," we now know that ignoring a theological problem can be tantamount to ending the retreat then and there for some retreatants. Thus in situations like the one outlined above, it can be helpful to try to tease out the theological roots of the problem. For example, some retreatants are unaware that our tradition holds that Jesus is still a human being; they think he left his humanity, his feelings, his memories behind at some point. In so doing, they do not appreciate that Jesus is the person he is today quite precisely because of the experiences he had some two thousand years ago. He carries his history with him forever, but they want to relate to some other Jesus instead of the historical Jesus who is risen. Sadly, the value of Ignatian contemplation risks being lost on them, as it is reduced to a history lesson, and an ambiguous one at that.

Other retreatants have a similar objection, insisting that they want to relate to Jesus as he is now, that is, they want to relate to the resurrected Jesus, the Jesus who apparently no longer suffers. Without taking over the retreatant's retreat and over-programming it, the director might want to challenge the retreatant to realize that the paschal mystery continues today, that the cross still constitutes the present reality of Jesus, that so long as anyone suffers, Jesus identifies with the sufferer. Jesus takes up the cause of the sufferer; and this constitutes as real a cross as any, assuming, as we must, that Jesus' identification with the poor and suffering of our world is fundamentally real and not simply pious talk. It is as though Jesus himself continuously prays for the grace of the Third Week with regard to the world: "for sorrow with the world in sorrow, to be broken with the world broken, for tears and deep grief because of the great pain the world endures." And this is hardly to be dismissed as being too far-fetched an approach given Jesus' clearly personal identification with the poor in Matthew's account of the Last Judgment, and given the profound question Saul experienced: "Saul, why do you persecute *me*?"

Another type of problem has to be faced when directors find their retreatants practically disowning their imaginations in this week, protesting that to this point they had made everything up themselves. A few pointers may have to be given on the differences between using the imagination to re-present and to enhance our

> *The director might want to challenge the retreatant to realize that the paschal mystery continues today, that the cross still constitutes the present reality of Jesus, that so long as anyone suffers, Jesus identifies with the sufferer.*

participation in reality and using the imagination to escape into pure fantasy.

It is important to remember that the stakes are high in the Third Week, and it is only to be expected that difficulties which were simmering just below the surface for several weeks—real difficulties—may arise at this time. They ought to be addressed respectfully, however they arise.

The Seventh Day

The seventh day, the day corresponding to Holy Saturday, is a unique day in the *Exercises*. There should be no formal prayer periods on this day after the repetition of the whole Passion at midnight and again in the morning. This is a time for retreatants to ponder what it would be like if Jesus were no longer to exist in their lives, how it would have felt to experience Jesus' death without knowing that his resurrection by the Father was imminent.

Directors can suggest that their retreatants think and try to feel what it must have been like for Mary and the other disciples to have lost Jesus, how empty and desolate they would have felt. The idea is for the retreatants to enter fully into an experience of having the bottom fall right out of their world. After all, they left behind the Second Week consolation of the apostolic life, now they have to let go of the "consolation" of union with Jesus. Since there is no palpable possible, the Holy Saturday experience is often one of absolute numbness, a feeling of being radically alone. It is not normally a bitter experience, for the pain is more diffused than that; and any vestiges of anger have already been routed out. There is no reason for retreatants to feel sorry for themselves. At this point in the *Exercises,* after inordinate attachments have been purified, after the imagination and will have been focused so singularly on being present to Jesus, after moments of a most personal and intimate union with him, Jesus' death dissolves everything. The retreatants should have no desires left, no purpose, no dynamism: they may even feel something akin to "freedom" or autonomy, but the feeling is alienating, isolating, and is without any dynamism of finality whatsoever. Even their elections are rendered meaningless without Jesus. And so they stand before God as open vessels, and, for Holy Saturday at least, profoundly empty vessels. At this point they are spiritually poor, and they are uniquely prepared for the absolutely gracious gift of Jesus' Resurrection by the Father on Easter Sunday. In fact, the degree to which the retreatants allow themselves to feel the emptiness that must have surrounded Jesus' death is the degree to which the Resurrection will be experienced as the pure and delightful gift of the Father that it was, and, therefore, also as a truly joyful event.

Transition

Since the Fourth Week continues directly from the Third Week with the visit to Mary [299], directors often suggest to their retreatants that they focus on Mary in a special way on Holy Saturday.

Conclusion

One of the tendencies directors frequently have to face is their desire that their retreatants have the most historically accurate, the most meaningful, the most comprehensive, realistic, rooted, sacred, powerful, and wonderful experience of the person and life of Jesus possible. There is nothing wrong with that desire except when a time constraint—say of thirty days—is placed on the retreatant. We know only too well that it is rarely possible to gain a depth of insight into the person and life of Jesus without many years of praying, studying, living, loving, and serving.

It is one thing to state this, and another to live with this desire being frustrated. And it is frustrated, and frequently so, when, for instance, a retreatant never quite grasps the importance of Jesus' own election, preferring to view Jesus' life as excruciatingly passive, and thereby assuming a concomitantly passive personal stance towards life as well. Or the desire is equally frustrated when a retreatant never allows Jesus to be fully human, opting instead to hold on to the popular algebraic notion of a half-human, half-divine Jesus (with the divine decidedly predominant), thus insuring that Jesus is un-followable. It is also faced when essentially all of a retreat is focused on overcoming a particular psychological or spiritual roadblock that never quite comes down, perhaps because the roadblock has become an idol, or because the retreatant insists that God remove the roadblock before he or she will respond. The frustration is equally faced when a simply beautiful retreatant's prayer sadly resembles distantly-familiar Aesop's fairy tales, replete with magic and little moral lessons.

What then happens to all the theory of what the *Exercises* can be? At those moments, and at the risk of sounding too pious, the director nonetheless has to be certain that God is bending over backwards looking for a possibility to break through to the retreatant, waiting for that moment of openness to invite by attraction. There is no comparing God's infinite desire for the retreatant to the director's desire. Nor can we assume that following the exact pattern of the *Exercises* is God's priority, for God has a habit of indicating that, for all our lofty pondering on the structure and dynamics of the *Exercises,* the real dynamic, and the matter for discernment, always remains the concrete relationship between God and the retreatant .

Notes

[1] The term "historical Jesus" is here used quite deliberately to affirm the inseparability of the "historical Jesus" and the "Christ of faith." The faith affirmation of the Christian today parallels the resurrection affirmation of the women and apostles: namely, that it was precisely the historical Jesus who was raised by the Father and who now is at the core of Christian religious experience. Failure to be clear on this matter can often lead to praying the *Exercises* (and indeed praying and reading the Gospels) as though one were reading a history book rather than encountering the real-live Jesus of history now and forever risen by the Father. The Resurrection itself is the Father's quite deliberate response to the specifics of Jesus' life.

[2] Here and throughout, the translations of the *Exercises* are the author's own.

[3] *En las tercera semana se confirma la elección de mejor vida. En esta tercera semana se consolida y reafirma la elección ya hecha de una vida mejor . . .* (p. 479, n. 240). See Miguel Lop SJ, *Ejercicios espirituales y directorios* (Barcelona: Editorial Balmes, 1964).

PHILIP L. BOROUGHS

Using Ignatian Discernment

discernment

Periodically throughout one's life, circumstances arise or realities become clear that cause one to reconsider one's work, ministry, or living arrangements. Diminishing energy, feelings of boredom or of being taken for granted, or an emerging desire for new challenges can signal a need to reappraise one's situation. Obviously, these times of transition are unsettling, and they can be stressful as one begins to let go of the security of the familiar and searches for new clarity and direction. However, these periods also can generate new possibilities and a renewed sense of responsibility for one's life.

At times such as these, the Serenity Prayer of Alcoholics Anonymous seems particularly appropriate: "O God, grant me the courage to change the things that I can change, the serenity to accept the things that I cannot change, and the wisdom to know the difference." Sometimes circumstances warrant a fundamental change in one's life, while at other times a change of attitude or behavior seems more appropriate. As one critically reviews his or her situation and assesses available options, one wisely might wonder whether there are any norms or principles to help one choose among the options.

In the *Spiritual Exercises* St. Ignatius of Loyola offers a number of principles for discernment which can be extremely useful for those entering into a time of transition.

One of the major goals of the *Exercises* is to assist those who undertake them to make the right life choices. The principles of discernment reflect Ignatius's own experience of prayerful decision making, and a brief review of the major transitions in his life will offer a context for his insights.

Ignatius's Life

On 20 May 1521 Ignatius was wounded in the battle of Pamplona, and in the long recuperation period which followed, a fundamental reorientation of his life began. Over the next several months, as he contemplated his future, Ignatius became aware of different interior movements affecting him. Gradually he recognized the patterns of these interior movements, noting that certain spirits or desires produced peace and hope while others, which initially delighted him, eventually left him sad and depressed. As a result of these fluctuations, Ignatius decided to follow the spirit or direction which ultimately consoled him, and thus his religious quest began in earnest.

Abandoning his life as a soldier and courtier, he moved to Manresa and formally commenced a spiritual journey which gradually helped him to identify and understand his limits and disoriented attachments as well as his deepest dreams and desires. After months of intense prayer and penance, mystical experiences, and interior growth, he embarked on a pilgrimage to Jerusalem. There he hoped to spend his life visiting the holy places and helping souls. However, after he had been in Jerusalem only nineteen days, the Roman Catholic authorities ordered him to leave. The political climate was tense, and they did not want to assume liability for this questionable religious enthusiast.

Accepting their legitimate authority over him, Ignatius concluded that it must not be God's will that he remain in Jerusalem. He decided that he needed further education if he were to serve God's people in some other capacity. He returned to Spain and began studying grammar at the University of Barcelona. Two years later he advanced to study the humanities at Alcalá. After many months, however, his austere lifestyle and his growing reputation as a lay spiritual director caused such controversy that he was investigated by the Inquisition. Although exonerated of any wrongdoing, he was forbidden to continue his spiritual ministry. Consequently he moved to the University of Salamanca. There the same pattern was repeated, and once again he had to revise his plans. Ignatius then transferred to the University of Paris, where he spent the next seven years earning his bachelor's and master's degrees. These were intense years of study and spiritual ministry, and they were also years when he gathered some lifelong companions who shared his ideals and his commitment to service.

As his formal education drew to a close, Ignatius became seriously ill and was advised by his doctors to return to his native country to recuperate. He journeyed home with the understanding that he and his companions would reassemble in Venice once he had recovered. From there they hoped to gain passage for Jerusalem, where they would spend the rest of their lives in ministry. Ignatius and his friends vowed to wait one year in Venice for passage to Jerusalem; but if they could not arrange their trip during that time because of political turmoil, they would travel to Rome and place themselves at the service of the pope. Since no ships left Venice for Jerusalem that year, they proceeded on to Rome in keeping with their vow.

As their reputation for holiness and ministerial effectiveness spread, requests for their services began to arrive from various corners of the world, forcing this rather loose-knit group of friends to consider the nature of their commitment to each other. After weeks of prayerful deliberation, they decided to form a religious community and elected Ignatius to be their religious superior. Although he initially declined the position, subsequent prayer and consultation with his spiritual director moved him to accept. He spent the last fifteen years of his life as the superior general of the nascent Society of Jesus. During this time of rapid growth and development, Ignatius not only provided this new community with inspired leadership, but he also prayerfully drafted its constitutions.

With the exception of his seven years at Paris and his final years in Rome, Ignatius moved frequently throughout his adult life. His constant effort was to discern and follow God's will within the social and historical realities of his time. Although he was the recipient of many mystical graces, few of them provided him with specific instructions about the decisions he faced. Rather, these mystical experiences confirmed the general direction of his life and God's ongoing companionship with him. Decisions about particular choices he faced required prayer and discernment to discover God's will. Ignatius's early lessons in the discernment of spirits, his respect for human learning and reflectivity, and his courage to act once he felt he knew what God wanted of him facilitated his prayerful decision making during the numerous transitions of his life.

Predispositions for Discernment

Ignatius's religious experience and his *Spiritual Exercises* suggest that, if an individual wishes to enter into a process of discernment in order to discover God's will, certain predispositions are necessary: interior freedom, sufficient knowledge of self and the world, imagination, patience, and the courage to act responsibly. Without these graces, true discernment is not possible.

Interior Freedom: The first paragraph of the *Spiritual Exercises* clearly asserts that interior freedom is a sine qua non for finding God's will: "We call Spiritual Exercises every way of preparing and disposing the soul to rid itself of all inordinate attachments and, after their removal, of seeking and finding the will of God in the disposition of our life for the salvation of our soul" (SpEx 1). When Ignatius speaks of ridding oneself of inordinate attachments, he can be very explicit. In the Meditation on the Two Standards, he identifies inordinate attachments primarily as temptations to riches, honor, and pride (SpEx 142). Today we might describe them as an attachment to possessions or a specific lifestyle, a desire for recognition or a preoccupation with the opinion of others, and an insistence on being in control of one's life or radical self-sufficiency. Ignatius believed that attachments such as these would so condition one's life that one's relationship with God would be seriously compromised and one's freedom to find God's will would be lost.

During times of transition in a person's life, other variations of inordinate attachments also can surface. For example, at the first sign of serious difficulty, some people immediately search for new living or work possibilities, fearful of the asceticism required for long-term commitments. Others, feeling misunderstood and unvalued, find it easier to cling to chronic anger and bitterness than to identify and address the source of these feelings and move to a more integrated life. Still others become so completely preoccupied with their own personal growth that they ignore the legitimate needs of those whose lives are interconnected with theirs. Whatever form an inordinate attachment takes, it can effectively inhibit the possibility of true discernment because it centers one's life in oneself rather than in God.

Knowledge: True spiritual freedom or detachment depends on self-knowledge. More than just an understanding of one's limits or even one's patterns of temptation, self-knowledge requires a profound awareness of one's gifts and one's deepest desires. However, during times of transition, individuals frequently say that they do not really know what they want. This is often part of the initial unrest which introduces a need for change. But it also can be an invitation for individuals to reclaim their deepest desires, those essential values which give ultimate meaning to their lives, their relationships, and their involvement with the world.

For example, when one becomes overwhelmed juggling the increasing demands of family and career, or exhausted by the mounting expectations of one's ministerial position, or seriously disillusioned by institutional intransigence, identifying again or reformulating one's deepest desires provides a starting point for making new choices. Articulating one's deepest desires helps one to prioritize commitments and can provide some perspective for letting go of those concerns which jeopardize what is more important. Sometimes people come to realize that they have to reconsider their original life commitment because of subsequent choices they have made over the years. Others may discern that their deepest desires have not changed, but that they have to find a new or healthier way of living them out. Still others may experience a call to live out their original commitment even more radically. Reappropriating one's deepest desires is a critical dimension of self-knowledge.

However, for Ignatius self-knowledge was not enough. He spent many years studying in some of the most respected universities of his day and achieved an advanced degree in theology because he believed that education was a critical component for ministry. He even reduced his intense spiritual activities during his university years because he discerned that his extended prayer was interfering with his commitment to study. Ignatius emphasized education as a significant component in the formation of young Jesuits and as an important ministry of the Society of Jesus because through it he promoted the ongoing transformation of individuals, church, and society. Consequently, not only knowing oneself, but also knowing the complexities of any given situation, possessing a critical understanding of systems and structures, and having sufficient education for one's current ministry or some new possibility are critical dimensions of a discernment process.

Imagination: Knowledge in concert with imagination can produce new possibilities. Ignatius clearly manifested an imaginative approach to ministry through the creation of the Society of Jesus and its novel structures and methods. He also used the power of imagination in his approach to prayer. Through an imaginative entry into the Scriptures and other specially constructed meditations, Ignatius hoped to dispose individuals for a more vital union with the living God. The Ignatian method of prayer encourages a felt knowledge of God which engages the whole person and generates a radical recentering of one's life.

The process of discernment comes alive when people can imagine new possibilities for themselves. However, when an individual is tired, confused, or burned out, it is often impossible to generate the energy necessary to reconceive one's reality. The imagination can work very creatively under pressure, but when one is overly stressed, the imagination withers. In order to be hopeful and capable of envisioning options for oneself, rest and play are essential. Furthermore, those activities which give an individual true peace and an enthusiasm for life ultimately are connected with God's will for her or him. When one has the imagination to understand that God speaks through one's deepest desires, desires which are inherent to the person God has created, then one is more likely to discern how God might be leading one.

Patience: In Western culture there is such an emphasis on speed and efficiency that it is often difficult to accept that patience and an attentive waiting also are essential to the process of discernment. Throughout his life Ignatius experienced both the necessity and the hidden blessings of waiting. It took him ten months to recover from his injuries at the battle of Pamplona, but it was during this time that he began to learn discernment of spirits. Ignatius's trip to Jerusalem also lasted about ten months, and although he was not allowed to remain there, the journey itself taught him to trust in God's providence and to identify with Jesus' suffering. Ignatius then spent ten years in studies, followed by another year waiting to see if he and his companions would be able to travel to Jerusalem. These long years prepared him for sacramental ministry in the church and blessed him with a community of companions who shared his commitment to service. Although Ignatius's plans frequently led to the unexpected, the experience of ongoing discernment and waiting for God's will to be clarified often issued in mystical graces and heightened union with God.

The attentive waiting frequently required during a time of transition demands discipline and deep interior freedom. As one's accustomed life starts to unravel, it is natural to desire an immediate alternative. One may be tempted to settle for the first option which materializes or to force an alternative before one has the appropriate energy to imagine something new. Sometimes individuals grow weary waiting for God to act while, ironically, God is waiting for them to let go of an inordinate attachment and surrender to God in trust. It is also humbling to wait for physical and psychological healing processes to run their course. Individuals in transition need to be patient with themselves and the integrity of their own process of development without at the same time losing sight of their gifts and talents. Waiting periods usually are longer than one thinks endurable, and during these times of darkness people are often tempted to question their judgment and self-worth. Therefore, it is critical to check in regularly with friends and a spiritual director for confirmation of one's decision to wait for God with openness and trust.

The process of discernment comes alive when people can imagine new possibilities for themselves.

Courage: The final predisposition necessary for discernment is the courage to act once one's discernment is complete and God's call seems clear. Ignatius seemed blessed with this gift. Over the strong objections of his family, he radically reoriented his life when he departed for Manresa, and his pilgrim journey to Jerusalem certainly reflected his deep resolve to follow God in trust. Possibly even more trusting was his obedience to church authorities who insisted that in spite of his long journey he leave Jerusalem after only nineteen days. His commitment to years of study and to his ministry as a lay spiritual director in spite of several investigations by the Inquisition reveals the depth of his determination. Ignatius was not afraid of controversy or misunderstanding, but he aggressively sought their resolution in order to confirm his discernment and protect the integrity of his ministry.

For the person who senses that a significant transition in life is necessary, the changes that one decides upon can be difficult for others to accept or support. While their input may legitimately suggest further discernment, their reserve also may stimulate the discerner to greater resolve and courage. This may be especially true when the call to leave one situation does not include a clearly defined alternative. Sometimes it is only after making a decision and living with it that one finds the space and energy needed for discovering a new direction. While others may interpret this initial ambiguity as a sign of faulty discernment, in fact it may embody great trust in God on the part of the person in transition.

Finally, discerning God's will often becomes increasingly subtle as one's union with God matures. After a person has had a faithful relationship with God for years, God may trust him or her so much that God does not appear to be involved in a decision that has to be made. Instead, God encourages the person to make a decision based on his or her deepest desires. By deciding on one's own, the discerner ultimately is acting in accord with God's will, but he or she may perceive it only through the subsequent peace that God grants to confirm the decision. In this instance God enhances the responsibility of the discerner to act out of the union that their loving relationship has achieved. Here again a spiritual director can offer helpful support and perspective to the individual in discernment.

The Ignatian Rules for Discernment

As one enters into a period of transition and discernment, it is wise to assess one's interior freedom and depth of knowledge, to reflect on the creativity of one's imagination and the durability of one's patience, and to pray for the courage to act responsibly. These predispositions will assist the mature discerner in identifying and applying appropriate principles suggested by Ignatius in his *Spiritual Exercises*, particularly those contained in his reflections on Making a Choice of a Way of Life (SpEx 169-189) and his Rules for Discernment of Spirits (SpEx 313-336).

During the Second Week of the *Exercises*, while the retreatant is walking with Jesus through the mysteries and events of his life, Ignatius invites the person to consider how she or he wishes to embody discipleship. For Ignatius, union with God is the ultimate goal of one's life. Therefore, during this week Ignatius encourages the retreatant to choose a way of life which most enhances that union. If one has already made a permanent disposition of one's life prior to entering into the *Spiritual Exercises*, one's discernment may focus on ways of reorienting one's life in order to enhance one's union with God.[1]

Ignatius describes three times or ways in which a good choice of life may be made *when* one's basic options are clear. One is ready to make a decision (1) when God so directly moves an individual that there is no hesitation that this choice is from God; (2) when the individual can discern patterns of consolation and desolation which indicate which choice will bring life; (3) when the individual is peaceful, that is, not moved one way or another by different spirits of consolation or desolation, and turns to various rational and imaginative approaches to find God's will (SpEx 175-177). Although the first way of making a decision may be rather rare because of its intensity and specificity, nonetheless many people do have unique spiritual experiences in their lives against which they can measure the wisdom of a subsequent and more particular decision.[2] When one is trying to determine if the conclusion of one's discernment seems appropriate, one can compare it with a previous incontrovertible manifestation of God's love and examine the more recent decision for resonance or dissonance with the former. If the current decision seems in harmony with the earlier experience, that resonance may function as confirmation. If the two experiences do not seem part of a graced continuum, the more recent decision probably needs further discernment.

The second method of discernment is more characteristic of those praying over their alternatives during a period of transition. Whether moved by internal needs or external opportunities, people often decide how to make a significant change in their lives by taking their options to prayer and watching their patterns of consolation and desolation. When they have prayed for some time and can sense that a particular alternative consistently leads them to deep consolation, they are ready to make a decision.

Of course, it is important to remember that Ignatius provides a specific definition of consolation and desolation. According to him, consolation is an interior movement which causes an individual to be inflamed by a love of God above all created things. Consolation includes any increase in faith, hope, and love which brings deep peace (SpEx 316). Conversely, desolation is described as that interior movement which produces darkness, turmoil, and restlessness that leads an individual away from God. Afflicting a discerner with temptations and disturbances, desolation diminishes faith, hope, and love (SpEx 317). True consolation, then, while producing deep peace, does not eliminate the possibility of ongoing challenge, suffering, or even dryness accompanying one's discerned choice. Similarly, what may at first appear pleasing or appropriate may ultimately lead to desolation (SpEx 332). It is critical, then, to discern the origin and evolution of interior movements in order to recognize patterns of grace and patterns of temptation (SpEx 333-335).

During times of transition careful discernment is particularly crucial because easy answers to one's difficulties may provide temporary escape, but old problems return if the real issues of the time were never faced. Sometimes, too, people hearing God's call shy away from it because it sounds too challenging, and as a result they may never find the meaningful life they desire. Others, failing to commit themselves to regular prayer, never quiet down enough to really hear what God may be saying. Discernment requires faithful prayer, critical reflectivity, and magnanimity of spirit in order to be effective.

Ignatius's third approach to discernment may seem at first simply an analytical way of making a decision, but it should be noted that this method, like the second way of discernment, requires prayerful confirmation to be complete. In order to emphasize its prayerful context, Ignatius carefully describes this technique in some detail (SpEx 178-183). As stated earlier, this more cognitive approach is helpful when one does not sense significant interior movements of consolation and desolation from which to discern a way of action. Having identified a possible choice of a way of life, one centers oneself before God and prays to be free of any inordinate attachments. Then one asks God to move one's will or deepest desires and enlighten one's intellect to recognize which choice would most bring about God's reign. At this point one weighs the pros and cons both of a particular decision and then decides on whichever option seems the most reasonable. Finally, and this is where the second form of discernment comes into play, one offers the decision to God in prayer, asking God to accept and confirm one's decision if it reflects God's will. By seeking confirmation in prayer, one is ultimately looking for a pattern of consolation or desolation to indicate the appropriateness of one's decision. If, after a period of time, one remains peaceful and energized by one's decision, that is a good indication of consolation and confirmation. On the other hand, if doubts, enduring questions, and desolation occur, then the discernment is not complete.

Ignatius also proposes other approaches to this third way of discernment. He suggests that one might imagine what one would say to a stranger in an identical situation to one's own. Then one should follow one's own advice (SpEx 185). Or one might imagine oneself at the moment of death, or facing God at the last judgment, and reflect on the choice one would like to have made from that vantage point (SpEx 186-187). Through the use of the imagination, Ignatius wants the individual to see beyond the confines of the present moment to gain a broader perspective on one's life. As in the more analytical approach earlier described, once a decision is reached, it is offered to the Lord for acceptance and confirmation (SpEx 188). Without this confirmation from God, the discernment is deficient.

Discernment requires faithful prayer, critical reflectivity, and magnanimity of spirit in order to be effective.

Obviously, Ignatius's three methods or times for choosing a way of life are helpful to one who has negotiated the transition process long enough to have clarified some options. But what about the people who have not yet sensed alternatives or are not sure what changes need to be made? Does Ignatius offer them any guidelines for their discernment process? From the Rules for the Discernment of Spirits, several insights are pertinent. First, Ignatius explains that, when God is leading a person who honestly seeks God's will, consolation, courage, and peace will characterize the situation. The evil spirit, on the other hand, uses the opposite approach and tries to distract and discourage the discerner with anxiety and false reasoning (SpEx 314-315; 335).[3] It is interesting to note that the evil spirit often uses false ideas to generate unhappiness, while God often blesses individuals with peace and hope to help them understand how God is at work. The relationship between positive and negative ideas and feelings should be reflected upon when one is trying to discern how temptations may be at work.

Ignatius warns the discerner not to make any significant decisions when one is in desolation (SpEx 318). His reasoning seems clear: When one feels distant from God and beset with darkness, confusion, and anxiety, it is not a good time to alter decisions made freely during a time of consolation. This reasonable advice needs some qualification. Ignatius's definition of consolation and desolation refers primarily to one's relationship with God and the effective consequences of that relationship. Therefore he cautions that one should not leave a significant commitment or meaningful ministry simply because one is feeling discouraged or misunderstood, for these feelings do not always indicate true spiritual desolation. Ignatius believes that freely made decisions should withstand periods of struggle and pain. However, if one is in a situation where one feels physically and psychologically overwhelmed or seriously threatened, she or he should move to some protected space from which one can discern an appropriate response. From this vantage point one can better discern whether one needs a radical change in one's life or whether some alteration in one's way of proceeding would be more appropriate. This is particularly true when one is involved in a destructive relationship or when a work situation has become intolerable. It is important to recognize one's own limits and to act responsibly before one allows oneself to be destroyed by outside forces. This does not deny Ignatius's earlier principle of not making decisions during times of desolation. Rather, this action enhances interior freedom since it empowers one to discern and act more intentionally. Furthermore, self-protective action usually generates consolation because it provides some perspective and control over an unmanageable situation.

Since desolation diffuses energy and darkens prayer, a natural temptation when one is discouraged is to reduce one's spiritual activities. However, Ignatius advocates the opposite approach (SpEx 319). During times of desolation he encourages individuals to intensify their prayer and boldly affirm their fidelity to God in trust. Ignatius believes that times of desolation, although unpleasant, could heighten self-knowledge and promote a greater appreciation of one's need for God (SpEx 322). In response to the temptations which frequently characterize periods of desolation, Ignatius urges strength in the face of fear, openness instead of secrecy, and diligence where one is particularly vulnerable (SpEx 325-327).

When one experiences disorientation during a time of transition, it is difficult to remain open to God and to others. One often wants to withdraw in self-protection. Obviously, added time for reflectivity and inner renewal is essential, but too much isolation also can heighten temptations about one's self-worth and inspire negative comparisons with others. If one is caught in a spiral of negative self-images and increasing depression, discerning the origin, movement, and end point of these negative spirits will assist one in discovering the patterns of one's temptations and strategies for dealing with them (SpEx 333-335).

Of course, one needs to be equally cautious during times of intense consolation. It is easy to make dramatic resolutions when one is extremely happy, only to abandon them later when the consequences of those resolutions become clear. Whereas consolation truly may be a gift from God, the conclusions one draws from that consolation may not be part of the grace being offered at that time (SpEx 336). For example, someone may be deeply appreciative of the unconditional love and acceptance he or she experiences in a special relationship, but that appreciation in itself does not necessarily indicate that one should marry this loving friend.

When one experiences disorientation during a time of transition, it is difficult to remain open to God and to others.

Finally, when one realizes that a radical change in one's life or ministry is necessary, but an energizing alternative is not yet clear, it may be necessary to choose an interim solution from which to continue the discernment process. While this possibility lacks the focus and security of something more permanent, it honors the integrity of the discernment process and allows the individual time to explore possibilities without the pressure of making a major decision hastily. Ignatius and his early companions spent an interim year in Venice waiting for a ship to take them to Jerusalem. While that opportunity never arose, it was a productive year of prayer and ministry, and it prepared them for their journey to Rome and the foundation of the Society of Jesus. By extending the discernment process, an interim period can decrease the pressure around making a decision while encouraging further openness and creativity.

Whether one is just beginning to raise questions about one's situation, or is waiting patiently in the dark as God mysteriously leads one forward, or has identified one or two clear options for final decision, Ignatius provides several principles of discernment for a person in transition. These principles emerged out of his own experiences of transition and were effective because of his interior freedom, his knowledge of himself and his world, his fertile imagination, his deep patience, and his courage to act responsibly. Ignatius's principles of discernment manifest the wisdom so beautifully requested in the Serenity Prayer.

Throughout his life Ignatius discovered that, by continually searching for God's will and trying to live in accord with it, he experienced an ever deepening union with God. That is the hope of all discernment. During inevitable times of transition, prayerful discernment clarifies options and prepares one to live with greater intentionality. Some transitions lead to radical change. Others lead to a careful refocusing of one's ongoing commitments. Whatever the outcome, the ongoing process of discernment supports adult Christians in living responsible discipleship.

Notes

[1] Ignatius accepted that some life commitments are permanent and therefore not open to further choice once they have been embraced. Ordination and marriage are two situations he specifically mentions. Obviously, some people in transition are going to be examining these commitments as well. There are reasons which can necessitate reconsidering these commitments and the Rules for Discernment of Spirits and Ignatius's reflections on making a choice of life can be helpful in this reconsideration. Admittedly, this issue needs greater explication than the scope of this article can accommodate.

[2] See William A. Barry SJ, "Touchstone Experiences as Divining Rods in Discernment," Review for Religious 49, no. 3 (July-August 1990): 610-614.

[3] In his notes on the General Examination of Conscience, Ignatius claims that human thoughts have one of three origins: they come from self, from God or the good spirit, or from the evil spirit (SpEx 32). Ignatius believed in a personification of evil who could tempt human beings, but not control their freedom to make choices. Consequently, his Rules for the Discernment of Spirits identify both the patterns of the good spirit and the evil spirit. Although many people today prefer to describe the evil spirit not in personal terms but rather as unconscious resistance or negative cultural influences, nevertheless Ignatius's rules for discernment offer practical guidelines for dealing with positive and negative interior movements

Discernment and Decision Making

Do not conform any longer to the pattern of this world, but be transformed by the renewing of your mind. Then you will be able to test and approve what God's will is—his good, pleasing, and perfect will (Rm 12:2).

Iscernment may be defined as a conscious experience of God's grace drawing one to a course of action or exposing the influence that a projected course of action will have on one's relationship to God in Christ. It is not, therefore, some kind of generalized awareness of God or of his presence, but an insertion into a process—the process of finding and owning the will of God or, in other words, of Christian decision making. A discernment which does not lead to a decision is incomplete, has been aborted at some point along the way. When a decision has been reached, it becomes a concrete expression, an incarnation of one's desire to respond to God's love and to serve his kingdom.

Personal Freedom

In spite of the laudable wishes of many Christians to move away from an exaggerated individualism, the historical circumstances in which we find ourselves today force the individual person to take much more responsibility than in the past for his or her decisions. In pre-Vatican II Catholicism there were structures, modes of exercising authority, theological and moral certainties, as well as a cultural and social underpinning of religious observance, all of which both lessened the need for personal decision making and made it easier on those occasions when it was required. Post-Vatican II Catholicism has seen a breakdown of

structures, a questioning of authority, fewer certainties, a part-
ing of the ways between the values of the Gospel and those of an
increasingly secular society, all of which places a heavy burden
of responsibility on the individual. As a result many people discover that they are disorientated by a freedom for which they are
ill-prepared, the freedom to make decisions for themselves.

Such a disconcerting experience reveals how frequently
ambivalent is our attitude towards personal freedom. It is a value
we proclaim and which we defend vigorously if it is, or even seems
to be, threatened. Yet we may well shy away from some of its
inevitable consequences: the increased level of anxiety it brings
into our lives; the ambiguities of right and wrong, of good and
better; the depth of commitment which a major decision entails.
It seems as if personal freedom must be paid for by pain and suffering.

Our awareness is also heightened that we live in: (a) a world
of desires (maybe to be human is to desire); (b) a world of limits
(some present within our own being and personality, others
imposed from outside of ourselves); (c) a world of choices (because
the desires and the limits must somehow be brought together in
some kind of tolerable ordering—harmony would be too strong
a word—otherwise there is chaos, even insanity). Out of this contemporary human and Christian situation arises the necessity for
a pedagogy of discernment.

Images of God

It is hardly an exaggeration to say that our understanding and
practice of discernment depend in large part on our image or
images of God and on how we experience our relationship with
him. Such images are often more implicit than explicit. They can
operate in a subtle, even subconscious, way, influencing our attitudes and actions without our being in touch with what is happening. The more we grow in self-knowledge, the greater the
possibility of rectifying the distortions in our images of God and
thereby freeing ourselves to be motivated and directed through the
mediation of images which more accurately reflect the reality of
God. In the context of discernment, a crucial distinction arises
between the set of images which both expresses and leads to deism
and an opposing set which expresses and leads to theism. What is
this distinction concerned about?

Deism is a conviction of the existence of God as a hypothesis required by reason, but allowing no place for any divine revelation. This deistic God created the universe and set it in motion, but then left it to its own devices, offering no further enlightenment or guidance. On the analogy of an absentee landlord, this is an "absentee God," majestic and all-powerful certainly, but remote, aloof, uncaring. Such a God, in practice if not necessarily in theory, is experienced as impersonal.

In contrast, theism is belief in a personal God who does reveal himself and, in so revealing, shows love for his people and guides them to their eternal destiny. By definition Judaism and Christianity are theistic religions, and both the Old and New Testaments witness to the reality of God's concern for and active presence in his creation. It is clear that discernment can be a realistic possibility only within a theistic vision of the universe.

But in fact many Christians live their lives almost as though they were deists, as though God were not immanent in the world, involved in communal and personal histories, sharing with us his wisdom, being Emmanuel: God-with-us. A simple but challenging way of discovering where we stand experientially (not theoretically) vis-à-vis a deistic or theistic image of God is to ask: Do I believe deeply in the prayer of intercession? Do I make such intercessory prayer? Or have I reservations and doubts about its effectiveness? How do I react affectively to the words of Jesus "Ask and it will be given to you"?

Models of Faith

As we continue to look at some of the presuppositions of discernment, our understanding of faith emerges as another central issue. Again we can examine two contrasting models. On the one hand faith can be seen as an assent to a collection of divinely authenticated facts or truths which otherwise would be inaccessible to human reasoning. Through faith these are now accepted on God's own and sole authority. The Christian creeds are articulations of such faith. This approach is sometimes called the "propositional" model of faith, and the stress is on the intellectual component of the act of faith.

The alternative model sees faith as a personal commitment to the living God who invites us into an ever-deeper relationship with him—God who reveals himself as the Thou to our I, and not as abstract or speculative truth. This God makes himself known as Lover, and not only or even primarily as Teacher. The believer then reaches out in response to God, not as someone might think vaguely about marriage, but as a person in love yearns passionately for union with his or her beloved. This approach can be termed the "encounter" model of faith, and the stress is on the personal and holistic nature of the faith commitment. For discernment to be possible, this "encounter" view is necessary, for only within the experiential relationship to which this model points can we discover the existential will of God and through our decisions allow our lives to be shaped in accordance with it.

Unique Relationship

But, one might object, does not the "propositional" view already provide us with knowledge of God's plan and will? Do we need more than the guidance of the Scriptures, the creeds, church teaching? Once more it can be helpful to posit a pair of contrasts. First, there is "global teaching." By this is meant all that the "propositional" model of faith provides on the doctrinal, moral, and spiritual levels. We communicate it to one another through catechesis, homilies, lectures, writing, and so forth. Such teaching is addressed to all and is presumed to be, in large part at least, applicable to all. Our knowledge and appreciation of it are necessary for Christian living.

But on the other hand each of us has a unique, personal relationship with God which is not and cannot be identified with that of others. It possesses a radical incommunicability. This relationship can only be experienced at the depths of our being, at that innermost core which the spiritual tradition refers to as the "heart." It is precisely there that God speaks most directly to each person and where each discerns what is immediately appropriate and relevant to him or her in the "global teaching." The issue in discernment is always the question: To what is God calling me—and only me in my unique relationship with him—concretely, here and now?

What we need, therefore, is faith in a personal God who reveals himself in an encounter which manifests his unique relationship with each of us. The next inquiry centers on the mode of God's communication with us or, more specifically, on the context of discernment: How does God make his will and intentions known to us? Throughout the history of religious experience, believers of many different traditions have pointed to three such modes of communication. The first might be termed "supernatural," or more accurately "preternatural," and is represented in the Christian tradition by the mediation of angels or good spirits. The second mode is intellectual or rational, whereby God enlightens our minds and so enables us to grasp his plan and our particular place or role in it. The third is affective or emotive, by which we are drawn and attracted to God himself and to all that is good, and then to that concrete good which is an expression and incarnation of our personal relationship with God here and now. It is not for us but for God to choose between these three modes. Our part is to be open to the possibility that God may make use of any of them or any combination of them.

Foundational Faith Experience

In any exercise of discernment or decision making, the experiential starting point has to be our awareness of who we are (our personal identity) and of who we are in relation to God (our faith identity). Both personal and faith identities can emerge and become firm only through experience and reflection on that experience. Each of us has what may be called a foundational faith experience, which is usually not just one particular experience of God (such as the conversion of Paul on the road to Damascus), but the accumulation of a whole series of experiences from the moment when God first became a reality for us. There is need to keep in touch with this foundational faith experience through the practice of personal anamnesis.

Discernment can be a realistic possibility only within a theistic vision of the universe.

This word anamnesis is taken from its usage in biblical and liturgical theology, where it refers to the power of memory to recall in faith past events in such a way as to make those events present. So at the Passover the Jewish people remember the Exodus, not just as a historical event, but as an event which is present to them here and now and whose effects they are experiencing here and now. Through their very act of recalling the Exodus they too, like their ancestors, are being liberated. Likewise in the Christian Eucharist it is through anamnesis, our calling to mind the death, resurrection, and ascension of Christ, that the entire paschal mystery is made present and effective for the remembering community.

In a similar way personal anamnesis is the recalling of our own history of religious experience and our personal salvation history. It puts us prayerfully in touch with the wonders of God's working in our lives and enables us to tap these inexhaustible sources of spiritual energy. We learn to appreciate, savor, taste, and draw comfort and strength from the experiential reality of God in our lives—that foundational faith experience which reveals who we are before God and in relation to God.

The link between personal anamnesis and discernment lies in that foundational faith experience becoming the touchstone for evaluating any new experience, any new situation, any new decision that has to be faced. Just as nothing can be measured without a measuring rod or weighed without a weighing scale, nothing can be discerned without a personal norm for discernment. Our foundational faith experience gives us our norm, our touchstone, our rod or scale.

Another image may help. We can visualize our foundational faith experience as a deep well. Any fresh experience, situation, or decision must be dropped into that well as we might drop a coin. If the sound we hear when the coin (the new experience) strikes the bottom is musical and harmonious, that indicates that there is a rightness about it, a fittingness, a harmony between it and our foundational faith experience—and so we can take it on board, accept it, integrate it. But if the sound is unmusical and dissonant, then we know that the new experience, situation, or decision is not in harmony with our foundational faith experience—and so we cannot take it on board, accept it, or integrate it. What the discerning person always seeks is a congruence of the "new" with his or her personal and faith identity.

Human and Divine Interaction

As a process of decision making, discernment involves the same human skills and techniques that are used in "secular" life (such as a counselor might suggest to a client who has problems with self-management). Examples would be the following:
- enunciating the questions clearly and concisely;
- discovering all the possible courses of action;
- gathering the needed evidence from different sources;

- clarifying the criteria to be applied in the decision;
- articulating the arguments for and against each option;
- weighing the importance of these arguments;
- committing oneself to one definite course of action;
- implementing the decision.

However, since discernment presupposes a faith context and is a search for the will of God, the process is one in which God needs to be explicitly present. What role does he play? Is God brought in

- as a substitute for the grind of the "secular" process?
- as a further step beyond that process?
- as a limiting factor (the decision cannot be against God's will)?
- as a source of enlightenment (the expert consultant)?
- as the person who already knows the answer to the discerner's questions?
- as the one to whom the discerner is ultimately responsible?

None of these suggestions is adequate to describe or explain the nature of the human and divine interaction which is the essence of discernment. The reality is deeper and more complex. God is in the process of discernment as the source of our ability to decide in freedom and of our desire to decide with integrity. He is our Creator who continues to sustain us in being and to breathe life into us as we think, reflect, and pray. He is immanent in his creation, in us, and so is acting from within, not from without. God acts from within our human personalities and our lived experience, and especially from within the reality of his graced relationship with us. Hence the importance of owning our foundational faith experience. And finally, God is the goal at which we aim throughout the discernment, since our decision will be a further insertion of ourselves into his plan for humankind, which is that we be forever in union with him. The discernment process is radically and inescapably contemplative.[1]

Note

[1] In this article I have drawn heavily on the writings of my Jesuit confreres Michael J. Buckley, John J. English, John C. Futrell, and Lawrence J. Murphy.

Communal Spiritual Consolation

The understanding and practice of spirituality has tended to focus on an individual person's experience and aspirations, but the individual needs to realize that spirituality is always in a communal context. If spirituality focuses on the experiences the individual has in, through, and of community, there is less danger of an individualistic spirituality. Consider the many examples in the Old Testament and the whole "Body of Christ" spirituality of the New Testament. Still one has to keep in mind that the individual is not to be considered as a cog in a collectivity.

It is important that each one of us realizes that "person" is constituted and known by relationship. Only in community does the individual find and appreciate personhood.[1] Otherwise, the focus can quite easily result in an individualistic spirituality which is self-centered and destructive of the person.

In my years of giving the Spiritual Exercises of St. Ignatius and of assisting communities to learn and do communal discernment, I have come to the awareness that even in spiritual affairs we take on an individualistic attitude when we judge and act. We know that the teachings of Hebrew Testament and the Christian Testament emphasize that our faith is a communal affair (for example, Ex 19-24, Jn 14-17, 1 Co 12, Ph 2). Yet we do not deeply enter into the communal expressions of our faith for insight, strength, and action. Rather, we put great effort into individual solutions and activities.

Ignatius Loyola, reflecting on his own life experience, gathered the wisdom of the masters of the spiritual life in his rules of discernment and decision making.

All the great spiritual desires, hopes, truths, and maxims and all the experiences of consolation and desolation, of true paths and of deceptive paths, that have been dealt with down the centuries can be applied to a community of persons.[2]

A heightened awareness of community and communal movements is needed for reading the signs of the times (history and social analysis) and making decisions by an inductive process (from a discernment of spirits perspective).

I hope to take these principles and show that they can be applied to communities and even best understood in a community setting.

My concerns are that:

- Communal attitudes are not considered vital to the ultimate meaning of our lives.
- We do not appreciate the communal as significant for personal salvation or for discovering the "will of God" in our interior life and in the building of "the divine-human community" here and now.
- In our concerns about personal salvation and leading a fully Christian life, we are still governed by individualistic images and desires.
- Our image of God is something "out there," a god we need to please, or a god who performs miracles, or a god who loves and condemns us as single entities.
- We still operate from an "I" position with God.
- We are fascinated by a psychological/spiritual understanding (Gnostic?) of our individual selves.
- We do not appreciate the historical/communal in spiritual matters.
- We have very little interest in the church as community.
- We are not sure what a Christian faith community is.
- We do not do much communal discernment.
- We lack conviction about the significance of communal discernment actually seeing it as an attack on personal freedom, personal discernment, and personal decision making.
- We think communal discernment is only a matter of group process that eventually leads to consensus.
- We do not easily relate and refer to other communal groups—for example, women's groups, peace groups, justice groups, governmental agencies, and the United Nations—to help us search or to be objective discerners in our own personal and communal actions.

I believe that:

- Community and communal experience are primary in living out our personal Christian life and discerning the "will of God" in our personal lives.

- Community is more than a collectivity of human beings.
- Community is a lived reality, that is, more than a mental construct.
- Communal discernment is not only a possibility, it is a necessity.
- The basic experience of discernment is spiritual consolation.
- Communal spiritual consolation can be known and used in discernment.

An Experience of Communal Spiritual Consolation

Since experience is the fundamental base for any spirituality, I would like to consider the phenomenon of communal experience from a faith perspective and to discuss what this means for Christian living, for Christian discernment and decision making. I will begin by recounting an experience which a community of religious women name as one of their communal spiritual consolations.[3]

During a workshop on communal discernment, I asked this community (about seventy members, 60% over fifty years of age) to recall some communal activities and reflect on one in which they sensed that they had experienced communal spiritual consolation. This was their response.

The *occasion* among others which they focused on was the death five years ago of three of their young sisters in an automobile accident and the funeral which followed this tragedy.

The *experience* they described included the extreme state of shock that the community was in for the next two days and the sense that something beautiful and good was happening to them as a community during the day of the funeral. They returned to the experience in order to describe it in terms of feelings, images, concepts, and phrases.

The extreme shock that the community was in for the next two days was described in these ways: disbelief in its reality, "it couldn't happen to us," "is God really with us?" anger with God in his superiority, shaken to the core, stupefying effect, disintegration, doubting, "equalizing of people," emptiness, powerlessness, unspeakable sorrow, grieving, forgiveness of others, new openness to persons not part of the community.

The feelings that something beautiful and good was happening to them as a community especially during the day of the funeral were described as communion in pain, communal loss, communion in humility, communion with people outside their immediate religious community—blood families, city, other religious orders, nation. The funeral itself was a type of bittersweet experience. There was great mourning and yet a sense of being loved and cared for as a community. They experienced a new kind of unity and belonging. They had a new awareness of the love and presence of God to them as a community. They could even recognize the suffering Christ in their midst and identify his presence in their community.

The images that remained with them were: people hugging and crying, people in hushed groups, many lay people in the hallways, two young sisters sobbing through the funeral, three caskets in the church for a long time, endless procession, broken families of the sisters gathered in our house, our own community as a family face to face with death, receiving from others, openness to others.

The phrases and concepts that were now present in recall were: unity, poverty, dependence, peace through pain, hope, trust, "the Lord is close to the broken hearted," best of ourselves came out, "You could ask anybody to do anything," regathering, reunion, reconciliation, Micah's words "act justly . . . love tenderly . . . walk humbly with your God," God is directing and carrying us, "in our weakness is our strength."

Upon *reflection* they got more in touch with what had been given to them as a community. Besides what is described above, they recounted something else that is quite extraordinary: a true expression of the larger faith community we call church. The religious women themselves were in a great state of shock and practically incapable of organizing the funeral and reception which would ordinarily follow a funeral of one of their members.

It was in this situation that the lay friends of the religious community took over. They moved in and took care of the reception desk, the funeral arrangements, the announcements and invitations. Later they prepared the residence for the funeral Mass and reception. They handled the organizing of the music, the preparing of the reception hall and the meal. They gathered in great numbers to be with the sisters to celebrate the entrance into glory of their deceased sisters.

The Influence of This Experience

This experience influenced the community in three major

ways. The first was its new awareness of communal identity—unity, trust, peace, hope, and communal images of itself such as "when we are weak then we are strong." The second was on decisions which flowed from the experience. The third was the significance of this consolation as a discerning criterion for judging other decisions.

New Awareness

This experience gave the group a new sense of who they were, especially in relationship to the larger church. They viewed themselves now in a new light. Previously they saw themselves as serving the larger community. Now they became conscious how the larger community had served them. The experience affected the community's aspirations, desires, vision, future planning.

What *elements* are easily recognized?

- A significant factor in this communal experience is its historicity and human/horizontal expression. It was a three-day experience. It was an expression of human compassion, love, kindness, and strength (fruits of the Holy Spirit, see Ga 5:13-26). The tragedy remembered is an all-too-common human occurrence in our world today.
- The experience was communal, especially the funeral.
- The consolation was preceded by an outpouring of love from others not belonging to their immediate group.
- The experience carried with it much communal affection.
- There was a sense of awe, as well as humility, at the surprising way the Lord (through the lay community) had taken over in this time of distress.
- They themselves had a new sense of unity and belonging.
- They sensed the presence of Christ and his paschal mystery in a new way and so a new dimension of faith, hope, love.
- They experienced a new peace and energy.
- They experienced a new sense of identity, vocation, mission, and celebration.

Impact on Decisions

After this experience of being loved by the larger faith community, they realized that they had to search and discover the basic spirituality that energized them as an apostolic community. Recognizing and appreciating the communal presence of Christ the "horizontal" Christ became an important element in their search.

This experience made them rethink their basic objectives as a community (the community's vocation). They realized that the laity "they were to serve" were a source of energy for themselves. Collaboration with the laity became a significant objective for the community. Their process for bringing about collaboration with the laity (their new sense of mission) became communal in planning and execution.

They realize that acknowledging achievements, failures, joys, and sorrows (communal celebrating) must include the laity in the future.

A Criterion of Future Discernment

There is a further significance to this communal experience, namely, that it is a criterion for judging other affective communal experiences while discerning.

As noticed above, the experience described influenced the community in its later decision making. In the future they will have this experience as a new element to add to their "myth" as a community. They now have a new event of their communal graced history to recall when the need to discern situations arises or new directions are to be taken.

Analysis of This Experience

This example of a community experiencing spiritual consolation answers many of the questions spiritual masters point to when testing the spirits in individual persons (see 1 Jn 4:1-18). What is the source of the experience? How does it develop and grow? What is the end result of the experience?

When we consider this communal experience, what can we recognize that parallels our understanding of individual discernment of spirits? What would we sense carries us beyond individual to communal discernment?

We notice that there was a movement from disbelief and aloneness to one of unity, trust, and hope; from communal desolation to communal consolation.

The movement itself was unexpected, a surprise. The community experienced an increase of faith, hope, love, and peace in the midst of great sorrow and loss.

We also recognize in the experience of this community some of the faith experiences we think apply only to individual persons. They have experienced the One, the Beautiful, the True, the Good, even if it was not in the dramatic way that the Chosen People experienced the God of Abraham, Isaac, and Jacob with Moses on Mount Sinai (see Ex 19:16-26).

They were given an experience of being loved as a corporate person. This led to a new sense of belonging and fellowship, *koinonia*, and then a new sense of unity and communal identity. Moreover, the origin of this consolation came from outside the community, that is, from the larger faith community. The love of the Trinity was experienced through the human actions of the larger faith community.

The community experienced new meaning as it realized its identity with the suffering Christ in this experience. In a newfound sense of humility, the community was able to take on the mind and heart of Christ somewhat as Paul urges that the community of Philippi do (Ph 2:5-11). The most complete communal experience at the liturgy brought the community to realize it was reexpressing the paschal mystery of Christ. We might say that they had a new consciousness of the Risen Christ in their midst. This sense of Christ led to a further desire, resolve, and energy for ministry.

In the way the three days developed, in this very historical experience, we can recognize the compassion, love, kindness, teaching, and strength of the Trinity. For this community there is a new conviction that their own and the larger faith community are an expression of the Risen Christ. They have been given a new knowledge of how to look for Christ in human events. This heightened awareness of Christ in the community leads them to pray that they will search out his presence in ordinary life and be instruments of insight, strength, joy, and peace in this world.

Further Ignatian Considerations

One of St. Ignatius's principles for discerning is that correct decisions are made in the time of spiritual consolation (*Sp Ex* §318).

Sometimes in a communal decision the communal spiritual consolation can be without proportional cause and known without any hesitation, as Ignatius suggests (*Sp Ex* §175 and §330). At other times it is known during or after the communal process much as Ignatius points out in the other two occasions for making a correct decision (*Sp Ex* §§176-188) .

Good group process itself will give a sense of consolation.

For during such a process all members feel that they have been heard, that all issues have been addressed, that the sufferings to be undergone have been faced, and that the members of the group have entered into the process freely, without holding anything back, and have given themselves to it in terms of Christian principles. So there can be a sense of unity and peace.

Still Ignatius recommends a further activity of seeking confirmation of the decision reached by such a good process. So the group is to pray for spiritual consolation. At this time a reflective knowledge of the community's unique sense of spiritual consolation is recalled by a special faith activity of remembering known as *memoria* to give a criterion for discerning the affective experience of confirmation. Does the experience of confirmation fit the known consolation of previous times? Is it in tune with the community's graced history? Does it express anew the vision, dream, myth of the community?

In the ongoing process of discernment as the decision is implemented other criteria for discernment, such as unity, peace, and joy in suffering, will refer back to this experience and discover nuances not previously noticed. Such communal spiritual consolations will be significant in both the judgments around the decision and the fruits of the implementation. Does the community experience some of the very humbling experiences of its past communal history as it implements and succeeds? Does it recognize the furtherance of its vision and goals in an affective way? Has the community retained its previous sense of humility, of compassion, of kindness, of outgoingness, of willingness to suffer with the body of Christ as the process of putting the decision into act occurs (see Ga 5:22-26)?

A reflective knowledge of the community's unique sense of spiritual consolation is recalled by a special faith activity of remembering known as memoria to give a criterion for discerning the affective experience of confirmation.

Summary

We see that such experiences are not static but moving. They are known both interiorly and exteriorly by the community. Some are of such a nature that they have to be considered as special affective movements from the Trinity. They are experienced as given from beyond the group, as unexpected, as surprise. They carry the community to express love in deeds. The meaning of such experiences needs to be discovered. Such experiences have to be appropriated and owned. This happens when the community acknowledges the experiences and makes them significant in its decision-making process.

Questions

In view of the significance I have perceived in this and other experiences of communal consolation in the processes of discernment, it might be wise to examine our own attitudes and convictions regarding the communal dimension of spirituality. The following questions may be helpful:

- Do I think I can be saved alone?
- Do I think I have a one-line connection to God?
- Do I consider spiritual experiences as mine alone?
- Do I think Christ is my individualistic savior?
- Do I see other persons and communities as the place where I am to "win my salvation"?
- Do I see the church as a source for my individualistic spiritual needs?
- Is discernment of "God's will" strictly an action I per form in my own interior being?
- Is faith community only a place to check out my individualistic decisions and actions?
- Am I saved and able to build God's realm only in, through, and as a community (People of God, human race)?
- Do I need to read the Bible as if every "you" is plural?
- Is there really the possibility of doing communal discernment?
- Is there really such a thing as communal spiritual consolation?

Many of our current attitudes and dispositions are the legacy of the Enlightenment, which considers all the truths of Christianity from an individualistic point of view. The challenge for us today is to heighten our awareness of the presence and action of the Trinity in our communal reality.

Notes

[1] See many writings of John MacMurray on the realization and experience of person, for example, "we are only persons at all through our relations with other persons," *Freedom in the Modern World* (London: Faber, 1932); "overcome individualism by communal action . . . it is only in meeting others that we find ourselves and our own reality," *Search for Reality in Religion* (London: Quaker, 1965).

[2] For the last eight years I have been discussing and experiencing the validity of this statement with James Borbely SJ, Marita Carew RSHM, John Haley SJ, Judith Roemer ANG, and George Schemel SJ. We have composed a manual to assist Spiritual Guides of Groups: *Ignatian Spiritual Exercises for the Corporate Person* (Scranton, Pennsylvania 18510: University of Scranton).

[3] The example used in the article receives further development in John English SJ, *Spiritual Intimacy and Community: An Ignatian View of the Small Faith Community* (New York: Paulist, 1992), ch. 3.

The Dynamic of the Question in the Search for God

adaptation

The two questions that Paul asks when he finds himself confronted by God on the road to Damascus are at the heart of every Christian conversion experience both as event and as life-long process:

1. "Who are you, Lord?" (Ac 22:8).
2. "What shall I do, Lord?" (Ac 22:10).

First, he must know who this God is who confronts him; then he must do something about it. Since God is that kind of God, Paul seems to be saying, *therefore* I must find out and do whatever he commands me to do. To "know" the living God, in the biblical sense, is to live with him in doing his will. Our action must be in response to God's action. We must be with God in doing what he is willing and doing. God loves us, *therefore* we must love one another (1 Jn 4:19). It would be absurd to talk about knowing God if you did not also love your brother.

Anyone who says, "I love God," and hates his brother, is a liar, since a man who does not love the brother that he can see cannot love God, whom he has never seen. So this is the commandment that he has given us, that anyone who loves God must also love his brother (1 Jn 4:20-21).

Our desire to know God is authenticated by our seeking to know and to do his will within the complexity and historical particularities of our intrapersonal, interpersonal, social, national, and international life. We cannot know God apart from all the levels of human life; for through his grace and demand he is operative at every level.

Throughout the New Testament we find that a long passage about God will typically conclude with a "therefore," which goes on to point out how the knowledge of God is one with seeking to do his will. Sharing his life means doing his will.

In his letter to the Romans, for example, Paul writes eleven "theological" chapters, explaining who Jesus Christ is and what he has done for us. Then, Chapter 12 begins, "I appeal to you, *therefore*, my brothers," and Paul gives a long list of attitudes, practices, and characteristics of the way in which Christians are to act: Let love be genuine. Hate what is evil. Hold fast to what is good. Love one another with brotherly affection. Bless those who persecute you. Live in harmony with one another. Repay no one evil for evil. And the word "therefore" is the pivot of the whole argument. Because of all these things that I have been writing to you about (for eleven chapters!) are true, Paul is saying in effect, *therefore*, this is the way in which you must act fully to experience their true goodness for yourselves.

The letter to the Ephesians offers another example. The first three chapters expound the work of Christ upon the cross, and the fourth begins:

"I, *therefore*, a prisoner in the Lord implore you to lead a life worthy of your vocation. Bear with one another charitably, in complete selflessness, gentleness, and patience. Do all you can to preserve the unity of the Spirit by the peace that binds you together" (4:1-3).

And the writer continues with advice about the way life is to be lived *because* of what God has done in Christ. We will know Christ and his Father only when we follow Christ in doing the will of his Father. Another striking example of this truth is found in Paul's letter to the Philippians:

"Do nothing from selfishness or conceit, but in humility count others better than yourselves. Let each of you look not only to his own interests, but also to the interests of others. Have this mind among yourselves, which you have in Christ Jesus, who, though he was in the form of Cod, did not count equality with God a thing to be grasped, but emptied himself, taking the form of a servant, being born in the likeness of men. And being found in human form he humbled himself and became obedient unto death, even death on a cross" (2:3-8).

An assertion of what Christ has done is also an assertion of what *we* must do to know, in the biblical sense, who God is. God has acted in this way toward us, *therefore*, we are to act this way towards others. God loves us, and we shall give that same love to others if we truly "know" God. One who knows God will not refuse to love one whom God loves. What God wills is what he loves. God is known, in the biblical sense, in doing what he wills or loves. In Jesus Christ we have the ongoing answer of an infinitely knowing and loving God to *our* ongoing questions, "Who are you?" and "What must I do?" The Christian desire to know the God of Jesus Christ is a daily quest inspired by the gift of his Spirit to know and to do his will. The Spirit of Jesus Christ and his Father unites and animates the Christian community in its thirst for God and for the accomplishment of his will. It expresses itself in the community's prayer, "Thy kingdom come, thy will be done." The community prays that it may increasingly come to know God in faith, and acknowledge him as the holy center and meaning of its life. Its prayer expresses its belief that God's purpose is to unite all human hearts under the sovereignty of his love. The life and teaching of Jesus spell out what the Christian community believes the doing of God's will and the coming of his kingdom entails.

The Question-raising God

The biblical narratives are an external expression of the interior life of a covenant people. The questions which God raises in these narratives reveal what is going on in the cognitive and affective life of a people at every level: intrapersonal, interpersonal, social, national and international. There is no knowing God, in the biblical sense, without experiencing him as a question-raising God at every level of human life. He reveals himself in the questions he raises about our lives. His question-raising reality is experienced wherever and whenever we seriously ask about the ultimate meaning and goodness of our lives. God is as inescapable as his questions. Significantly, God's first word to us in the Bible is a question: "Where are you?" (Gn 3:9). The covenant people experiences God in his question about its identity. Its quest for God begins with its experience of his quest or question for them. To hear his word is to hear his question about the meaning and purpose and goodness of its life. The people of the New Covenant hears that question-raising word in Jesus Christ whose first utterance in the Gospels of Luke and John is a question: "Why were you looking for me?" (Lk 2:49), and "What do you want?" (Jn 1:38).

From the moment of the annunciation, God's word is a question-raising event in Luke's gospel: "She was deeply troubled by these words and asked herself what this greeting could mean" (1:30); and, "How can this come about, since I am a virgin?" (1:34). Mary experiences the question-raising mystery of her son when she finds him in the Temple and asks, "My child, why have you done this to us?" (2:48).

The entire life story of God's incarnate Word challenges us as God's question and answer about our identity. Jesus Christ is the incarnate Question and Answer of God about the true goodness and direction of our lives. Even the shortest Gospel, *Mark*, reflects the tension of *the* Question that Jesus is for all human life with its no less than one hundred eighteen questions, of which more than half are raised by Jesus himself.

Being with Jesus entails following him in learning to live with responding love to the question-raising Mystery (God) at the heart of all human life.

If the gospel narrative is the external expression of knowing and loving Christian subjects (the evangelists) in the life-long process of conversion, the questions that pervade it imply that an authentically Christian life is one of loving responsiveness to the question-raising meaning of God at every level of human life. If the church employs this narrative in its pedagogy for cultivating the gift of God's love in the interests of human transformation (conversion) at every level, it implicitly recognizes the dynamic of the question for learning to know God in the biblical sense as the question-raising Mystery at the heart of all human life. Christian maturation, then, implies fidelity to the question that God raises and to the answer that he gives about the true meaning and goodness of our lives. If God is known by doing his will, the Christian must learn to live in the daily tension of the question, "What is God's will for me?" There is no doing God's will without seeking it in the concreteness and complexity of our lives. (The self-righteous are their own "little gods"; they evade his question by implicitly identifying God's will with their own self-will.)

Being with Jesus, or Christian discipleship, entails following him in learning to live with responding love to the question-raising Mystery (God) at the heart of all human life. It means accepting the Question that is God himself of seeking to know and to do his will. We accept our true and God-given identity in doing his will. The kingdom of God—life under the sovereignty of his love—is coming wherever his will is being done. If God's will is done, all human persons will enjoy the fulfillment of their true interpersonal identity in his kingdom. We are free to reject our God-given identity in favor of self-will where the self is king in its own impersonal kingdom. There is no authentically interpersonal life where the sovereignty of God's love is rejected. Jesus' "thy will, not mine" (LCD 22:42) expresses the radical responsibility to God which grounds freedom for genuinely interpersonal life. His way of the cross reveals his acceptance of his God-given identity as the "Beloved Son"; this is his way of self-transcendence as the Beloved Son that he is glad to be in responding (responsible) love with his Father. His way of the cross reveals how his disciples must accept their God-given identity.

The dynamic of the question in the gospel narrative is ultimately that of God's love flooding our hearts through the Holy Spirit given to us (Rm 5:5), for the narrative is a symbolic expression and witness to the Christian community's knowledge (in the biblical sense) of that love manifested in Jesus Christ and communicated through his Spirit. The Gospel narrative is implicitly the Christian community's answer to the question, "What does it mean to love God with one's whole heart and whole soul, with all one's mind and all one's strength?" (Mk 12:30). What does it mean to fulfill the new commandment of Jesus, "Love one another just as I have loved you" (Jn 15:12)? What is God's distinctive way of loving as manifested in Jesus Christ and in the believing community that lives in his Spirit? How ought we to respond to that love? What is God doing in my life?

The gospel writers employ the dynamic of the question to symbolize the pattern of God's love and its distinctive way of operating in our lives. Love is the central motivation of the question-raising and question-answering dynamic of the gospel narrative. The gospel writers implicitly reply to the question, "What is the appropriate response to our being loved by God in Christ and his Spirit?" They present Jesus as the norm that we are to follow for such a response. His "Come, follow me" (Mk 1:16) expresses the dynamic of divine initiative and human response at the heart of our transformation in the lifelong process of our learning to live in God's love. Following Jesus in response to the grace and demand of God's love constitutes Christian conversion both as event and lifelong process.

Such conversion is always precarious; for we can fall out of love with God. Consequently, we are bid to watch and pray, to make our way in fear and trembling. We can always fail to heed Jesus' invitation to follow him in his self-surrender to this Father's love. His invitation raises the question daily, "Are we following Jesus in response to God's love?" The gospel narrative was written to raise the question for all Christians at all times: "Are we living in the Spirit of Jesus, leading lives of responding love?" Hearing God's word means hearing his question and responding appropriately. Raising the question implies that no Christian should self-righteously assume that he or she is always following Jesus; for God alone is unquestionably good. Although our lives are the manifestation of God's grace, they are measured by the demands of his intention.

The church employs the dynamic of the question in the gospel narrative for its spiritual pedagogy. We must learn to hear the Question and the Answer (God) that is at the heart of every human life in order to become authentically human, following Jesus' way of responding love to human and divine others. That Question must always challenge our self-understanding, individually and socially, and be the norm of our decision and action. The Word of God takes the form of the Question and the Answer that is given to us in Jesus Christ and his Spirit. That Word expresses the Spirit of the Father's love that has been given to us and elicits our responding through and in the same Spirit of love to the Question and the Answer that constitutes our God-given identity. Our hearing the Question (in the biblical sense of a loving response to the grace and demand of God) is even now our accepting the Answer that is our God-given interpersonal identity. The just are even now rising in responding love to the Question that is also the Answer to their identity. The dynamic of the Question in the gospel narrative implies the Christian community's grateful response to that enduring love that it knows in its fidelity to the Spirit.

Every New Testament affirmation about God is implicitly the Christian community's answer of responding love to the Word that is both the question and answer of God. Jewish and Christian Scriptures are the expression of responding love inspired by the gift of the Spirit of love for the God who speaks in his question and answer. Paul affirms that Jesus Christ is the *Yes* spoken by God in response to the implicit question of Israel: Is God faithful? (2 Co 1:20). This corresponds to John's doctrine of Christ as the *Amen* (Rv 3:14).

John's doctrine of the Son as the Word of God who is the fullness of truth (Prologue to his Gospel) implies his life of responding love for the question that is the self-revealing answer. John's living in the Spirit of love for the question of God yields the answer of God. He knows the Spirit (in the biblical sense) in the love that the members of the New Covenant community have for one another. On the basis of their loving correspondence for one another before the Word-Question-Answer of God, John can affirm that "God is love" (1 Jn 4:8, 16).

The Father communicates himself by sending his Son (Word) and Spirit (Love). He speaks his Word of truth and Spirit of love, empowering us in the special biblical sense to know him and to accept our true identity. There is no hearing or lived experience of the Father's Word, as question or answer, apart from the Spirit of his love through and in which his will becomes our meaningful life-principle. Jesus is known as Lord (1 Co 12:3) in the biblical sense only by those whose hearts and minds are governed by the Holy Spirit of his love; his meaning as God's Word is effectively grasped only by those who live in the Spirit of his love for the Father. The gospel narrative of the way of the cross implicitly answers the question of Jesus' meaning for us. It symbolizes what it means to have an authentically interpersonal life with God and all others. There is no such life without the self-transcendence of responding love for all others, divine and human.

The dynamic of the question in the Gospel narrative is indispensable for Christian conversion both as event and as a life-long process of maturation; for there is no human transformation or maturation, at any level, without questions. Because we are neither self-explanatory nor self-sufficient, we must go outside ourselves in self-transcendence for both our meaning and our fulfillment. The quest for both takes the form of the question. The dynamic of our questioning implies that we are not autonomous, but relational beings, seeking the answers correlative to our questions. The same dynamic implies a correspondence of knowing and loving subjects. If we are able and willing to question, there must be others who are able and willing to answer. Our questioning presupposes answerable and responsible (response-able) others. Reciprocity is possible among knowing subjects who are able to question and to answer, and loving subjects who are willing to question and to answer. If persons are knowing and loving subjects, their authenticity is achieved in coresponsibility. Persons are interpersonal or conscious and relational; consequently, the failure to be interpersonal is the failure to be personal. Irresponsibility is the failure to be a knowing and loving subject.

Jesus is known as Lord in the biblical sense only by those whose hearts and minds are governed by the Holy Spirit of his love; his meaning as God's Word is effectively grasped only by those who live in the Spirit of his love for the Father.

Our personal identity is interpersonal and rooted in coresponsibility. It is defined by those *to* and *for* whom we are responsible (answerable). The Good News of Jesus Christ is the perfection of divine and human coresponsiblity. He is the response (answer) of the knowing and loving Father to our human need for him; and he is the response of perfect human receptivity to and availability for the Father. He is the Good News that God assumes responsibility for the fulfillment of every human life; that God sends his Son and his Spirit for that purpose. He is the Good News of God's responding love to the need of every human person for him, and of man's perfectly corresponding availability for God's love. The interpersonal life of Jesus Christ is the solidarity of God and humankind in corresponding (coresponsible) love. He is both the prayer of all humankind for God and the response of God to that prayer. Significantly, all the evangelists show Jesus, before all the great decisions of his life, spending the night in prayer alone on the mountain.

There is no passivity in Jesus' receptivity, response and listening to his Father. His receptivity is at one and the same time supreme activity, commitment to accept demands, making himself available, and being ready to serve in responding love. Solidarity or coresponsibility with God demands the supreme activity of his self-giving in commitment to his Father's will. At Gethsemane he prays: "Abba, Father, all things are possible for you. Take this cup away from me. But let it be as you, not I, would have it" (Mk 14:36).

Always doing what is pleasing to his Father (Jn 8:29), Jesus is a knowing and loving subject who coresponsibly collaborates with his Father in giving the new life of their Holy Spirit to all others. Christian discipleship consists in our being with Jesus in his costly and supreme activity of receiving his life from the Father and communicating it to others as fully coresponsible knowing and loving subjects living in his Spirit. Through the gift of his Spirit we are invited and empowered to share the freedom of Jesus Christ's coresponsibility with the Father and all others. Actively accepting the Holy Spirit as our new life principle, we accept our God-given identity as coresponsible knowing and loving subjects and the freedom for an authentically interpersonal fulfillment. Through the gift of the Holy Spirit we are free to share in the interpersonal coresponsibility and life-principle of the knowing and love subject that is Jesus Christ.

The gospel writers employ the dynamic of the question to evoke the coresponsibility of their readers. They have written their question-raising narratives as a call to coresponsibility with God in Christ and his Spirit for others. The coresponsibility of New Covenant brothers and sisters for one another and all others reveals that of the covenant-creating and covenant-sustaining Spirit of Jesus Christ and his Father. The Spirit of love with which the Son responds to the Father and the Father responds to the Son is made manifest among those who respond to one another with the same love. The Father and the Son are wherever their Spirit is operative in the coresponsible activity of all who receive it to become covenant-creating and covenant-sustaining persons. Such persons respond to the word, whether as question or answer, that God speaks within their life story by becoming the communicators of faith and hope for others. They communicate complementary aspects of the grace and demand of that word for authentic human development and fulfillment under the sovereignty of God's corresponding love in response to human need.

The costly commitment of Christians to God in the service of others both within the realm of covenant community responsibilities and the world beyond is rooted in the mutual indwelling and self-transcending love of the Father and Son that constitutes the community of Christian faith. The outgoing compassion of Christians for others without limits or conditions bears witness to the indwelling trinitarian love that is the ultimate source and term of the Christian community's life and that of the world that it is called to serve in coresponsibility with the Three Persons. The giving of new life is the very meaning of the dynamic of the question at the heart of all human life. The meaning of the Gospel is revealed in this dynamic within the realms of our experience, understanding, judgment, decision and action, where the word of God summons us to coresponsibility. Jesus' first words in Luke (2:49) and John (1:38) are, respectively, the questions: "Why were you looking for me?" and "What do you want?"

Just as in the measure that we advert to our own questioning and proceed to question it, there arises the question of God,[1] so too, in the measure that we advert to our being questioned by God and proceed to respond, there arises the question of our authenticity. We achieve authenticity in the self-transcendence whereby we become knowing and loving subjects whose cognition and affectivity are concomitantly experienced in our unrestricted drive to know and to love. In the Gospel narratives, Jesus questions us to stimulate our questioning, reflection, response and conversion to unrestricted loving. Jesus summons us to the unrestricted questioning and loving that would free us from being locked up in ourselves. As the question of God is implicit in all our questioning, so being in love with God is the basic fulfillment of our conscious intentionality as knowing and loving subjects.[2]

The biblical narrative presents questions for intelligence or understanding, reflecting the life of the People of God asking what and why and how and what for: "When the Israelites saw it [food in the desert], they said to one another, 'What is it?'—for they did not know what it was" (Ex 16:15).[3] In the wonder created by Jesus' first miracle, Mark records that "They were dumbfounded and began to ask one another, 'What is this?' " (1:27). The occurrence of Mary's questions is striking in Luke: " Why have you treated us like this?" (2:48), and "How can this be . . . when I have no husband?" (1:34). Nathanael asks: "How do you come to know me?" (Jn 1:48). Jesus asks: "If I spoke well, why strike me?" (Jn 18:23). A more reflective attitude indicating the inner tension of inquiry, the dynamism of the search for understanding, occurs when Luke tells us that: "Mary treasured up all these things and pondered over them" (2:19). The word, "pondered," is the same one he uses for the "discussion" of the Jewish rulers on how to handle Peter and John (Ac 4:15), and for the "debate" in which the Athenian philosophers engaged Paul (Ac 17:18). Linked with this is the occurrence of wonder in its milder forms, as when outside the sanctuary "the people were waiting for Zacharias, wondering why he was staying so long inside" (Lk 1:21).

Upon questions for intelligence and understanding follow questions for reflection, asking whether or not this really is so or that really could be. This question regards truth, what is so. It requires evidence enough to justify a judgment on the matter; it asks which side of a contradiction is right. John presents some instances: "There was much whispering about him in the crowds. 'He is a good man,' some said. 'No,' said others, 'he is leading the people astray'" (7:12). Later, we have the significant statement: "Thus he caused a split among the people" (7:43). John's affirmation that "Jesus is the Christ, the Son of God" (20:31) raises a question for reflection that leads to the split of Christ's followers from Judaism. The high priest challenges Jesus with such a question: "By the living God I charge you to tell us: Are you the Messiah, the Son of God?" (Mt 26:63). The same question for reflection is implied in the centurion's affirmation: "Truly this man was the Son of God" (Mk 15:39). Jesus' cross-questioning of the Pharisees provides another instance of the same type of question: "Whose son is he (the Messiah)? 'The son of David,' they replied. . . . 'If David calls him 'Lord,' how can he be David's son?' " (Mt 22:42-45).

Questions arise in the order of doing as well as knowing. Questions for deliberation arise when we ask whether this or that is worthwhile, whether it is not just apparently good but truly good, what has objective value. Jesus' statements "Go and do the same yourself" (Lk 10:37), and "Mary has chosen the better part" (10:42), and ". . . do this and life is yours" (Lk 10:28) answer questions for deliberation.

Jesus poses questions for identity: "Who is my mother? Who are my brothers?" (Mk 3:33); "What is your name?" (Mk 5:9); "Who do you say I am?" (Mk 8:29). He poses questions for intelligence or understanding: "Why are you frightened? Have you still no faith?" (Mk 4:40); "Where did he get all this? What wisdom is this that has been given him? How does he perform miracles? Isn't he the carpenter, the son of Mary . . . ?" (Mk 6:2-3). He raises the question about what people are doing and where they are going, about the meaning of their life: "You have eyes, can't you see? You have ears, can't you hear?" (Mk 8:18) and "Can you see anything?" (Mk 8:23). Questions define the relationship between the Master and the disciple; for the true understanding of discipleship is correlative to the true understanding of the Master. When Peter acknowledges that Jesus is the Christ and then immediately rejects Jesus' way of suffering and death, he reveals his failure to understand the true meaning of both the Master and of discipleship (Mk 8:27-9:1). At a deeper level, the failure to grasp Jesus' true meaning is the failure to grasp our own God-given identity. Jesus is the answer of God to the question of what we are called to be.

Questions for deliberation arise when we ask whether this or that is worthwhile, whether it is not just apparently good but truly good, what has objective value.

Our sincere engagement with the question is already a form of commitment to the answer. The questions that are most important to us concern the matters that are dearest to us. There are no such questions apart from the affective power and motivation which sustains them. Love seeks understanding. Love *asks* all she meets, as we read in the Song of Solomon, where she can find her Lover. A loving heart is a questioning heart; an indifferent heart knows no such interest. Even the questions of Jesus' adversaries show that they are not indifferent and are, therefore, at least in touch with the love that could save them.

Our lives are qualified by the quality of the questions that engage us. Preoccupation with trivial questions and concerns trivializes our lives. The Christian community employs its gospel narrative to learn to live with the most fundamental questions about human life and to respond to them in the Spirit of Jesus Christ. The answers to the basic questions that Jesus Christ raises are given to those who are willing to share his life of costly self-transcendence, or way of the cross. The answers to his questions are learned in the authentic corresponsibility of those who live in the Spirit of Jesus Christ within his New Covenant community.

The New Covenant community gives witness to its Lord by becoming the question-raising and answer-giving sacrament of God for the world. The Word of God, both as question and answer, is spoken to the world in and through the New Covenant community. The Three Persons reveal and communicate their coresponsibility in the life of the New Covenant community for all humankind.

Covenant love is coresponsible love both among covenant members and between them and all others, human and divine. The covenant love of Jesus Christ is known, in the biblical sense, by those who accept with responding love his brothers and sisters, no less than his Father and Spirit. His interpersonal life of covenant love reveals an interpersonal God as a community of Persons living in responding love and coresponsibly creating and sustaining and fulfilling all humankind through the grace and summons to coresponsibility. Their coresponsible love is the gift and summons for ours.

The dynamic of the question in the gospel narrative represents a coresponsible Father and Son and Spirit (uncreated grace of self-gift) summoning us to the coresponsibility of an authentically human life, to "knowing God" (in the biblical sense) in loving all others. The dynamic of the question is an implicit summons to the way of the cross; for, without the costly responding love that is self-transcendence, we cannot become coresponsible and "know God."

Rejection of the Cross is radical irresponsibility in the refusal to become seriously engaged with the answer that Jesus offers in the question that he raises about the ultimate meaning and value of human life; for there is no human authenticity apart from self-transcendence in communion with the Spirit of the Father and Son which enables it. The Word that is question draws us to itself as answer in the tension of coresponsible love that the gospel narrative represents as Jesus Christ's way of the cross. The Spirit of that Word has been given to enable our hearing that Word both as question (promise) and answer (fulfillment), as the Alpha and the Omega of every human story. The Spirit is wherever it acts; and it acts in the lives of coresponsible persons responding wholeheartedly to Jesus' commandment of love (Mt 22:34-40; Mk 12:28-34; LCD 10:25-28). The love of God finds expression in the love of neighbor, and the love of neighbor receives its foundation and energy in the love of God that is given to us in the

Spirit of the Father and his Son. Wherever that Spirit is being accepted, coresponsible persons are accepting in responding love the answer to the question that is the origin and ground and direction and the fulfillment of all human life.

Irresponsibility can be regarded as our futile attempt to give ourselves a meaning that implies our radical rejection of our God-given meaning. We can futilely attempt to take our life stories "out of context" with respect to the question and answer that is their ultimate background, ground and foreground. We can attempt to make our own human egos the ultimate context of our human story.

Rejection of the Cross is radical irresponsibility in the refusal to become seriously engaged with the answer that Jesus offers in the question that he raises about the ultimate meaning and value of human life.

To take anything out of context is to lose its true meaning. The rationalizations of a bad conscience express the experience of such a taking-out-of-context. The discomfort and unease of a bad conscience is the voice of God recalling us to the true meaning of our life story. Our radical misinterpretation of the universal human story and its ultimate context (God) distorts our grasp of all human stories by taking them out of their true context, that which ultimately makes them truly good and meaningful. God alone is the answer to our quest for our true meaning and goodness. Because God addresses himself to every human being, we are enabled to be free, conscious, coresponsible, Knowing and loving subjects (persons) whose existence as such is constituted by the endless answer to the question that grounds our lives.

Jesus asks ninety-eight different questions in the synoptic gospels. He raises twelve additional questions in his parables. Forty-seven different questions are addressed to Jesus in these gospels. Of the approximately one hundred fifty seven questions raised in the synoptic gospels, one hundred ten originate with Jesus himself. Even the forty-seven questions addressed to Jesus are occasioned by him. The healing context of many questions suggests their importance in the psychotherapeutic dialogue of faith and trust. The dynamic of the question lies at the heart of human transformation in the event and lifelong process of Christian conversion. Jesus' questions challenge us to growth and development at every level (intrapersonal, interpersonal and social) under God.

A Gnostic pattern is present in the Gospel of Thomas where the emphasis is on Jesus as the one who answers all our questions about mysteries; whereas, in the New Testament, the emphasis is on Jesus as the one who raises questions for our responsible decision and action, calling us to new life, to sell all and to follow him in the self-transcendence of total surrender to God.

Our Questions and Our Desire to Know God

Every act of questioning presupposes the possibility of our finding the truth. Without an implicit "faith" that intelligibility and truth can be found we would not have the courage to seek understanding or to make judgments about the world around us. By the fact that we do ask questions and make judgments (even, for example, "it is a *truth* that there is no intelligibility or truth") we give ample evidence that we cannot eradicate our primordial trust in the intelligibility and truth of reality. That we find ourselves spontaneously asking questions is direct evidence for the fact of our having a desire to know the truth.

But there are different types of questions. Some of our questions inquire as to what a thing is or ask about its meaning, intelligibility, or significance. This type of question is resolved when we are given an "insight" into the essence of something. If you find yourself asking what the author of this book is trying to convey in these sentences, then this is an example of the first type of question. It may be called a "question for understanding." It will reach its goal when you find yourself saying: "Now I see the point."

But gaining understanding is not the end of the questioning process. For not every insight is in touch with reality. There can be illusory as well as realistic understanding. So a second type of question spontaneously arises, and it leads you to ask whether your insights or those of others are *true*. I may see the point that an author is trying to make, but an uneasiness will eventually lead me to ask whether this point is well taken. Is it faithful to the facts of my own experience? Is it based on reality? Is it true? This type of questioning provides evidence that I am not content with mere insight and understanding. Thus I ask: Is it really so? Does this viewpoint correspond with reality? Is it a fact? We may call this second type "question for reflection" or a "critical question." It is especially our critical questions that give evidence of our desire to know and of our basic discontent with mere understanding. We want to make sure that our insights, hypotheses, and theories are true to reality.

Asking a question is possible because we do not yet know the answer. If we knew the answer we would not ask the question in the first place. And yet we know something about what we are questioning in order to ask about it at all. But at the same time our consciousness has to dwell within the horizon of truth in order for us to inquire about it at all. In other words, our minds must already have moved into a specific field of knowledge and been influenced by the objects of this field in order for us to ask about what lies within the horizon. I could not seriously desire the truth about myself, others and the world unless the horizon of truth had already encircled my consciousness.

If we know that God means *truth* our affirmation of this ultimate horizon cannot, by definition, be an illusion. For the desire for the truth undercuts all illusions. If we identify "God" with the unrestricted horizon of truth and love toward which our desire to know is directed, we need not fear that our belief is a projection of wishful thinking. If the desire for God is at root the desire for truth, then this desire will not be able to take refuge in illusions or mere thinking.

The desire for God coincides with our desire for truth. God is the ultimate horizon of truth which continually activates our desire to ask questions and allows us no peace until we have surrendered to it. God is the ultimate objective of all our questioning. Truth is ultimately a *mysterium tremendum et fascinans.* As in the case of the "sacred," we both hide from it and seek it at the same time. We know that the truth hurts, but we also intuit that it alone can provide a firm foundation to our lives. The ultimate truth, depth, future, freedom, and beauty into whose embrace we are constantly invited consists of an unconditional love that is the *tremendum* from which we flee as well as the *fascinans* that promises us ultimate fulfillment. If we find the elusiveness or depth or "futurity" of truth intolerable, it may be because our strong impulse to master takes precedence over our desire to be grasped by the truth.

Religion may be understood as the conscious decision to move within the truth. It is a rejection of the strong temptation to make truth the object of our will to mastery. It is a surrender to truth as the *mysterium tremendum et fascinans* in which alone our freedom and fulfillment lie. Religion is an ongoing conversion to the dimension of the truth that transcends the everyday world of fear and all the illusions based on fear. Wherever there is a sincere desire for the truth about ourselves, others, and the world there is authentic religion, even if it does not go by that name. The religiousness of this desire for the truth consists of a fundamental trust in the ultimate intelligibility of reality without which we would not have the courage to ask questions and to seek the truth. From the perspective of human consciousness and longing, religion has its origins essentially in the God-given desire for the truth, that is, God himself. The core of religion is an uncompromising passion for the truth.

If mystery is understood merely as a vacuum that begs to be filled with our intellectual achievements and not as an ineffable depth summoning us to surrender ourselves completely to it, then it is hardly adequate as a term for the divine. The gaps in our present understanding and knowledge would better be called *problems* than mysteries. A "problem" can eventually be solved by the application of human ingenuity. Mystery, in contrast to problems, is incapable of any "solution." Mystery becomes more prominent the deeper our questions go and the surer our answers become. Mystery appears to consciousness at the "limit" of our ordinary problem-oriented questions. It reveals itself decisively at the point where we seriously ask what may be called "limited-questions," questions that lie at the "boundary" of our ordinary problem-solving consciousness.

For example, while science is dominated by problems for which some resolution or definitive answer is expected, the scientist might find himself eventually asking: Why should I do science at all? Why search for intelligibility in the universe? Similarly, the field of ethics attempts to give answers to our moral dilemmas, but at the limits of ethical investigation there arise such questions as: Why bother about ethics at all? Why be responsible? Why pursue the good life? Why keep promises? Why should we be faithful? Is the universe at heart faithful and trustworthy? If it is not, then why should I worry about fidelity and promise-keeping? At this juncture we have shifted from ethical problems into the realm of the mysterious and unsolvable. Ethics can no more easily answer these limiting questions than science can tell us why we should seek intelligibility in the universe.

Another illustration: literary criticism attempts to respond to questions concerning whether a work of literature is aesthetically worthy of our respect. But at the limit of literary criticism there arise questions that it cannot itself address: Why pursue the beautiful? Why bother about aesthetic criteria at all? What is beauty? Again we have moved out of problem and into mystery.

Each discipline is specified by the types of questions it raises, the kinds of problems with which it deals. It pursues its questions with a degree of success proportionate to the problems it solves. But at the boundaries of all these various fields of human inquiry we come to an impasse that we cannot get beyond no matter how much intellectual effort we exert. Our problem-solving techniques cannot get us over the encompassing horizon of mystery opened up by our limit-questions.

The place of mystery, and hence the appropriate place for the introduction of a specifically religious discourse, is at the limits of our problem-oriented questioning, when our inquiry shifts to another key entirely. At such a point we realize we are asking questions that no human ingenuity will ever solve or "remove." But even though we cannot give final solutions to these impossible questions, we may still respond (that is, "answer back") to them. This response is appropriately not one of trying to ignore, repress or eliminate them, but rather allowing them to take over our consciousness and pull us into the mystery that lurks on the other side of our problems.

Besides the mysterious questions that arise at the limits of our intellectual life there are also the "boundary experiences" that confront us at the edges of our everyday life. The encounter with suffering, frustration, and ultimately death arouses questions of an entirely different sort from those we "normally" ask. Usually we are preoccupied with the ordinary "problems" of life, such as how to pay bills, how to pass a course, and so forth. In other words "how" questions dominate the ordinary course of our lives. But there are certain "shipwreck" or "earthquake" experiences that occasionally break into the routine of our lives, and when they do we experience the superficiality of our pragmatic "how" questions and the invasion of "why" or "ultimate" questions. Such experiences raise questions that stand at the "limit" of our ordinary consciousness of life, and they can sensitize us to the mystery that always silently accompanies and encompasses our lives. When we are beset by these marginal experiences we ask "ultimate" questions more intently perhaps than before. Can this be all there is to life? Are death and tragedy the final word? Is there any final meaning to my work? Is there an answer to the problem of suffering? Perhaps the questions aroused by tragedy make us most vulnerable to the touch of mystery. Nevertheless, positive and ecstatic moments of deep joy can just as readily transport us beyond the boundaries of pedestrian existence.

The feeling of being deeply loved by another or of being enthralled by great beauty can also lead us to ask limit-questions. Will love prevail? Is beauty only an illusion? Why cannot these moments last forever? Such questions open us to mystery and lead us to a religious interpretation of the universe. At the "limit" of our ordinary experience and our problem-solving questions we are alerted to the nearness of mystery. We sense that it has been intimately present all along but that it has not entered deeply into our explicit awareness. In limit-experience and limit-questioning we are confronted with the opportunity of making the dimension of mystery the most important and enlivening aspect of our lives.

Notes

[1] Bernard Lonergan, *Method in Theology* (London: Darton, Longman & Todd, 1971), p. 103.

[2] Ibid, p. 105.

[3] Frederick E. Crowe, "Neither Jew nor Greek, But One Human Nature and Operation in All," in *Philippine Studies* 13 (1965), pp. 561-566. In this section, Crowe treats of biblical interest in questions. Crowe comments that questions may be introduced by the same interrogative and show the same grammatical form; but it is the *intention* of the questioner that determines the type of question: does he intend to put an objection as one contradicting, as one concerned with the truth? Or does he intend to ask for explanation as one puzzled and desiring understanding. Crowe assigns Mary's question in Luke 1:34 to the latter type, the Lord's in Mt 22:45 to the former, but this is for him a matter for exegesis to decide. Generally, he believes that questions put in sarcasm (Jn 1:46) or hostility (Jn 6:42, 52) intend to contradict and regard the level of truth, whereas a more neutral attitude such as that shown by the Jerusalem delegation to the Baptist (Jn 1:25) could pertain to either level. In fact, Crowe believes that the average person freely mingles both levels in confusion, and there is no reason for insisting that a given question must be a pure case of one or the other type (p. 564).

Doing the Spiritual Exercises in Four Summers

Recently. I completed the giving of *Spiritual Exercises* of St. Ignatius by using the time of eight-day retreats over a period of four summers. Since the experience of this kind of adaptation of the full *Exercises* may be usable by others, I would like to describe: the situation which precipitated this adaptation, what the director and the retreatant did, and the advantage of such an adaptation. I shall also include some statements which the retreatant had written after her experience.

The Situation

The retreatant was a retired teacher in the Philadelphia area. She had been a member of the Loyola Professional Sodality. now the Loyola Christian Life Community. For twenty-five years, she had made days of recollection and preached retreats of several days' length. In the previous summer, I had guided her in a directed retreat. She had never had an opportunity to make the entire *Spiritual Exercises,* nor had she been able to find a director to lead her through the retreat in daily life. Yet. her experiences in Christian Life Community and her own desire to progress in the spiritual life made her eager to do the entire *Exercises.* So, I suggested that she consider making these *Exercises* in four summer sessions of eight days each. She agreed to try the plan. In her words:

> I see my personal experience of the full Ignatian Exercises as the culmination of many years of making retreats using the *Exercises.* As I recall the days of preached retreats, I real-

ize now that they were but a preparation for the profound experience of the full Exercises. While they were good experiences, for the most part, it was not until I made my first directed retreat that I really got the full impact of the *Exercises* and felt conscious of personal involvement. Many times in those days I was tense, anxious and even a little resentful, especially on the day we meditated on sin. I just did not feel like such a sinner. However, I am sure that I must have received many graces, and I developed a great respect for the *Exercises* and a deeper commitment to CLC.

What Was Done

The ideas behind this adaptation are basically very simple. The retreatant would do one Week of the *Spiritual Exercises* in each of the four summers. The format would include a three-part plan: preparation, the retreat itself, and a follow-up.

Prior to the retreat, I gave the retreatant several passages from Scripture (such as Is 55, S 3:1-16; Jn 1:35-39; Lk 1:4-15) to use for her prayer to see if God were calling her to this enterprise. It seemed as though God was actually *pushing* her. Thus, she came to the retreat house with a twofold emotion: fearfulness at beginning something new, and overwhelming enthusiasm to enter into a deeper relationship with her God. She put it this way:

> Making the full *Exercises* over a four-year period was a whole new experience, a new dimension. Now I was going into them in depth, often repeating the same material and always gaining new insights. At first, I had some anxiety. I was not sure of what I was doing. But my director encouraged and reassured me, and from then on all went well, and I was at peace.

During those eight days she prayed four times a day, using both the text of the *Exercises* and scriptural passages like Is 43 and 49; Ps 42, 63 and 139; Jn 15; Gn 3; 2 S 11-12; Ps 32 and 51; Lk 15 and 16; Rm 5 and 7; Jm 2; and Lk 5. Then she saw me for an hour each morning to see how her prayer had gone. Her realization of how deep, intense, and personal God's love for her was brought her to a humble gratitude and a deeper love for God in return:

> Meditating on the Principle and Foundation I gained a deeper realization of my lack of freedom and deep sense of my unworthiness in the face of God's goodness. During the

exercises of the First Week I slowly came to the realization of my own sinfulness; but now instead of depressing me, as it had in the past, I was filled with joy and gratitude to God for all his mercy and goodness. The awareness of God's love and goodness made me conscious of my unworthiness as a disciple and my longing to do more for my Lord. I was continually asking myself: "What have I done? What ought I to do? What will I do?" And I was asking the Lord for generosity in serving him.

Thus, she was able to attain the grace of the First Week in that time period.

At the conclusion of that first summer, I gave her some additional readings from the Scriptures listed above so that in her daily prayer she could continue to deepen her experience of God upon her return home. The reason for this follow-up was to enable the retreatant to do additional repetitions of the prayer which had been fruitful. This follow-up would last for several days to a few weeks until the fruit had been gathered; then she would return to the subjects of her regular daily prayer.

The format of preparation, retreat experience, and follow-up was done in each of the succeeding years.

So, prior to the second summer, I contacted the retreatant and asked her to pray over some of the previous scriptural passages so that she might revisit the graces she had received during the previous summer; in this way she would be able to have a smoother transition from the First Week to the work of the Second Week.

She found that Ignatian contemplation was beneficial for her, and she attained an affectionate relationship with Christ.

When she arrived at the retreat house, we reviewed the graces which she had attained, found that she had "repeated" them during the preparation for the second session, and then began to look at the contemplations of the Second Week.

During this second session, we simply concentrated on the Ignatian grace: "to know Jesus intimately, to love him more intensely, and so to follow him more closely" (*Sp Ex* §104). She found that Ignatian contemplation was beneficial for her, and she attained an affectionate relationship with Christ. We made no attempt to do an Election at that time.

On the eighth day of this session, I asked her to continue

with a large section from Mark's gospel (8:27-10:45). By using one paragraph each day, she could build up a pattern of contemplation for her daily prayer, and she could grasp more fully the values, attitudes, and standard of Christ.

The same format of preparation, retreat, and follow-up was repeated in the third and fourth years. The retreatant writes:

> The experience of meditation on the Passion was almost overwhelming. My pain and suffering with Jesus was so acute that I found myself turning to the Father and asking him in anger: "Why are you letting him suffer so?" I was conscious of the contrast between the sublime Lord and the hatred that surrounded him. It was a painful and emotional experience.
>
> How can I describe the Fourth Week? It was a glorious one for me. However, I find it hard to describe my experience during this time. It was truly a faith experience. I was deeply conscious of the consoling presence of the Risen Lord and overcome with love and longing. I felt his peace and love surrounding me, and that has not left me. I wish I could find the words to thank him for his great gift to me.

Advantages and Disadvantages

Obviously, there are several disadvantages to adapting the *Exercises* in this way. First, four summers is a long time to spend on such an undertaking; it is difficult to maintain enthusiasm and continuity for this commitment. Second, this kind of a retreat is not conducive for a person who needs to make a decision about a state in life or about any other matter. Third, there is no guarantee that a retreatant will complete the First Week during the first session; the director and the retreatant will have to struggle with ways to attain the graces of the various Weeks when the interruptions are a full year in duration. I myself was fortunate on this point. Except for the second summer, the retreatant attained the grace which was sought. In that second summer, I relied upon the fact that she was a person who prayed each day. I simply gave her the additional passage from Mark's gospel (8:27-10:45) so that she could complete the attainment of the Ignatian grace in the next several days.

The process of corresponding with the retreatant prior to each summer's retreat proved to be an advantage rather than a disadvantage. It took some time to check my notation on the retreatant's previous development and to propose some passages for bringing her to that spiritual level again. But as a result, her prayer prior to each summer's session put her in the proper disposition to enter into another grace-filled experience and also enabled her to pull the entire four-year task into a unified journey.

Thus, the real advantage in this adaptation is that the retreatants are enabled to pray through the entire *Spiritual Exercises* of St. Ignatius and to experience this dynamism of God's grace in their lives. People who might find a benefit in using this method are: retreatants who return to the same retreat house year after year, religious men and women who have the obligation of making an annual eight-day retreat, and those lay people who use part of their summer vacation to make a retreat; also, retreat directors might find this variation a challenging enterprise to offer to their regular clientele.

Although the experience of making the full *Exercises* is a value in itself, there are additional advantages. First, this method enables retreatants to attain the goal of Ignatius, namely that they come to an understanding of God's will for them and that they receive the graces to carry out that will in their lives. Second, the retreatants learn Ignatian spirituality by experience. They see that God's personal love for them is the primary cause for their repentance from sin, their call to follow Christ their King, their commitment to serve Christ by serving others, and their love for God in gratitude. Third, by reason of the interview with the director, the retreatants learn the process of discernment; that is, they learn how the Divine Majesty is acting in their lives and, thereby, is assisting them to make important decisions in accord with God's will. Fourth, Ignatian spirituality is apostolic; during this four-year time span, retreatants are able to integrate their prayer and their work and, thereby, monitor their apostolic effectiveness.

Conclusion

Although this method is not an ideal adaptation of the *Spiritual Exercises*, it does present an opportunity for some people to make the entire *Exercises*. Our experiment of doing the full *Exercises* in four consecutive summers, in fact, proved to be highly successful. The retreatant writes:

> I am sure that experiencing the *Exercises* as I did has had an effect on me and my life. Although there has been no radical conversion, I see a gradual change in myself in many

imperceptible and subtle ways as I try to become a more Christ-centered person. With a deepening in my prayer life, I am getting to know myself better and, hopefully, growing closer to God. As I strive to change my attitudes and ideals to conform more closely to Jesus: I feel a greater freedom. At the same time I realize my complete dependence on God and his grace. Now I have a greater desire than ever to serve my Lord in my neighbor, and I look for opportunities to do this especially in the social problems of our day. But the greatest effect and the most wonderful realization is the conviction of God's presence in my life, his nearness, and his great love for me.

Our success may be an incentive for others. People who are not able to have thirty consecutive days to make these *Exercises*, or who do not have directors available to guide them through a Nineteenth Annotation retreat may find that this adaptation would enable them to receive the benefits of Ignatius's plan and to perceive the spiritual growth in their own lives.

Contemplative Imagination in Persons with Multiple Disabilities

I maginative contemplation is an experience of prayer which can be a personal encounter with the Lord that touches the deepest part of our reality. For those individuals who have some degree of mental retardation or brain damage the use of the imagination is an invaluable resource in their life of prayer. While people of normal intelligence rely strongly on their cognitive ability, mentally retarded adults rely more on their affective, intuitive abilities.[1] In the context of spiritual direction I find it necessary to understand the heart of the handicapped people whom I direct in order to genuinely grasp the nature of their relationship with God. The heart is said to be (metaphorically) the seat of the entire inner life of a person, where sentiments, memory, thoughts, planning, and decision occur. It is the mysterious place where God addresses the person and response is made.[2] In sharing prayer experiences with my directees which involve imaginative participation in a passage of Scripture, I find that their interaction with God on a personal level is revealed. Through imaginative prayer they allow their hearts to become vulnerable; they give God permission to manifest a loving presence to them in a vivid, sensory way. Unencumbered by cognitive, analytical thinking, they are willing to meet the risen Jesus with a sense of joy and spontaneity that celebrates the gospel as a living, eternal reality. In that encounter with Jesus they discover an assurance of his love which gives them the freedom to share their own hidden pain and struggles.

The *Spiritual Exercises of St. Ignatius Loyola* are an excellent vehicle for the use of imagination in prayer and are adaptable to the needs of handicapped persons. Ignatius himself favors the adaptation of the *Exercises* according to the needs of the individual person.

> The *Spiritual Exercises* should be adapted to the requirements of the person who wishes to make them, that is to say, according to their age, their education, and their aptitudes.[3]

In my adaptation of the *Exercises* I would meet with my directees on a weekly or bimonthly basis, not during an extended time in a retreat setting. In these sessions we would use meditations or contemplations which came mostly from the Principle and Foundation and from the Second Week of the *Exercises*. The focus of the Principle and Foundation is a growing awareness of God's encompassing love. The Second Week deals directly with the events in the life of Jesus which are part of the coming of the reign of God.

In every session our opening prayer reflected the Principle and Foundation of the *Exercises*. This idea is described by St. Ignatius in the following way:

> Man is created to praise, reverence, and serve God our Lord and by this means to save his soul. All other things on the face of the earth are created for man to help him fulfill the end for which he is created.[4]

This premise of the *Exercises* serves both as a comfort and affirmation to my directees by helping them to see that their purpose in life is to praise, reverence, and serve God. My directees often express anxiety about their purpose in life because the severity of their physical handicaps prohibits the possibility of having jobs. My directees who became disabled through accidents are also searching for a new definition of purpose in their lives. One directee frequently tells me: "God allowed me to live for a purpose, but I'm not sure what that is."

Through redefining their purpose in Ignatian terms they become free to use their gifts and abilities to the fullest potential without submitting to the standard of productive efficiency in our society. Through viewing all things as connected with their purpose of giving glory to God, my directees begin to look at the world with new eyes. Elmer O'Brien describes Ignatius's mystical experience using the analogy of a young man who is wonderfully in love with a new resiliency to his step and a new brightness in his eyes.[5] This transforming experience of God enabled Ignatius to accomplish many other tasks. It is this transformed worldview which is communicated through Ignatian spirituality. It allows my directees to see whatever they are unable to accomplish as a part of God's plan which has unique significance.

Our opening prayer is followed by a slow and prayerful reading of a short Scripture passage. The elements of the passage are then clarified for those who have cognitive deficits in comprehension. This involves reviewing the sequence of events, the characters, and difficult vocabulary words which need explanation. This is followed by a period of silence during which the directee imagines all of the details of the setting of a Scripture passage along with imagining herself as some part of the Scripture event. The directee indicates to me the completion of the time of silence and shares what transpired during the time of imaginative prayer. This is followed by another period of silence during which the directee enters into a conversation with one of the people in the Scripture story and asks for the specific grace that he or she needs. This part of the contemplation is referred to by Ignatius as the colloquy. The period of silence is once again terminated by the directee and is followed by a sharing of the essence of the conversation which took place in the contemplation. Our closing prayer is usually shared verbally, including a prayer of petition for the specific grace sought in this contemplation and a prayer of thanksgiving for this manifestation of God's love.

This simplified structure consolidates the enumerated points and preludes of the Ignatian contemplations and makes them more accessible to my directees. One major difference in this adaptation is that the Exercises are facilitated by a director who participates in the prayer experience of the directee. The director is necessary to help to maintain the structure and focus of the contemplation. The director also helps the person to understand the prayer experience in the larger context of life, along with discerning the meaning of the consolations and desolations which surfaced during the prayer. This second aspect of the director's role is not only applicable to work with special populations but would also pertain to any direction relationship in which the Exercises are explored.

A person of normal intelligence might have a very similar prayer experience to one of my disabled directees. The difference is that the person of normal intelligence is able to find a way to define and conceptualize a prayer experience so that it can be communicated to a spiritual director at a later time. For the most part my directees cannot do this because of deficits in memory, thought organization, and verbal communication. The immediacy of an imaginative prayer in the context of our session helps me to get a sense of the person's relationship with God and to help the person reflect on the significance of that relationship. I believe that the depth of the experience of God which my directees have is in no way diminished by their inability to remember or to thoroughly describe the experience. My role as a director simply involves helping my directees to see with new eyes so that they might find a way to reflect on God's sacred action in their lives. After a shared imaginative prayer with Scripture I encourage my directees to repeat the prayer at home during the week. I emphasize the moments of consolation found in the Scripture and I encourage my directees to return to those moments in prayer. This also is based on the Ignatian method of staying with moments of consolation. The repetitions help my directees to use their sensory imagination more independently in their personal prayer. For those with memory deficits I have no assurance that this type of prayer is carried out; however I feel that as the fruit of imaginative prayer is experienced within our sessions, it will naturally become integrated in the private prayer life of the directee.

I believe that the depth of the experience of God which my directees have is in no way diminished by their inability to remember or to thoroughly describe the experience..

I would like to describe the experience of using contemplative imagination with three directees, showing particularly how this form of prayer facilitated a deepening relationship with God and brought a sense of healing and wholeness to fragmented areas of the person's life.

My first directee, whom I shall call Ann, participated in five prayer sessions from the second week of the *Exercises*. Ann is brain damaged from an accident and has difficulty with her short-term memory and thought organization. Prior to her accident Ann had been a Buddhist. Two years ago she converted to Roman Catholicism.

In our first session she contemplated the three persons of the Trinity viewing the world and deciding to send Jesus into the world to save the people from destruction. Since she was unfamiliar with this type of prayer she was initially restrained in the use of her imagination and in her own emotional participation in this prayer. Her greatest response in this first session was to our structured periods of silence. She became so immersed in the silence that she did not indicate any completion of the quiet time as I had instructed her to do. The silence seemed to bring a sense of peace and calm to Ann who is normally an anxious person. I also suspected that the silence perhaps reminded her of the Buddhist spirituality of her past. Her verbal response at the end of this session was: "Thank you. I am truly grateful for this time."

In our second session Ann contemplated the Annunciation. Having some familiarity with the structure, she entered into this prayer more readily. After a silent contemplation Ann described the angel Gabriel as a fragrance and a melody which was present to Mary—however Mary could not see him. She described Mary in a simple, white room, frightened and uncertain about this whole experience. As Mary begins to understand that she has been chosen by God she is overcome with a sense of awe and a desire to surrender to God's plan for her life. Her colloquy became a dialogue with Mary which flowed quite easily. The scene unfolded in this fashion:

> Ann: Mary, you were able to do all that God called you to do. You were able to give your all. I want to do that also, but I am so spaced out, so forgetful, my thoughts are all mixed up. I want to be able to do my art work and to give my all.
> Mary:Come with me and I will spend some time with you talking to God about that and together we can ask him to help you.
> Ann: (speaking to me) I can't believe it! I can't believe that she is actually willing to spend time with me. I can hardly believe that she would take the time to do that for me.

In this session Ann experienced Mary as an intercessor, as a woman who accepted her and cared about her. She identified with Mary's experience of being uncertain about her future, yet desirous of following God's ultimate plan for her life. The role of Mary brought forth a mother image for Ann which helped to bring healing of the tragic loss of her own mother which occurred in her disabling car accident. Mary's willingness to be with Ann increased her self-esteem and her sense that she is worthy of attention in the eyes of God.

Our third contemplation focused on the birth of Jesus. Ann, who by this time was becoming more comfortable with the prayer process, chose to be a friend of Mary who accompanied her on the journey to Bethlehem. Initially this evoked a feeling of fear and inadequacy in Ann because she felt unable to help Mary with the delivery of baby Jesus. She felt consoled by Mary and Joseph who she said gave her permission to wait outside. She said that she knew that they were not angry with her because they later invited her in to see the child.

Throughout this contemplation Ann seemed to focus on the pain of Mary's pregnancy which seemed to be a reflection of her own pain. When I asked Ann what was happening she answered me with her head down: "I was once that way, too." She then described her own experience of having been pregnant and having had an abortion. In her colloquy she told Mary that she did not know what she was doing at the time, that she was all mixed up and trying to find herself, that she did not think that she could take care of a baby. She finished by telling Mary how sorry she was.

I asked her if she knew that God had forgiven her. She said yes, she knew, because God had allowed her to live through her terrible accident. She also told me that she believed that her aborted child has a soul. For our closing prayer we entrusted the soul of her child to the Lord and we asked for the grace of a deep, personal experience of God's love and forgiveness .

In this situation my role as director required great sensitivity to the individual who was coming in touch with strong feelings of guilt, while simultaneously remaining attuned to the Holy Spirit who was setting the pace of the prayer. For the first time I realized that Ann's abortion had shortly preceded her accident. In the accident Ann had lost her mother, her successful Madison Avenue job, and her ability to live independently. One of my major concerns was that Ann not perceive her tragic accident as God's punishment for her abortion. My focus stayed on the merciful and forgiving love of God which I believed could penetrate the pain of my directee's life circumstance. Throughout this session it was clear that the Holy Spirit was bringing to the surface wounded and vulnerable parts of Ann which the Lord wanted to heal. Parts of her life were beginning to have new meaning in the light of God's love.

In our fourth contemplation, the flight into Egypt, Ann chose to stay with the same theme. She first had a sense of awe at Mary's courage and perseverance in bringing Jesus to safety. Her focus, however, became Rachel weeping for her children, which referred to the babies who were ordered to be killed by Herod. In her imagined version of this Scripture passage she focused on Mary and the mothers who had lost their children. As soon as Herod died, Mary returned to visit all the other mothers, to offer them comfort and consolation in their loss and encourage them to bear other children.

Ann's colloquy again became a dialogue with Mary. She once again told Mary how sorry she was about her abortion. She told Mary that even though she cannot have any children now she would like perhaps to care for a foster child or volunteer in a day care center. When I asked her what Mary answered she said:

> "Mary understood me! My thoughts are usually all jumbled up in my head, but she knew just what I meant and just what I wanted to say."

For Ann this was a healing experience of being understood in spite of the thought disorganization which was caused by her accident.

In our fifth contemplation, we prayed with Psalm 139 and reflected on gratitude for life events. While thanking God for family, friends, and education, Ann also thanked God for her accident.

> "I am especially grateful for my accident, because now I can see. God allowed me to see in a way that I never could have before. It is really true—he is always there. I know that God has a purpose for my life. I think maybe that he allowed me to live so that I can let others know that he is real. I want to do the best that I can."

In the imaginative part of this contemplation Ann imagined Jesus helping her to design a recent art project. She was beginning to see Jesus present with her and caring about the events of her daily life.

> "When I do a project, I know that he is with me. I know that the Holy Spirit who lives inside of me comes out through my an work. That is the gift that I can share with people."

My second directee who used contemplative imagination in our session is a young, black Pentecostal woman whom I shall call Gloria. Gloria has cerebral palsy, is physically handicapped, mildly retarded, and mildly impaired in both speech and hearing. She lived most of her life in a state institution and currently lives in supervised housing for disabled adults.

After an opening prayer of offering all that we think, say, and do for the glory of God in a passionate, Pentecostal style, I read the passage from Isaiah 49:14-16 to her. Her eyes began to fill with tears as she quietly asked me to read it again. Without prompting, she was entering into a meditation on those words of Scripture and allowing the consolation which they contained to wash over her.

For the first part of our imaginative reflection I asked her to imagine that she had given birth to a new baby and was holding it. This exercise is recommended in the *Take and Receive* Series.[6] She closed her eyes and grasped a bunch of pink tissues which she was holding in her hands. She began to gently rock her imagined baby with an expression of joy and tenderness on her face. She then addressed the baby on her own initiative with the words from Psalm 139: "I praise God, for you are fearfully, wonderfully made."

This prayer brought forth her own qualities of nurturing gentleness along with giving form and expression to her own desire to give life. It brought her in touch with God as the creator and giver of life who enables us to be sacred vessels of that life. It did not matter that in reality this directee most probably will never have a child. This prayer awakened in her a sense of awe at the beauty of new life and recognizing God as the source of life. These are the two points which I affirmed as a director.

In part two of this contemplation she was instructed to imagine that she was a child being held by God who loved her like a mother. At this point the story took a new direction. According to Philip Sheldrake, once the passage has sunk in, the Bible may be put aside and the scene permitted to happen.[7] The new direction can best be described in the words of Gloria's own vivid description.

> "I am two years old and crying, 'Mommy, Mommy,' but she is not there. Then I see Jesus walking toward me. He is right over there. (She points to her left.) He is walking toward me—no, he is running toward me. He picks me up in his arms and holds me. (At this point tears are running down her cheeks.) He says to me: 'Why are you anxious? Why are you worried? Why do you get so upset? I am here

with you.' (I then asked her what she said to him.) I could not say anything. All I could do was look into his eyes. I do not want to leave. I feel like I have gone to heaven. Can we do this again some day, Carol?"

In this prayer she was probably reflecting her own experience of abandonment when her mother institutionalized her at an early age. She was able to allow Jesus to comfort her in her distress. Jesus' words to her also addressed her current concerns about becoming easily excited and losing emotional control. Through imagination she was able to come closer to God, who can heal the wounds of her past and restore a sense of peace to her present. The contemplation ended without words—a sacred moment of silence.

This prayer brought forth her own qualities of nurturing gentleness along with giving form and expression to her own desire to give life.

As the director, I helped to facilitate a peaceful and prayerful atmosphere along with discerning if the emerging image of God coincides with the image of a loving God that is found in Scripture. Her image of God was authentically loving and accepting and could be encouraged. In her closing prayer she said, "Thank you, Lord, for this beautiful medication." She had not yet mastered the word *meditation*, so she substituted the closest word that she knew. I found this to be a delightful and appropriate error.

I used this same imaginative prayer based on Isaiah 49 with another directee whom I shall call Jenny. Jenny is severely physically handicapped with cerebral palsy and arthritis. She is mildly retarded and nonverbal. She communicates by pointing to words on a board. Jenny also had been institutionalized by her parents at an early age.

In the first part of the prayer she experienced a lot of desolation at the thought of holding a baby. She is well aware of her physical limitations and in this imaginative scene she was afraid of dropping the baby.

As we progressed to part two, she experienced a transformation in the prayer. Part two involves imagining being held by God who loves us as a mother. In observing her I noted a glowing expression come across her face. She entered the period of silent reflection with an evident sense of peace and comfortable reverence. In sharing her experience she told me:

> "I felt beautiful. She (God) loved me so much that I had no more wheelchair."

She felt God's love so strongly that it was as though she had been healed physically. The operation of the Holy Spirit was clearly apparent in this session, because I do not usually recommend that severely handicapped persons imagine that they are healed. It once again shows me that the Lord communicates with people in the depths of their hearts in surprising and unique ways.

> "The secret of the heart is so impenetrable, so extraordinary—the place where God resides in each of us . . . the secret heart in each of us, the mystery of our own being, is where God says: 'I love you' because no one else has said this."[8]

In this situation I might be concerned that such an image of healing might lead to unrealistic hopes and disappointment. Quite to the contrary, it led Jenny to a deep consolation of knowing God's love for her. In our closing prayer Jenny could bring her fears, which are related to her physical disability, before the Lord along with her gratitude for the consoling experience of God's love. These two elements bring a sense of integration and balance to Jenny's life. Knowing God's love as a mother also helps to bring about healing of the wounds of abandonment which she, too, experienced from her family.

In conclusion, these three individuals who participated in the adapted prayer forms based on the *Spiritual Exercises of St. Ignatius* have all expressed a desire to use this form of prayer on a regular basis. All three of these women have faced serious challenges in their lives which called forth a radical trust and dependence on God. Their vivid imaginations combined with their deep faith have been vital assets in their spiritual journey.

The prayer of St. Ignatius has become a song for them to live by.

> Take Lord, receive,
> All my liberty,
> My memory, understanding, my entire will.
> Give me only your love and your grace,
> That's enough for me.
> Your love and your grace are enough for me.[9]

My directees are learning to surrender their physical and mental disabilities, their emotional frustrations, and their wounded hearts to a compassionate, accessible God. They are beginning to discover their own creative possibilities for being instruments of God's love in a broken world. They are open vessels of the grace of a new vision. Together we are learning to see with "grace-healed eyes"[10] our profound purpose and value in the reign of God.f

Notes

[1] Grace Harding, "Religious Imagination of the Mentally Retarded Child." *National Apostolate for Mentally Retarded Persons*, Fall Quarterly, 1987, p. 2.

[2] Walter Kern, *Pastoral Ministry with Disabled Persons* (New York: Alba House, 1985), p. 11.

[3] Anthony Mottola, *The Spiritual Exercises of St. Ignatius* (New York: Image Books, 1964), p. 41.

[4] Ibid, p. 47.

[5] Elmer O'Brien, *Varieties of Mystical Experience* (New York: Holt, Rinehart, and Winston, 1964), p. 252.

[6] Jacqueline Syrup Bergan and S. Marie Schwan, *Love: A Guide for Prayer* from Take and Receive (Winona, Minnesota: St. Mary's Press, 1985), p. 40.

[7] Philip Sheldrake, "Imagination and Prayer." The Way 24, no. 2, April 1984, p. 96.

[8] Jean Vanier, "Opening the Hearts of the Poor." *Communio*, Winter, 1982, p. 405.

[9] "Take Lord, Receive" (prayer of St. Ignatius) from *Earthen Vessels* (NALR, 1975)

[10] Henri Nouwen, "Downward Mobility." *Sojourners*, June 1981.

JOHN R. WELSH

Finding Prayer In Action

*T*he most abiding challenge to those who direct the prayer life of people in "active" apostolates or engaged in pastoral activity has to be that of indicating the relevance of prayer within the context of apostolic action. "Relevance" may not be the most apt word to denote that vague, haunting feeling that somehow the period of my formal prayer ought to "say something" or "bear upon" all the rest of my day, devoted to activity. I use "relevance" rather to *connote* through an association of images, instead of trying to define precisely what we all sense: that prayer and action, certainly as an ideal, are conjoined.

On the other hand, in offering these reflections of a method for consciously uniting our activity with our prayer, I prefer to use the language of precision and definition. Supposing agreement that in day-to-day practice we rarely advert to definitions and hardly at all do so with any precision, I hope in what follows to awaken in readers a sense that "I'm already doing that"; then, through some precision, to help them to attend more reflectively on its advantages in prayer-action dynamics. In other words, this article has no pretensions of describing a brand-new method, but only of setting out in a descriptive way the interaction or relevance of prayer and apostolate.

Circular Interaction

The interaction may be imagined as circular, starting with (a) prayer, (b) going on rounds of activities, and (c) closing the day with reflection. True, these three "instants" are well known and practiced widely. What makes of them a dynamic is the interconnection, the uniting, of each "instant" with the others and thus a closing of the circuit, so to speak. It is on the value of this "fitting together" of prayer-action-reflection that I am focusing.

(a) The "prayer" I speak of is simply the time of formal prayer at the start of the day, the morning meditation or set of prayers or readings which are often done in common, either as preparation for the Eucharist or within the Liturgy of the Hours. It comprises both "hearing the word of the Lord" and "pondering on it in one's heart"; listening to the Lord and responding as that word motivates and arouses sentiments in my heart. As a simple illustration, I fix attention in morning prayer on a chalice on the altar as a symbol of my daily offering to Christ in union with the Holy Sacrifice offered "from the rising to the setting of the sun."

The "reflection" at the close of the day may come in many forms: examination of conscience, recitation of Evening Hour, community night prayers, an evening Mass, or a private review of the day.

(b) "Activities" include all the occupations of the day, be they study, raising children, teaching, nursing, directing, counseling, traveling, attending planning sessions, doing business, or keeping house. Here it is vital that the sentiments evoked in prayer "overflow" and stream into the kind of person who is performing the tasks of the day. To put it another way, the one who prayed earlier should be saturated in the affectivity or the spirit that the prayer stimulated and in this spirit continue thinking, feeling, and deciding; and, of course, he or she should act and judge and treat others in that same spirit. Continuing the illustration above (the chalice on the altar), I set out for a meeting on the other side of my vast city, choosing the wrong bus, missing the interurban train, and arriving long after the appointed time, only to discover that I have come to a parish with the same name as another in the same sector and that the meeting, now concluding, is at the other parish, a good two miles distant. Staying where I have arrived, I visit the staff of a recreational program for children, which is modeled on a type common throughout the city. Though frustrated, I sense I have made an important contact for my work, one more useful perhaps than the meeting I missed.

(c) The "reflection" at the close of the day may come in many forms: examination of conscience, recitation of Evening Hour, community night prayers, an evening Mass, or a private review of the day. In this moment one passes in review the significant moments of the day's activities, letting what is "significant" come to the fore spontaneously: an image deeply impressed, a personality encountered, a conversation whose very overtones I recall, or the salient emotional tone of the day, such as anguish, euphoria, anger, frustration, or quiet satisfaction in unfolding events. Reverting to the illustration I have been using: late at night I look back on my day. The sentiments of frustration tinged with resentment somehow evoke the Lord's challenging words to the two "sons of thunder": "Can you drink the chalice that I will drink?" And I think, this is the chalice I saw on the altar when I prayed my daily offering, but through the day's events now it is a chalice of frustration and incomprehension, like the one Jesus chose in union with the Father's will. Now I have, in deed and in fact, just such a chalice to complete the offering I made to the Father through this morning's words of offering.

Visit to a Bairro and Back

Coincidentally, on the very day I was planning what to say in a conference on "prayer and action" to lay ministers of an impoverished community on the outskirts of an important urban center in northwest Brazil, the events I recount below took place.

My day began with a reflection on the situation of the great majority of families living in this *bairro* spread out all over this dry, unproductive area, whose only "industry" is fashioning bricks from the native clay using the most primitive of all tools, the human hand. People here grub for a hand-to-mouth subsistence from meager gardens and a few farm animals, with a few folk holding low-paying jobs in the city. Without amenities of civilized living, they manage to keep their families housed, fed, and clothed at a greater level of dignity than anyone could expect. And here I am, a lone minister of the Gospel come to conduct a parish mission. What do I have to give? Searching memory for a text, I find, "And Jesus said to his disciples, 'Carry no money in your purses, no pack, no second tunic . . . and announce the kingdom of peace.' " Well, that's me. All I've got on me is a return ticket to São Paulo. With confidence in the Lord and in the truth of his word, I'll begin.

The first visitor of the day is swarthy, smiling João, a St. Vincent de Paul visitor, who invites me to accompany him on a house-to-house visitation of sick, elderly, one-parent homes in the most abandoned part of the *bairro*. In the afternoon a senhora Rita will visit in another section, and if I like I can go with her. I am ready to make a full day of it, and start off conversing with an elderly widow hobbling about on swollen legs as she gets the best chair for the padre. We talk about her absent family, and she wants to confess in preparation for the Communion a lay minister will bring later in the week, and we pray together. That is the pattern of the day. Sometimes we have a reading from the Bible or a few verses of songs the children like to sing, always letting adults talk about their lives and their families: not married in the church, out of work, father working hundreds of miles away, children too poor and ashamed to go to school. And somehow the fact that I am the padre makes them feel the presence of our Lord in their lives, giving hope and courage, bringing his word and leaving his blessing on them.

At the bell calling all to Mass that evening, my mind and emotions are still out in the *bairro*, with the widows, the children, the overworked mothers, old and worn before their time, and I feel empty and useless, yet strangely content in being a presence that in Christ has enriched them. The gospel of the day takes my breath away. It is from Matthew's ninth chapter: "And seeing this vast multitude, Jesus was moved to compassion because they were so weakened and downhearted, like sheep without a shepherd. And he said to his disciples, 'The harvest is enormous but the laborers are few; pray then to the Lord of the harvest that he send laborers into the harvest.'"

It goes without saying that no one can expect that events of each day will fall out in such a neat pattern as the day I have detailed above. But with this day as a sample before us, we can explore more precisely the points of contact between the three "instants," observing what it is that gives them cohesion. It is to these points that on any given day we can become alert and so make within our own consciousness a unity of prayer and action.

First of all, I am aware that, because of the early meditation on Jesus' charge to go "without pack or staff," I was keyed up to go willingly to make the rounds with empty hands, relying on nothing but the Gospel message. Looking back, I realize it was the flowing over into action of the refreshed motivation provoked by this passage that gave flesh and blood to what might have been a sterile reflection on a pious subject. From this I feel invited to be more on the alert to find in daily events and contacts a kind of matrix to pour the energies awakened in prayer, aware all the while that it is the Spirit of God that is moving within me. And the same Spirit guides me through his gifts to discover the personal features of this matrix of action in the faces of the people I meet and move among during the hours of each day.

Here I must stop to notice that in this last paragraph I have used words like "aware" (twice), "realize," "alert to find," "to discover." And that makes me believe that the key to this whole dynamic must be in the third "instant," the review-reflection (c). Why so? Because it is here that one attends in a focused way on the general movement that makes of discrete moments a true dynamic. In the day I have described, the image of the dispersed sheep provoking Jesus' compassion was the mechanism that helped me to advert to my having relived that very symbol and to notice, to my surprise, the interaction of motivation and experience in what had happened to me. It is my observation that constant practice of reflection on daily experience must make one ever more aware of the unity of daily living and that, once so aware, one will perforce live on a more conscious level the inner dynamic of prayer that informs daily action. It is the habit of reflecting on my action as it is motivated by prayer that forms the integrating factor of a unified conscious existence.

Persuaded that this dynamic is part of Christian spirituality at its roots in the New Testament, I close by underscoring the unity of prayer, action, and reflection revealed in Mary the Mother of Jesus, who is also the Model of the church and of Christian spirituality.

Mary's Visit and Her Meditating Heart

This three-part dynamic—(a) the revealed word that sets the tone of the day, followed by (b) action that is motivated and informed by prayer, concluding with (c) a review that confirms or sums up the content of the day—all is expressed for our instruction in the first chapter of Luke's Gospel (vv. 35-56), the twin events of Annunciation and Visitation.

(a) In Mary's encounter with the angel, who brings the message of her miraculous conceiving of God's Son, we have the model of all prayer: hearing and listening to the word and its full import, then responding from a heart ready to act from faith in that word. Clearly, Mary grasps the uniting of two words of the angelic message: God's intention in her regard and the sign of the sterile Elizabeth's pregnancy. Mary knows that these words become united in the truth that what confounds human endeavor is do-able for God and is the sign of his saving work. The "nothing impossible" reveals the handiwork of the Almighty. And she, with a faith deriving from her great ancestor Abraham, responds by a word which allows the work of God to be fulfilled in her body: "She conceived of the Holy Spirit."

I feel invited to be more on the alert to find in daily events and contacts a kind of matrix to pour the energies awakened in prayer, aware all the while that it is the Spirit of God that is moving within me.

(b) Then with haste the virgin handmaid moves into action. Her journey to Elizabeth's house is motivated both by her confidence in the word she has received from on high and by the heartfelt response of one ready to serve. The phrase "with all haste" may be read on various levels, but the point I make is that Mary's action in journeying flows directly from the moment of the divine message she has just received. Connecting to the dynamic I have been describing, observe that she has just declared herself a "servant" of God's word and that now the journey in haste testifies to her desire to bring to Elizabeth the fuller import of her cousin's having conceived at an age considered sterile. In other words, Mary's presence in the Judean home and her greeting as an unexpected visitor become for Elizabeth a sign of recognition of the wholly divine and mysterious character of the condition in which the two women find themselves. Thus Mary, who glimpsed the union of these two events "of the Lord," moves to unite physically the principal personages of this conjoined mystery of salvation.

(c) It is the poetic response of Elizabeth that sums up for Mary the significance of the angelic message and her own active part in the mystery of God's saving work. Mary and the fruit of her womb are blessed and this in a double sense: The maiden visitor is truly "mother of my Lord," chosen by God to bear his divine Son; blessed too because of her faith through which "she has believed that what she has been told by the Lord will be fulfilled." In fact, in this very encounter Mary receives the confirming sign of the action of the Spirit of God fulfilling the promise of the overshadowing which has worked the conception of God's Son "become man" and also bringing her faith to its peak expression: "Be it done to me according to your word."

Thanks to Luke's pedagogy we gain the insight that Mary has formed a habit of reflecting on the significance of key events of her life, thus producing a unity of vision and action that characterizes her life. Does not the evangelist go out of his way to conclude the shepherds' witness to divine intervention at Jesus' birth with the remark "Mary kept all these words, meditating on them in her heart"? And then repeats the phrase at the conclusion of the scene of Jesus' absence in the temple? No isolated instances these, but a pattern revealing Mary's habitual growing in the gifts of the Spirit, a union with God which effectively unifies all aspects of her life in the Spirit.